HUNGRY FOR PARIS

RANDOM HOUSE TRADE PAPERBACKS

New York

HUNGRY for PARIS

The
Ultimate Guide to the City's
109 Best Restaurants

ALEXANDER LOBRANO

PRINCIPAL PHOTOGRAPHY
BY BOB PETERSON

LIBRARY OF CONGRESS CATALOGING-IN-PUBLICATION DATA
Lobrano, Alec.
Hungry for Paris: the ultimate guide to the city's 109 best restaurants/
Alexander Lobrano. —Second edition.
pages   cm
Includes index.
ISBN 978-0-8129-8594-8
eBook ISBN 978-0-8129-8595-5
1. Restaurants—France—Paris—Guidebooks. 2. Paris
(France)—Guidebooks. I. Title.
TX907.5.F72P37524 2014
647.9544'361—dc23   2014002338

TO BRUNO MIDAVAINE
FOR HIS REMARKABLE PALATE,
EXTRAORDINARY COOKING,
AND INVALUABLE PATIENCE

CONTENTS

...

1st and 2nd

ARRONDISSEMENTS

TUILERIES, LES HALLES, BOURSE

Table for One 188

8th Arrondissement

LA MADELEINE, CHAMPS-ÉLYSÉES

Eating the Unspeakable 250

The Rise and Fall of the Parisian Brasserie

13th, 14th, and 15th
ARRONDISSEMENTS

PLACE D'ITALIE, GOBELINS, MONTPARNASSE, GRENELLE, CONVENTION

Fashion Plates: A Brief History of Stylish Dining in Paris

16th *and* 17th

ARRONDISSEMENTS

TROCADÉRO, VICTOR-HUGO, BOIS DE BOULOGNE, L'ÉTOILE, TERNES, WAGRAM, CLICHY

18th, 19th, *and* 20th

ARRONDISSEMENTS

MONTMARTRE, BUTTES-CHAUMONT, NATION

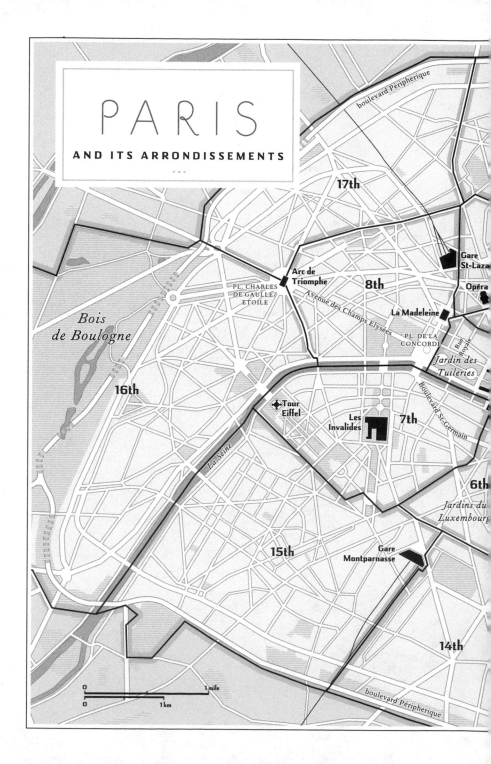

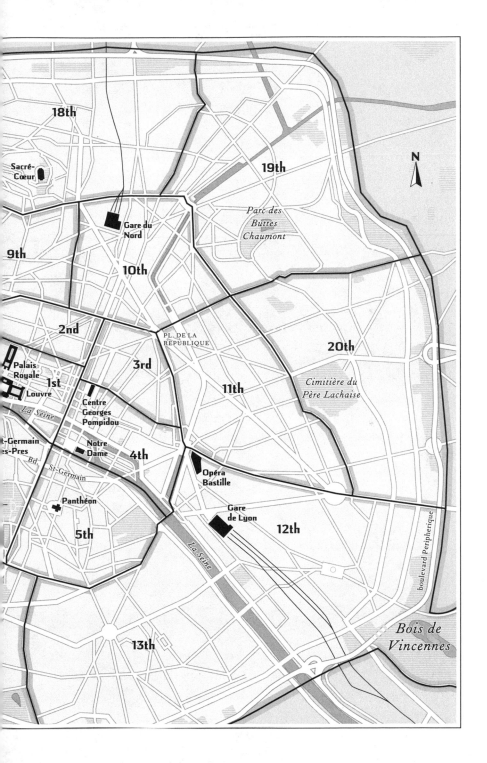

A LETTER FROM PARIS

P ARIS HAS CHANGED A LOT DURING THE SIX YEARS SINCE I wrote the first edition of *Hungry for Paris*, and mostly in ways that are for the good. To be sure, the sort of traditional bistros I remain besotted with—cozy places that serve long-simmered dishes like boeuf bourguignon and cassoulet—continue to become rarer as their owners retire and a new generation of bistro chefs mostly prefer dishes of their own invention to this classic repertoire, but many of these new places are superb.

What's also changed is how the men and women in the kitchens of the new modern bistros of Paris perceive their work. They see themselves as chefs rather than as cooks, with the imperative of expressing themselves creatively through their cooking. If this has made it harder to find a good coq au vin, it's also led to a delicious renewal of the city's culinary landscape and gastronomic preeminence.

People often ask me if the French capital still deserves its vaunted epicurean reputation, and I instantly tell them it does. The rigor of a French gastronomic education is second to none—all you have to do is spend as much time in Paris kitchens as I have to see this truth in action. And then there's the culinary exigence of the Parisian public, something that's informed by France's long and glorious love affair with great food. Finally, the variety and quality of the ingredients available to Parisian chefs remain unequaled almost anywhere in the world, not just in regard to the country's dozens of cheeses or magnificent poultry, but also considering the stunningly good foods made by French bakers, charcutiers, and others, along with the glorious bounty of its farms, pastures, and waters.

A growing interest in locavore dining, or food that's both seasonal and locally grown, as well as in eating more healthfully, has encouraged the birth of a new generation of remarkable food suppliers such as Terroirs d'Avenir, a small company that stocks the larders of many of the city's most talented young chefs. Paris may lack the abundant ethnic options of cities such as New York, London, or Los Angeles, but in terms of offering spectacular food for midrange prices, it still bests all comers in the Western world.

Another reason that Paris still warrants its laurels is that the culinary talent pool has become international in the same way that its fashion industry has. Dozens of brilliant Japanese chefs are now working in Paris, and surprising though it may be, two of the best young chefs are American, Daniel Rose, from Chicago, at Spring and Boston's Braden Perkins at Verjus. These days almost every country in the world is represented in Paris kitchens, and Perkins explains why: "I wanted the experience of cooking with French produce for a French clientele." There are also more women cooking in Paris restaurants today than in the past, notably Adeline Grattard of Yam'Tcha and Mexican-born chef Beatriz Gomez of Neva Cuisine.

Other noticeable changes in the city include the gradual disappearance of the printed menu—many chefs change their bill of fare daily and so prefer a chalkboard format—and also shorter menus that focus more on the best seasonal produce. Wine lists increasingly reflect the intense interest of a new generation of Parisian restaurant goers in natural wines (without additives) and those made with organically grown grapes.

And as the city evolves in sociological terms, new neighborhoods have become important destinations for food-lovers. If the 11th and 12th Arrondissements were emerging destinations six years ago, today they're serious gastronomic turf. And the 9th, 10th, 18th, 19th, and 20th Arrondissements are coming on strong as locations for young chefs going out on their own who are looking for both affordable rents and a receptive local clientele.

Paris may still be waiting for a vegetarian restaurant of the caliber of the excellent Vedge in Philadelphia, but vegetarians are much better catered to today than they were in the past, and gluten-free dining is an emerging trend as well.

Are there still some things I'd like to see change in Paris? Certainly. My fondest hope is that someone will come along and make the brasseries of Paris seriously good places to eat once again. There's some reason to be optimistic here, too, since Lazare, chef Eric Frechon's recently opened brasserie at the Gare Saint-Lazare, has become a hit by shrewdly revising this genre for a new century. The food's very good, affordable, and served with charm in a setting that succeeds by visually referencing some of the best-loved decorative tropes of Paris brasseries—metal-clad bars, mosaic floors, globe lights—but with modern dash. Likewise, a new generation of restaurateurs and chefs are revising the service in Paris restaurants toward a style that's more customer-centric and friendly, a change that can't happen soon enough for me, since the distant and occasionally patronizing service meted out to foreigners assumed to be errant and unknowing children has never been more inappropriate.

Finally, you might want to know how I chose the restaurants in this book, so allow me to explain. My priority is seriously good food. Other factors that may affect the desirability of a restaurant—a striking decor, for example, or a fashionable clientele—never sway my preference for addresses that consistently deliver gastronomic excellence. This covers a whole gamut of different dining experiences, from simple crêpe counters or falafel stands to storied haute cuisine tables, along with bushels of bistros, both traditional ones and the best of the new modern breed, which are the ballast of this book.

Since you can get burgers, pizza, sushi, and smoothies at home, I privilege French cooking, too, and this runs from old-fashioned bistros such as Joséphine "Chez Dumonet," one of my favorites, to brilliant newer restaurants such as Le 6 Paul Bert. I also aimed to offer a selection of great places to eat in every neighborhood of the city, and to propose a variety of different settings, from cozy bistros to glamorous restaurants with stunning decor and elaborate table settings. Insofar as service is concerned, if I had any doubt that you'd be warmly welcomed and well served in a restaurant, it didn't make my cut.

As a frequent traveler, I know there are some nights when all you want is a good, uncomplicated meal just out the door from your hotel or apartment, while on other occasions you'll be looking for a meal that's an adventure or even a gastronomic epiphany. In terms of pricing, I've favored the sort of midrange table where we Parisians eat most often, because one of the enduring glories of Paris in comparison to other large Western cities is that its midrange dining is so outstanding.

Finally, you might also be wondering about how I arrived at 109 restaurants, and my answer to this question is simple. The normal reaction when presented with a very long list is to wonder which ones are really good. Well, in this case, all of them are. To answer the other question I'm asked very often indeed—

what are my favorite restaurants in Paris?—you'll find them all in these pages, which I hope lead you to some wonderful meals and a deeper understanding of and pleasure in the city that I long ago chose to make my home.

—ALEXANDER LOBRANO

PREFACE
MY PASSION FOR PARIS

. . . .

Paris, August 1972. The city was stinking hot, the mysteriously empty Champs-Élysées (my family knew nothing about the month-long August holiday of the French) was paved with bumpy cobblestones, and most French cars looked like funny metal beetles.

After six weeks of maternally led but basically autonomous splendor in Italy, Austria, Switzerland, and Germany, my mother, two brothers, and I were meeting my father and sister in Paris. Our first meal was spent at the Androuët, a restaurant that specialized in cheese. We all loved cheese. So off we went in two small taxis; the one I was in included a smelly, drooling German shepherd looking over the front seat and a driver who managed two deliciously ripe-smelling Gitanes before we got to the restaurant, maybe a fifteen-minute drive. The blue cigarette packet on the dashboard was decorated with a fan-wielding gypsy encircled by a blue curl of smoke, possibly the stuff of erotic musings, but the best was yet to come.

The strange little restaurant with rough white stucco walls and wrought-iron fixtures shocked with a hairy dairy stink: cheese. We ate salad with hot *goat* cheese (with all due respect to Miss Healey, my third-grade teacher and the one charged with the awkward business of teaching us about mammals, it had never occurred to me that goats had milk, much less that you could make cheese from it) fondue, which made us kids nearly drunk with its kirsch fumes; Roquefort soufflé—served with walnut bread; a small salad dressed with sharp vinaigrette, and sublime cheese; cheese; and more cheese. We went back the next night, and maybe the following one, but on our last night in Paris we ended up in a stifling cellar in the Latin Quarter, where we all ordered onion soup and boeuf bourguignon.

The beef was chewier than what I knew at home, but I'd never eaten a sauce like that in my life. What did it taste like? Smoke, beef, blood, salt, onions, mushrooms, and wine. I spooned, dunked, and licked until not a drop of the velvety garnet-colored sauce was left and later spent a restless night knowing that I'd never be free of a powerful, permanent craving for more. Little did I know then that this addiction would become the compass by which I would live my life.

Four years later I was in Paris again, dumb from the misery of British food on a student pauper's pocket in late-seventies London and desperate for goat cheese and more of that sauce. But, on a night so cold it made your eyeballs ache, I discovered choucroute garnie, a vast smoking platter of tart sauerkraut mounted with several kinds of sausage, fatback, and brined pork loin. Eaten with waxy white potatoes and nostril-stinging mustard, it's one of the world's great winter dishes and immediately became a firm favorite. I amazed the waiter but not myself by polishing off every blond shred of cabbage, every nubbin of pork, along with a second serving of potatoes, yet secretly, I was still yearning for boeuf bourguignon.

The punitive wages of New York publishing subsequently kept me away from Paris again for a long time. Then, the next time I finally visited the city, and after a night of revelry, I found myself flat broke and walking back to my hotel without a map as the city was waking. Shop owners opened wheezing metal gates, a florist was secateuring lily stems into the gutter, and waiters in snug waistcoats set up regimented burgundy-and-ivory wicker chairs on café terraces. The air smelled of melted butter, coal smoke, cigarettes, stale wine. Too tired to be completely panicked, I just walked, dazed but intrigued by the quickening pulse of the city. Somewhere I came across a small market, just setting up so early in the day. "J'espère qu'elle l'a valu!" shouted one of the stallholders, to the laughter of colleagues, and though it was five years before I understood the remark ("I hope she was worth it," a reference to my disheveled appearance, assumed to be the aftermath of an amorous evening), I knew that being teased was also being included in a Parisian morning. I stopped and stared into an open wooden crate at fat bronze pears that not only had little gold labels with black Gothic lettering but had had their stems dipped into crimson wax (why?). Before I could even wonder if I had enough to buy one, a barrel-shaped woman in a knit cap handed me one that had been bruised. I didn't realize that it was a gift and tried to pay her, but she waved me away. I carried the surprisingly heavy pear in my pocket until I was in the middle of the Pont des Arts, and then, leaning on the railing, I bit into the fruit and rich, sweet juice sluiced through my fingers and ran into my sleeves. Happier than I'd ever been, I crossed the river and found the Hotel La Louisiane, knowing, when I slid back into my lumpy bed, that I was meant to live in Paris. After all, I'd just walked home like someone who'd been born there, and my forearms were sticky with pear juice.

But it was some years later back in New York at a dreary

Third Avenue coffee shop where my fate was sealed. "Alec?" Where else would I find a friend whom I not only hadn't seen in five years but who knew about a job opening in Paris, the idea being that I could live in France? I applied for the job that afternoon and was hired.

MY PASSION FOR FRENCH FOOD

SEPTEMBER 1986. I MOVED TO PARIS WITH TWO SUITCASES, left them unopened at the hotel, and went out to discover that the Latin Quarter place with boeuf bourguignon had become a Greek restaurant. I was disappointed but undaunted. My first weekend in Paris was spent in a heightened haze of elation and loneliness, but I did buy five restaurant guidebooks. I may not have known a soul in Paris, but rather than moping around the Luxembourg Gardens all afternoon, or hurriedly scarfing down an omelette in a café, I decided to make the best of things, like the fact of being in Paris, along with a company expense account for all meals, and find the best boeuf bourguignon in town. Being on a quest is the best way to learn any city, and in search of my stew that fall, I mastered the Métro system, and even more valuably, how to eat alone and be happy.

I found my calling as a food writer in a rather unlikely setting, as a writer for Fairchild Publications, the New York–based fashion publishing group, when I started work in their Paris offices. Most of the work I did for them revolved around fashion, and I found my occasional assignments to report on restaurants in Paris, Milan, or Florence vastly more interesting than

anything having to do with fabrics or silhouettes. The job came with a very generous expense account, however, which enabled me to begin my assiduous discovery of French food and Paris restaurants.

Three years later I left Fairchild to become a freelance writer and immediately sought out as many food-oriented assignments as I could. I was fortunate to write for the now sadly defunct *European Travel and Life* as well as for *Travel and Leisure*, *Time Out Paris*, and many guidebooks, including *Frommer's* and *Fodor's*. Along the way, I became European editor for *Departures* magazine and also wrote regularly on French food and restaurants for *Food & Wine*, *Bon Appétit*, and *Gourmet*, for whom I worked as European correspondent from 2000 until its most regrettable closing in 2009.

During the course of this work, I've been privileged to spend hours talking to the best chefs in Paris, often behind their kitchen doors, and also to take dozens of cooking classes. I love to cook and consider that a personal working knowledge of the ingredients and techniques used in French cooking has been essential to my ability to understand and appreciate the meals I am lucky to enjoy in the city's restaurants.

In any given week in Paris, I usually try a half-dozen new restaurants and return to a few old favorites. All of the restaurants profiled in this book are places I've been to many times, and though that doesn't guarantee that you won't try one of

MENU 19€ PRIX
BOISSON et service compris
APERITIF : Kir, sangria ou cocktail
ou ¼ VIN : côtes du Rhône ou Rosé de Proven
UNE ENTREE au choix.
avocat farci au crabe et aux crevettes
salade de saumon fumé
soupe à l'oignon et ses petits croûtons gratin
salade aux lardons et son œuf poché
tarama servi avec ses toasts chauds.
salade Bahamas garnie de fruits frais
UN PLAT au choix.
truite pochée aux amandes
faux-filet sauce poivre ou roquefort
escalope de dinde Cordon bleu
tagliatelles au saumon
brochette de bœuf (sauce au choix)
assiette du pêcheur
DESSERT ou FROMAGE au choix
profiteroles au chocolat chaud
tarte normande et sa crème fraîche
colonel (sorbet citron arrosé de vodka)
pruneaux au vin servis avec glace vanillée
mousse au chocolat maison.

them on an off night, I can vouch for the seriousness, reliability, and quality of their cooking.

Needless to say, I never moved back to New York. Instead I fell hard for Paris, and began almost three decades of singularly spectacular eating as well as earning a living writing about it. And there's no city in the world where you eat better. Period. As is true of all big cities, what you really need, however, is a local friend to tell you where to go, and that's the whole idea of this book. Consider me to be your friend in Paris, the amiable obsessive who's spent years tracking down everything from the best boeuf bourguignon in town to those haute-cuisine tables that are actually worth a major wound to your wallet, from the world's best oysters, to onion soup so good you'll get teary-eyed. I know that I've been lucky, and I want to share. Bon appétit!

—ALEXANDER LOBRANO

Paris, AUGUST 2010

HUNGRY FOR PARIS

A READER'S GUIDE
HOW TO USE THIS BOOK

. . . .

THIS BOOK CONTAINS MORE THAN A HUNDRED PROFILES of Paris restaurants. Each portrait is intended to convey the personality of the table and its cooking, and together they offer a portrait of Paris seen through the prism of the city's best food.

As someone who travels constantly, I spend a lot of time with travel and guidebooks, and what I need from them most often is good recommendations of where to eat. While there are many sources for information on a given city's museums, for example, it's much more of a challenge to find restaurant advice that I can trust.

Some books are excellent, some less so. With their shortcomings in mind, I decided to write the Paris restaurant book that I'd hope to find if I were a food lover traveling to Paris, a book that would, I hoped, be companionable, reliable, and usefully opinionated, and also a book I'd enjoy reading as much for pleasure as I would using it for valuable reference. In the age of the Internet, hundreds of Web sites offer suggestions and restaurant reviews, but I also wanted to offer something I often find missing in cyberspace, which is a friendly, knowledgeable, and authoritative voice one can rely on.

With this ambition, I faced the delicious but challenging task of selecting which restaurants merited inclusion. My original list ran to more than two hundred tables, which I winnowed down to some hundred-plus restaurants where I know you'll have not only a great meal but also a great experience of Paris.

This book covers the entire spectrum of Paris restaurants, from globally renowned haute cuisine restaurants to the city's best falafel sandwich. The largest number are, of course, the bistros that are emblematic of eating in Paris and that also serve up some of the city's best food at relatively reasonable prices.

Every restaurant included in this book has a full-length profile, followed by "In a Word," a quick summary of that table for anyone in a hurry, plus a list of recommended dishes and a tagline that includes its number on the map, address and phone number, the Métro station nearest to the restaurant, its opening hours, and the average price of a meal for one without wine. French dishes that may be unfamiliar are explained in the longer profile but not in the list of recommended dishes, so if you want further information on a given dish, refer back to the main text.

Prices are indicated according to the following scale:

· ·

INEXPENSIVE:	$	*Less than €30*
MODERATE:	$$	*€30–50*
EXPENSIVE:	$$$	*€50–75*
VERY EXPENSIVE:	$$$$	*over €75*

· ·

Indexes at the end of the book group the restaurants according to type, price range, and places that are open all or part of the weekend.

THE HAPPY EATER'S ALMANAC:
HOW TO HAVE A PERFECT MEAL IN PARIS

. . . .

O HAVE A WONDERFUL MEAL IN PARIS, IT HELPS TO HAVE an informed and sympathetic understanding of the different expectations that the French and most North Americans bring to the table. For starters, consider the balance of power. Americans believe the customer is entitled to have a meal his or her way. The French, deeply admiring of the culinary profession, are more willing to submit to the chef—you never hear Parisians asking if they can have it without the garlic, with no salt, or made with lemon juice instead of vinegar—and are brought up to believe that any restaurant meal follows the same script. You study the menu over an apéritif and begin with a first course, followed by a main course, then maybe cheese, and finally dessert and coffee. You don't ask if you can have cheese as a starter or two desserts instead of a main course, since it disturbs the essential, ancient logic of a well-constructed meal.

Parisians also have a much more relaxed attitude toward what they eat than do North Americans, who are often surprised by what appears to be their relative indifference to health considerations at the table. The reality isn't that the French are oblivious to the benefits of eating less fat, salt, or sugar. Instead, they believe in moderation and eating a well-balanced diet—

the French rarely snack between meals—and also that gastronomic pleasure is more important to one's physical well-being
than obsessive calorie counting. In contrast, North Americans
tend to have a more anxious relationship with food. No country
in the world other than the United States could have invented
the concept of the chocoholic, a term that is freighted with
puritanical connotations, since it implies an unhealthy depen-
dency on chocolate. Considering all of the other possibilities
for destructive vice, I think an outsized love of chocolate is
relatively harmless. Similarly, Americans want their food engi-
neered to create and sustain health. Compared to the French,
they think they've seen the "Lite," and they want meals that are
low cal, low fat, low salt, and high fiber. The French will tell
you that all of these worries are addressed by eating three balanced meals a day.

To be happy in a Parisian restaurant, it also helps to take
a few pointers from the locals. For example, even though Parisians are deferential to chefs, they're otherwise assertive and
engaged diners. This begins with insisting on being well seated
when they arrive in a restaurant and then establishing a cordial
complicity with the waiter or waitress. What's understood is
that you'll be working together to create a successful meal. This
is why servers in Paris restaurants proudly explain their menus
in painstaking detail and are usually pleased when their clients
are inquisitive or curious. Ordering is a process of friendly but
serious discussion and consultation that's undertaken with the
goal of composing a suite of dishes that flatter one another. If
you order smoked salmon as a starter and grilled salmon as a
main course, the waiter may try to guide you toward a more
varied set of choices. Similarly, if you order a strong-tasting
first course and a delicate main one, the waiter may suggest an

alternative appetizer that won't overwhelm your second course. You're never obliged to follow his suggestions, but it helps to understand his well-intended motivation.

Parisians also know that good cooking takes time and so happily allot at least two hours for a typical restaurant meal. They'd never dream of trying to rush the kitchen either, since they understand that dining in a restaurant is a glorious public ceremony that has been refined over the course of centuries to enhance two of the most essential and wonderfully recurring pleasures of civilized daily life: great food and good conversation. The following section addresses various subjects and issues that you may encounter when dining in Paris.

APÉRITIFS (before-dinner drinks). Parisians rarely drink cocktails or hard liquor before a meal—they consider that these drinks dull the taste buds. Instead, they prefer a glass of Champagne or white wine or maybe a kir, white wine dosed with crème de cassis (black currant liqueur), crème de mûre (blackberry liqueur), or crème de pêche (peach liqueur). Popular nonalcoholic quaffs include tomato juice and Perrier, which the French never drink with meals because they think its large bubbles make it too gaseous to go well with food.

BREAD. I learned the importance of bread to the French through poignant firsthand experience. In the 1970s, my family hosted a French foreign exchange student, the son of an oyster fisherman from the southwestern town of Arcachon, at our home in suburban Connecticut. The first night that the genial Francis sat down with us for dinner, he scanned the table with a slightly panicked expression and then asked my mother if we had some bread. She excused herself and returned to the table with several slices of Pepperidge Farm white bread in a basket. He thanked her but still looked crestfallen when he peered into the bread basket.

Several days later, in my brother's French class, Francis talked about what he liked most and least about the United States. It turned out that he'd fallen hard for New York City, pizza, Chinese food, and pancakes with maple syrup but he found American houses overheated—even though it was a bitterly cold winter, my mother had to close the windows in his room every morning—and that he was suffering from severe bread deprivation. "Eating American bread is like eating a towel," he told the class to great hilarity. The following Friday, my father thoughtfully brought a baguette home from a bakery in New York, and Francis almost yelped with joy when he saw it.

Suffice it to say that bread is a vital and much-loved part of any meal in Paris. The most commonly served bread is a sliced baguette, or long crispy golden wand of wheat-flour bread. If you order oysters, you'll be served pain de seigle (rye bread) with butter, but otherwise butter is almost never served with bread in French restaurants. Some restaurants also serve pain de campagne, which comes to the table as slices of a crusty loaf baked with unbleached flour.

CHEESE. Though the cheese course is a waning institution at most Paris restaurants—even Parisians have become more calorie-conscious, and it is expensive to maintain a good selection of properly aged cheese—many better restaurants still serve a cheese tray between the main course and dessert. On a well-stocked tray, the cheeses are arranged clockwise, with the mildest one, usually a chèvre (goat cheese) or a gentle cow's milk cheese at "noon," to the strongest one, generally a blue cheese, at "eleven." A well-composed French cheese course stops several times on this clock according to individual taste. Cheese in France still remains a highly seasonal product. The best time of the year to eat most chèvres, for example, is in the spring, when the goats are eating fresh grass again after the winter months, while Mont d'Or, a creamy Alpine cheese, is at its best during the winter. Don't hesitate to ask the waiter for suggestions, and if you're wondering why cheese tastes so much better in France than it does at home, it is because French cheeses are still generally made with raw, as opposed to pasteurized, milk. Pasteurization kills off the friendly bacteria that give cheese its unique taste. Despite USDA regulations, eating cheeses made from raw milk is not only perfectly safe but essential if you're to appreciate them fully.

CHILDREN. Parisians very rarely take their children when they go to restaurants, but this is no reason why your well-behaved young ones won't be welcome. Be forewarned, however, that few Paris restaurants have children's menus and that the leisurely pace of Parisian dining can try smaller nervous systems. As a general rule of thumb, brasseries are good bets for kids, since their service is brisker, their menus generally offer things that kids like to eat, and the animation in the dining room provides helpful distraction.

COFFEE. The French never drink coffee with their meals and order coffee with milk (café au lait) only at breakfast. The standard French coffee is a small, dark espresso-style coffee known as a café or express. If you want coffee with milk during the day, order a café crème (coffee with steamed milk) or a noisette, which is an espresso-style coffee with a shot of milk. American-style coffee (café américain) is generally available in hotel restaurants or places with large tourist clienteles, but few Paris restaurants are likely to have it on hand, since the French find it too thin. Decaffeinated coffee, or un décaféiné, is commonly available, but very few Parisian restaurants serve cappuccino, to say nothing of low-fat mocha lattes. Artificial sweeteners are generally available.

COMPLAINTS. Many Anglophones are uncomfortable making complaints in restaurants. Parisians don't suffer from the same inhibition—if their meat is over- or undercooked, they won't hesitate to send it back and neither should you. Similarly, if you're unhappy for any other valid reason—you don't like your wine, or you're disappointed by something you've ordered—signal the waiter and politely but firmly explain your problem.

CREDIT CARDS. Most Paris restaurants accept at least one credit card, but to avoid an awkward surprise, it's a good idea to check when you're booking a table. The most commonly accepted card is Visa, and most restaurants also take MasterCard. American Express and Diners Club cards are less common.

DIGESTIFS (after-dinner drinks). According to the consensus of good manners, Parisians stop drinking wine when their coffee is served at the end of a meal, and though the tradition of concluding with a Cognac or an Armagnac is waning, they remain a glorious way of winding up a memorable meal. Single-malt scotches are also popular, as are Alsatian eaux-de-vie, clear spirits distilled from plums, pears, raspberries and other fruits—the latter being a real treat when served chilled on a warm summer night. A glass of Champagne also makes for a lovely nightcap, but the French never order cocktails following a good feast.

DINING HOURS. With few exceptions, lunch is served from noon to 2 P.M., dinner from 8 P.M. to 10 P.M. If you're hungry outside regular dining hours, try a café—most of them serve sandwiches, salads, and omelettes all day long—and if you want to eat late, your best bet is a brasserie or hotel restaurant.

DOGS. Don't be surprised to find yourself sitting next to a poodle in a Paris restaurant. Parisians love their pooches and often bring them along when they go out. Birds and reptiles are less well received, and cats stay home.

DRESS CODE. The Parisian idea of informal dressing is still very different from what passes for relaxed in most English-speaking countries. Deeply groomed in the art of public life, Parisians take pride in their appearance, and you'll rarely see them wearing T-shirts, shorts, or running shoes anywhere but at the gym. If you'd like to look local, women will never go wrong with the proverbial little black dress or a nicely cut pair of trousers and a blouse, while dress-down for men means a long-sleeved shirt with dark trousers and maybe a sweater or the quintessentially French white shirt with jeans and a blazer. Very few top-flight restaurants still insist that men wear ties, but you can avoid the ignominious fate of having to wear the ill-fitting house jacket by packing a lightweight blazer. And throw a tie into your luggage just in case.

FISH. Fish is often served whole in Paris restaurants. Parisians rightly believe that this offers a visible guarantee of freshness and also that fish cooked on the bone is more flavorful. If you don't want to bone your poisson yourself, ask the waiter to enlever les arêtes (remove the bones) for you. Certain fish, including tuna and salmon, are regularly cooked rare. If you want your fish cooked through, ask for it bien cuit (well done). The quality of fish and shellfish in Paris is excellent, but since the wholesale market is closed on Monday, meaning the last delivery was probably on Saturday, you might want to wait for Tuesday to get the freshest catch of the day.

LANGUAGE. Almost all restaurants in Paris now have a staff member or two who speaks English, but if you're not French-speaking, it is still not a bad idea to tuck a dictionary in your pocket on the off chance that you end up on a linguistic sandbar. Aside from a few brasseries and hotel restaurants, English-language menus are still uncommon in Paris. Don't assume that anyone speaks English, however. Instead, ask, "Parlez-vous anglais?" ("Do you speak English?") and hope that the answer will be "Yes." A few common French words and phrases will always make you more welcome, including "S'il vous plaît," the French equivalent of "please" and the politest way to attract a waiter's attention; and "Merci" (thank you).

LEFTOVERS. Since the portions served in Paris restaurants are more moderate than those found in North America, it's unlikely you'll end up with many leftovers at the end of a meal. Parisians almost never ask for a doggy bag, and few restaurants are equipped to serviceably pack up anything you haven't eaten. But if you end up with a tasty morsel on your plate that would be good as part of a picnic, you can always ask if you can take it home—"Est-ce-que je pourrais garder ça pour mon chien?" ("May I please keep this for my dog?"). In my opinion, avoiding waste and exercising a little thrift trump cultural differences.

MANNERS. Parisians are very polite and always greet the maître d'hôtel or hostess with a pleasant "Bonjour" or "Bonsoir" when they arrive in a restaurant, and an "Au revoir" when they leave. Conversational levels are also lower in Paris than they are in many other cities, so keep your voice down to assuage the locals.

Should you have the occasion to dine with French people, be advised that their casual conversational style is very different from that of North Americans. The French never ask personal questions—Are you married? What do you do?—until they've become reasonably well acquainted, and they are often flummoxed by what they see as our disorganized chatter. When it comes to any serious discussion, the French approach is leisurely and empirical, beginning at the broadest base of an issue or idea and winnowing it down to a careful conclusion. This may strike you as long-winded or dull, but bite your tongue and don't interrupt. Religion and politics are rarely discussed among people who don't know one another well, and to their credit, the French are brought up to believe that listening attentively is as important as expressing every thought that comes into your head, so when in doubt pinch your pie hole (be quiet).

MEAT. The French generally eat their meat rare, correctly believing that well-done meat has lost its flavorful juices. If you want your meat well done, order it bien cuit (well done). Rare is saignant, medium, à point.

MENU VOCABULARY. Somewhat confusingly, first courses in Paris restaurants are known as entrées—how the term came to mean a main course in English remains a mystery. Main courses are called plats, and plats du jour are the daily specials, often special seasonal dishes or recent inspirations of the chef. Fromage, or cheese, follows the main course. *Dessert* is a word that the English language borrowed from French.

NOISE. With some exceptions, notably the city's large brasseries, Parisian restaurants are quieter than those in large cities such as Los Angeles, Chicago, New York, and London. The French generally dislike noise while they're eating and attempt to keep the conversational volume at a discreetly low level.

OYSTERS. The French are mad for huîtres (oysters), and, contrary to the old dictum that they should be eaten only during a month with an *R* (September to April), they scarf them down all year long. (The reason for the *R* rule, by the way, is that oysters become laiteuses, or milky, during their reproductive season, and many people find that this masks their true taste.)

France produces some 130,000 tons of oysters annually, which makes it Europe's largest and the world's fourth largest producer. The main oyster-producing regions are Normandy, Brittany, Charente-Maritime, the Arcachon Basin, and the Mediterranean. Connoisseurs insist that you can immediately tell in which of these waters an oyster originated in the same way that you attribute a wine to a specific region of France, since the varying salinity and plankton levels affect the taste and size of these tasty morsels.

As befits a great Gallic delicacy, French oyster terminology is as detailed and complex as that used to identify and classify the country's wines. France produces two types of oysters—plates, which are flat, and creuses, which have convex shells. Plates are usually more expensive, since they're harder to grow. The two main varieties of plates you'll find on a shellfish menu are belons, from Brittany, and marennes, from the Loire-Atlantique. Oysters are then calibrated according to size. Creuses, the most common oysters, range in size from No. 5, the smallest, to No. 0, the largest. Plates oysters run from No. 4, the smallest, to No. 000, the largest, and spéciales, which are larger and meatier than creuses, start at No. 4 and run to No. 1. Big or small, they're all delicious, although recent fashion has favored smaller oysters, including boudeuses, which weigh in at just over an ounce, and the slightly larger papillons. Other terms you'll run into include fines, which indicates small to medium-sized oysters; spéciales, larger and meatier than fines; fines de claires, which are fattened at lower density in saltwater claires, or marshes, than spéciales; spéciales de claires, which usually have a more pronounced taste of the sea since they're finished in lower-density claires than are fines; and the connoisseur's choice, pousses en claires, which are fattened longer and at lower density than any of the others. Gillardeaux are especially plump, delicious oysters from Brittany. Confused? Throw caution to the winds and just enjoy them—French oysters are the world's best.

PRICES. Contrary to popular wisdom, you can eat extremely well in Paris without spending a small fortune. Many bistros offer a good-value prix fixe menu that includes a starter, main course, and dessert for a single set price, and plats du jour, or daily specials, are also often a good buy. Keep your bill down by skipping a drink before dinner and bottled water, and also by ordering the house wine. Sharing first courses and desserts is perfectly acceptable, too.

Restaurants in this book are rated according to the following price scale, which represents the cost of an average meal per person without wine.

· ·

INEXPENSIVE:	$	*Less than €30*
MODERATE:	$ $	*€30–50*
EXPENSIVE:	$ $ $	*€50–75*
VERY EXPENSIVE:	$ $ $ $	*over €75*

· ·

RESERVATIONS. Reservations are absolutely essential in Paris, especially if you want to eat at one of the city's more popular tables, in which case you should book as far ahead of time as possible. For Parisians, making a reservation not only ensures a table but is a sign of commitment and respect toward a restaurant and its staff. Parisians take reservations seriously, too. If you no longer need or want the table you've reserved, you should *always* cancel your reservation. An empty table punches a hole in the fragile finances of a restaurant, especially in a city like Paris, where one seldom runs into the double or triple seatings for the same table that are common in North American cities. Though some restaurants have double sittings during a given service, most Parisians will not put up with being rushed at the table—as far as they're concerned, once you've been seated, you shouldn't have to keep an eye on your watch.

RESTAURANT TYPES. Anyone accustomed to the generic hybrids that pass for "French" restaurants back home—in many places, "French" is still synonymous with "fancy"—may be confused by the different styles of restaurants in Paris, so a word of explanation is in order.

The bistro is the bedrock of Paris dining. Bistros are generally small, casual restaurants that are best known for their traditional plats mijotées, or simmered dishes, such as boeuf bourguignon (beef braised in red wine with onions, mushrooms, and cubed bacon) or blanquette de veau (veal in a lemony cream sauce). They also serve roasts and grills, are often crowded and convivial, and reflect the personality of the owner, who is often in the kitchen while his wife or her husband runs the dining room.

Within recent years, a new generation of chefs has reworked the bistro idiom by serving contemporary French cooking that's often lighter and more creative than what's on offer at traditional bistros. Many famous chefs have also branched out by opening bistros where you'll find their signature touch applied to bistro cooking, with delicious results.

The brasserie is perhaps the other best-known Paris restaurant category. These large, swift-paced establishments came into their own in the second half of the nineteenth century, when France's expanding rail network brought an influx of travelers to the capital and the city's growing population and booming tourist trade caused a restaurant boom. Many famous Parisian brasseries have Alsatian roots—the word means "brewery" in French—and Alsatians fleeing the eastern region of Alsace after it was occupied by Germany following France's defeat in the Franco-Prussian War (1870–1871) brought the brasserie tradition (breweries in Alsace often served food in taverns adjacent to their brew halls) to Paris. Traditionally, brasseries serve oysters, grills, and choucroute garnie, an Alsatian specialty of sauerkraut garnished with sausages and various cuts of pork. Many of them have a grand decor, are open daily, and serve late. Animated and convivial, brasseries are a good choice for weekend and holiday dining and perfect for large groups.

Regular restaurants tend to be more expensive, formal places that often cater to a business clientele at noon and serve traditional French bourgeois cooking—that is, richer, more elaborate dishes than you generally find in bistros and brasseries. Haute cuisine restaurants are the pinnacle of the French food chain. Often found in hotels, they have elegant decors, soigné service, and lavish menus. These places tend to be very expensive and require reservations to be made several weeks in advance.

SALADS. Once or twice a year during the summer, I see the same handwritten sign. "Pas de salade comme plat/No salad as a meal!" a warning to salad-mad North Americans that they cannot order salad as a main course in the restaurant where the sign is posted. This is because salads are usually eaten either as appetizers or after the main course in France, not as main courses, and restaurant owners don't like serving a bowl of modestly priced greens when they could sell a sturdier and more expensive main course.

If you want a salad as a main course, your best bet is a café. Most of them offer a variety of salades composées, salads garnished with cheese, hard-boiled eggs, tomatoes, potatoes, ham, chicken, fish, or shellfish. The standard French salad dressing is oil and vinegar, but you'll occasionally come across blue cheese dressings. If you'd like a simple green salad with your meal, ask for a salade verte. A salade mixte is a green salad with tomatoes.

Popular first-course salads on Paris menus include salade

folle (crazy salad), with greens, green beans, and thin slices of foie gras; frisée aux lardons, curly endive with croutons and sautéed chunks of bacon; salade de tomates, tomato salad; salade de mâche et betteraves, lamb's lettuce with chopped beets in a creamy vinaigrette; salade aux noix, mixed greens with walnuts; salade lyonnaise, mixed greens with bacon, soft-cooked eggs, and occasionally anchovies, herring, chicken livers, or sheep's feet. A salade niçoise is a meal-sized bowl of mixed greens garnished with anchovies, tomatoes, tuna, black olives, potatoes, and green beans.

SALT AND PEPPER. Some restaurants don't put salt (sel) and pepper (poivre) on the table, the implication being that the chef's food is already perfectly seasoned. If you want salt and pepper, don't hesitate to ask. In addition to regular white table salt, you may also come across coarse sel gris, which is made by evaporating seawater and is considered to have better flavor and also be rich in trace minerals, or fleur de sel, the fine white salt crystals that form as seawater evaporates in open salt pans and are laboriously gathered by hand. You'll find regular black pepper in most pepper mills, but some southwestern restaurants and contemporary bistros may serve small open dishes of bright orange piment d'Espelette, which is made by grinding long red peppers from the Basque country village of Espelette.

SMOKING. One of the great banes of Paris restaurant dining has been stubbed out. As of January 1, 2008, all restaurants in Paris officially became nonsmoking.

SOFT DRINKS. If you want to drink Coca-Cola with your foie gras, that's your prerogative, but expect visible consternation, even indignation, from your waiter. The French almost never drink soft drinks or iced coffee or tea with a meal, and diet soda is still not common in most French restaurants. Parisians who don't wish to drink wine with their meals order water, which is the best diet drink of them all.

SPECIAL REQUESTS. Though most Paris restaurants will try to accommodate common dietary considerations, many kitchens bridle when customers become too specific with special requests. It's fine to ask for the sauce on the side, but don't expect a friendly reception to a request that the chef omit an ingredient such as garlic or onions.

TIPS. Service is *always* included on any bill in a Paris restaurant, and you are not obliged to leave an additional tip. Customarily, however, a little extra change is welcome. On a €100 bistro meal, I might leave €5 extra, while excellent service at a haute cuisine restaurant may warrant a €20–40 tip. Tips are always in cash, since French credit card terminals do not allow the addition of a tip. Coat check attendants are usually happy with €2 per chit.

VEGETARIANS. Though Paris is still not as vegetarian-friendly as cities such as New York, San Francisco, and London, vegetarians are much better catered for today than they were in the recent past, when the only dedicated vegetarian restaurants in Paris were sad-sack sixties-vintage Latin Quarter holes-in-the-wall. Restaurants in this book that are particularly vegetarian-friendly include Au Coin des Gourmets (Vietnamese), Arpège, L'Astrance, L'Atelier de Joël Robuchon, Le Bambou (Vietnamese), Breizh Café, Le Dôme (fish), Les Fables de La Fontaine (fish), Fish la Boissonnerie, Liza, Pierre Gagnaire, Spring, Verjus, and Ze Kitchen Galerie. Many other restaurants are happy to offer salads, soups, omelettes, and vegetable plates, however—just alert the waiter as soon as you arrive that you're a végétarien (male)/végétarienne (female).

WAITERS AND WAITRESSES. Waiting tables is a respected profession in France, which explains the seriousness with which many waiters and waitresses do their jobs. Don't mistake this professionalism for unfriendliness. The French prefer a polite distance when being waited on and are unlikely to discuss anything other than what they're eating and drinking with the staff. Servers never introduce themselves, and though you may occasionally see staff wearing name tags in hotel dining rooms, it's considered impolite to address anyone by his or her first name.

WATER. Parisian tap water is perfectly potable, so unless you prefer mineral water, request a carafe d'eau, a carafe of water, which restaurants are required by law to serve you. The most popular still mineral waters are Evian and Volvic, with Alsatian Watwiller, a nitrate-free still water said to aid digestion, turning up at some haute cuisine tables. Badoit is the most popular brand of French sparkling water, though the Italian San Pellegrino is also common. Chateldon, marketed as a premium water and the favorite sip of King Louis XIV, comes from the Auvergne region and is served at many upmarket restaurants.

WINE. The arrival of the wine list in a Paris restaurant is often a source of quiet panic for the simple reason that many people assume that they don't know enough to make an informed choice. If you're one of them, rest assured that you're in good company. Most people, even Frenchmen, know a lot less about wine than they let on. So relax and remember that the whole point of wine is pleasure and that learning to pair wine with food is a joyous lifelong process of trial and error.

Armed with this outlook, consider the waiter or the sommelier (wine steward) to be your helpful, if not unfailingly disinterested, teacher. Ask for suggestions, and don't be cowed into thinking that price is the unfailing guarantee of a good wine. When presented with the bottle you've chosen, read the label carefully to make sure it's the wine you've ordered, and remember that the main reason you taste it after it's been uncorked is to make sure it isn't bouchonné, or corked. Corked wine has a moldy taste and musty smell that occurs when the cork used to close the bottle was contaminated with TCA (2,4,6-trichloroanisole), a chemical compound that occurs when natural airborne fungi come into contact with the chlorophenol contained in cork. If you're not sure if your wine is corked, ask the sommelier or waiter to taste it, too.

Happily, a new generation of Parisian sommeliers is not only demystifying the whole business of choosing wines but takes pride in helping you find something that will suit both your tastes and pocketbook. Many of them are also likely to propose wines from some of France's lesser-known wine regions, especially Provence and the southwestern Languedoc-Roussillon, the latter being France's largest wine-producing region. Their thinking is that these wines are somewhat bigger and stronger-tasting than most French wines and so will please anyone used to drinking New World wines as those from Chile, California, New Zealand, and Australia are known. If you prefer quieter, subtler Old World–style wines, make this known.

Parisian wine lists are most often organized according to the major French wine regions, specifically Alsace, Beaujolais, Burgundy, Bordeaux, Côtes du Rhône, Languedoc-Roussillon, Loire Valley, and Provence. Other important wine regions include Corsica, the Jura, and the southwest. Wines are grouped under these regional subheads by color—blancs (whites), rosés, and rouges (reds). Unlike many Americans, Parisians never order wine by the cépage, or grape variety. If being deprived of such familiar classifications as Pinot Noir, Merlot, Chardonnay, or Sauvignon Blanc leaves you without bearings, don't hesitate to explain to the waiter or sommelier (wine steward) what style of wine you like and also your budget. Don't feel pressured into accepting his or her suggestions, either. Good fail-safe wine choices include Sancerre, Chablis, and Graves if you want to drink white and Côtes du Rhône if you're after an affordable medium-bodied red.

Many Paris restaurants have a house wine that's often a decent buy for the money, and more and more of them also

serve wine by the glass. Brasseries and bistros often offer perfectly drinkable wine by the carafe, too.

WHAT IS FRENCH FOOD?

For many years, French food was a mystery to me, and from
the regular visits of friends and family I know that for many
people it remains an alluring enigma. Though the idea of sitting down to a Gallic meal provokes heightened expectations—
France's gastronomic reputation precedes any actual experience
of its food—the same prevailing wisdom also holds that French
food is rich, fancy, and expensive. Further, very few people can
actually name more than a handful of French dishes. Almost
no one wants to admit to this slightly embarrassing quandary,
however, which is why I'm happy to share my own learning
curve in the hope that it's enlightening.

My earliest memory of eating anything specifically described
as French was the éclairs my mother bought at the A&P supermarket in Westport, Connecticut. Long, narrow soggy pastries
shaped like hot dog rolls, they were filled with a gelatinous yellow pastry cream and glossed with chocolate frosting. I liked
them well enough, but as my only firsthand reference, they
offered little by way of elucidation about French food.

Sure, my parents bragged in the most general of terms about
excellent meals they'd had during trips to Paris, and Mom occasionally made "Beef Burgundy," a stew of cubed beef with
mushrooms, onions, and a short pour of Holland House red
cooking wine, and sometimes even a cheese soufflé, but when
we had a quiz about "Foods from Around the World" in my
second-grade class at the Greens Farms Elementary School, I
chewed my pencil. Italian was easy—pizza, meatball grinders,
and spaghetti—and so was Chinese—the egg rolls, fried rice,

barbecued spareribs, shrimp toast, and Moo Goo Gai Pan we'd get as Sunday-night takeout from the West Lake restaurant downtown. But French? I finally wrote "French toast, French dressing, and French fries," and was surprised to get my test back with a red penciled "Good!" in the margin next to my flat-footed guesses. Even though I was only seven years old, I suspected the inadequacy of my answers.

As a bookworm, I eventually gathered that French food was special and fancy, but since the French kitchen had contributed no signature dish to the repertoire of foreign foods figuring in the American diet of the 1960s, I wasn't exactly sure what form this edible elegance might take on a plate.

At some point in the 1960s, a very good cheese store opened in downtown Westport, and my father liked to stop by after our Saturday trip to the library and pick up a random assortment— random because we didn't really know what we were doing— of cheeses. We all liked Brie, which suddenly became popular in the late sixties, but the cheese that made Mom really happy was a triple crème called L'Explorateur, which had a little drawing of a rocket ship on the round gold label riding its velvety white rind. Slowly other "French" foods registered on my radar. Pepperidge Farm introduced a line of heat-and-serve croissants, which suburban Connecticut decided were a dressy alternative to Parker House rolls at the Saturday-night dinner parties that were so much a part of this era, and on hot summer days, Mom liked a bowl of Bon Vivant brand canned vichyssoise (cream of potato soup) for lunch, or she did until the night we were listening to WQXR, New York's classical radio station, and the flannel-voiced newscaster announced that a Westchester couple had died of botulism after eating said soup. "Bon vivants no more!" my father quipped when my mother told him about it.

The company went out of business within a month, but Mom fearlessly transferred her allegiance to Pepperidge Farm canned vichyssoise, which seemed so smart and, well, French, with a sprinkling of freeze-dried chives.

Not long after the vichyssoise incident, I had my first French epiphany. On a lazy June Saturday, Mom drove my brother John and me into New York to go to the Metropolitan Museum of Art. On that hot day in the wanly air-conditioned museum, I could have stared at Monet's *Garden at Sainte-Adresse* for hours. A man in a waistcoat and straw boater sat in a wicker chair next to a woman hidden under a white parasol staring out at the flinty waves of the breezy English Channel—you knew there was a wind because you could almost hear the two flags in the painting snapping—and if I loved the freshness implied by this scene, I was also smitten by its elegance—the immaculately groomed garden with its scarlet swords of gladioli and banks of nasturtiums, the two well-dressed couples, several sailboats near the shore. The formality and reserve of the scene fascinated me, too. It was summertime, but no one was wearing shorts or T-shirts.

"Are either of you hungry?" Mom eventually asked, and when we said we were, I assumed we'd eat in the museum cafeteria, where the food wasn't especially good but the life-sized bronze figures skipping across the fountain basin in a reproduction of a Roman atrium made a meal special even if it was eaten from a warm, wet fiberglass tray. To my surprise, we left the museum and hailed a cab, which took us to Le Charles V, a French restaurant somewhere in the East Fifties. I was very excited when we arrived and a waiter with a thin mustache in a black jacket showed us to a table in a dining room decorated with miscellaneous medieval heraldry and wrought-iron paraphernalia.

Mom had vichyssoise to start, of course, but here with real chives scissored over the thick creamy soup. John ordered a chef's salad, and I chose champignons à la Greque. The hilarious discovery was that John's salad was topped with a hard-boiled egg, tomato, sliced Swiss cheese, and thin strips of a dark pink meat that the waiter told us was tongue. *Tongue.* A merciless tease, I stuck mine out every time my mother looked away, until she finally saw me and told me to stop it. John, a good sport, said it tasted sort of like a cross between ham and roast beef. My mushrooms—real ones, not canned—came in a tangy tomatoed vinaigrette with pearl onions and large white seeds, which Mom explained were coriander. Next, boeuf bourguignon (Beef Burgundy) for John, sole with grapes and toasted almonds for Mom, and coq au vin for me. The coq au vin came in a little copper casserole, and the meaty pieces of chicken were bathed in a glossy, winy-tasting mahogany-colored sauce. It was delicious, but what amazed me most was that I was finally eating French food, which made me feel as worldly and sophisticated as an eleven-year-old boy could be without being insufferable. The real triumph of the meal, however, was the poires belle-Hélène, pears poached in a syrup spiked with vanilla bean and lemon and served with vanilla ice cream and hot chocolate sauce, which I had for dessert. Sprinkled with slivered almonds, it was everything I'd so desperately hoped French food might be—something elevated and absolutely delectable.

Our lunch left me elated for weeks afterward. Suddenly, I was more knowing and tentatively connected to a world much larger than the one I lived in. It also made me rabidly anxious to get at some more French food, though this took a while.

We never ate at the one French restaurant in Westport. It

was too expensive and apparently not very good, so my aspirations remained fallow until the beginning of the 1970s, when two women, one of whom was half French, opened Bon Appétit, a cooking school and lunchroom, in an old brick mill building on the muddy banks of the Saugatuck River, Westport's own rather meager little river. It quickly became a refuge for a small but growing tribe of smart, restless women who wanted more out of life than macaroni and cheese and meeting their husbands' commuter trains every night.

The first time I went was after playing tennis with my friend Clay, his mother, June, and her friend Mrs. Weinstein, whom I remember because she'd stopped shaving her legs, a sign of her affinity with Women's Liberation, as it was then cumbersomely known. June and Clay talked about the years they'd lived in Venezuela—Clay's father worked for one of the big oil companies—and Mrs. Weinstein reminisced about living in New York's Greenwich Village as a young woman, her memories of parties on fire escapes, little theaters, and good bread implying that life in our small suburban town was wanting. Having never lived anywhere but Connecticut, I had little to add to what struck me as their knowing chatter, and so when the three of them ordered quiche Lorraine and salad, I did, too, even though I didn't know what it was. It turned out to be an egg, bacon, and cheese pie—a French recipe, of course—and the accompanying salad was a mixture of small feathery leaves and fronds that had nothing to do with the wedges of iceberg lettuce I knew as salad. What was even more interesting was that there were little ceramic salt dishes on the table filled with coarse gray crystals—sea salt, June explained. Rather dim-wittedly, I wondered how you got the salt out of the sea and also if it was clean, but I kept my mouth shut.

The quiche was wonderful—how could anything made with eggs, cheese, and bacon be bad?—but I was slightly disappointed by its homeliness. I'd been hoping to pick up where I'd left off at the Charles V. Mrs. Weinstein told us that the accompanying salad, which was simply dressed with oil and vinegar, was known in French as mesclun and that one of the owners actually grew many of the little leaves and herbs in her own garden. Worried that I'd been mute for too long, I decided curiosity was the best gambit. So I parried, "I wonder who Lorraine was?" June laughed out loud, and, after rolling her eyes, Mrs. Weinstein explained: "Lorraine is a region of eastern France, and quiche Lorraine is one of its specialties." Ouch. But save for this sting, I was very interested by what she had to say, and she must have sensed it. "Mesclun is traditionally eaten in Nice and the south of France, where another specialty is bouillabaisse, the famous fish soup," she said, adding, "Almost all of the regions of France have a famous specialty or two. It's one of the great pleasures of traveling there."

Further corrections to my developing but wobbly knowledge of French food occurred when a French foreign exchange student came to live with us for a month. Francis's father was an oyster fisherman in Arcachon, a small seaside town west of Bordeaux that's famous for these bivalves, and he'd eat absolutely everything, with the exception, however, of a few things he found in our pantry. He set me straight, for example, on French dressing—"We'd *never* put that on a salad. It would kill it"—and French toast—"We call it pain perdu and have it for dessert." Francis also intervened in the preparation of Mom's Beef Burgundy, politely suggesting that the beef be marinated overnight. He also asked her to buy some real garlic, fresh mushrooms, and, after tasting the Holland House red cooking wine in a Dixie cup, a bottle of real wine, which required a trip to the liquor store. The next afternoon he was a blaze of activity in the kitchen, and when dinner was served that night after Dad got home, the results were stunning. Though she'd been upstaged, Mom graciously complimented Francis on his cooking, though she couldn't help observing that his version required an awful lot of work.

That Christmas, someone gave us a fondue kit—a cast-iron pot to be placed on a trivet over a tin of burning Sterno (a little tin of jellylike fuel that you lit and placed under the pot, ostensibly to keep its contents warm—it never worked very well) and six long thin forks, each of which had a different-colored plastic handle—and on many Sunday nights that winter Mom made fondue, which she considered to be a useful way of using up various bits and pieces of old cheese. The cardboard box the kit came in had a skier schussing down a slope past several chalets and some stylized pine trees and was stamped MADE IN FRANCE. An accompanying recipe booklet explained that fondue, or melted cheese, was a popular dish in both the French and Swiss Alps.

I gleaned more information when I started taking French in junior high school. One of the basic pedagogical tools in class was the memorization of rather daft dialogues between imaginary people. One of them memorably took place in a restaurant in Lyon, where six Lyonnais—a boy and a girl, their parents and grandparents—were celebrating the mother's birthday. It was a grand restaurant for this family of swells, too, even if they started off with several things I found repugnant at the time—foie gras (fattened duck's liver) for the adults and frogs' legs sautéed in garlic and parsley for the children, followed by a few more things I couldn't imagine eating—the two men ordered veal kidneys in mustard sauce, the ladies, quenelles de brochet (pike dumplings) in sauce Nantua (crayfish sauce made pink with a dab of tomato paste). The kids, those little garlic lovers, had roast lamb—"Bien rosé, s'il vous plaît" ("Nice and rare, please"), the bratty little boy told the waiter—with pale green flageolet beans, which sounded delicious and were certainly a better garnish than the alarmingly green mint jelly we always had with roast lamb. For dessert, the men had cheese, the ladies île flottante (floating island, or clouds of meringue floating in crème anglaise), and the kids tarte pralinée, which Madame Barrow, my French war-bride French teacher, explained was an open tart made from crushed dark-pink-colored candied almonds. She also emphasized that this was a very special meal—most of the time, French people went to bistros, which specialized in slowly simmered dishes, or brasseries, which were big busy places that usually had oyster stands out front and served steaks, fish, and choucroute garnie. "There are few things better than a good choucroute garnie on a cold day," she added, sounding pensive and a little wistful on an October afternoon in New England. I asked her what it was, and she explained that it was an Alsatian dish of gently pickled cabbage—"not like your sour American sauerkraut"—topped with grilled bacon, several kinds of sausage, and pork, eaten with boiled potatoes and mustard.

The following summer, I made my first trip to France, and the vague but eager outlines of what I knew about French food finally came into clearer focus. We went to Au Pied de Cochon, a bustling brasserie in Les Halles, the neighborhood that had once been the main food market of the city of Paris, and ate onion soup, which came to the table under a gooey molten cap of Gruyère cheese, delicious little crispy baked ribbons of which ran down the sides of the white porcelain bowl. Under the cheese, which floated on a slice of toasted bread, the soup itself was hot salty beef broth loaded with sautéed onions, and it was one of the best things I'd ever eaten. Then, filet mignon with a side dish of sauce béarnaise, a wonderful little pot of edible yellow unguent made with egg yolks, butter, shallots, vinegar, white wine, tarragon, and parsley, flanked by a dainty little log cabin of French fries and garnished with sprigs of parsley. For dessert, we had crêpes flambées au Grand Marnier, which the waiter prepared in a shiny copper saucepan over a table-side burner and then lit in dancing blue flames for a finale I felt was the height of gastronomic glamour. Another night, I ate the best boeuf bourguignon—you may have gathered that this dish obsesses me—in a Latin Quarter bistro, and the next day, an amazingly good roast chicken, a dish that was a revelation for being so stunningly simple.

By the time we left Paris to visit the châteaux of the Loire and Normandy, something vital had shifted in the way that I thought about French food. What I'd learned was that the best French food often *is* stunningly simple. Sure, we went to a fancy restaurant or two in Paris, but the places that made me happiest were the city's bistros with their hearty, homey, happy cooking based on the freshest seasonal produce.

The many years I've lived in Paris have only confirmed the truth of this adolescent awakening. Though I've had the privilege of ascending the pyramid of French gastronomy and discovering some spectacular food at its higher altitudes, in the end, it is bistro food, or rustic cooking with deep roots in the various regional kitchens of France, that remains the blessedly eternal bedrock of the French kitchen.

A recent survey of their favorite recipes reveals that the French love their simplest food best, too. So here are the ten dishes that answer the question, "What is French food?"

• *Roast chicken.* The most popular dish of all with French home cooks is a well-roasted bird. There are two reasons why it tastes so good in France. First, the French prefer good free-range chicken, and second, they never stuff the bird, rightly believing that the best way to enhance its flavor is to butter it well before cooking and baste it several times while it's in the oven.

• *Moules marinières.* Mussels cooked with chopped shallots, parsley, white wine, thyme, and a bay leaf or two, sweet and succulent.

• *Boeuf bourguignon.* As far as I'm concerned, humanity has invented few dishes that produce joy and solace at the table more reliably than this famous Burgundian beef stew.

• *Sole meunière.* After being dredged in flour, salt, and pepper, this princely fish is sautéed in hot melted butter and dosed with a bit of fresh lemon juice.

• *Pot-au-feu.* Nothing offers more primal comfort than this winter-defying dish of beef and vegetables braised in bouillon and served with coarse salt, mustard, and horseradish.

• *Choucroute garnie.* Like so many of the most ancient French dishes, this one displays a humble but shrewd gastronomic genius, since choucroute, or pickled cabbage, is rich in vitamin C and so was a perfect medieval panacea during the many months when France was greenery-deprived. It is garnished with grilled bacon, sausages, and salt pork and eaten with boiled potatoes and lashings of sharp mustard.

• *Navarin d'agneau.* The best way to experience what a godly gift the arrival of spring was for the French in centuries past is to sample this stew of lamb and spring vegetables, including turnips, tomatoes, carrots, and onions.

• *Blanquette de veau.* Veal simmered with mushrooms and onions in a white sauce of egg yolks, cream, and lemon juice. Delicate and delicious, it is usually served over rice.

• *Cassoulet.* Though there are endless riffs on this southwestern French standard, it is generally a slow-simmered combination of white beans, lamb, pork, mutton, and sausage.

• *Bouillabaisse.* As the name tells—it roughly translates to "slow boil"—this fish soup native to Marseille is simmered for hours so that the homeliest fish of the catch of the day thrown into the kettle dissolves into a rich, ruddy potion that is an honest, ancient gust of the Mediterranean.

· · ·

Frenchie

ON A MISTY OCTOBER NIGHT, I ARRIVE AT FRENCHIE, ONE of the best modern bistros in Paris, ahead of my friend David, and I decide to stroll the surrounding streets of Le Sentier, a maze of ancient lanes in the 2nd and 3rd Arrondissements that was once the garment district of Paris. As such, it's a place where

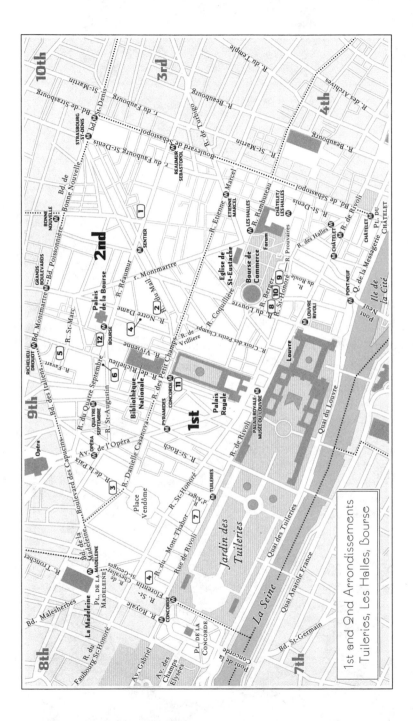

1st and 2nd Arrondissements
Tuileries, Les Halles, Bourse

the city's old stone is still pregnant with the flicker of small, cautious dreams—for generations of immigrant seamstresses, the modest hope of something better was the only way to stay sane in the face of relentlessly hard work at the sewing machines.

In recent years, Le Sentier, following the pattern of similar old working-class neighborhoods like Nolita in New York City, has begun a new chapter in its long history as creative types move in, drawn by its affordable rents, and open shops, galleries, and restaurants. Against this backdrop, it's no surprise that young Nantes-born chef Gregory Marchand hung out his first shingle in the tiny cobbled rue du Nil after stints at Jamie Oliver's Fifteen in London (where he acquired the nickname Frenchie) and the Gramercy Tavern in New York. With its exposed brick walls, factory lamps, and scuffed plank floors, this vest-pocket dining room invokes a gritty but pretty post-industrial aesthetic that feels more Anglo-American than French.

I'm sipping a chilled glass of Rueda, a Spanish white, when David comes in. A pastry chef and popular blogger, he's another Connecticut-born American in Paris and is as passionate about food as I am. He's never been to Frenchie, whereas I've been a dozen times, and so I'm really looking forward to the meal. We study the short menu: two starters, two main courses, and two desserts, all of which change daily, and David remarks, "This is real market-driven cooking. This place could be in Berkeley or Napa. It looks good."

I was hoping David would want the beetroot, fresh chèvre, and preserved lemon starter, but on this damp night, we both ordered the cream of celery root soup, which was ladled over fresh croutons, a slice of foie gras, and a coddled egg to create comfort food at its most consoling. Next, some of the best brandade de morue (flaked salt cod with whipped potatoes and garlic) I've ever had. Marchand's version was wonderfully creamy, and came with vivid swirls of red pepper purée and parsley jus, both of which flattered the cod. David, happily, ordered the paleron de boeuf, or braised beef with carrots, and it was tender and redolent of wine, balsamic vinegar, and pickling spices, an original touch. And finally, a cheese plate, including a chèvre and a first-rate Tomme with a smear of heather-flower honey that pulled the grassy flavors out of both cheeses for me, and a chocolate tart with raspberry purée for David.

Busy with my cheese, I waited for the verdict of the chocolate-loving David on his tart. "This is really good. In fact, I love this place—it's too bad it's not in my neighborhood," he said. I feel exactly the same way, as do many other Parisians, so be sure to book well in advance if you want to sample Gregory Marchand's brilliant cooking.

IN A WORD: Talented young chef Gregory Marchand serves up delicious, inventive modern comfort food at this loft-like little bistro in Le Sentier, Paris's old garment district. He also runs a popular wine bar across the street that's a good opportunity to sample his cooking if you haven't been able to get a reservation in the bistro, and a takeaway place with great sandwiches next door.

DON'T MISS: The menu changes daily at Frenchie, but dishes to look out for are Marchand's delicious cheese-stuffed gnuddi, cumin-scented lamb with chickpeas and tomatoes, and dark chocolate tart with salted caramel sauce.

[1] **Frenchie, 5 rue du Nil, 2nd, 01.40.39.96.19.** MÉTRO: **Sentier.** OPEN **Monday to Friday for lunch and dinner;** CLOSED **Saturday and Sunday.** www .frenchie-restaurant.com **(reservations possible on this website)** ▪ **$$**

Chez Georges

CHEZ GEORGES IS THE GASTRONOMIC EQUIVALENT OF THE little black dress—unfailingly correct, politely coquettish, and impeccably Parisian. This is why it was no surprise to find ourselves seated next to the affable and slightly owlish Didier Ludot on a balmy summer night. A self-described antiquaire de la mode (antiques dealer specializing in fashion), Ludot runs La Petite Robe Noire (The Little Black Dress) and another boutique specializing in vintage fashion in the Palais-Royal. Since he was entertaining a customer, a stylish Park Avenue blonde who gamely insisted that they speak French so that she "might mend the wreckage of what I half learned in college"—much to her credit, her French was good, and much to his credit, his patience didn't fail once during a two-and-a-half-hour meal— Ludot's choice of a restaurant was perfect. Chez Georges is exactly what most foreigners want a bistro to be, which is basically a place where time has stood still on a very French clock (Parisians like it, too, but find it expensive).

Here, the menu is still written out by hand daily and then mimeographed in lilac-colored ink. Brown banquettes upholstered in what the French euphemistically call moleskin but North Americans know as leatherette line both walls of the long, narrow railroad-car-like dining room, and there's a little bar just inside the front door where your bill is tallied and taxis are called. The decor, such as it is, dates back to its founding in the early 1900s and doesn't add up to much more than mirrors interspersed with Gothic columns and a pale tiled floor.

The older waitresses who have ruled the roost for decades are gradually retiring, but the younger staff perpetuate a delightful house serving style based on smiles and solicitude. And most important of all, the menu hasn't changed an iota during the twenty years that I've been coming here. This place remains an unfailingly good address for a trencherman's feed of impeccably prepared bistro classics.

On a warm night, Alice, Bruno, and I raced through a bottle of the good house Sancerre and the plate of sausages and radishes that came with a little pot of butter as soon as we'd ordered. Though everyone and his great-aunt is staking a claim to Julia Child these days, I couldn't resist telling them about how she'd taught me to butter my radishes on my first visit to Chez Georges. Invited to dinner by the late Gregory Usher, an American who founded the cooking school at the Hôtel Ritz and a close friend of Julia's, I arrived uncharacteristically early and found Child already seated and alone. I introduced myself and watched in fascination as she buttered a radish and chomped away. Then, after a swig of Sancerre, she said, "The radish is one of nature's most underrated creations." I smiled, and she added, "It's a good thing no one overheard me. When you're my age, a remark like that could land you in an old folks' home. Still, a nicely buttered radish is just the thing to remind any cook to stay humble and simple in the kitchen. Most foods don't really need any improving."

I suspect Child loved Chez Georges for the same reasons I do. Not only is the food delicious, but it's a good spot in which to channel frivolous, flirtatious postwar Paris, the wondrous city that not only made Julia Child into Julia Child but Audrey Hepburn into Audrey Hepburn, Leslie Caron into Leslie Caron, etc.

Bruno, good Frenchman that he is, ordered a salade de museau de boeuf—thin slices of beef muzzle, a curious crunchy mix of meat and cartilage, which Alice gamely tried, and I went for a sauté of girolles, tiny wild mushrooms, which were delicious, but not garlicky enough. In fact, the microscopic bits of chopped parsley included to make it a real persillade (mix of chopped garlic and onion) alarmed me. No knife I know could have chopped that finely, so suffice it to say I deeply hope Chez Georges isn't starting to take shortcuts, like ready-made restaurant-supply-company persillade, for example. Alice had a good ruddy ratatouille, in which the eggplant cubes retained their shape but had a correctly soft texture, with the lovely addition of a handful of plump capers.

Our main courses were outstanding, too, including Alice's veal sweetbreads with girolles and Bruno's similarly garnished veal chop. Neither was as good as my grilled turbot, a big slab of meaty white fish on the bone with sexy black grill marks like a fishnet stocking. It came with a little huddle of boiled potatoes and a sauceboat of béarnaise sauce so perfect that I polished off what my fish didn't need with a soup spoon.

I couldn't resist the wobbly and wonderfully cratered crème caramel in a fine bath of slightly burnt caramel sauce, while the others ate wild strawberries and first-of-season French raspberries with dollops of ivory-colored crème fraîche, confirmation of my deeply held belief that butterfat is bliss. Just as we'd finished our coffee, the blond waitress of a certain age, a handsome woman with a severe chignon, reappeared; she'd changed out of her black uniform and white apron and was wearing a perfectly pressed pink paneled linen skirt and a matching sleeveless top. She bade everyone good night and went, Cinderella-like, into the night. When we left a few minutes later, our transformation went in the opposite direction, or silk purse into sow's ear, since

after several delicious blowsy hours of la vie en rose, our beeping cell phones signaled the impatience of the world outside. This is why I hope we'll always have the delicious antidote to modernity offered by Chez Georges and buttered radishes.

· · ·

IN A WORD: The perfect all-purpose Parisian bistro and a great place to hunt down impeccably made bona fide bistro classics like blanquette de veau (veal in a lemon-spiked sauce) that are increasingly hard to come by.

DON'T MISS: Terrine de foie de volaille (chicken liver terrine); harengs avec pommes à l'huile (herring with dressed potatoes); foie gras d'oie maison (homemade goose foie gras); escalope de saumon à l'oseille (salmon in sorrel sauce); coquilles Saint-Jacques aux échalotes (scallops sautéed with shallots); grilled turbot with béarnaise sauce; profiteroles (cream puffs) with hot chocolate sauce.

. . .

[2] 1 rue du Mail, 2nd, 01.42.60.07.11. MÉTRO: Bourse or Sentier. OPEN
Monday to Friday for lunch and dinner. CLOSED Saturday and Sunday. ▪
$$$

Goust

I'VE KNOWN AND ADMIRED ITALIAN-BORN SOMMELIER AND
restaurateur Enrico Bernardo for a long time, ever since I
first met him when he was working at the Four Seasons Hotel
George V, the setting from which he won the prestigious title of
Meilleur Sommelier du Monde (world's best sommelier) in 2004
at the remarkably young age of twenty-seven, with this honor
following on the heels of Best Sommelier in Europe, 2002; and
Best Sommelier in Italy, 1996–97.

Not only does the elegant and charming Mr. Bernardo have
a truly extraordinary nose and palate when it comes to wines,
he also has a deep hands-on knowledge of cooking that he
acquired while working as an apprentice at the three-star res-
taurant Troisgros in Roanne and Stockholm's Grand Hotel. So
it's the profoundly sophisticated and sensual complicity he spins
between food and wine that makes Goust, Bernardo's hand-
some restaurant near the Place Vendôme, such an outstanding
address.

There's an ambience of worldly hospitality in this good-
looking and stylishly decorated dining room on the first floor of
a Napoleon III townhouse on a quiet street in the heart of Paris.
The staff are polite and precise but also warm and relaxed, a

service style that's an important prerequisite for enjoying the highly curated meals Bernardo serves. To wit, Goust is all about wine and food pairings, so the best way of dining here is to opt for a tasting menu with a different pour being served with every course.

This is what I did with my friend Ammo, an Anglo-American concierge at a Parisian grand hotel, who invited me to join him for dinner and who also was just about the perfect person with whom to have shared such an experience. Why? This tasting concept works best when you're with someone who's curious, alert and observant, and yet the pleasure of savoring and discussing each pairing would have been ruined by someone who took it too seriously. Bernardo's joy is in constructing liaisons that are so perfect and so passionate they seem metaphysically inevitable, which means that a meal here is an intense and intriguing experience. Fortunately, the dry sense of humor Ammo and I share forestalled any drift to lyrical wine chat. Instead we ate and drank extremely well, and appreciated every sip and every bite.

After a glass of Champagne, we agreed to put ourselves in the hands of Mr. Bernardo, who orchestrated a meal I knew would be superb from the moment I tasted the beautifully seasoned tuna tartare with a quail's egg dribbled with mango coulis. And if I didn't know that chef José Manuel Miguel was Spanish (he's from Valencia, worked at Martín Bersategui in the Spanish Basque country, and was most recently with Eric Frechon at Le Bristol), I'd have guessed it when he sent out a ruddy and deeply satisfying dish of riz Bomba, the short-grain rice from the fields around Valencia, with chopped razor-shell clams, a good gust of pimentón (smoked paprika), and a citrus foam. Though foam, or aerated sauces, can be exasperating, because they're one of the preferred affectations of so many ambitious young chefs, the tart, evanescent citric veil beautifully accentuated the gently iodine-rich flavor of the clams, which were a great foil to the al dente rice. The Manchego foam on the grilled rougets and potato with a sublime coulis of piquillo peppers was a bit timid, however—this dish would have been just as good in both visual and gustatory terms if it had been served nude.

The meal shifted to a more decidedly Gallic register with a gorgeous dish of poached egg with a generous garnish of black truffle on a bed of long-stewed beef and then a beautifully cooked duckling breast—juicy and rare, with a light jus and an intriguing garnish of lightly mentholated shiso leaves. And finally a warm just-set chocolate cake for dessert with a final pour, a twenty-year-old Graham's Tawny Port, a real invitation to musing and meditation if ever there were one.

As is true of any really great restaurant, Goust would be as good for a romantic night out as it is for a gray-flannel business meal. The lighting is good. The good bourgeois bones of the room, with its handsome fireplace and parquet floor, have been tweaked by the sort of 1970s lighting fixture you'd expect to see in the old East German parliament building, which gives this space its visual wit. There's a nice buzz in the room, too. Altogether it's a winningly adult, fairly priced, and terrifically sincere restaurant that succeeds for being something completely unique in Paris.

IN A WORD: Enrico Bernardo, one of the world's great sommeliers, has created a stylish adult restaurant where the excellent cooking of a talented Spanish chef teams brilliantly with his shrewdly selected pours.

DON'T MISS: The menu at Goust changes regularly, but dishes to look out for include red tuna tartare with a quail's egg and a mango coulis, deconstructed paella with razor-shell clams, pan-roasted duckling breast with shiso leaves, and a luscious warm dark chocolate cake for dessert.

. . .

[3] 10 rue Volney, 2nd, 01.40.15.20.30. MÉTRO: Opéra or Tuileries. OPEN Tuesday to Saturday for lunch and dinner. CLOSED Sunday and Monday. www.enricobernardo.com • $$$

Liza

PARIS IS ONE OF THE BEST CITIES IN THE WORLD FOR anyone who loves Lebanese food. Why? Lebanon was a French protectorate from 1922 to 1943, and the Lebanese still learn French, aspire to sending their kids to school in France, and love vacationing in Paris. Many wealthy Lebanese also fled the country during its recent cycles of turbulence and settled in Paris, which means that the capital has a large, affluent community. The French themselves love Lebanese food, especially mezze, or the assorted hors d'oeuvres that begin most Lebanese meals.

Liza is one of the best of a new generation of foreign tables in Paris that are ditching ethnic stereotypes—in terms of both decor and cooking—for edgy style and culinary authenticity. Located near the old Bourse, this place is a sexy gallery of almost invisibly contrasting tones of ecru and ivory rooms with dark parquet floors and perforated white steel tables that were imported from Beirut, owner Lisa Soughayar's hometown.

The kitchen shows off just how dazzlingly good and varied Lebanese cooking can be, with mezze and regional dishes that go beyond the usual standards. The best way to enjoy this restaurant is to come as a group, so on a warm summer night Bert and Noël, friends who live in Los Angeles, joined Bruno and me for dinner. For starters, we loved the lentil, fried onion, and orange salad; the kebbe, raw seasoned lamb, which is sort of a Near Eastern take on steak tartare; grilled haloumi cheese with apricot preserves

and moutabbal (a spicy mash of avocados), and fried shrimp. The main courses were excellent, too, including roast sea bass with citrus-flavored rice and fruit sauce, grilled lamb chops with lentil puree and cherry tomatoes slow-baked with cumin, and ground lamb with coriander-brightened spinach and rice. Among the desserts we enjoyed were the rose-petal ice cream with almond milk and pistachios and the halva ice cream with tangy carob molasses.

· · ·

IN A WORD: This small, stylish, friendly Lebanese restaurant has quickly become popular with Paris's large Lebanese community and fashionable Parisians who love the decor and light, bright, authentic cooking. An excellent choice when you want something other than French food.

DON'T MISS: Lentil, fried onion, and orange salad; kebbe (seasoned raw ground lamb); grilled halloumi cheese with apricot preserves; moutabbal of avocados and fried shrimp; grilled lamb chops with lentil puree and cherry tomatoes; roast sea bass with citrus rice and tagine sauce; rose-petal ice cream with almond milk and pistachios; halva ice cream with carob molasses.

· · ·

[4]   14 rue de la Banque, 2nd, 01.55.35.00.66. MÉTRO: Bourse. OPEN Monday to Friday for lunch and dinner; Saturday dinner only. CLOSED Sunday. www.restaurant-liza.com ▪ $$

Aux Lyonnais

THE FIRST TIME I WENT TO THIS COZY 1890-VINTAGE bouchon (Lyonnais bistro) twenty years ago, it was staffed by kindly older waitresses in black dresses and white aprons, the beautiful Art Nouveau tiles needed a scrub, and the kitchen sent out a variety of Lyonnais specialties that the French would describe as "correct," or decent if unremarkable. I liked its homely charm, however, and the saucisson de Lyon (pistachio-studded pork sausage) served with warm potato salad and quenelles de brochet, or pike dumplings in a pale pink sauce Nantua (creamy crayfish sauce), made for a fine feed.

Then, in 2002, Alain Ducasse, perhaps France's most ambitious gastro-entrepreneur, took it over, freshened it up, and shrewdly revised the menu to appeal to contemporary Parisian preferences for lighter, healthier food within the parentheses of traditional Lyonnais cooking. The transformation was a big surprise to anyone who knew the old place, since the very idea of reinventing a venerable old-time table like this seemed, well, like something an American would do. In fact it brought to mind the bizarre way the traditional old farm stand in the Connecticut town I'd grown up in had been knocked down and replaced by a luxurious, sanitized, and expensive pastiche of a New England farm stand. Both replications have turned out to be a huge success, however, and Ducasse's version of Aux Lyonnais is very popular, packed at lunchtime with men in suits and international types who view the Ducasse name as the gastronomic equivalent of Chanel, and in the evening with a mixed crowd of journalists, bankers, and bourgeois couples.

As is true of all of Ducasse's satellite restaurants, this place follows a carefully devised, high-concept script, the intention being to make one of France's sturdier and most venerable regional kitchens fresher and sexier. Presentation is always important to Ducasse, which means that many dishes come in squat glass mason jars or enameled cast-iron casseroles, bread is slotted into a tan canvas pouch that hangs from the table, and wines are served by the *pot*, the thick-bottomed glass flask you find in traditional Lyonnais bouchons. Even though neither the menu nor the atmosphere approximates the real experience of a Lyonnais bouchon—they're bawdy, sleeves-rolled-up places serving copious quantities of sturdy old-fashioned food like museau de boeuf (beef muzzle) and tablier de sapeur (breaded marinated tripe), neither of which is on the menu here—you still get a very good meal and the chance to sample several classics that are rarely seen on Paris menus anymore.

Start with some charcuterie—several types of sausage, pork crackling, and cervelle de canut (silk worker's brain, a reference to the pale complexions of Lyon's silk workers), a delicious mixture of fromage blanc (fresh white cow's milk cheese), shallots, garlic, chives, oil, and vinegar. The salade de cervelas, sauce gribiche is excellent, too—thick slices of cervelas sausage (a finely textured pork sausage) and waxy potatoes served hot in a little casserole. I also like the casserole of seasonal vegetables, the coddled eggs in a mason jar with morels and crayfish, and the marinated herring.

My favorite main course here remains what it's always been—pike dumplings with crayfish in sauce Nantua—and this version is exemplary. Calf's liver en persillade (bread crumbs, garlic, and parsley) is impeccably cooked, too, and the Saint-Marcellin is a runny, lactic treat. The tarte de pralines, an open-faced tart made with vividly red-colored sugar-coated almonds, is a treat, too, and the service is young, friendly, and swift.

.   .   .

IN A WORD: Alain Ducasse's neo-Lyonnais bouchon cleverly updates the gastronomic idiom of the famously gastronomic city at the confluence of the Rhône and Saône rivers for the twenty-first century. The satisfying richness of such hearty dishes as sabodet (sausage made from pig's head and skin) is retained, but the kitchen's subtle sleight of hand renders them lighter and more refined.

DON'T MISS: Charcuterie plate; salade de cervelas; poached eggs with morels and crayfish; marinated herring; casserole of seasonal vegetables; quenelles de brochet aux écrevisses (pike

dumplings with crayfish sauce); calf's liver en persillade; navarin d'agneau (lamb stew); tarte de pralines.

. . .

[5] 32 rue Saint-Marc, 2nd, 01.58.00.22.16. MÉTRO: Bourse or Richelieu-
Drouot. OPEN Tuesday to Friday for lunch and dinner. Saturday dinner only.
CLOSED Saturday lunch, Sunday, and Monday. www.auxlyonnais.com ▪
$$$

Le Mesturet

NOT FAR FROM THE OLD BOURSE (THE FORMER FRENCH
stock exchange) Le Mesturet, previously a corner café and now
a simple, friendly restaurant, is like a souped-up Gallic version
of a New York coffee shop, an affordable, casual place where
locals go for simple, tasty comfort food when they don't feel

like cooking. What's made this place with wan lighting and negligible decor a big hit is generally good food for very reasonable prices and the contagiously jolly atmosphere generated by people letting their hair down.

The amiable owner, Alain Fontaine, sources directly from small producers in southwestern France, which explains the succulent confit de canard (duck preserved in its own fat and then grilled), Rocamadour (a creamy cookie-sized cow's-milk cheese from the Dordogne), and excellent Corbières, a hearty red wine with a cherry perfume from the abbey of Fontfroide in the Languedoc-Roussillon. "In a country as agriculturally blessed as France, there's no reason you shouldn't eat well, even for modest prices," says Fontaine.

On a Friday night just before Christmas, we went as eight—five Parisians, two visitors from Chicago, and a friend from Marseilles—and this demanding octet loved the meal that followed.

Grilled eggplant topped with melted goat cheese and surrounded by a tangy tomato coulis on a bed of salad leaves was redolent of good olive oil and Mediterranean herbs, and a homemade terrine de chevreuil (roebuck) with a big lobe of lush foie gras in its center tasted of the wild—this entrée was a real surprise on the menu in such a modestly priced restaurant, since game is expensive in Paris.

Alain Fontaine's menus assiduously follow the seasons—I still remember a delicious open tart of sardines with a compote of shallots and grilled red peppers on a summer night—and mignons de biche (venison medallions) in a sauce of preserved wild blueberries and a tender civet de marcassin (braised baby wild boar) were both excellent. Though tempted by one of the better blanquettes de veau (veal, mushrooms, and baby onions in a lemon-spiked cream sauce) in Paris, I couldn't stay away from the confit de canard, duck preserved in its own salted fat, which came with pommes dauphinoise (potatoes baked with cream); the crisp skin of the bird contrasting with its melting flesh is one of the great pleasures of the French table.

While we were idling after dinner, over coffee and Vieille Prune eau-de-vie, a delicious amber spirit distilled from plums in southwestern France, Fontaine came to the table. "Tell your friends I bought them some Bénédictine," he said, reminding me that the last time I'd been in his restaurant had been several months before with friends from Seattle, who had yearned for a tot of the herbal liqueur made by Benedictine monks in Normandy. I dutifully informed Seattle and received the following e-mail: "Fontaine is a true restaurateur—he knows any good restaurant is all in the details, and his hospitality is exceptional. Tell him we can't wait to come back!" Most clients of Le Mesturet feel exactly the same way.

.   .

IN A WORD: With a menu that brims with the goodness of the best French regional produce, this amiable bistro is a perfect place for a relaxed meal that's easy on the wallet.

DON'T MISS: Coq au vin (rooster braised in red wine); sea bream with Mediterranean vegetables; grilled tuna with anise oil; Rocamadour cheese; clafoutis aux quetsches (baked custard with plums).

. . .

[6] 77 rue de Richelieu, 2nd, 01.42.97.40.68. MÉTRO: Bourse or Quatre-Septembre. OPEN daily for lunch and dinner. www.lemesturet.com ▪ $$

Le Meurice—Alain Ducasse

WITH ITS LAVISH ORMOLU MOLDINGS AND GRAND CRYSTAL chandeliers, Le Meurice is one of the most beautiful dining rooms in Paris. For all of its rococo splendor, however, the special affection I have for this space runs back to a soft Indian summer morning fourteen years ago when I came to have a tour of the hotel while it was undergoing renovations. I entered through a side door in the construction hoardings and, looking for the woman with whom I had an appointment, I found myself on the edge of the dining room, where a team of men in dusty blue overalls were arguing in Italian.

"No, no, that's not the right color. That's cream, not almond," an older man said to his colleague as, down on their knees, they stared at a tiny piece of stone on the mosaic floor they were creating. "The almond is too dark, the cream would be better. This is a corner of the room and the light in Paris is so often gray," said his colleague. They changed it back and forth several times, finally settling on the cream. I'd never seen such a large and elaborate mosaic being created before, and I never enter this room without remembering their pride and their seriousness.

So a passionate attention to detail really does underlie the experience of a meal at one of the most legendary dining rooms in Paris, and this is why I was so curious to go there again to dinner the other night. Chef Yannick Alléno, who presided at Le Meurice for many years and won three stars there, moved on in January 2013, and now the restaurant has joined the stable of tables run by Alain Ducasse, who has placed Christophe Saintagne from Restaurant Alain Ducasse at the Hôtel Plaza Athénée in the kitchen.

Waiting for Bruno in the street, I couldn't help wondering if the impending meal might feel like finding a bird in the nest another bird had built. Then Bruno showed up in his Mini convertible, and it was amusing to watch the top-hatted valet park this nice little car between a Bentley and a Lamborghini. When we went inside and were ushered through the door behind a panel in the lobby, the dining room was not only every bit as magnificent as I remembered but also pleasantly more subdued. Several years ago, designer Philippe Starck tinkered with the original post-renovation decor, and since I don't want irony-inflected wit to knock askew the sort of double-barreled grandeur I experience so rarely, I'd never really taken to his tweaks.

Alain Ducasse is both extremely discreet and a real aesthete in the best sense of this word, so it was fascinating to register the small but subtle changes he'd made at the restaurant just a few weeks after it became one of his. The decor has been simplified—the fancy Starck armchairs have been replaced with traditional ones, and the table settings have been dramatically planed down. The only ornament on our ecru-linen-dressed table was a plump ripe yellow tomato on a small smooth shake of timber (we later learned it came from one of the many trees felled in the forests of Versailles during a terrible storm several years ago), and it was a pregnant clue as to the visual and gastronomic sensibility of the meal that followed.

The first dish to arrive at the table was a small square sandwich of toasted country bread filled with fleshy, pleasantly earthy-tasting cèpes and a veil of smoked country ham. At the same time it appeared, a waiter brought the salt and pepper in gray porcelain cubes that briefly grabbed my attention with their stark beauty before I was distracted by the arrival of the first course in our tasting menu, served in a black cast-iron casserole. When the lid was removed, we saw a pretty little still life of vegetables that had been cooked on a bed of gray sea salt, and the waiter then supplied us with long thin forks to spear the vegetables and dip them into a tart green herbed dairy sauce. The vegetables—carrots, potatoes, onions, baby leeks—were homey and satisfying, and the gently astringent sauce cleansed the palate for everything to come. This communal dish also whispered that the pleasures of the table are often best shared. As much as this opener surprised us, we were both transfixed by the plate and the small fragile ramekin the sauce came in. "It must be him," said Bruno, but we couldn't gracefully upend anything to check until a few minutes later, when we saw Belgian ceramicist Pieter Stockmans's name printed on their bottoms.

We'd first discovered Stockmans's exquisite ceramics in a boutique in Antwerp, and I'd later seen them at Restaurant Jean-François Piège in Paris. What transfixed me, though, was deciphering what these very carefully chosen objects were saying. What I surmised is that in the twenty-first century, luxury should be pure and delicate, or a series of simple evanescent pleasures that are humble and healthful rather than ostentatious and self-indulgent. Clearly Ducasse had decided to make Le Meurice his laboratory for reinventing French haute cuisine.

This extended to the deeply considered casting of the staff in this dining room, where I was happy to see more women working than I ever had before in such an exalted restaurant. Among them were the charming and enviously polyglot Spanish woman who explained the haiku-like menu to us, and then the sommelier, Estelle Touzet, whose love and knowledge of wine and eloquent and thought-provoking way of describing it became one of the major threads of pleasure that animated our evening.

Bruno loved his sautéed autumn fruit and vegetables served with a deglazed sauce of cooking juices and cider vinegar—a varying palate of acidities and different shades of bitterness is another recurring element of this kitchen—while my pâté chaud de pintade au chou came as an elegantly fragile cartridge of pastry filled with chunks of tender guinea hen and Savoy cabbage bound by a baked mousse of liver and gizzards.

The nearly nude way in which our fish courses were prepared further emphasized the angelic intentions of the kitchen. A magnificent lozenge of butter-basted turbot came on an identically sized piece of fine toast lightly spread with tapenade, all that was needed to emphasize its natural flavor with the foil of a little salt and texture. It reminded me of the innocent simplicity with which fish is often cooked in Scandinavia, while John Dory, also cooked on the bone, was presented on laser-fine slices of fig with coin-sized pieces of turnip and a salad of herbs. Here, the fine graininess of the fig seeds flattered the fish, while the gentle bitterness of the turnips punctuated its natural sweetness.

Main courses were even more plainspoken in an almost Amish sort of way. Bruno's colvert (wild duck) was cooked rare and garnished with halved black grapes, kernels of corn, and a luscious salmis (the bird's bones pounded to a smooth paste with red wine and stock), while my veal sweetbreads surprised me even after the detailed explanation of this preparation I'd been given at the beginning of the meal. A perfectly round slice of sweetbread was topped with a fine crust of toasted golden bread crumbs and came with a comma-shaped side dish of roasted heirloom tomatoes with a few melted shards of Parmesan. Restraint was the clear intention of this preparation, with the tomatoes intended to provide an acidic foil to the rich, creamy flavor and texture of the sweetbreads. This was the one moment in the meal when I yearned for a bit more, but in terms of the logic behind my menu, it was impeccable.

Ducasse is now producing superb chocolate at an atelier in Paris near the Bastille, and it supplied the raw materials for a stunningly good finale—chocolate ice cream decorated with fine broken panes of caramel on a bed of almonds, with an accessorizing cocoa mousse and a pitcher of warm melted chocolate. Following the waiter's instructions, I spooned up some of the mousse and ice cream with a nut or two and dribbled it with melted chocolate before experiencing an avalanche of pleasure that was propelled into even higher relief by the deceptively modest tone of the preceding meal. The glass of ten-year-old Barbeito Bual Old Reserve Madeira, which sommelier Touzet explained she'd chosen for the faint flavor of the salt in the island's soil expressed through the grapes behind the foreground tastes and aromas of caramel, leather, and tobacco, added a deeper blaze of sensuality to this shudderingly good concoction. Bruno enjoyed his roasted figs, which were served in a fragile bowl of mesmerizingly aromatic dried fig leaves with a granité of red wine atop a hazelnut cream, and we were more relieved than surprised when the traditional trolley of post-prandial sweetmeats brought tableside contained freshly made fruit compotes and sorbets instead of the usual mignardises, candies, and pastries. This gentle and simplified proposal was much more in keeping with the prevailing—and even invigorating—theme of restraint that had informed our meal than a selection of sugary little cakes would have been.

There was nothing ascetic or puritanical about the modera-

tion that was the rudder of this meal, however. Instead it recognized that many people coming to a restaurant of this caliber today are there to be entertained as much as they are to be fed, and that almost anyone who can afford such an experience probably leads a life of habitual abundance.

Ultimately, this was a superb and very daring meal, because after making his reputation with a disciplined take on the simple but naturally baroque character of European Mediterranean cooking, Ducasse has completely revised and reinvented his repertoire. What he instinctively understands, you see, is that as the conventional summit of the French culinary experience, haute cuisine has always been a mirror of our aspirations, pleasures, and even fears, and in his stunningly astute reading of these evolving codes in a still-emerging new century, he's come up with an intriguing new recipe for pleasure. Gallic gastronomic luxury should be simple and wholesome.

. . .

IN A WORD: Alain Ducasse showcases his vision of French haute cuisine for the twenty-first century in one of the most magnificent dining rooms in Paris.

DON'T MISS: The menu here will change with the seasons, but the delicate pâté chaud remains a fixture on the menu and shouldn't be missed, along with the butter-braised turbot on toast spread with tapenade and the spectacular all-chocolate dessert made with chocolate from Ducasse's own Paris atelier.

. . .

[7] 228 rue de Rivoli, 1st, 01.44.58.10.55. MÉTRO: Concorde or Tuileries. OPEN Monday to Friday for lunch and dinner. CLOSED Saturday and Sunday. www.lemeurice.com/le-meurice-restaurant • $$$$

Spring

EIGHT YEARS ON, IT'S STILL SPRING IN PARIS, AND THAT'S more than a minor miracle considering that the chef at this intimate modern French bistro in an ancient stone house in a side street of Les Halles is a young American, Daniel Rose, a native of Wilmette, Illinois. This isn't the first Spring in Paris, however. Rose, a smart, curious, and very likable guy who isn't afraid to take a chance—to say the least, since being an American cook in Paris still elicits the vestigial response in many French minds that all we Yanks ever want to eat and know how to cook are hamburgers—debuted with a tiny sixteen-seat restaurant and off-the-cuff market menu in the 9th Arrondissement in 2006. I went a week after the gas had been turned on and was charmed by both the food and the atmosphere, which was warm, friendly, and relaxed. But it quickly became so popular that you had to book weeks ahead of time to land a table.

Given his guilelessly swashbuckling backstory—Rose had done a year at the Institut Paul Bocuse in Lyon, and cooked in Brussels, Guatemala, and Paris before striking out on his own—he batted away doubters and earned a respected local reputation as a nervy and inventive cook with a signature love of the best seasonal produce and a solemn, almost Gallic attention to detail. Then, at the height of his first success, he closed down his atelier table and undertook the long, arduous, and expensive renovation of the old house that is home to his restaurant today.

It, too, was a hit from the day the doors first opened in 2010, with Rose manning a stainless-steel-clad open kitchen in the corner of the intimate, minimalist dining room with a mostly

French staff. I had several superb meals here, but then this place escaped me as well, because of the reservations problem. So I was very curious to return with another expat, Trish, a charming Irish woman and rightfully esteemed cookbook author, on the sort of cool early autumn night that stokes your appetite. I was not surprised to find the dining room packed with a mostly English-speaking crowd. Spring has nudged its way onto the bucket list of many travelers and the kitchen is also willing to cook for vegetarians, something that's not always a given in Paris, where non-meat-eaters often get fobbed off with an afterthought salad and a dish of miscellaneous vegetables.

As soon as our hors d'oeuvres were served—a polite if not adequately flirtatious trio of small plates containing melon cubes with a timid whisper of lime zest, a miniature portion of vitello tonnato that oddly lacked the taste of tuna in its nicely made mayonnaise sauce, and some braised Japanese eggplant—the riddle was born that I found myself trying to solve all through the meal. Is Spring an American restaurant in Paris, and does it matter one way or another? Aside from the restaurant's exposed stone walls, which date from the seventeenth century, and the improbably formal serving style of the staff, this relaxed unembellished space cues you to expect something warmer and more casual. You might find it in Oakland, Philadelphia, or the currently trendy neighborhood of a dozen other American cities, this place that looks and works like a pullback from the gestalt of a typical French restaurant. This is deliberate. On the eve of opening four years ago, Rose told me he believed in "democratic gastronomy," as opposed to a more hierarchical French one, and that he was aiming for a restaurant that's "totally customer-centric."

When our first course arrived, I was relieved when it knocked our lively conversation sideways. Trish had never been here before, and I wanted her to like Rose's cooking as much as I do. Cork-shaped plugs of perfectly ripe red tomato sat in a rich but light olive-oil-dotted vegetable bouillon with an impeccably cooked piece of sea bass dressed with fine sprigs of salicorne, a succulent salty sea vegetable popular in France. The surprise was that the tomatoes had been cold-smoked, a brilliant idea for being so unexpected and creating a punchy link between the fine umami bath of soup and the angelic fish.

"This is lovely," said Trish, and so was the elegant but seemingly effortless main course, a juicy, golden-skinned duckling breast cooked pink and accompanied by a silken sauce of its pan juices, cucumber sticks that added a refreshing Asian feint, almond puree, fresh blackberries, and whiskers of chive. Beyond their goodness, if anything was notably French about these preparations, it was the stunningly good produce and flawless culinary skills. What registered as American was the instinct to dare contrasts of texture and flavor beyond the approved notes on Escoffier's gastronomic keyboard. This is what gives Rose's food its soulful and witty touch of jazz, and why I always look forward to a meal here.

Spring desserts can be strikingly original, like a memorable olive-oil-flavored chocolate ganache garnished with a sprig of fresh red currants, or pleasantly homey, like the gratin of white peaches that concluded our lunch, which was ultimately a delicious little minuet between contemporary American cooking and the best of Gallic tradition.

· ·

IN A WORD: Chicago-born American-in-Paris chef Daniel Rose has won a big reputation for the inventive but deeply reasoned market-driven modern bistro cooking he serves in a relaxed minimalist dining room in the heart of Les Halles, Paris's old market quarter.

DON'T MISS: Rose's menus evolve constantly, but standouts from the meals I've had here include yellow tomatoes with smoked tuna from Saint-Jean-de-Luz; tartare of tuna belly topped with crunchy black ashes made from leeks; sea bass with cold-smoked tomatoes and salicorne (seaweed); veal breast with langoustines and cheese-stuffed zucchini flowers; roasted pigeon garnished with tiny girolles and slices of fresh cucumber; and olive-oil-flavored chocolate ganache with red currants.

. . .

[8] 6 rue Bailleul, 1st, 01.45.96.05.72. MÉTRO: **Louvre-Rivoli or Les Halles.** OPEN **Tuesday to Saturday for dinner only.** CLOSED **Sunday and Monday.** www.springparis.fr ▪ **$$$**

La Tour de Montlhéry

IF YOU'VE NEVER BEEN TO THIS BAWDY, BRAWNY BISTRO in a side street running off of what used to be Les Halles, the heaving main food market of Paris (now long gone), you might wonder why a noticeable number of people seem to show up with damp hair. I certainly did before I'd lived in Paris for several years, and eventually I discovered that this is one of the best places in town to go after the quick shower that follows some amorous ardors. Why? Because this ballsy old place drives any happy couple in on itself at the same time that it provides the foil for a really good time—the drama of waiters in black aprons sweeping through the bric-a-brac-decorated dining room filled with red-checked tables, the absurdly generous portions of the sort of stick-to-your-ribs comfort food you want when you're really hungry, and the quiet hilarity of a shared, consensual party to which everyone's been invited.

Be forewarned that when I say the portions are generous, I mean huge, so the daintier appetizers are prudent—maybe a salade frisée (curly endive) with garlicky croutons, smoked salmon, or one of my very favorite and increasingly difficult to find old-fashioned starters, oeuf en gelée, a poached egg in salty beef aspic with ribbons of ham or tongue.

It serves one of the best côtes de boeuf (rib steaks) in Paris, and it comes to the table with an avalanche of hot, golden, freshly made frites. If the onglet (hanger steak) is my hands-down favorite, however—rare, chewy, well-aged meat with a sauce of shallots sautéed in wine and butter—I also like the haricots de mouton, mutton stewed with white beans, a trencherman's dish par excellence that I recommend to anyone suffering from jet lag or who's preparing for a move or any other exhausting and stressful event. The first time I ever tried the mutton, I'd come to the table with wet hair, and though the elderly man in a bread-crumb-dotted sweater vest at the next table seemed to be contentedly churning his memories, he eventually revealed his sly sense of humor. "J'ai faim," I'd said while studying the menu. A minute later, he leaned over and spoke, "Excusez-moi, s'il vous plaît, mais il faut vite gouter ça. L'amour vous a rendu souriant mais un peu pâle." ("Excuse me, but you must try this, since love has left you smiling but a little pale"). No cool day anywhere in the world goes by without pricking a yearning for its pot-au-feu, beef boiled in bouillon with vegetables. Sprinkled with coarse gray sea salt and eaten with tiny cornichons (cucumber pickles) and a tiny wooden spade or two of nostril-clearing

mustard, it's one of the most brilliant antidotes to winter I've ever found. Oh—and dessert? I've never gotten there, but others have extolled the profiteroles (choux pastry with vanilla ice cream and lashings of hot chocolate sauce).

·   ·   ·

IN A WORD: An authentic old-fashioned bistro with a retro decor that recalls the days when it fed workers from the now-gone Les Halles, Paris's main food market, just down the street. Busy but good-humored waiters serve a jovial crowd feasting on good, sturdy French comfort food served in gargantuan portions. A great choice for a late dinner or a good dose of sepia-toned Paris.

DON'T MISS: Salade frisée aux croutons aillés (curly endive salad with garlic croutons); oeuf en gelée (poached egg in beef aspic with ham); onglet (hanger steak) with shallots; tripes au

Calvados; côte de boeuf (rib steak); haricots de mouton (mutton with white beans); profiteroles.

. . .

[9] 5 rue des Prouvaires, 1st, 01.42.36.21.82. MÉTRO: Louvre-Rivoli or Châtelet-Les-Halles. OPEN Monday to Friday for lunch and dinner. CLOSED Saturday and Sunday. ▪ $$

Yam'Tcha

TUCKED AWAY IN A QUIET SIDE STREET NEAR LES HALLES, this sweet and very sincere little restaurant is one of the first twenty-first-century tables in the French capital. Why? Because chef Adeline Grattard, who trained with Yannick Alléno at Le Meurice and Pascal Barbot at L'Astrance before spending two years in Hong Kong, has coined a brilliant new culinary idiom with a healthy pulse of aesthetic and gustatory originality.

Grattard eschews fusion in favor of an elegant and very delicate gastronomic minuet between the French and Cantonese palates. In contrast to the heavy-handed mixing and mashing that often occurs when a French chef mines a foreign kitchen for inspiration, the dishes that make up Grattard's tasting menus (four or six courses, changing almost daily) are beautiful, deeply considered, and intricately composed studies in taste and texture that create their own subtle but unfailingly elegant gastronomic logic.

This intimate dining room with its soft lighting and exposed stone walls is also a pleasant place for a meal. At the service bar Grattard's husband Chi Wah Chan oversees the optional tea service—Yam'Tcha means "to drink tea"—and you can choose to sample a different tea with each course. The hospitality is relaxed but stylish and unself-conscious, and depending on where you're seated, you can also watch Grattard hard at work in the compact glass-walled kitchen just inside the front door.

My first meal at Yam'Tcha was on a mild pollen-scented spring night right after it opened, and what Bruno and I were

served perfectly captured the quickening season. We began with an amuse-bouche of slivered broad beans with ground pork and sesame seed oil, followed by grilled scallops on a bed of bean sprouts in a luscious emerald-green wild garlic sauce. Next came whole rougets served on a bed of Chinese cabbage with enoki mushrooms, a slice of Cîteaux (a Burgundian abbey cheese), and finally a sublime dessert of homemade ginger ice cream with avocado slices and passion fruit. Delighted and a little awed by this meal, I knew I'd come back, and so I have, with every visit reprising the pleasure of this first discovery and yielding a dish or two I muse on for days afterward.

·   ·

IN A WORD: The signature of young chef Adeline Grattard's cooking is a subtle, sensual mingling of the French and Chinese palates.

DON'T MISS: Grattard's tasting menus change constantly, but one signature dish to look for is roast duck served over Szechuan-style eggplant.

. . .

[10] **4 rue Sauval, 1st, 01.40.26.08.07.** MÉTRO: **Louvre-Rivoli.** OPEN **Wednesday to Saturday for lunch and dinner. Tuesday dinner only.** CLOSED **Sunday, Monday, and Tuesday lunch. www.yamtcha.com.** ▪ **$$$**

Verjus

NEW ORLEANS–BORN AND BOSTON-BRED CHEF BRADEN PERKINS and his wife, Laura Adrian, first began to register with Paris food-lovers after they arrived in the city from Seattle in 2007 and launched a popular by-reservation-only series of private dinner parties called the Hidden Kitchen (now closed) in their Palais Royal apartment. Beyond the clever marketing of this product—the couple remained anonymous and responded to requests for hard-to-land reservations with teasing emails—Perkins, who'd most recently cooked with Seattle chef Tom Douglas, showed up with another card up his sleeve: he planned to introduce the French capital to some seriously good contemporary American cooking.

The French are still wont to think of American food as what they see in the movies—hamburgers, hot dogs, milk shakes, and other stateside comfort foods—or as cooking that's light-years removed from anything that could be qualified as gastronomy according to Gallic codes. Still, Braden, who opened his restaurant, Verjus, in a beautiful duplex space in a nineteenth-century house overlooking the Palais Royal in 2011, has admirably succeeded in finding a clientele for his intensely imagined American-style market cooking among gastronomically exigent Parisians and the city's expat crowd.

"What we're doing is unabashedly *not* a French restaurant," Perkins told me after my first revelatory meal here. "Americans aren't afraid to work across different spectrums and create new dishes and hybrids—think of the Korean tacos in Los Angeles. This approach runs counter to the Cartesian French way of thinking—you know, that there's a right and a wrong way to do everything. The idea that the 'wrong' way might produce something interesting—even delicious—doesn't register much in Paris." Still, Perkins is besotted with the quality of the French produce he works with and is part of the influential constellation of young Paris chefs who are supplied by Terroirs d'Avenir, a small provisioner specializing in impeccable and often offbeat items such as lamb sweetbreads, coucous de Rennes (a rare breed of chicken), and choux de Pontoise (a leafy conical cabbage from the Parisian suburb of the same name), among other highest-quality delicacies.

So, never having been able to land a table at the Hidden Kitchen, because I travel too often and unpredictably, I was intrigued the first time I went to dinner at Verjus. The name is the French word for the jus of unripe grapes, and so a winking reference at Perkins and Adrian's friends who run several well-established wine bars nearby—the couple know they're the new kids on the block.

Arriving, I loved this dining room immediately, since it overlooks the Palais Royal and the Théâtre du Palais Royal just across the street through huge picture windows, and mismatched flea-market chairs were stationed at smooth oak tables. Somehow it didn't really feel like a restaurant, though, maybe because the atmosphere was so relaxed, and maybe because it quickly became apparent that all of the role-play usually involved in dining out in Paris was not going to happen here. Bruno and I ordered the four-course dinner (the restaurant is open only for dinner, but the couple's wine bar downstairs serves delicious small plates and sandwiches at lunch), and our meal began when Braden arrived tableside with an amuse-bouche—two baked baby beets lightly sprinkled with caraway seeds on bamboo skewers in a shallow glass dish filled with frothy buttermilk. What I liked best about this hors d'oeuvres was that this trio of flavors, so unexpected in Paris, astutely referenced the cooking of Central Europe—Poland, Lithuania, and beyond.

Next, a really brilliant little miniature as our first course—roasted baby leeks with a quail's egg, Israeli couscous, oven-dried radicchio leaves, and a scattering of ash I'd guess was made from the trimmed greens of the leeks. This was a fascinat-

ing composition, at once feral and very comforting, sort of like a detail from a Breughel painting of a winter feast in the Low Countries. A succulent chunk of baked lightly smoked salmon garnished with flying-fish roe and accompanied by tofu flan with a corsage of salad leaves and fennel bulb shavings followed, and it was such an immensely satisfying dish I found myself regretting that I'd never been able to attend one of Braden and Laura's dinner parties. This was, in fact, dinner party food, or the dinner party food of powerfully talented cooks, because it was so much more immediate, fragile, and personal than restaurant food.

Perkins arrived tableside again with the final main course, a perfectly roasted chunk of pork belly with carrots cooked in carrot juice. The gentle bitterness of a spray of frisée sprinkled with crumbled ricotta salata served as the sophisticated foil for the sweetness of the carrot, which elongated the caramelized juices of the meat. This dish was so brilliantly balanced as to be almost algebraic, but remained friendly and sincere rather than cerebral. After a superb cheese sampler for two from Hisada, the cheese salon run by Japanese maître fromager Sanae Hisada next door, dessert—chocolate ganache with beet sorbet, drops of citrus coulis, and a dose of fennel—was, in the context of the way our meal began, a sort of fairy-tale ending, since we'd returned safely after several adventures and some magic to the same place where we'd begun. Fascinating though it was to discover the affinity between beets and chocolate, I found the fennel, an echo of the caraway in the amuse-bouche, a bit too potent. Still, this was a deeply imagined and beautifully executed meal, and for the first time ever in Paris, I was proud in strictly gastronomic terms to be an American. Note that the private dining room here seats twelve, which makes it perfect for a large family or group event.

·   ·

IN A WORD: If New Orleans–born and Boston-bred chef Braden Perkins has triumphantly hung out the banner of seriously good contemporary American cooking at his handsome restaurant in the Palais Royal, what makes it really special is the superb quality of the French produce he cooks with.

DON'T MISS: Perkins's tasting menu evolves according to the seasons and the whimsy of his suppliers, but dishes I've particularly enjoyed include buffalo milk and ricotta dumplings with sweet peas, heirloom carrots, hazelnuts, wild herbs, and lemon; pan-fried Banka trout with chanterelles, guanciale, pickled chiles, chives, and roasted corn soup; pan-roasted duck with smoked celery root, orange, rye, and red cabbage sauerkraut; and roasted pork belly with carrots cooked in carrot juice and a garnish of curly endive and crumbled ricotta salata.

· · ·

[11] 52 rue Richelieu, 1st, 01.42.97.54.40. MÉTRO: Palais-Royal–Musée du Louvre or Pyramides. OPEN Monday to Friday for dinner. CLOSED Saturday and Sunday. www.verjusparis.com • $$$

Verjus Wine Bar, 47 rue Montpensier (just downstairs from the restaurant but with its own entrance), 1st, no phone and no reservations. OPEN Tuesday to Friday for lunch. CLOSED Saturday, Sunday, and Monday. www .verjusparis.com • $

A PARIS FOOD CALENDAR

·   ·

MY PARIS FOOD DIARY, A MEMO ON THE BEST SEASONAL
eating in Paris, begins in October, when it all began for me. It's
a glorious time of the year, because, depending on the weather,
it offers a wonderful edible crosshatching between late summer
and autumn. You'll find late raspberries and Provençal tomatoes
at the same time game begins to appear, and mushroom lovers
know bliss as black trompette de la mort (trumpets of death, but
delicious), cèpes, and girolles come to town. October also sees
the beginning of serious shellfish eating, notably scallops and
oysters, and is a fine month for cheese. (Yes, in France cheese is
seasonal, too.) Brie, that all-American French favorite, is ideal
(it should be made with lait cru, raw milk, since pasteurizing
kills off all of the friendly bacteria that give any good cheese
its taste and character), and the best are labeled as coming from
Meaux—my favorites are from Melun and Montereau. Chestnuts are also in season, and a superb variety of fruit finds its way
into homey desserts, including figs, pears, quinces, and apples.

On the cusp of winter, November has many consolations.
The call of the wild is never stronger, including sanglier (wild
boar), lièvre (hare), chevreuil (roe deer), and biche (venison), as
well as the best birds—pheasant, partridge, and wild duck among
them. The winter vegetables found in medieval still lifes—leeks,
Savoy cabbage, carrots, and Brussels sprouts—start to appear,
and any good cheese tray startles the nostrils with Époisses, an
odoriferous, full-flavored cheese from Burgundy.

December is Lucullian, a time for feasting on foie gras, oysters, truffles, lobster, and langoustines, perhaps followed by a juicy Corsican clementine or two (they're at their best during the holidays and show up on many restaurant menus as part of citrus desserts), while January and February whet the appetite for some of the most ancient French dishes, many of which have a historical pedigree as a reflection of the way the Gauls tided themselves through the winter once the barnyard had gone quiet. With dusk beginning at 4 P.M., I crave pot-au-feu (beef in its own bouillon with carrots, leeks, and potatoes), choucroute garnie (sauerkraut with sausage and pork), cassoulet (white beans, preserved duck, and sausage stewed under a crust of bread crumbs), coq au vin (rooster, traditionally, or chicken in red wine sauce), and poule au pot (chicken poached in stock with carrots, potatoes, and celery). Oursins (sea urchins) provide some bracing iodine-rich punctuation to winter's stewed meats, and I never pass up the cheese tray, especially the creamy vacherin, a soft cow's milk cheese from Savoy that reaches perfection during the winter; Morbier, from the Jura with its distinctive dark gray ribbon of pine ash; Beaufort, a rich nutty cheese from the Alps; and Mimolette, a hearty, orange-colored cheese with a rind like a melon from the north of France.

March is a tease. The first mesclun, or mixed baby salad greens, reaches Paris from Provence, and the stalls at the organic market on the boulevard de Batignolles in the 17th Arrondissement, which has many of the same vendors you find on the boulevard Raspail in the 6th Arrondissement but with lower prices and a more convivial atmosphere, are often decorated with feathery sprays of lemon-bright mimosa, a signal that the grip of winter is easing. Milk-fed baby lamb from Sisteron in Provence and the Pyrenees appears on the butchers' stalls, and the fishmongers display turbot, cod, and John Dory. Toward the end of the month, there's a moment of jubilation when I spot the first asparagus, usually from Pertuis in Provence, in tight purple-headed green bunches. They cost an arm and a leg, but I fork over my euros without hesitation. Likewise, the first of a new season's chèvres (goat cheeses) have a delicious lactic tang that quickens the palate.

April brings new potatoes, slightly tart tapered gariguette strawberries from southwestern France or plump sweet ones from Carpentras in Provence, rhubarb, and occasionally even early cherries from Roussillon. At the fishmonger's, pearly pink langoustines languish on crushed ice next to glossy gray sole, and I crave small, runny Saint-Marcellin cheeses made with milk from cows that have finally gotten a little greenery back into their diets. The veal is also excellent at this time of the year.

In May and June, farm wives sell lilacs and peonies from their own gardens, and salads of peppery roquette (arugula) are part of every weekend meal. Baby artichokes, fava beans, and fresh garlic are perfect for impromptu pasta or risotto recipes, while Norman cheeses like Livarot and Pont l'Évêque are at their best, and one of the rarest French abbey cheeses, Cîteaux, from Burgundy, makes a brief but welcome annual appearance at the end of May.

The return of real tomatoes, as opposed to sad, cottony stand-ins from greenhouses in Brittany or Belgium, is cause for celebration in June and July, as is the annual avalanche of cherries. Fuzzy early peaches are a treat, as are French haricots verts (much of the year in Paris, string beans come from Kenya) and fresh almonds. And the honied perfume of melons from Cavaillon in Provence means that summer's in full bloom.

August is all about salad days—the variety of lettuce and greens on sale in Paris markets makes anyone an herbivore, plus nasturtiums, zucchini blossoms, and other edible flowers, and heirloom tomatoes. This sleepiest month in Paris also means sardines and mackerel, perfect for grilling, along with fresh anchovies from Collioure, a Mediterranean port near the border with Spain. With their tart skin and sweet amber flesh, quetsches, the yellow plums from Lorraine, are great for baking, but there's no better late-summer dessert than a bunch of opalescent Chasselas grapes.

Every September when I return to Paris from vacation, I buy a good ripe raw-milk Camembert before I even open the mail. This month is when the most emblematic French cheese is at its best, and it is hard to imagine a better lunch than a creamy wedge of perfectly ripened Camembert smeared on a torn chunk of crackle-crusted baguette and a glass of red wine. I also crave oysters and langoustines, pigeon, and buttery pears with Roquefort cheese. After languid summer days, I'm hungry for Paris.

THE FOUR SEASONS

· ·

STRAWBERRIES AND MANURE. GUSTS OF FLOWERING privet hedge—a cloying smell like perfume on dirty skin. The summer smells of France are surely one of the main reasons I made it my home. The French not only have no fear of strong smells, they prize them, relishing the sensual provocation offered by this most defenseless and instantaneous of our senses.

It's early July in France, and I'm traveling all over the country on assignment as I always do at this time of the year, which is why my nostrils are being punched into bliss. France is a country that still lives the seasons on the most ancient and intense of terms, as a suite of gifts from nature.

Outside Bitche, a forgotten corner of the country on its border with Luxembourg, the smell of ripe strawberries from the surrounding fields is so strong on a hot afternoon I almost drive off the road. Five days later, the reek of Breton pig barns packs a punch that makes my eyes water, and a week later, during a walk along the beach on the Ile-de-Sein, a tiny island off the coast of Brittany, at low tide when the sun bakes the shaggy tufts of seaweed clinging to rocks, the seaside stink is so primal that evolution never seems more obvious.

France, thank God, has not lost the seasons, and the purest proof is found in the country's markets and on its menus, where a colorful, slow-moving carousel of pleasure requires 365 days to make a full turn. The urgency and avidity of our need to bodily consume the seasons corresponds to deep things, to ancient animal cravings to chomp on what surrounds us for pleasure and a visceral understanding of what we need to remain healthy, and also as a way of measuring time against the specter of our own mortality. After winter's sluggishness, what brings on a quickening physical gladness faster than the season's first asparagus and its intriguing uric visiting card, the olfactory sign of a potent diuretic purging that's a relief to sluggish gizzards at winter's end? Can anything express the poignancy of autumn better than the last raspberries? By living outside the seasons, we've not only forsaken—and increasingly forgotten—centuries of nutritional wisdom as encoded in seasonal recipes and produce, we've made our bodies mute. Historically, appetite, the desire for one food over another, has been the purest form of humanity's self-preserving and sustaining biofeedback.

Where Cheez Doodles, Mountain Dew, and Reese's Peanut Butter Cups fit into this equation is hard to say, but galloping obesity, along with the alarming rise in the incidence of diabetes and heart disease in the United States, are sure symptoms that something's gone very wrong in the country's eating habits. Less egregiously, it's not right that Costco sells huge bundles of asparagus year-round, to say nothing of peaches, nectarines, and, amazingly enough, zucchini blossoms (I swear I saw them recently at the Costco in Norwalk, Connecticut).

Like most Americans, I grew up guilelessly eating Chef Boyardee canned ravioli and drinking neon-pink strawberry-flavored milk. And then I had the same awakening as many other lucky Americans when I went to Europe. Before, I had no inkling that the anonymous, aseasonal produce of suburban American supermarkets, the cellophane-wrapped iceberg lettuce and the New Zealand blueberries on sale in January, symbolize our alienation not only from what we eat but even from one another.

Living in London for a year in the late seventies, I was a flat-broke student sharing a run-down duplex with a motley crew of similarly hard-up types. They were Irish, Maltese, Australian, Rhodesian, and Scottish, which made the kitchen an interesting place. Just out the door was the North End Road market, one of the last of London's great old-fashioned street markets, and we shopped there with pooled change for whatever we could afford. During the winter we ate carrots, cabbage, leeks, potatoes, Swedes, rutabagas, Jerusalem artichokes, or whatever was cheapest because it was what was in season. In those days, there was no lettuce because lettuce doesn't grow in England in February and the Spanish hothouse stuff in the supermarkets was too expensive for us. Spring brought forth fleeting treats like Jersey new potatoes. I still remember being puzzled by the fuss over these potatoes, which was all we had for dinner one night. Then I tasted them. Nutty and sweet, glossed with butter and simply dressed with sea salt (the first time I saw its gray color, I was reluctant to try it because it looked *dirty*), black pepper, parsley, and chives, they were astonishingly good. Early summer—runner beans, real lettuce, early stone fruit. Fall—the first apples and chestnuts, which Jenny from Dublin cooked up as a casserole one night. And on a cold winter night, a gratin of parsnips with a loaf of good bread, some butter and blue cheese, and a jug of red wine was a fine feed that cost the tribe barely more than a pound. It took a year, but through privation, I discovered there was more to eating than just meat with a starch and veg, and, freed from this model of what a meal should be, I became increasingly curious about what I ate.

To be sure, I wasn't completely ignorant of how the seasons could animate a year at the table. In the summer, we'd occasionally stop at one of the farm stands once common in New

England for cherries, tomatoes, and corn on the cob, and again in the fall for big glass jugs of cloudy caramel-colored apple cider made on a clanking machine surrounded by a swarm of yellow jackets that had been put into service just after the Civil War. I also had once rather reluctantly discovered what real milk tasted like because one of the best dairy farms in Connecticut was a short bike ride from our house. The gentle old farmer with his fat Guernsey cows in a tidy barn where the tiled walls were covered with faded satin rosettes—his serial farm show awards—stunned my brother and me one June afternoon by offering us mugs of milk still warm from the cow and thick with sweet-tasting cream. But most vegetables on our family table were frozen, herbs were dried, and fruit, something none of us much cared about, often came in cans. So I came home from England with what must have been an insufferable disdain for the family larder. Little did I realize how little I actually knew, however, until I moved to Paris in 1986.

That first fall, I happily lost my virginity over and over again. I had my first fresh cèpes (porcini mushrooms), my first bécasse (woodcock), and my first quince. It was a season of lavish discoveries, and best of all, it never ended. Even after twenty years, I'm still exploring the bounty of a country that has a proud and ancient consensus that eating of the moment is the key to eating well.

This is why when people who love to eat ask me what's the best time of the year to visit Paris, I tell them there's no bad time—it all depends on what you're hungry for. And if you're unsure of your cravings, tour a market or two as soon as you get to town, since they're an unfailingly good reference for what's best of season.

· ⚘ ·

L'Ambassade d'Auvergne

THOUGH MANY OF PARIS'S REGIONAL RESTAURANTS REMAIN stuck in a dusty time warp, this "embassy" of France's south-central Auvergne region is one place I desperately hope never changes. Occupying an ancient house on the edge of the Marais, this two-story restaurant's decor of dark beams, dried flowers, and rustic bric-a-brac, including copper saucepans and cast-iron cooking utensils, hasn't been touched since the Petrucci family, dyed-in-the-wool Auvergnats, their Italian surname notwith-standing, opened for business in 1968. This means that it has acquired the honest patina of a real auberge, or down-to-earth country inn. The comfortably spaced tables are dressed with pink jacquard tablecloths woven with its name, the service is well rhythmed, the welcome is warm, the prices are moderate, and, most of all, the food's absolutely delicious. In fact I can't think of many places where I'd rather end up on a cold winter's night, since its regional roster of hearty peasant dishes showcase some of the quieter treasures of the French kitchen. To be sure, it's sim-

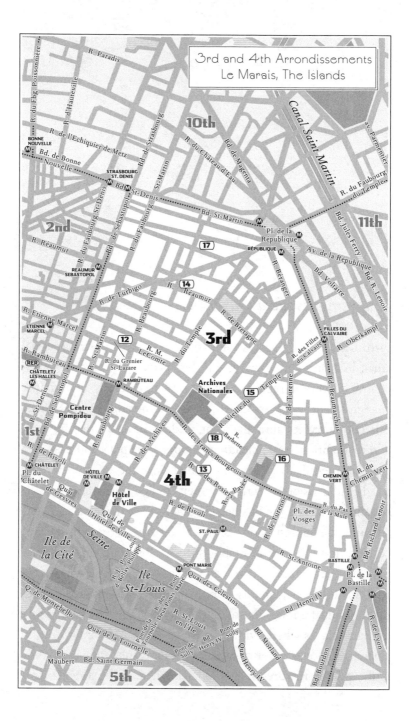

ple, stick-to-your-ribs food, but then that's why I love it—these are dishes that have been consoling and fortifying hardworking farmers, shepherds, masons, and blacksmiths for centuries.

In a nod to its popularity with business diners, foreign visitors, and French visiting from the provinces, the menu makes a feint at contemporary preferences for lighter eating, but by all means ignore those dishes in favor of such classics as the sublime salad of brown Puy lentils seasoned with vinegar, a judicious and delicious dose of creamy goose fat (remember the French paradox, the confounding reality that the French happily consume rich and fatty treats like foie gras yet remain both thin and healthy, before you blanch), and lardons (chunks of bacon). Or, if this sounds too rich, try a slice of jambon de coche de la châtaigneraie, one of the world's finest hams. Rubbed with salt, it's aged six months in a smokehouse over a chestnut-wood fire, and the result is luscious, silky, richly flavored meat that I think may be the best ham in France.

One place where the light touch works brilliantly, though, is its version of stuffed cabbage, one of the region's most famous classics. Instead of the usual mound of pork, salt pork, bread, onion, and cloves placed in the middle of a blanched cabbage and baked, this version comes as a delicate, flavorful mille-feuille, where the stuffing is thinly layered between cabbage leaves and baked as a terrine. Succulent and perfectly seasoned, it's deeply satisfying, and every time I come here, I struggle to decide between the grilled sausage with aligot and the cabbage. Happily, the waiter usually offers a big dollop of aligot, one of the most irresistible comfort foods ever devised, to everyone at the table. Aligot, an Auvergnat staple, is a whipped blend of potatoes, young Tomme de Laguiole cheese, and garlic, and it provides the opportunity for a pleasing bit of old-fashioned table-side theater, since the waiter brings it to the table in a thick copper casserole and whips it a few times, holding his wooden spoon high so that you can see that it has the surprising texture of molten latex.

Dessert may seem improbable at the end of such a meal, but it'd be a shame to miss their sublime chocolate mousse. Note, too, that this place is open on Sundays and is a great alternative to the usual brasserie option.

. · .

IN A WORD: This cozy, welcoming old auberge north of the Centre Pompidou in the 3rd Arrondissement makes good on its name by being a brilliant "embassy" of Auvergnat cooking in Paris.

DON'T MISS: Chestnut soup with cèpes; jambon de coche de la châtaignerie (country ham smoked over a chestnut-wood fire); pounti (terrine of pork, swiss chard, and prunes); lentil salad; stuffed cabbage; aligot (potatoes whipped with Tomme cheese and garlic); guinea hen with braised cabbage; tray of Auvergnat cheeses; chocolate mousse.

. . .

[12] 22 rue Grenier-Saint-Lazare, 3rd, 01.42.72.31.22. MÉTRO: Rambuteau or Étienne Marcel. OPEN daily for lunch and dinner. www.ambassade-auvergne.com • $$

L'As du Falafel

EVERY DAY BUT SATURDAY, THERE'S INSTANT SATISFACTION in publicly breaking one of Paris's silliest and strangest taboos, which is the stuffy informal ban on the ambulatory snacking

that makes for great eating in so many of the world's other best cities. Here, municipal disapproval keeps Parisian streets empty of anything resembling a New York City hot dog stand or a Saigon sidewalk pho vendor, and the prevailing bourgeoisic casts a hairy eyeball on any public consumption less decorous than a picnic. But my bet is that even those sourpusses who look askance at anyone eating a cheese sandwich in a park would make an immediate exception for the falafel sandwiches sold at this hugely popular Israeli-style storefront in the Marais if they'd ever tried one. To keep the crowds at the takeout window moving, you pay first and get a chit to hand to the counterman. Then a hot pouch of the best pita bread in Paris is slit open and filled rapid-fire and generously with grated carrot; purple cabbage; cubes of golden fried eggplant; and hot, crunchy falafel. Finally the whole works is lashed with tahini and some hot pepper sauce if you want it (you do). Once you've taken possession of the city's best street food, the next goal is to find a place to stand out of the way and consume this delicious meal without covering yourself with slaw or sauce when all you have to help are a few flimsy paper napkins. Good luck.

. . .

[13] **34 rue des Rosiers, 4th, 01.48.87.63.60.** MÉTRO: **Saint-Paul.** OPEN **Monday to Thursday and Sunday for lunch and dinner. Friday lunch only.** CLOSED **Saturday.** ▪ **$**

Au Bascou

PREDATING THE INTERNET AND THE TGV HIGH-SPEED RAIL system, which have dramatically shrunk the perceived size of France, the regional tables of Paris are a poignant reminder that even today the country is still composed of proud and distinctive regions, many of which have their own cultures and cuisines.

If the opening of the French national railway system during the nineteenth century and the ensuing massive migration to Paris from previously poor and isolated parts of the country such as Brittany and the Auvergne originally established these nostalgic outposts in the capital, today they function as a living gastronomic library of the deep, diverse, and solidly rustic roots of French cooking.

While many of these slightly wistful tables have closed during the last few years as their owners have retired and returned to the villages from which they came, it's still possible to do an intriguing tour-de-France without leaving the capital, and this friendly, cozy little Basque table on the northern edge of the Marais is a fine place to start.

Stepping inside off the busy rue Réaumur, you could suddenly be in a little tavern in Saint-Jean-Pied-de-Port or Bayonne. Under a ceiling of exposed beams decorated with dangling strings of oxblood red Espelette peppers, wooden tables are set with Basque linens and the menu offers an excellent array of Basque country classics, including piperade, which is made from eggs scrambled with tomatoes, onions, and peppers and garnished with pieces of fried country ham, or another starter, pimientos stuffed with pureed salt cod. Then there are excellent main courses like supions (baby squid) sautéed with chorizo (spicy paprika-flavored sausage) and Espelette peppers on a bed of rice, and axoa, a Basque stew of ground veal, onions, and peppers. Desserts include beret Basque, a beret-shaped chocolate-covered, cream-filled sponge cake, and gateau Basque, a flat, flaky golden cake filled with almond cream.

Since the arrival of the new chef, Bertrand Guéneron, former second to Alain Senderens, not only has the cooking here become more refined, but several contemporary French dishes have been added to the menu, among them a delicious chestnut soup garnished with foie-gras-stuffed ravioli, sautéed shrimp with a salad of finely sliced fennel bulb and mixed leaves, and duck breast with red pears. The red Irouleguy from Domaine Brana is a fine wine choice with this cooking, and the service by the smart, friendly young staff makes this a place you want to linger.

· ~ ·

IN A WORD: The best outpost of Basque country cooking in Paris and a great choice for a long, relaxed lunch.

DON'T MISS: Sauté of escargots and Bayonne ham; pintade à la Bayonnaise (guineau hen with a garnish of tomatoes, peppers, and onions); grilled cod; Ossau Iraty cheese with black cherry preserves; millefeuille à la vanille.

. . .

[14] 38 rue Réaumur, 3rd, 01.42.72.69.25. MÉTRO: Arts-et-Métiers or Réaumur. OPEN Monday to Friday for lunch and dinner. CLOSED Saturday and Sunday. www.au-bascou.fr ▪ $$

Breizh Café

PARISIAN PREFERENCES IN REGIONAL COOKING TEND TO reflect trends in the preferred French vacation spots of magazine editors. In the 1990s, Provençal cooking suddenly became stylish, but now, with sunbathing out of favor and real estate prices in the Lubéron well beyond the reach of most people with editorial salaries, shaggy green Brittany is getting a look in. You know what that means—crêpes, which are made from white flour, and galettes, which are dun-colored, from buckwheat. Paris's traditional crêpe belt surrounds the Gare du Montparnasse, the gateway to the capital from Brittany and a heavily Breton neighborhood until an egregious redevelopment in the 1970s.

Breizh Café, the city's best crêperie, is a happy reflection of how much Brittany has changed during the last twenty years, since it's located right in the heart of the Marais and pokes fun at the traditional folklore of crêperies with a slick decor of slate floors, rough oak-paneled walls, and amusing Manga-style paintings of Breton women wearing coiffes, the traditional Breton lace bonnets. The Manga look and the wasabi dressing available for the house green salad also reveal the fact that the clever owner, Bertrand Larcher, had already perfected his new-wave crêperie concept not only in his native Cancale, a delightful seaside town in Brittany, but in Tokyo before opening this Paris branch. Since the French are uninspired sandwich makers, this is an ideal spot for a quick, tasty, reasonably priced lunch, too. Larcher's Japanese crêpe makers use only organic produce—flour, eggs, milk, and butter—and the results are outstanding, including one delicious galette (savory buckwheat flour crêpe) filled with a fried egg, ham, raw-milk Gruyère, and sautéed button and shiitake mushrooms, and another with ham, an egg, Gruyère, and artichoke hearts. You can add a first course of oysters if you're hungry, and do try one of the excellent dry organic ciders on the cider list (cider being the traditional drink with crêpes in Brittany). Dessert crêpes, made with white flour, include classics like one flambéed with Grand Marnier, which is brought to the table dancing with blue flame in a miniature copper casserole, and my favorite, which is drizzled with salted caramel sauce and topped with a ball of excellent vanilla ice cream.

IN A WORD: The crêpe and galette get a makeover for the twenty-first century using top-quality, mostly organic produce, and the stylish interior reflects Brittany's emergence as a newly chic holiday destination for increasingly SPF-conscious Parisians.

. . .

[15] 109 rue Vieille du Temple, 3rd, 01.42.72.13.77. MÉTRO: Filles du Calvaire. OPEN Wednesday to Sunday. CLOSED Monday and Tuesday. www .breizhcafe.com. ▪ $

Café des Musées

AS HEARD FROM A BASEMENT MEN'S ROOM, THE LEVEL OF echoing laughter and conversation may seem a very odd way to gauge the quality of a Paris kitchen, but it's a surefire measure of a place where a wonderfully diverse crowd of Parisians comes with the certain knowledge that they're going to eat well and have a good time. So when I briefly excused myself from the table at the Café des Musées, this happy human music heard from afar made me eager to get back upstairs as soon as possible and rejoin the fun.

In fact, this corner café cum bistro with a forgettable decor might well serve as a model for what the Parisian café genus could and should become. This understandably popular place keeps the neighborhood—the western edge of the Marais, not far from the Picasso Museum—fed everyday, too, a rarity in Paris.

On one of the more forlorn restaurant days of the year, New Year's Day, we met a pair of hungry friends from Boston, and our progress through the daily chalkboard menu made an already happy occasion, a reunion, even better, especially since these Bostonians love to eat but were on a budget. A half-dozen deep-sea oysters from the waters off Paimpol in Brittany were superb, served room temperature with a basket of crusty baguette and good butter, and carefully shucked so that not a drop of their delicious brine went missing. Still, these beautiful bivalves were upstaged by a terrific soup of smoked garlic and beer from the northern French town of Arleux—creamy with pureed potato, comforting with the ancient whiff of a wood-burning hearth, and celebrating the sturdy eternity of honest peasant cooking with a soft gust of garlic, along with a coarse, richly flavored chicken liver terrine with onion jam. Poulette fermière aux chanterelles arrived in a miniature black cast-iron casserole with plump pieces of barnyard fowl riding a deep, creamy bed of chanterelle mushrooms, and the entrecôte, an often problematic cut of French beef for Americans accustomed to a thicker and much more tender steak, was immaculately cooked and wonderfully chewy. It also came to the table with a generous bowl of hot hand-cut golden frites that we squabbled over and a ramekin of excellent homemade béarnaise, a real treat now that many restaurants buy in their sauces.

Two of us followed with the excellent assortment of cheeses— Saint-Nectaire, Camembert, and a chunk of ash-blackened Pyramide (goat cheese), and the others swooned over an individual serving of chocolate mousse and pears poached in red wine with cinnamon, vanilla beans, and cloves, a really lovely winter dessert.

The wine list offers a bluff assortment of good bottles, including several by the glass or *pot* (a 50-centiliter carafe), and our saucy waitress never missed a beat throughout the whole meal. Come here once, and you'll ending up wishing this place was just around the corner from your own front door for a long time to come.

· · ·

IN A WORD: If only every café in Paris served food this good and reasonably priced.

DON'T MISS: Smoked garlic and beer soup; tarte moelleux (like a quiche); terrine ménagère aux foies de voláille (chicken liver terrine with onion jam); free-range chicken with chanterelles; entrecôte; chocolate mousse; pears poached in red wine.

· · ·

[16] 49 rue de Turenne, 3rd, 01.42.72.96.17. MÉTRO: Saint-Sébastien-Froissart or Chemin Vert. OPEN daily for lunch and dinner. www .cafedesmusees.fr. ▪ $$

Pramil

WITH ITS ANCIENT EXPOSED STONE WALLS, WHITE-PAINTED beamed ceiling, low lighting, and potted orchids, chef Alain Pramil's contemporary French bistro in the northern Marais is an address to which I always return with pleasure. It's also a table that comes to mind immediately when I want a seriously good meal in a setting that's propitious for a good tête-à-tête. This is why I booked here when my friend Martine told me she was coming to town and suggested we have dinner.

Martine, a lively, elegant woman who loves good food and wine, is someone I've known for years, ever since she invited me to an epic wine tasting at chef Alain Senderens's château outside Cahors, her hometown in southwestern France. It lasted nine hours; I was the youngest by at least twenty-five years of the twenty-some guests in attendance and surely knew less about wine than anyone else at the table, which is why it was a shock (from which I'm still recovering) when around three in the morning I was asked to stand up and give a discourse on the dozens and dozens of wines we'd just tasted. I've long since deleted from memory whatever I mumbled, but it still gives us a good laugh when we get together. Our paths cross too infrequently, so I really wanted to take her somewhere that was very Parisian and served food she might not run into in Cahors.

A warm welcome got things off to a good start, and I was gratified when Martine started reading the menu and said, "Oh, my! This is going to be difficult," because there were so many appealing options. That spring night, Martine began with a salad of ficoïde glaciale, a crunchy, succulent salad plant, a similar one that's a feature of southern Californian landscaping, with grilled shrimp and roasted tomatoes, and I tried the warm white asparagus soup with a ball of foie gras ice cream. Martine's salad was excellent, and I liked my soup, but found the ice cream a little gimmicky. A few ribbons of foie gras would have underlined the wonderful earthy flavor of the asparagus more effectively than the cold sweet ice cream, but the soup was beautifully made and pleasantly tinted with piment d'Espelette—the red pepper from the Basque country, the heat of which backstopped its richness. Next, perfectly grilled scallops in a light vermouth-scented cream sauce with wilted spinach for me, and a succulent onglet de veau (veal steak) with olive-oil-enriched potato puree for Martine.

Our stunningly good white Burgundy, a Savigny-lès-Beaune, was ideal with these main courses, and also worked perfectly with the excellent selection of cheeses, the best of which was a first-of-season chèvre from the Loire, that I chose instead of dessert. Martine was happy with her nougat glacé—an old-fashioned French favorite of ice cream studded with candied fruit and nougat—and asked for the restaurant's card while I was paying the bill. "This is exactly the kind of restaurant I love finding in Paris," she said as we walked together for a while afterward. I agreed that it's these unexpected little places as much as the star-studded ones that make dining out in the French capital so satisfying at all levels of the local gastronomic food chain.

· ⁓ ·

IN A WORD: Chef Alain Pramil's well-mannered and attractively decorated vest-pocket bistro in the northern Marais near the Place de la République is a fine choice for a quiet, possibly romantic meal, since his inventive modern French cooking is not only delicious but makes for good conversation.

DON'T MISS: Cauliflower cake with hot-pepper jelly, fi-coïde glaciale salad with grilled shrimp and roasted tomatoes, house-smoked salmon, rabbit terrine, grilled scallops with vermouth sauce, sea bass with eggplant and Kalamata olives, veal steak with olive-oil-enriched potato puree, homemade nougat glacé, and coffee-cream-filled millefeuille.

. . .

[17] **9 rue du Vertbois, 3rd, 01.42.72.03.60.** MÉTRO: **Temple or République.** OPEN **Tuesday to Saturday for lunch and dinner. Sunday dinner only.** CLOSED **Monday. www.pramilrestaurant.fr • $$**

Robert et Louise

GENTRY IS THE ONLY WOMAN I KNOW WHOSE IDEA OF A good time is the do-it-yourself courses offered in the hardware department at the middlebrow BHV (Bazaar de l'Hôtel de Ville) department store during the weekend—how to use a staple gun, how to tile a shower stall, and so on. Born in Hollywood, she also has the edgy "Black Dahlia" look of a heroine in a Nathanael West novel. You know, scissored black bangs, bright red lipstick, high-heeled lace-up boots, and a waist so tiny it's not much bigger than a large bunch of flowers. It's only her upturned, elfin nose that blunts the immediate certainty she's a dominatrix (she's actually a talented lingerie designer with her own Paris-based company).

We haven't known each other very long, but when I was mulling over whom I'd invite to lunch at Robert et Louise in the Marais, she instantly came to mind. Why? She's hilarious and a keen student of atmosphere, and she eats like a quarterback. Further, she knows that elegance—the apotheosis of any Parisian who loves the city's public life—is generated by rigid discipline in terms of texture, color, and line. Of course you create your own personal style, but the rules must be mastered and respected if elegance is the desired effect, and most Parisians couldn't even begin to fathom anyone who doesn't aspire to it. Gentry not only knows all of this but embraces it, which makes her profoundly Parisian. So I suspected she'd thrill to this funky and rather dusty dining room where the cooking is done over a wood fire in a large chimney and in a tiny jerry-built kitchen under a flight of stairs and you occupy bare wood tables in a long, dim, narrow dining room under huge centuries-old beams.

For half a century, it was the lair of Robert Georget and his wife, Louise, who contentedly cooked for the northern Marais as it evolved from a run-down and slightly sad part of the city into one of the trendiest parts of Paris. Following Robert's death, his daughter Pascale joined her mother in the kitchen, and with any luck at all, this legendary old table will survive instead of meeting the too-common fate of many restaurants in gentrifying parts of Paris and becoming a clothing boutique. Just to get a rise out of her, I ask Pascale, a sturdy, friendly woman with an engagingly husky voice and ready smile, if she's planning to keep cooking or convert the space into a boutique. "Mais vous êtes fou ou quoi!" ("Are you crazy, or what!") she shouts, and then, when I tell her I was just teasing, she says, "Vilain garçon! C'est une bonne chose pour vous que je ne suis pas venu à table avec un couteau. Alors, qu'est-ce-que vous allez mangez?" ("Naughty boy! It's a good thing for you that I didn't come to the table with a knife! Now, what are you eating?")

I start with a plate of silky Parma ham, freshly sliced, and Gentry goes for snails. Then we split a massive exquisitely charred côte de boeuf for two. It comes sliced in a pool of its own rosy juices on a wooden cutting board, along with a bowl of pommes sautées and a side of salad. We ignore the salad, immediately ask for more potatoes, and continue sipping a great jammy Gigondas. "This is why I moved to Paris," Gentry announces when the steak is almost finished. "For this atmosphere, this sense of history, the consensus that pleasure is more important than work. I've always wanted to be in this ancient and brilliantly dowdy room," she continued, smiling. "It makes me think of the old photographs by Boubat and Doisneau I'd stare at for hours as a fourteen-year-old girl wishing herself far from Newport Beach, California." All of which is to say that having a truly good meal is always almost as much about good casting as it is about the food, since who you eat with and where you eat change everything.

IN A WORD: For carnivores only, this simple bistro offers the fleeting chance to sample an unself-conscious prewar Paris atmosphere, and the côte de boeuf (rib steak) for two is spectacular, too.

DON'T MISS: Marinated herring; fromage de tête (head cheese); côte de boeuf; omelette forestière (filled with wild mushrooms).

. . .

[**18**] **64 rue Vieille du Temple, 3rd, 01.42.78.55.89.** MÉTRO: **Rambuteau.** OPEN **Tuesday to Sunday for dinner. Thursday to Sunday for lunch.** CLOSED **Monday. www.robertetlouise.com.** ▪ **$$**

LATIN QUARTER, SAINT-GERMAIN-DES-PRÉS, FAUBOURG-SAINT-GERMAIN

Allard

I WAS SITTING IN THE MÉTRO ON THE WAY HOME FROM DIN-ner at this venerable old corner bistro in the heart of Saint-Germain-des-Prés, which was founded in 1932 by Marthe Allard, a cook from Burgundy. It had recently been taken over by Alain Ducasse, and I'd returned out of curiosity to see if a place I'd once loved might be good again; it was. So it was a pleasure to scroll through the photos of the meal I'd taken on my phone in lieu of notes.

Even though I hadn't left the table more than an hour earlier, my mouth watered when I got to a shot of the roasted duck with green Sicilian olives that I'd shared with my friend Judy, a New Orleans–born journalist who's lived in Paris for almost forty years. The big golden bird from Challans, a town in the Poitou-Charentes region famous for its fowl, had been cooked just pink; strewn with olives, it barely fit into the serving dish in which it arrived at the table. We'd eaten as much of it as we possibly could, but I still regretted

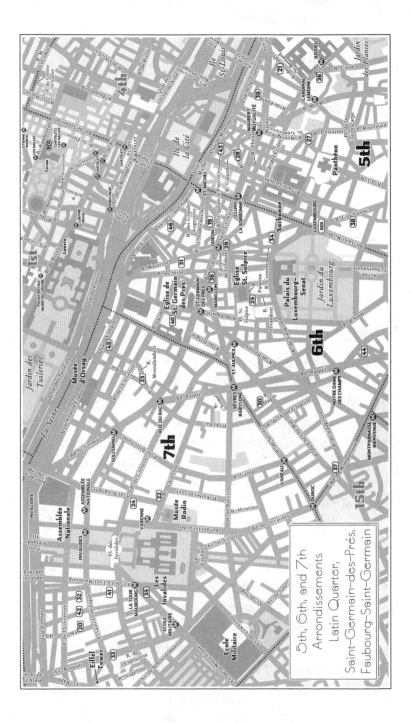

5th, 6th, and 7th
Arrondissements
Latin Quarter,
Saint-Germain-des-Prés,
Faubourg-Saint-Germain

the leftovers I'd liked to have taken home and turned into a nice duck parmentier, or shepherd's pie. Unfortunately, doggie bags still just aren't done in Paris, with a few exceptions, such as the table d'hôtes at Boucherie Hugo Desnoyer.

"Cet canard, il est magnifique! S'il vous plaît, où est-ce-que vous avez mangé ça?" said the distinguished-looking man in a loden coat who had been reading a newspaper when I sat down next to him. When I answered him, he replied, "Ah bon!" and told me that he hadn't been there in years but would be tempted to return for the duck, a house classic that had once been one of his favorite dishes as well. "What else did you eat?" he asked, and I showed him more photos of our meal. Judy had had sautéed first-of-season cèpes from Corrèze in central France, and I'd had a superb pâté en croûte—buttery pastry enclosing a gently gamy poultry terrine—made by young award-winning Parisian charcutier Arnaud Nicolas. Somehow or other we'd also managed dessert—profiteroles with vanilla ice cream and dark chocolate sauce for Judy, and a savarin (sponge cake) with whipped cream and a good head-clearing soaking of excellent rum from the island of Réunion for me.

"Thank you for sharing your meal with me. It does my old heart good to know that a few of the old bistros soldier on," said the man when I stood up to leave the train. It had done my somewhat younger heart good to have eaten this meal, too, since as much as I applaud the creativity and talent of the new generation of chefs who are renewing the gastronomic laurels of Paris, the brilliant bedrock of great food in the city for me will always be traditional bistro cooking. This is why I'm hoping that the next time I go I'll get exactly the same table Judy and I had, the one for two next to the big zinc bar in the cozy front room with its caramel-colored walls and mottled mirror, and I'll have the escargots and then either the sole meunière or the roasted Bresse chicken, both of which are served for two.

·   ·   ·

IN A WORD: Alain Ducasse succeeds as the savior of a much-loved old bistro with a charming fly-in-amber decor in the heart of Saint-Germain-des-Prés.

DON'T MISS: Escargots, pâté en croûte, frog's legs in garlic butter, turbot with beurre blanc, sole meunière, roast duck with green olives, roasted chicken, beef cheeks and carrots braised in red wine, profiteroles with vanilla ice cream and hot chocolate sauce.

. . .

[**19**] **41 rue Saint-André-des-Arts, 6th, 01.43.26.48.23.** MÉTRO: **Odéon.** OPEN **daily. www.restaurant-allard.fr** ▪ **$$$**

L'Ami Jean

IF YOU MISSED THE GLORY DAYS OF LA RÉGALADE, THE most famous bistro to open in Paris during the last fifteen years under the founding chef, Yves Camdeborde, this brawny south-western bistro in a polite part of the 7th Arrondissement is about as close as you can get to finding out what all of the original fuss was about. Chef Stéphane Jégo worked with Camdeborde for ten years before going out on his own, and his style remains very much inspired by that of his master.

This place also approximates the original La Régalade in terms of being a busy, bustling place with several sittings (if you come for dinner, book the second one so that you won't be rushed), a good-value chalkboard menu that changes regularly, closely spaced wooden tables, and slightly frantic waitresses.

Despite the fact that it has the bawdy atmosphere of a rugby players' canteen, it's very popular with staff from nearby UNESCO and decorous loden-coat-wearing locals, and you'll spot a lot of très 7th Arrondissement ladies of varying ages wearing Alice headbands and inherited Hermès scarves. In fact, the friendly older couple sitting next to Claire, Denis, Bruno, and me on a busy Saturday night seemed to be lapping up the rambunctiousness of this place, and when we fell into conversation, Madame accurately described Jégo's bistro as "très bon enfant," French argot for "very pleasant."

Chef Jégo sautées tiny pétoncles (scallops) in their shells in foaming butter, and once they open, he sprinkles them with sautéed shallots, a little garlic, a few branches of thyme, and several slices of grilled bacon to create a dish that's irresistible. Claire and I couldn't stay away from these sweet little morsels, while Denis had baby squid sautéed with plump white beans and Bruno was in ecstasy over his potent game bouillon with crumbled bacon, sliced chestnuts, and chives. The main courses were similarly delicious, including a perfect petit salé, a stew of salted pork and lentils; axoa, a traditional Basque veal stew spiked with red and green peppers, the quiet fire of ground Espelette pepper, garlic, and onions; and a succulent griddled daurade (sea bream) with olive oil and lemon.

Instead of dessert, I chose the Ossau Iraty cheese from the Basque country with black cherry jam, while Bruno was happy with his slice of gâteau Basque (a flat pastry cake filled with cherry jam), and Denis pronounced the rice pudding even better than that of his grandmother in Rennes. "That was a very good meal" was Claire's verdict once we'd found the calm of the sidewalk out front. "It was even worth putting up with the noise," Denis added, and he's absolutely right.

·   ·

IN A WORD: Chef Stéphane Jégo's southwestern-French-inspired bistro cooking is hearty and delicious. This sincere, happy place isn't cheap but it's one of the best buys on the Left Bank for the quality offered. If you're coming for dinner, book the calmer second service.

DON'T MISS: The chalkboard menu changes constantly, but dishes to look out for include baby squid sautéed with white beans; bouillon de gibier (wild game bouillon); pétoncles (tiny scallops); axoa (Basque veal stew); daurade à la plancha (grilled sea bream); petit salé (salted pork and lentil stew); sanglier (wild boar); crème de citron avec nougatine noix-pistachio (lemon cream with walnut-and-pistachio nougat); and rice pudding.

· · ·

[20] 27 rue Malar, 7th, 01.47.05.86.89. MÉTRO: Invalides. OPEN Tuesday to Saturday for lunch and dinner. CLOSED Sunday and Monday. www .lamijean.fr • $$$

L'AOC

WITH ITS FLESH-TONE WALLS, BOUQUETS OF DRIED ROSES, and collection of cast-iron agricultural fair award plaques on the wall by the tidy rotisserie, this cheerful Latin Quarter restaurant could be found anywhere along thousands of kilometers of route nationale in France. In the big city, this ruddy, profoundly Gallic tavern is a rarity, a happy place where the French come to feel good about themselves by celebrating the extraordinary agricultural bounty of l'Hexagone, as they affectionately refer to France. "I have no formal background in cooking," explains chef-owner Jean-Philippe Lattron, a strong, stout man with beetle brows, a big smile, and a reassuringly firm handshake. "My idea in opening this restaurant was to work exclusively with the best produce and let it speak for itself."

It was a great idea, too, since Lattron combs France in search of the best AOC foods and then cooks them with respectful precision to bring out their natural flavors. AOC, which stands for Appellation d'Origine Contrôlée, is the star of French agriculture, a designation that's sparingly awarded by the French government to produce that adheres to a legally defined set of qualifications that govern almost every aspect of its production and require that it come from a specifically defined geographical area. In the same way that most Americans possess a frightening store of television show trivia—almost everyone over a certain age knows the names of the Three Stooges or, more recently, the Kardashians—the French can be counted upon to offer up a reverent sigh when reference is made to such AOC products as porc noir de Bigorre, pork from a special breed of black pigs raised in the southwest French region of Bigorre, part of the Béarn. And for this reason, the menu at L'AOC is an implicit celebration of good eating and environmentally intelligent farming, a concept that couldn't possibly be more timely.

For foreigners who want more details on the various AOC labels on the menu, Lattron's delightful wife, Sophie, speaks perfect English—she lived in New York for several years—and loves to reminisce about her experience of "la vie américaine" and how much she loves the Big Apple.

On a sullen winter night when the pavement outside was glistening with rain, we settled in over glasses of white Quincy wine and shamelessly helped ourselves to the two big terrines she set down on the table—chicken liver and campagne (country style), which was unctuous and almost gamey with pork liver. With a little linen slip of Poujaran bread, we could happily have made a meal of the terrine but went on to excel-

lent first courses of oeufs en meurette, a Burgundian classic of poached eggs in a sublime sauce of deeply reduced beef stock spiked with red wine and loaded with chunky lardons (chunks of bacon) and baby onions, and marrow bones seasoned with Guérande sea salt and served with a small salad. Rotisseried AOC chicken from Lattron's native Sologne just north of the Loire River valley, known for the quality of its fowl, came with sautéed potatoes, and a thick slab of Bigorre pork had a crunchy skin and delicious blazes of fat and came with a mountainous side of sautéed potatoes.

Afterward we split a plate of brebis, ewe's milk cheese made by Benedictine monks in the Pyrénées mountains, served with black cherry jam, and concluded with a delightful café gourmand, espresso served with a tiny glass ramekin of hazelnut-topped rice pudding, another one of chocolate pudding, and a miniature financier cake.

All during the meal, I was distracted by the self-satisfied chauvinistic grumpiness of the neighboring table of six, clearly politicians since they spoke about how hard it is to get a "handi-capé" parking place, thus confirming my suspicion that most of these reserved parking spots in the streets of Paris aren't for handicapped people at all but for VIPs with pull. Their happy ranting also took them to subjects as diverse as the quality of America's cheeses (épouvantable, or dreadful), the madness of even thinking of admitting Turkey to the European Union, and how the Germans were getting the better end of the stick when it came to the job cuts at Airbus. In almost any other setting, these snatches of overheard conversation would have rankled, but so lavishly served and well fed on such an inhospitable night, I actually felt forgiving and even a little humbled by my own good fortune in living in a city where a young couple so passionate about the quality of the food they serve would find such an enthusiastic following.

.   .   .

IN A WORD: This cheerful, friendly bistro in the Latin Quarter makes a welcome fetish of the finest-quality French produce, foodstuffs worthy of receiving the coveted AOC (Appellation d'Origine Contrôlée) label, and the chef, Jean-Philippe Lattron, wisely knows that food this good should be prepared simply.

DON'T MISS: Marrow bones with Guérande sea salt; terrine de foie gras; roast lamb; roast pork loin; roast chicken; crème brûlée; baba au rhum (sponge cake with whipped cream and rum).

. . .

[21] 184 rue des Fossés-Saint-Bernard, 5th, 01.43.54.22.52. MÉTRO: Cardinale Lemoine or Jussieu. OPEN Tuesday to Saturday for lunch and dinner. CLOSED Sunday and Monday. www.restoaoc.com • $$

Arpège

ROGER, AN AUSTRALIAN BUSINESS LAWYER WITH WHOM I shared a shabby bedsit in London many years ago when he thought he was a thespian and I was writing mediocre poetry in the style, I hoped, of Gerard Manley Hopkins, calls from Sydney. He's coming through Paris for a night on his way to a week's work in Africa and invites me to dinner at Arpège. He hears me hesitate—time and distance have not dulled the antennae of the heightened intimacy born of the privation we shared.

"I know it's bloody expensive, but the firm's paying, and since I remarried I've become almost completely vegetarian," he explains.

Not having known about his vegetarianism, I scuttle my reluctance. It'll be great to see him, and I suspect he'll very much enjoy the many vegetarian dishes on chef Alain Passard's menu. Whether I will enjoy the meal or not remains to be seen, but frankly under the circumstances, it doesn't matter—this will be an occasion where friendship trumps gastronomy.

What I didn't tell him is that I have a complicated and often conflicted relationship with Arpège. I've had some sublime meals here, but I'm bothered by the brazenly expensive wine list, often find the service aloof, and am underwhelmed by the visual austerity of this small dining room just across the street from the Musée Rodin. Most important, I often find Passard's food so simple, even ascetic, that it fails to ignite the blaze of pleasure I expect from haute cuisine. On the other hand, I'm fascinated by the fact that Passard is such an iconoclast, and, almost more than any other restaurant in Paris, this place forces me to ruminate on what the experience of a restaurant should be at the beginning of a new century.

The last time I'd been there, I'd been intrigued but troubled by a plate of tiny new potatoes from the chef's five-acre garden in the Sarthe, an hour southwest of Paris. They were smoked in oat straw and served with a horseradish mousseline, to create a dish that was a brilliant declension of a rustic Breton taste memory—Passard is from Brittany, where they eat a lot of potatoes, and learned to cook from his grandmother, who insisted that the most important skill in the kitchen was learning to do an impeccable roast. Serving up smoky spuds in the Faubourg-Saint-Germain, the citadel of the French aristocracy, was clearly intended to shock and provoke, and it succeeded at doing both. Despite its homeliness, it was brilliant and deeply satisfying, since the sweet taste of the potatoes was amplified and framed by the sharp horseradish, and the umami (the fifth sense of taste, including tastes like sharp cheese, chicken soup, soy sauce, seaweed, cured meats, etc.) added by the smoke ennobled the dish with perfect balance. On the other hand, this dish cost nearly 42 euros—for potatoes! In the same vein but even more extreme was a gratin of Cévennes onions with aged Parmesan. It was delicious, but ultimately I could have cooked it myself. So was this deliciousness adequate to my expectations of a great chef? I wasn't sure.

On my way to meet Roger, this spool of thought renewed itself. Making great produce eloquent is an extraordinary talent, but when it veers towards a simplicity accessible to any layman, the specter of the emperor's new clothes is uncomfortably invoked. Out of curiosity, I glanced at the recipes posted on Passard's website before going out the door, and they confirmed my confusion, or the seesaw, love-hate relationship I have with this restaurant. A recipe for carpaccio de langoustines might take twenty minutes—you just slice the raw langoustines and season them—while his famous "tomates confites aux douze saveurs," Arpège's signature dessert, wouldn't take a half hour. When it comes to cooking, the input of time doesn't always equate with ecstasy, but I think we go to restaurants of this caliber to experience something we could never hope to achieve ourselves.

Roger, already at the table, was let down by the dining room. "It looks a lot like the executive lunchroom of a gray flannel bank," he astutely observed of the curved pear-wood paneling ornamented only with a few inserts of Lalique glass. He loved Passard's signature amuse-bouche of an eggshell filled with a raw yolk, cream, and maple syrup, however, and we were both in great spirits and honestly hungry.

So we ate. He had spinach with salt butter and carrots with orange zest, a vegetable plate of snow peas, asparagus, fava beans, tiny peas, cabbage, onions, and a few other legumes, while I went for the foie gras with dates and roast chicken. And as is invariably the case, my reflexive dubiousness with regard to Arpège was eclipsed by the point-blank fact that the food is often excellent. It helped, too, that the Aussie bank popped for a superb bottle of Condrieu, and even though he described the service as "chilly," Roger and I had a hilarious time reminiscing about Monique, a friend who used to shoplift trays of pork chops at a Sainsbury's supermarket in London's North End Road for Saturday-night feasts. And thirty years after scarfing down this purloined merchandise, here we were, former turnstile jumpers, splashing out in one of the most expensive restaurants in Paris. Our collective memories formed the jolly scrim to this meal, and I held my tongue throughout—there's nothing worse than the local expert when all anyone wants to do is have a good time— but I was curious about what I knew would be his very blunt take on the place once we were outside on the sidewalk a few hours later.

"Damned good food, and it's brilliant that someone really cares about veggies, but what a bloody-minded place," said Roger, as I walked him back to his hotel. My sentiments exactly.

· ⟶ ·

IN A WORD: Alain Passard is an iconoclast who thumbs his nose at the conventions of haute cuisine dining by serving delicious but often dead simple vegetable dishes, along with fish and fowl, in a rather wan dining room. Though his swooningly high prices are a brainteaser to justify, there's no denying that Passard's a superb chef.

DON'T MISS: Potatoes smoked in oak straw with horserad-ish mousseline; gratin of Cévennes onions with Parmesan; lob-ster in vin jaune (a maderized golden-colored wine from the Jura region of France) sauce; veal sweetbreads with réglisse (a licorice-tasting herb); roast pigeon with hydromel (mead); to-matoes confites aux douze saveurs (baked tomatoes with twelve flavors).

. . .

[22] 84 rue de Varenne, 7th, 01.47.05.09.06. MÉTRO: Varenne. OPEN Mon-day to Friday for lunch and dinner. CLOSED Saturday and Sunday. www .alain-passard.com • $$$$

L'Atelier de Joël Robuchon

TAKING A LEAF FROM NEW YORK CITY COFFEE SHOPS, JAPA-nese sushi bars, and Spain's tapas counters, chef Joël Robuchon opened his counter-service-only snack de luxe just off the rue du Bac in 2004 and it's been packed ever since. I love the way Robuchon democratized great food by freeing it from its nor-mal formal sitdown rituals, and occupying a comfortable stool at the bar here is one of the most convivial restaurant experiences Paris has to offer. Since the no-reservations policy, aside from the 11.30 A.M. and 6.30 P.M. sittings, often means a long wait, I usually pop in at the last minute at an unlikely moment, late on a rainy Tuesday night, for example, and treat myself to a luxuri-ous if pricy feast by foraging among the many delicious small plates on offer. The innocuous black-lacquer-and-red decor has always reminded me of something you'd expect at a pole dancers' club, but this hardly matters when you're so intently focused on what's on your plate. There are some lovely things to eat here, too, including Iberian ham with pan con tomate, tomato-smeared toasts like those you'd get in a Barcelona tapas bar; a layered timbale of grilled eggplant, tomato, zucchini, and buffalo-milk mozzarella; frogs' legs beignets (fritters) with garlic cream; and the sublime merlan Colbert, a whole deboned breaded whiting delicately fried and served with fried parsley, herb butter, and a side of the world's best potato puree. And thanks to a charming Brazilian gem dealer, who recommended it so heartily she couldn't be ignored, I discovered Robuchon's elegant take on spaghetti carbonara, which is made with smoky Alsatian bacon and crème fraîche. The brilliant Chartreuse soufflé, which is spooned open and topped with a ball of pistachio ice cream, creates an elegant finale with its sophisticated contrast of sweet and bitter flavors, but every time I taste it I can't help but feel slightly wistful for Robuchon's original restaurant, Jamin, which the chef sold at the age of fifty, ostensibly to retire. Anyone as creative as Robuchon could hardly be expected to remain idle, however, and so L'Atelier was his comeback vehicle. L'Atelier is great fun, but it offers tantalizing cameos of his extraordinary talent rather than the mesmerizing full-barreled experience Jamin once did.

· · ·

IN A WORD: Chef Joël Robuchon's counter-service-only snack bar de luxe is one of the most original restaurants in Paris and a delightful place for solo diners and couples (conversation becomes awkward if you're more than three). The small-plate format offers a dazzling experience of his talent that's ideal for lunch or a light dinner.

DON'T MISS: Griddled encornets (baby squid) and artichokes; Iberian ham with tomato toasts; frogs' legs beignets (fritters) with garlic cream; timbale of grilled eggplant, tomato, zucchini, and buffalo-milk mozzarella; braised duckling; merlan Colbert (boned, breaded, fried whiting with herb butter sauce and potato puree); grilled tuna belly; scallop with truffle shavings; caramelized quail; spaghetti carbonara; Chartreuse soufflé.

. . .

[23] 5–7 rue de Montalembert, 7th, 01.42.22.56.56. MÉTRO: Rue du Bac. OPEN daily for lunch and dinner. www.joel-robuchon.net ▪ $$$$

Auguste

DESPITE ITS SOMEWHAT UNLIKELY LOCATION ON AN EX-clusive street in the silk-stocking 7th Arrondissement, Auguste is among the more reliably inventive restaurants in Paris right now. For almost twenty years, the vital middle layer of the French food chain, serious restaurants, often with a single Michelin star, has been steadily atrophying, leaving a sorry gap between the lofty summit of increasingly corporate-bankrolled haute cuisine and the bistro, which will always be the solid base of good eating in France. Now something is stirring, and Auguste is one of a few new tender shoots in this once forlorn territory.

"When I first opened, a lot of the younger French food journalists told me my cooking was too old-fashioned and that I should become more cutting edge, or attuned to the cooking of chefs like Ferran Adria or Thierry Marx. But I knew this wasn't what my clients wanted. So I've found my own way to be modern," says chef Gaël Orieux, a Breton who looks as if he could be Errol Flynn's grandson and who named his restaurant in honor of that grandest of classic French chefs, Georges-Auguste Escoffier.

By choosing to ignore all the Merlin-like trends of the moment, including molecular cooking and now tired bells and whistles like miniature wands of cotton candy as garnishes, he has succeeded in creating an impressive template for the modern French restaurant that's chic and comfortable, with swift, friendly service that suits busy people who want exceptionally good contemporary cooking without all of the pomp once associated with this category. "I've consciously streamlined the whole experience of a Michelin one-star table," says Orieux, who won his first star in 2007 and whose impressive résumé began at Paul Bocuse and includes stints at Alain Senderens, Les Ambassadeurs at the Hôtel de Crillon, Taillevent, and finally Le Meurice under chef Yannick Alléno.

Wintergreen walls, sleek Art Deco *Normandie*-style armchairs, and a scarlet banquette that makes me think of the huge lips in the Man Ray painting *The Lovers* make a refreshing break from the faux rustic or Louis-something settings usually favored by Paris power brokers and presage Orieux's exquisite modern cooking. He tinkers with his menu all the time, so it's hard to recommend my favorites, but on a rainy night in May, I loved his asparagus with a "gariguette" garnish made from chopped country ham, shallots poached in red wine, tomatoes, and tarragon. This condiment brilliantly teased out the natural taste of the asparagus, and I found myself wishing that I could take home a mason jar of it to use on pasta and grilled chicken. Served in a martini glass, oysters in seawater aspic came with garnishes of horseradish mousse and pickled pears. "This is excellent," said my friend Michèle, a longtime resident of the nearby rue Vaneau, "but the locals are so parsimonious, I don't know if they're ready for these prices."

Two snowy filets of John Dory posed on a thick emerald green pudding of riced artichoke hearts, marinated vegetables, and pureed fresh coriander were magnificent; the gentle bite of the vegetables complemented the taut fish and the subtly acidulated tones of the sauce flattered it without masking its natural flavor. Baby lamb from the Pyrénées had a similarly delicious natural logic, since it was served on a bed of coarsely pureed rattes potatoes dotted with pleasantly chewy salty laitue de mer (seaweed) and lightly dosed with elderberry-infused oil. I finished up with a lovely composition of wild strawberries, raspberries, and rhubarb in lychee juice, and Michèle relished a private gastronomic souvenir by ordering a Grand Marnier soufflé, something she said she hadn't eaten since her First Communion lunch in the small Breton city of Quimper many years before. Chatting briefly with Orieux after dinner, Michèle politely wondered about his prices, which frankly, given the quality of his food, I find perfectly reasonable. "If I serve a lot of politicians at noon the Assemblée Nationale is just up the street, in the evening my regulars are all local, including people like François Pinault," Orieux replied, doing a harmless bit of name-dropping—Pinault, one of the richest men in France, is head of Artemis, the luxury goods holding company that owns Gucci and Christie's. And, proving his implicit point that restaurants are an intriguingly accurate gauge for reading any neighborhood, we passed three Bentleys parked along the rue de Bourgogne while walking home. Clearly, this neighborhood needed this restaurant, and in Orieux, they've found a real star.

. . .

IN A WORD: Gaël Orieux's excellent contemporary cooking has made this stylish restaurant a new address for Paris power brokers and anyone who loves good food. With its racy contemporary decor and friendly, well-drilled service, it's as good a choice for a tête-à-tête as it is for a business meal. Note, too, that it offers a great-value prix fixe lunch menu.

DON'T MISS: Asparagus with gariguette garnish; oysters in seawater aspic with horseradish mousse and pickled pears; pigeon roasted with spices; veal sweetbreads roasted in vin jaune with salsify; strawberries, raspberries, and rhubarb in lychee juice; soufflé Grand Marnier.

. . .

[24] 54 rue de Bourgogne, 7th, 01.45.51.61.09. MÉTRO: Varenne or Assemblée Nationale. OPEN Monday to Friday for lunch and dinner. CLOSED Saturday and Sunday. www.restaurantauguste.fr • $$$$

Au Bon Saint Pourçain

SAINT-GERMAIN IS WITHERED-CARROT TERRITORY, WHICH is why the refrain of the locals is "God bless, François," the bushy-browed owner of this small and delightfully unpretentious little bistro behind the church of Saint-Sulpice.

Solacing the hardworking bourgeoisie of the neighborhood, that anxious elegant tribe who inhabit gorgeous apartments with

dated decors they either inherited or bought a long time ago—
and ascetically empty refrigerators: think a bottle of duty-free
vodka, an old jar of mustard, organic jam brought home from
stylish corners of Europe (fig preserves from Croatia or lemon
marmalade from Puglia), a few eggs no one remembers buying,
and a withered carrot or two in the vegetable drawer—is his
vocation. What François knows is that the locals live for the
weekend and the pretty, busy markets of the towns where they
have country houses and the time to cook. During the week in
Paris, they chronically get home from work too late to shop,
too tired to cook. So they eat a quick plate of pasta in one of
Saint-Germain's innumerable Italian restaurants, or, when
they're craving real food or want to share a bona fide "insider's"
address with foreign friends, they come to François.

   This is why his tiny restaurant feels a bit like a club, replete
with heavy velvet curtains in the doorway and a crowd of
regulars who recognize one another with a smile or a nod

without feeling obliged to take things any further. In fact, chatting between tables normally isn't done, because it breaks the unstated rule that this precious place is for letting your hair down with friends, not networking or preening. This doesn't mean that unknown faces are unwelcome, however—this is actually a quietly friendly spot, and the worldly regulars happily welcome the variety provided by foreigners.

François, who originally worked here as the sole waiter before buying out the owner, knows all of this, which is why he quickly pours a glass of complimentary white Saint-Pourçain and brings a saucer of saucisson (sliced sausage) when you're seated on the old moleskin banquettes, and why he wouldn't dream of taking certain things off the menu. Claire, the friend who introduced me to Au Bon Saint Pourçain fifteen years ago, always has the same meal—marinated leeks to start and then brandade de morue, salt cod with mashed potatoes and garlic. The dish I crave is the boeuf aux olives, braised beef with green olives. Such homey plats mijotées (long-simmered dishes) are the stars of the menu and are cooked in a tiny kitchen just off the dining room. Other house classics include the compote de lapereau (rabbit in tarragon-flavored aspic), tête de veau sauce gribiche (calf's head with a sauce of vinegar, eggs, cornichon pickles, and capers), and a fine tarte Tatin. It's a bit raspy, but everyone drinks the house Saint-Pourçain, a rustic red wine from the south-central Auvergne region, or, wanting something better, the very good Irancy, a light red from northern Burgundy.

· ·

IN A WORD: Just the ticket when you want a good, friendly, low-effort bistro meal in the heart of Saint-Germain-des-Prés. Cash only, no credit cards.

DON'T MISS: Poireaux vinaigrette (marinated leeks); compote de lapereau (rabbit in tarragon-flavored aspic); boeuf aux olives (braised beef with green olives); brandade de morue (shredded salt cod mixed into mashed potatoes with garlic); entrecôte; sauce marchand de vin (steak with red wine sauce); tarte Tatin.

. . .

[25] 10 rue Servandoni, 6th, 01.43.54.93.63. MÉTRO: Saint-Sulpice or Mabillon. OPEN Monday to Friday for lunch and dinner. CLOSED Saturday and Sunday. ▪ $$

Le Buisson Ardent

LOOK CAREFULLY AT THE PEDIMENT OF THE BUILDING that houses this delightful Latin Quarter bistro, and you'll discover the origins of its name—a poignant stone miniature of Moses and the burning bush (in the book of Exodus, Moses learns of his divine calling when he comes across a burning bush in the Egyptian desert).

Passing through the heavy curtains at the door here, one immediately senses the relaxed, happy atmosphere of this 1925 vintage dining room, where the tables are generously spaced, the service is smiling and friendly, and two large chandeliers with frosted tulip lamps overhead add intimate scale to a high-ceilinged room with red banquettes, forest green walls, winsome romantic friezes, and white wedding cake moldings.

The contemporary French menu changes often, but its guiding themes are quality, generosity, and a well-groomed creativity with cosmopolitan inspiration. Arnaud Vansanten trained with Guy Savoy, and his haute cuisine background is quickly apparent in the way he works a traditional bistro register with delicious details—the bread here is homemade—and intelligent innovation, which is immediately seen in starters such as a plump artichoke heart stuffed with fresh chèvre in a sauce vierge (a light vinaigrette with tomato cubes), white asparagus with a red-fruit vinaigrette, and grilled salmon cooked rare, garnished with dill and lime and a salad of sorrel-brightened tabouleh.

During my last meal here, the quartet of academics at the table next to me eagerly tucked into two côtes de boeuf (rib steak) Simmenthal with a grainy mustard jus and generous sides of potatoes dauphinoises, but I loved my succulent chop of free-range pork with orange, fresh sauerkraut, and pickled turnips, and I had trouble keeping my fork away from Jutta's chicken breast lacquered with satay sauce and served with a smoked bacon emulsion and creamy polenta. "I really like this place, Alec," she said, glorying in a visit to Paris, where she lived for many years before moving to Provence. "The food's delicious, and everyone's so friendly."

The desserts were excellent, too. Jutta had the quince Tatin with marscapone colored a soft pink by Lyonnais pralin, or sugar-coated almonds, and my lychee bavarois was mounted on a crunchy disk of white chocolate, praline, and puffed rice and drizzled with hibiscus syrup. Manager Nicolas Desnoues stopped by for a chat at the end of the meal and discussing what makes us happy at the table, he told us that "generosity and a desire to please are what I look for in a restaurant." And they're what he offers so successfully at this excellent restaurant.

· ·

IN A WORD: Excellent contemporary French cooking, warm hospitality, good service, and a comfortable, good-looking dining room make this cozy bistro in the Latin Quarter a real gem. The reasonably priced prix fixe menus are a great buy, too.

DON'T MISS: The menu changes regularly, but dishes worth looking out for include the pissaladière, an open tart of red peppers and sardines with olive emulsion; chèvre-stuffed artichoke heart; grilled salmon with dill and lime and tabouleh with sorrel; squid risotto with Parmesan; chicken breast lacquered with satay sauce and served with a smoked bacon envision and creamy polenta; calf's liver with spice-bread crumbs and polenta; côte de boeuf (rib steak) with grainy mustard jus and dauphinois potatoes; braised beef cheeks with green olives; chocolate mousse with candied orange peel; lychee bavarois with hibiscus syrup; dark chocolate soufflé; ice cream and sorbets from Damman's, one of Paris's best artisanal ice cream makers.

. . .

[**26**] 25 rue de Jussieu, 5th, 01.43.54.93.02. MÉTRO: **Jussieu.** OPEN **Monday to Saturday for lunch and dinner. Sunday dinner only.** CLOSED **Sunday.** www.lebuissonardent.fr ▪ **$$**

Christophe

ONE OF THE MOST EXCITING THINGS ABOUT LIVING IN PARIS is hearing the first drumbeats about a promising new restaurant. Though for a long time, it's been fashionable to scold the city as gastronomically stagnant, the reality is that the renewal of its culinary scene has recently been accelerating as a new generation of superb young chefs strike out on their own. And this is what makes Paris such an incomparably wonderful city to eat in: unlike in New York or London, where many new restaurants are major production affairs with huge bankrolls and publicity budgets, the undergrowth of good eating in Paris is still created the old-fashioned way, by passionate young chefs who yearn to share their cooking with the world and who are willing to work ungodly hours and risk crushing personal debt to do so.

The simple shop-front dining room in the Latin Quarter, where the only visual interest is the black-and-white photographs on the melon-colored and lemon yellow walls, doesn't promise much at first glance, but this makes it the perfect foil for a wonderful surprise. On a Sunday night—this earnest place is open on the weekend—the dining room was almost empty when we arrived but gradually filled up. Next to us, a Sorbonne professor patiently translated the menu from French into English for a tweedy college professor from Toronto and his wife, almost a cartoon of an academic spouse, with sensibly cropped short hair and a high-collared, long-sleeved red dress. "This beef is very famous in France, like Kobe beef in Japan. It comes from Coutance in Normandy, and the assiette de charcuterie Basque is an assortment of sausage and ham from the Basque country, in the southwestern corner of the country on the Spanish border." It was a pleasure to hear his commentary, too, since he took justifiable pride in educating his guests on the myriad fine points of French produce found on the menu.

I'd heard about the young chef, Christophe Philippe, from a friend who lives near his restaurant. "He worked for Sophie Pic in Valence, and he's very talented," she told me, and our first courses more than delivered on her high praise. Fine slices of smoked wild salmon were wrapped around salad leaves and horseradish cream and served with a hot chestnut-flour waffle, while a ruddy cream of lentil soup was garnished with tiny bits of grilled bacon. Perfectly cooked duck breast from Challans, a famous poultry-raising town in the Vendée region, in a deeply reduced and perfectly seasoned jus came with ravioli stuffed with duck thigh meat, a wonderful garnish, and shoulder of lamb with aromatic spices was an elegant French riff on Moroccan cooking. Philippe had grilled the braised lamb so that its skin was crunchy and the heat released the fine perfumes of cumin, coriander, pepper, and other spices you'd find in a market in Marrakesh. The modestly priced Château Saint-Martin Côtes de Provence recommended by the friendly young waitress was a stunningly elegant wine, too.

After a sumptuous preserved-lemon cream, we wanted to know more about Philippe and quizzed the waitress. "I'll let him speak for himself," she said, and when the chef came to the table a few minutes later, we raved about our dessert.

The boyish Philippe told us he'd grown up in Menton, a faded but genteel Riviera resort town on the Italian border. With its gentle climate, Menton was once famous for its lemons, which are still prized by France's best chefs—Alain Ducasse and Joël Robuchon among them—for their highly perfumed skin, thick pith, and low acidity. Today only a few growers still cultivate the prized citrus, but Philippe has his own source. "My mother sends me lemons, which are what makes the meeting of citrus and cream so suave in the dessert," he explained. So why does Christophe undertake all of this backbreaking work alone in a tiny kitchen? "I cook because it's my passion—why else would anyone work so hard?" he told us with a smile and then broke away to speak with another client, who was waiting to tell him, "C'était superbe!" ("It was superb!")

IN A WORD: Catch a rising star at this cozy Latin Quarter bistro. Chef Christophe Philippe's contemporary French cooking is disciplined, elegant, and delicious.

DON'T MISS: Trio du cochon Basque (pork from the Basque country prepared in three different ways); langoustines au basilic (Dublin Bay prawns with basil); veal sweetbreads with potato puree; sole roasted in butter and served with panisses (baked chickpea-flour bars); pineapple carmelized with cinnamon; chocolate mousse.

. . .

[27] 8 rue Descartes, 5th, 01.43.26.72.49. MÉTRO: Cardinal-Lemoine. OPEN Friday to Tuesday for lunch and dinner CLOSED Wednesday and Thursday. www.christopherestaurant.fr ▪ $ $

Au Coin des Gourmets

THE FRENCH LOVED INDOCHINE THE SAME WAY THE BRITISH loved India, as the romantic colony that curiously defined and flattered them, and long after their imperial construct was edited off the map, the same corner of Asia—now Cambodia, Laos, and Vietnam—still plays Parisian heartstrings.

This affinity, and the different vintages of the Indochinese diaspora who have settled in Paris—first at the end of France's futile war to prevent Vietnam's independence and then after the failed American attempt to thwart the country's fall into the fold of communism—mean that the French capital has one of the most vibrant and complex overseas Indochinese communities in the world. Many of those who came to Paris issued from the privileged casts in these colonies and so often had Chinese or mixed ancestry (the Chinese communities in all three of the Indochinese countries were prosperous and well established enough to be the middle layer, between the colonial French and the indigenous populations).

The delightful Ta family is typical Parisian Indochinese, since Cambodia, China, and Vietnam all have a place in the family history, which explains the varied menus at their two very good Paris restaurants. The long-running shop-front Au Coin des Gourmets is in the Latin Quarter, and the newer and more stylish branch is tucked away between the Place de la Concorde and the Place Vendôme on the Right Bank.

Both restaurants serve delicious home-style Indochinese cooking, mostly Vietnamese, but also a few Cambodian and Laotian dishes; as a new generation of the family comes into the business, the menus become longer and more authentic, including such dishes as natin, a Cambodian specialty of ground pork cooked in coconut milk and served on puffed rice. These new temptations notwithstanding, I have a hard time passing up such favorites as steamed Vietnamese ravioli stuffed with ground pork and sprinkled with fried shallots and herbs; nems, crunchy deep-fried rolls of pork, bean sprouts, and rice noodles that you wrap in lettuce leaves with fresh mint and dip in nuoc cham, a sweet-and-savory sauce; boned, stuffed chicken wings; grilled pork meatballs with salad; and the crêpe saigonaise, a very thin crunchy omelette filled with shrimp, squid, bean sprouts, onions, and herbs.

The original Latin Quarter address is a small, convivial, often crowded shop front with framed vintage travel posters on the walls, and it has a steady crowd of regulars running to local

academics and the occasional celebrity. The Right Bank address is more dressed up and a bit pricier, with a stylish decor, fresh flowers, and a refined atmosphere, but both are very good.

.   .   .

IN A WORD: The excellent Vietnamese cooking served by the Ta family offers a perfect alternative to French menus when you want something light.

DON'T MISS: Nems (deep-fried spring rolls); saucisse Laotienne (spicy Laotian sausage); soupe de crevettes au tamarin (shrimp soup seasoned with tamarind paste); Cambodian squid salad; Vietnamese ravioli; grilled beef salad; amok Cambodgien (cod with coconut milk and lemongrass steamed in a banana leaf); grilled pork meatballs with salad; boned, stuffed chicken wings; shrimp with basil.

. . .

[28] Left Bank: 5 rue Dante, 5th, 01.43.26.12.92. MÉTRO: Saint-Michel or Maubert-Mutualité. OPEN daily for lunch and dinner.

[4] Right Bank: 38 rue du Mont Thabor, 1st, 01.42.60.79.79. MÉTRO: Concorde. OPEN Monday to Saturday for lunch and dinner. CLOSED Sunday. • $$

Le Comptoir du Relais

YEARS AFTER YOU'VE LEFT YOUR NAPKIN ON THE TABLE, certain meals remain revelations. My first meal at chef Yves Camdeborde's aptly named La Régalade (the name roughly means "the good time") in 1994 overturned all of my expectations of bistro cooking. It was a sleety October afternoon, and after being tipped off to this newly opened place in an inconvenient corner of the 14th Arrondissement by Françoise, my next-door neighbor, I'd persuaded Marc to join me for lunch. We both had trouble finding the place, and he arrived in the same sour mood I did, with a dripping umbrella and a certain grouchiness over having been made to trek out to this wet, charmless stretch of pavement in the middle of the day. Then we eyeballed the chalkboard menu and our spirits lifted. "Ça a l'air bon" ("It looks good"), said Marc sort of grudgingly, and a second later the waitress thumped a heavy ceramic loaf pan of terrine de campagne on the table and told us to help ourselves. We did, shamelessly, because the loaf of coarsely ground pork and pork liver with a top crust of carmelized juices and distant hints of onion, garlic, and thyme was so good. We started with creamy chestnut soup with croutons and tiny cubes of foie gras, an amazing combination, and then Marc had grilled duck hearts with pleurotes (oyster mushrooms), which he insisted I try. New to duck hearts, I was surprised by how good they were, and my tiny scallops cooked in their shells with salt butter were superb—tender, sweet, and quietly briny, with an intriguing garnish of chopped walnuts. "This place is excellent," said Marc, now beaming, over the ewe's milk Ossau Iraty served with black cherry jam and an impeccable Grand Marnier soufflé that ended a meal that left us both awed. We'd discovered a remarkable cook, someone who'd created a sexy hybrid of gutsy southwestern French grub and refined haute cuisine dishes (Camdeborde trained with chef Christian Constant when he was at Les Ambassadeurs, the gastronomic restaurant of the Hotel Crillon).

I went back a night later and often after that, until it started to become difficult to get a reservation and the service became so rushed and frantic that it dulled the pleasure of the food. Ultimately, Camdeborde was cooking lunch and three dinner ser-

vices, a debilitating pace even for a barrel of a guy with a rugby man's build and stamina, so it came as no surprise when he sold it two years ago and took some time off.

Teasing rumors of his return to the range started a few months later, and then, suddenly, he was back! The opening of Le Comptoir du Relais overlooking a pricey piece of sidewalk just steps from the Odéon was electric news, and I immediately went. It was good, too—the single set menu at dinner began with chicken bouillon with mousseron mushrooms and perles du Japon (manioc-flour pearls, aka tapioca), and continued with crabmeat gelée with a zucchini puree, tournedos Rossini (steak topped with foie gras), a good cheese tray, and a red fruit and pistachio macaroon. As flawless a performance as this was, however, I found myself missing the high-testosterone cooking that had once had the whole world mewling for a place at his table. Still, given this quality, success was ensured, and it's since become viciously difficult to score a place for dinner in this pretty Art Deco dining room.

Every other person who visits me in Paris these days wants to go, though, so I've been there often. My last meal—oxtail gelée in red wine sauce with petits pois and Parmesan, sautéed foie gras with rhubarb, Bibb lettuce, and a Xérès-vinegar-spiked jus, grilled veal steak with flat parsley; cheese; and strawberries with ewe's milk ice cream and nougatine tuiles (wafers)—was excellent but curiously dainty and very polite, an opinion that was echoed by a Frenchman at the table next to me, who pronounced it "très première communion" (very First Communion), a reference to the extravagant lunches served by bourgeois families in the provinces to celebrate this important childhood milestone. So should you go? Yes, of course, but show up with the expectation of a very nice meal rather than a revelation.

IN A WORD: The star bistro chef Yves Camdeborde's latest place has rapidly become just as popular as his original rough-and-tumble La Régalade, but the earthy, lusty cooking of the old address has given way to a much politer and more polished cooking style. The food here is very good but will never make you moan.

DON'T MISS: The prix fixe dinner menu changes regularly, but good dishes often served à la carte at noon include a deboned pig's foot that could change your mind about this French favorite.

· · ·

[29] 9 carrefour de l'Odéon, 6th, 01.44.27.07.50. MÉTRO: Odéon. OPEN daily for lunch and dinner. www.hotel-paris-relais-saint-germain.com • $$

L'Épi Dupin

SEVERAL LIFETIMES AGO, OR SO IT SEEMS, THE NICE LADY in the post office first told me about L'Épi Dupin. I was living in the rue du Bac, and my post office, the place I most dreaded going to in the entire city of Paris due to its interminable lines, was in the rue Dupin. Then one day, a miracle—I stepped up to the counter and was greeted by a new face, a pleasant, efficient-looking, middle-aged lady with deep blue eyes and a bemused expression. Over the course of a month, she obviously eyeballed what I was sending—and receiving, too—since after the first few encounters, she asked me to recommend a good, inexpensive place in the neighborhood for lunch. I told her about Au Babylone, the simple lunch-only canteen in the rue de Babylone where much of the sales staff of the Bon Marché department store goes daily, and the next time I came in, she returned the favor. "As soon as you leave, go next door and book a table for dinner. The place just opened, and the young chef is going to be a star."

I did as told, and my first experience of François Pasteau's cooking was sublime, especially his signature starter of carmelized endive stuffed with runny goat cheese and main course of guinea hen with fennel bulb. It turned out he was a nice guy, too, a real feet-on-the-ground cook who'd been inspired by a stint in the United States before returning to Paris. The small dining room with its exposed, worm-eaten beams also reminded me of my snug, quiet apartment, part of an old stable in a courtyard overlooking a convent (how else would I know that even nuns dye their hair?). A fresh coat of white paint had replaced the grass-cloth-covered walls of the previous tenant, a Chinese restaurant, and the place had an appealing rustic feel. I went often those first few months, and then word got around and it became difficult to get a table and then basically impossible, in spite of the two services at dinner.

So I'd sort of forgotten about this place until deciding to see if I could snag a last-minute table on a quiet night in August, low tide on the calendar of Parisian life. Bingo! Arriving, it was a letdown to be seated in such a crowded, agitated dining room, and the new lemon yellow walls hardly helped. Our dinner had a balking, sclerotic rhythm, and, jammed in between two other deuces, it was impossible for the six of us to use our knives and forks simultaneously.

Pasteau's food, however, remains superb. A pâté de cèpes, a small molded timbale of eggy, probably chicken-liver-enriched custard studded with sweet, fleshy cèpes and brightened with a flat-parsley jus was sublime, a perfect example of how good contemporary French bistro cooking can be at its best. A daily special of grilled cod steak on a bed of garlicky white Paimpol beans in a veal-bouillon-enhanced sauce was well conceived, perfectly cooked, and generously served, as was a sesame-crusted tuna with eggplant and red pepper and noisettes of lamb with creamy polenta. Our bottle of white Crozes Hermitage was an excellent buy, too. But despite the kitchen's admirable skills, the meal was melancholy.

Why? Because the relentless get-'em-in-and-get-'em-out formula of this restaurant makes it almost impossible to have a good time. The dining room's overlit, too, and much of the crowd exudes the wilting smugness of the triumphant penny-pincher (many of the people who eat at L'Épi Dupin are more excited by the admittedly wonderful bargain price of the set menu than they are by the quality of their food). The waiters have also assumed a certain ironic detachment when it comes to dealing with the foreigners who dominate the place. So how to cope? Come in a group of at least three so that you can be seated at one of the comfortable round tables, and book for a late lunch or within minutes of last orders during the second dinner service.

· · ·

IN A WORD: One of the better modern French bistros in Paris but often crowded and marred by rapid-fire table turning.

DON'T MISS: Langoustines with pineapple-ginger chutney; cod steak with spinach and Morteau sausage; grilled skate with hazelnuts and dried fruit; cumin-seasoned pork breast with carrots and baby onions; runny chocolate-pistachio cake; apple and prune tart with pepper ice cream.

· · ·

[30] 11 rue Dupin, 6th, 01.42.22.64.56. MÉTRO: Sèvres-Babylone. OPEN Tuesday to Friday for lunch and dinner. Monday dinner only. CLOSED Saturday and Sunday. www.epidupin.com • $$

Fish La Boissonnerie

THOUGH I HAVE MANY WONDERFUL AMERICAN, ENGLISH, Canadian, and other English-speaking friends in Paris, I don't frequent Paris's expat watering holes for the simple reason that after so many years in the city, my life is more French than American. There are a few places I make an exception for, however, and Drew Harre and Juan Sanchez's very popular Fish La Boissonnerie in Saint-Germain-des-Prés is one of them. To be sure, the crowd here is often mostly English-speaking, but the convivial atmosphere, friendly service, and good modern French bistro cooking with international influences make a meal here as reliably comforting as slipping into a nice warm bath.

This is also an address I recommend to non-French-speaking friends, because I know that most people appreciate escaping the linguistic challenge every once in a while during a trip to Paris, and also because it's open daily, is a great place to meet new friends, and offers a good solid feed for a very fair price. It's also a pleasant place to go if you're traveling on your own, since you can have a meal at the bar. In other words, this is a great let-your-hair-down destination

Harre, a New Zealander, and Sanchez, a Miami native, have made their restaurant, which opened in 1999 in a former *poissonerie* (fishmonger) with a beautiful Art Deco façade, a showcase for new culinary talent, too, and if the staff in the kitchen changes with some regularity, the quality of the cooking is always reliable. The delicious bread served here comes from the ovens at Cosi, their sandwich shop across the street, and the wine list is composed of many of the same bottles that Sanchez sells at La Dernière Goutte (The Last Drop), his very successful nearby wine shop.

Dining here on a rainy spring night with Bruno and our friends Dorie and Michael, who divide their time between New York, Connecticut, and Paris, we ate our way through almost the entire menu and were impressed. Our meal began with *cha-*

wanmushi, a sublime and very delicate steamed Japanese egg custard flavored with gingko nuts and garnished with tiny salty cockles, and a superb starter of lamb sweetbreads with green asparagus in a pungent sauce of cider and pan drippings. Other standout starters we sampled included a kimchi (Korean cabbage pickled with hot chiles) soup with grilled pork breast and a homey but deeply satisfying coddled egg with parsley root, Swiss chard, and roasted garlic.

Main courses were impressive, too. Pan-roasted yellow pollack came with curried cauliflower and garbanzo beans and a lively lime condiment, while roast lamb was perfect seasonal comfort food with baby peas and gnocchi. Not only was the produce used in every dish outstanding—the kitchen here sources seasonal produce from small farmers whenever possible—but the intriguingly cosmopolitan flavors were impeccably mastered, too. Rhubarb panna cotta and a hauntingly good homemade rosemary-orange-and-black-currant ice cream finished off this fine feast, but many people also opt for the dependably good cheese course.

During the course of our meal we chatted with a table of charming South African winemakers on one side of us and a nice couple from Boston on the other, and both Dorie and I ran into friends, which isn't surprising, because Fish La Boissonnerie is an exceptionally convivial restaurant with a lot of atmosphere created by the exposed stone walls, zinc-clad bar, beamed ceiling and retro-style globe lamps overhead. Make sure you book here, since this place is so popular, and note that they serve a prix fixe menu at lunch that's an excellent value. And if Fish is all booked, you might also try Semilla, Harre and Sanchez's other restaurant a few doors down; it has similarly good food but is a bit noisier.

·   ·

IN A WORD: Drew Harre and Juan Sanchez's Saint-Germain-des-Prés bistro has become a popular neighborhood institution and travelers' favorite for its reliably good contemporary French bistro cooking, great wine list, and warm lively atmosphere.

DON'T MISS: The menu here follows the seasons and changes according to the chefs' inspirations, but dishes to look out for include a soup of roasted garlic and green tomato, beet-and-feta salad, sautéed foie gras, lamb tartare, pork belly with lentils, rhubarb panna cotta, and black-cherry chocolate ganache.

. . .

[**31**] **69 rue de Seine, 6th, 01.43.54.34.69.** MÉTRO: **Mabillon or Saint-Germain-des-Prés.** OPEN **daily for lunch and dinner. ▪ $$**

Les Fables de La Fontaine

CHEF CHRISTIAN CONSTANT IS ONE OF THE UNDERSUNG heroes of contemporary French cooking. While he was chef at Les Ambassadeurs at the Hôtel de Crillon, he enabled a remarkable succession of talented young chefs who passed through his kitchen, including Yves Camdeborde (Le Comptoir du Relais), Thierry Breton (Chez Michel), and Eric Frechon (Le Bristol), before they went out on their own and invented the modern French bistro.

Since leaving the Crillon, Constant has been gradually colonizing a charming village-like corner of the 7th Arrondissement in one long block of the rue Saint-Dominique, where he now has four restaurants: Le Café Constant, a pleasant place for lunch if you're in this neck of the woods; Le Violon d'Ingres, which I find overpriced; Les Cocottes, which specializes in casserole-cooked dishes; and Les Fables de La Fontaine, my favorite of the quartet, a relaxed and consistently excellent seafood restaurant overlooking a square stone fountain with handsome lion faces. Constant recently sold this restaurant to a young team, but chef Anthony David perpetuates the tradition of superb seafood woking, for which this since has become reputed.

During the summer, this tiny place puts a row of tables outside, and when I can snag one, it's a brilliant place for some urbane al fresco dining and a fine fish feed. On a balmy night last May, some friends and I got lucky, and the four of us had a superb meal that lasted until well after midnight as we finished off our delicious white Jaboulet Crozes Hermitage, tossed back espressos and riffed on some favorite big-city preoccupations: travel (Laurent and Carole were heading off to Venice for a weekend and wanted restaurant recommendations), real estate (will Paris apartment prices keep rising, and does it make more sense to try to buy a country house somewhere within an hour or so of Paris or go for something further afield?), restaurants, and sex (Laurent extolled the deliciousness of older women, while Carole told of the time a friend had invited her to visit the set of a porn film near the Cap d'Agde, the center of France's pornography industry; between takes, the female lead had spent her time reading the latest issue of *Cuisine de France*, a cooking magazine).

To the credit of chef Anthony David, though, the main thing we talked about was our food. Everyone loved the amuse-bouche (complimentary hors d'oeuvre) of Parmesan flan with sundried tomato puree, and our first courses—meaty Roumegus oysters with citrus aspic, langoustines fried in phyllo pastry with basil leaves and served with a citrus dipping sauce, and sea bream carpaccio with preserved lemon and lobster-infused coconut milk.

My only regret was that I got only five langoustines when, as I once learned in rough-and-tumble fishermen's canteens in Brittany where they were freshly landed and going for a song, I can eat them by the dozen. Not well known outside Europe, these pearly pink crustaceans are like miniature lobsters, with small, sweet, fleshy tails, and the best ones come from Le Guilvinec in Brittany. They're highly perishable and easily overcooked, too, which is why I was so impressed by their freshness. The main courses, which vary according to the season and the catch of the day, were outstanding, especially my grilled John Dory filets with sauteed carrots and squid and a carrot juice and maple syrup sauce. Smoked Scottish salmon with butternut squash and hazelnut puree and a bacon emulsion was outstanding, too, and the lighter eaters loved their turbot steamed with hay with seaweed, shellfish and fennel bulb puree. Desserts are simple, coffee tiramisu with pear marmalade and caramel mousse or a bowl of strawberries and cream, and even when you can't sit outside, the vest-pocket dove gray dining room has the happy, inoffensively clubby feeling of a place where everyone's having a great time.

·   ·   ·

IN A WORD: With a stylish crowd, an impeccable catch-of-the-day menu, and a pleasantly clubby atmosphere, this stylish seafood restaurant is a hit on the Left Bank.

DON'T MISS: The chalkboard menu changes daily, but dishes to look for include pastry-wrapped langoustines with basil;

John Dory filets with sauteed carrots and squid; crab ravioli; sea bass with morel risotto; coffee tiramisu with pear marmalade and caramel mousse.

. . .

[32] 131 rue Saint-Dominique, 7th, 01.44.18.37.55. MÉTRO: École Militaire. OPEN daily for lunch and dinner. www.lesfablesdelafontaine.net ▪ $$$

La Fontaine de Mars

SINCE I WAS SENSITIVE AND SOLITARY AS A LITTLE BOY, the shy wobbly birth of a new friendship always seems to me kind of a miracle and leaves me elated. As the years have gone by, though, I experience that fine fleeting moment when the mutual recognition of two psyches ignites the reciprocal curiosity from which friendship is born rather less often, because I'm part of a couple, have many friends already, and am much too busy. Against this backdrop, I prize the rarity of a new friend even more, which is why I gave it some thought when Felisa, a new friend who lives in California, e-mailed and suggested we meet for Sunday lunch while she was in Paris.

This particular meal is always a challenge, because so few really good places are open then. I'm also definitely not a fan of brunch in restaurants—I can do that meal much better at home, where I can eat it without changing out of my usual home gear of a teddy-bear pile Ralph Lauren jacket, oversized AMHERST COLLEGE T-shirt, sweatpants, and L.L.Bean moccasins, and most of the city's brasseries, always the weakest link in the Parisian food chain, are at their worst at Sunday noon. The main reason for this is that the Sunday lunch crowd at most brasseries preponderantly orders the cheap prix-fixe menu, so owners staff their kitchen lightly and with chefs and servers who are only partially trained, making mediocre cooking worse and slow to arrive at the table.

Knowing that Felisa loves old-fashioned Paris, I booked at La Fontaine de Mars, the 1908-vintage bistro selected for a very public private dinner by President Barack Obama and his wife Michelle when they were here in 2009. Though I hadn't been to this old-timer for a while, I knew that the elegant but relaxed mis-en-scène of the place—red-and-white checked tablecloths woven with the name of the restaurant, bentwood chairs, cushy old leather banquettes, and a pretty setting overlooking a fountain on the rue Saint-Dominique—would make Felisa happy. Owners Jacques and Christiane Boudon are consummate professionals, and La Fontaine usually offers first-rate people watching and eavesdropping as well as solid well-prepared old-fashioned bistro cooking with a southwestern French accent.

So on an Indian summer day when it was cool enough to air out the mothball scent of a tweed jacket not worn since May, I set out to meet Felisa. On the cusp of two seasons and facing the stolid Sunday dourness of the 7th Arrondissement, where I lived for many years, I felt wistful for all of those things I'd never know again, and I arrived at La Fontaine de Mars feeling pleasantly melancholy after these private pensive hors d'oeuvres.

Dramatically dressed in black-and-white, with wonderful 1950s costume jewelry, Felisa, an architect with a passion for vintage clothing, was waiting for me at a terrace table, and even though we'd only met several times before, conversation was exceptionally easy as we sipped kirs and studied the menu. "There's nothing in the world I think I'd rather read than the menu of a good Paris restaurant," she said, and I agreed wholeheartedly.

Suffice it to say, we had a very, very good meal, and La Fontaine has vaulted to the top of my Sunday lunch list and found a place on my roster of favorite bistros. The stylish Felisa didn't want a starter, but I couldn't resist the oeufs au Madiran façon meurette, which are as good a reason as I can imagine to get out of bed on a Sunday before noon—two perfectly poached eggs in a sauce of reduced Madiran wine with onions and bacon. A charming Dutch woman at the table next to us had the foie gras maison mi-cuit: probably because I couldn't take my eyes off it, she kindly offered me a taste on a toast point, and it was excellent.

Next Felisa, whose petite size is strikingly misleading when it comes to her appetite, ordered steak béarnaise with homemade frites, because "the beef in France has so much more flavor than it does in the U.S.," and I had free-range chicken in a cream sauce that was generously loaded with morel mushrooms. My fowl was juicy, tender, and wonderfully infused with the taste of the morels. After Felisa put a good dent in her beautiful pile of golden frites, I greedily finished them off, using the rest of her béarnaise as a condiment, and noting it was homemade—rather sadly a rarity in Paris these days—with a lovely bite of tarragon preserved in vinegar.

Finishing up over first-rate chocolate mousse and baba au rhum, I concluded that the presidential minders had chosen well for the First Family. I also knew I'd never eat here again without thinking of Felisa and that my next meal would be imminent, because I crave both the confit de canard and blanquette de veau from this lovely old-fashioned bistro the minute the trees of Paris go naked in the night.

IN A WORD: This well-mannered Hollywood set of a bistro is a perfect expression of the pleasantly bourgeois 7th Arrondissement and serves up fine renditions of such vieille France dishes as blanquette de veau, along with specialities from southwestern France.

DON'T MISS: Foie gras mi-cuit, oeufs au Madiran façon meurette, escargots, salade de tête de veau, blanquette de veau, boudin Basque (black pudding), cassoulet, confit de canard, steak béarnaise, poulet aux morilles, sole meunière, baba au rhum, chocolate mousse.

. . .

[33] 129 rue Saint-Dominique, 7th, 01.47.05.46.44 MÉTRO: Ecole Militaire or Pont-de-l'Alma. OPEN daily for lunch and dinner. www.fontainedemars.com • $$

La Ferrandaise

SINCE IT'S NEARLY IMPOSSIBLE TO FIND A REAL NEIGHBORHOOD restaurant in the heart of the heavily touristed Saint-Germain-des-Prés, I'm half reluctant to share the name of this excellent bistro, which has the vital ballast of a loyal following of diverse Parisian regulars—it's their exigence that keeps the kitchen on course and the atmosphere quite wonderfully local. At noon, you'll dine with book editors—Flammarion is based nearby—and epicurean but pennywise senators—the French Sénat is just across the street—and in the evening, hard-driving professional couples fill the place, notably whippet-like blondes who don't cook and their slightly cowed husbands. What everyone loves is the warmth and simplicity of this place, which is created by beamed ceilings, bare biscuit-colored stone walls, and a happy, casual staff who couldn't care less about fashion or politics, the local preoccupations, but are deeply in love with good food and wine.

The friendly welcome and attentive, slightly bemused service—the staff here enjoy babying and teasing the stressed-out power brokers—give this snug dining room the style of an auberge in a small French town like Laguiole in the Auvergne, and this rusticity, a relief from the competitive pressures of urban chic, lets all present feel as though they're getting away from it all during the space of a meal. The owner, Gilles Lamiot, is in fact an Auvergnat, and he perpetuates the tradition of good food at fair prices that his countrymen brought to Paris when many of them moved here from that mountainous central French region at the beginning of the twentieth century. This explains the winsome photographs of brown-and-white Ferrandaise breed cows on the walls—this race is native to the Auvergne's Puy de Dôme region—and also the restaurant's excellent cheese plate—Bleu de Langeuille, a creamy blue; nutty Saint-Nectaire; and the delicious, and rarely seen in Paris, Fourme de Rochefort Montagne, all of which hail from the region.

Aside from scoring such a perfect Left Bank location, Lamiot's coup was in hiring Kevin Besson, a talented chef who previously worked at Gourmand. Besson's menu is shrewd, too, since it offers the comfort food that Germanopratins (residents of Saint-Germain) crave, but in a discreetly revised register that makes it lighter and healthier. His marbré (terrine) of oxtail

stuffed with leeks and served with a homemade sauce gribiche (a mustard vinaigrette containing sieved hard-boiled egg, capers, and chopped pickles) is a perfect example, since the richly flavored meat is almost fat free, the leeks add a contrasting texture, and the tangy sauce gribiche lights up the combination. On a more modern note, his crab-filled ravioli in a ruddy ocher reduction of étrilles (tiny crabs) are superb, and escargots de Bourgogne en meurette (red wine sauce) is a brilliant idea.

Cloves spike the bed of white coco beans on which braised shoulder of lamb is served, and fennel add richness to the quinoa that accompanies a perfectly cooked filet of sea bream. Besson's pot-au-feu (beef poached in bouillon with winter vegetables) is quite simply superb, and the frites that come with the poire de boeuf, an exceptionally flavorful and tender steak, are first-rate. Among the desserts, the millefeuille minute, baked and assembled to order so that the fragile pastry leaves remain crisp, is filled with delicious vanilla cream, and the grapefruit terrine with tea sauce is perfect if you want something lighter.

Lamiot's wine list is one of the friendliest on the Left Bank, too. He serves a fine white Côtes du Rhône by the glass for €4, for example, and all of his bottles—a well-chosen selection that includes a fine Chorey-les-Beaunes 2004 by Claude Maréchal, an excellent Morgon made by Marcel Lapierre, and a nice Graves de Vayres Château Toulouze 2005, all very affordably priced—come from producers who work in "l'esprit bio," which means adhering as closely as possible to organic methods of traditional winemaking.

Finally, though I'm happy to have shared this little-known Saint-Germain gem with you, let's keep it between us so that we can always get a table.

·   ·

IN A WORD: A friendly, very experienced Auvergnat restaurateur has created an excellent traditional French bistro in the heart of Saint-Germain. Very popular with the locals, it hasn't yet been discovered by tourists and so is as good for savoring a Saint-Germain state of mind as it is for the delicious comfort food served up by a talented young chef.

DON'T MISS: The menu here changes regularly but dishes to look for include oxtail marbré stuffed with leeks; fricassee of wild mushrooms; escargots de Bourgogne en meurette; crab ravioli with sauce étrilles (crab sauce); cod with mashed potatoes; pot-au-feu; pintade (guinea fowl) with gratin of macaroni with Parmesan; poire de boeuf (steak) with frites; braised lamb shoulder with coco beans; cheese plate; millefeuille minute à la vanille de Madagascar; roasted pineapple flambéed in rum; grapefruit terrine with tea sauce.

. . .

[34] 8 rue de Vaugirard, 6th, 01.43.26.36.36. MÉTRO: Odéon. OPEN Tuesday to Friday for lunch and dinner. Monday and Saturday dinner only. www.laferrandaise.com CLOSED Sunday. ▪ $$

Le Florimond

THE HOPEFUL, RACING EXPECTATIONS BEFORE TRYING A new restaurant are one of the great pleasures of city life, especially in Paris, where the odds of success are solidly better than they are in other cities. I'd heard about Le Florimond from the friendly Auvergnat (from the south-central Auvergne region of France) owner of my local wine shop. "Nasty weather," he'd said a few days earlier when I had stopped by for a few bottles of his wonderful and inexpensive Colombelle, a Gascon white. "If I weren't stuck behind this counter, I'd hurry across town for the best stuffed cabbage in Paris. Now, that would taste good today." He grinned.

"So where would that be?" I said.

"Do you like stuffed cabbage?"

"It's one of my favorites."

"Then you'd really love this place, but I'm not sure if I remember the name." He was like a cat with a ball of yarn, and it took a few minutes more of this teasing before he'd had his

fun and jotted down "Le Florimond" on a notepad. I booked for lunch the next day. I've loved stuffed cabbage, one of the Auvergne's signature dishes, ever since I first had it at Jean-Yves Bath's excellent restaurant in the south-central Auvergnat city of Clermont-Ferrand fifteen years ago.

The welcome when I stepped in off the pavement was so warm it almost startled me—Parisians have finely embroidered manners but are not demonstrative, especially with strangers. Then, not a minute after I'd settled at a corner table waiting for my English friend Sue, a plate of nutmeg-scented gougères, or tiny cheese puffs, came to the table. I usually ignore such nibbles—the pleasure they offer never equals the calories they pack—but in this case I was tempted. These were hot and, from their soft, eggy consistency, obviously homemade, a good omen. The small butter yellow dining room was attractive, too. The banquette was covered in poppy-colored velvet, and there were Delft-style serving plates on the table and more Delft displayed on the walls, all of which created the sort of prosperous, scrubbed, comfortable interior you find in Vermeer's paintings. Sue came in with Tally, a taffy-colored Labrador, and we opened our menus.

"This is tough. I want everything," said Sue, a talented chef who once had a cooking school in Paris.

I agreed. Finally we ordered, and then we got down to talking about where and what we'd eaten since we'd last seen each other. She was on meal four out of ten she'd had during a recent trip to Barcelona when our first courses came: a terrine of mushrooms and Morteau (pork sausage from the Jura) on a beautiful salad of tiny tender green-and-garnet-colored leaves in a pale garlic cream dressing for me and terrine of boudin noir (blood pudding) and chestnuts with a nice waft of mace and clove for her. She went first, and her shoulders slumped.

"Oh, my God, this is absolutely delicious. This is real food," she said. My terrine was also stunningly good, the soft hash of the mushrooms a perfect foil to the smoky, chewy cubes of sausage. In fact, I felt a twinge the moment it was gone, knowing it had already been committed to that mental repertory of dishes I'll permanently crave between servings.

When the storied cabbage came, it was glistening in a pool of brown gravy so lush it had already skeined on its way to the table. Eyeing it, I instantly yearned for a boiled potato or two to mash into this unctuous bath with the back of my fork. So I asked, because I'd understood that this was a place where any reasonable request is fulfilled with pride and pleasure. The waiter returned with a thick square of pommes dauphinoise, too rich to go well with the cabbage but a lovely gesture. Sue and I mumbled during the meal. She was preoccupied with her homemade sausage ("I love sausage, all kinds of sausage"), veal steak, and plump white Tarbes beans from the southwestern French city with the same name in a sauce related to my gravy, and I was stunned by the elegance of my cabbage, a rustic work of art. Its delicate and perfectly seasoned stuffing of pork, veal, onion, cabbage, and Swiss chard was interleaved with parboiled cabbage leaves to create a sublime version of one of the most ancient and profoundly satisfying of all European winter dishes (some version of stuffed cabbage exists in almost every continental kitchen). We gorged ourselves and laughed out loud when the charming waiter asked if we wanted cheese. No, no cheese, but a vanilla millefeuille with two forks—the one I'd seen going by earlier had looked too good to resist. It was, and so is this bistro, easily one of the best in town.

"How was the stuffed cabbage?" my wine man asked me a few days later.

"Incredible."

"I knew you'd like it, but please don't give this one away. . . ."

Happily, he doesn't speak English, and you won't tell anyone who sent you either.

· · ·

IN A WORD: Aristocratic loden-coat-wearing locals with dachshunds tucked under their tables mix it up with the occasional well-advised tourist, UNESCO types, and top military brass with intimidatingly perfect posture (the École Militaire is just down the street) in this warm, welcoming neighborhood bistro, a place that's well worth traveling across town for. Some of the best home-style bistro cooking in Paris, with several outstanding Auvergnat specialties, makes this a great address for a hungry tête-à-tête or a quartet of friends who love to eat together.

DON'T MISS: Terrine of mushrooms and Morteau sausage; terrine of boudin mignon of pork braised with figs and sweet onions; stuffed cabbage; duck sausage with foie gras; gâteau (cake) of carmelized crêpes with grapefruit sections; vanilla millefeuille.

· · ·

[35] 19 avenue de La Motte-Picquet, 7th, 01.45.55.40.38. MÉTRO: École Militaire. OPEN Monday to Friday for lunch and dinner. Saturday dinner only, except for the first Saturday of every month. www.leflorimond.com CLOSED Sunday. • $$

Huîtrerie Régis

AS SUMMER STARTS TO FADE, THERE'S A MAJOR CONSOLA-tion I look forward to every year in Paris: oysters. No one produces finer ones than the French, which is why this vest-pocket dining room with whitewashed walls, a small serving bar, and seven tables (it seats fourteen maximum and they don't take reservations) set with white tablecloths and pretty blue serving plates is one of my favorite Left Bank addresses for a bivalve feast. To be sure, you can eat oysters year-round, but they really are at their best in the fall and winter, and few places in Paris offer a better shuck than Régis.

His oysters come from the Marennes-Oléron in the Poitou-Charentes region on France's Atlantic coast, and their quality is flawless. The rules of the house here require that you order a dozen apiece, which is one regulation I'm more than happy to abide by, especially since the only other foods served here are the occasionally available shrimp, clams, and sea urchins. There's something inherently festive about a meal at this little oyster bar, too, since a happy, easy camaraderie exists between people who are all enjoying the same pleasure, and it's fun to watch the amiable Régis opening the oysters and arranging them on platters of crushed ice to be served only with good bread and Echiré butter from the Poitou-Charentes region, some of the best in France.

Several varieties are on offer—fines de claires, pousses en claires, and spéciales de claires no. 3 (the number refers to their size; in France, oysters are calibrated from 000 to 6, with the smaller number indicating the larger-sized oyster)—but I also get the last, which have a sublime taste of the sea and lightly roasted hazelnuts. Though lemon wedges come with the oysters, I eat mine neat, savoring each creamy, fleshy mollusk and then tipping the shell back for the iodine-rich pleasure of its juices. To pass for a regular, don't return your empty shells to the tray stand—the French consider it bad manners to return empty shells to a shared tray—but pile them up in your plate, which the waitress will empty for you when it fills up. And be sure to order a nice bottle of Sancerre to savor them with. Plan on a slice of the flaky apple or other fruit tart for dessert, and get here when the doors open if you don't want to wait.

· ·

IN A WORD: A terrific hole-in-the-wall oyster bar right in the heart of Saint-Germain-des-Prés serving some of the best bivalves in Paris.

DON'T MISS: You're here to eat oysters, but if sea urchins are available, don't miss these delectable delicacies with their soft, briny orange meat.

. . .

[36] 3 rue Montfaucon, 6th, 01.44.41.10.07. MÉTRO: Mabillon or Saint-Germain-des-Prés. OPEN Tuesday to Sunday for lunch and dinner. CLOSED Monday and mid-July to end of September. www.huitrerieregis. com ▪ $$

Joséphine "Chez Dumonet"

DINNER AT JOSÉPHINE THE OTHER NIGHT LEFT ME FEELing optimistic about the future of France. First of all, after an absence of six years, nothing about this Left Bank bistro had changed, a truly blessed expression of the French talent for leaving well enough alone. The cracked tile floors, extinct brass gas jets, zinc-topped service bar, and custard-colored nicotined walls survived as one of those precious Parisian decors that instantly, almost tauntingly, promises a good meal with the confidence of a place that's been a setting for pleasure for more than eighty years.

Dorie, a cookbook writer who divides her time between New York and Paris, and I sat side by side on a brown-vinyl-covered banquette and talked our favorite subjects, books and food and books about food. Since I'd had a rich and rather soulless lunch in Reims, my appetite for the evening was more about seeing her than eating, or so I thought. Dorie's an interesting woman, with an intelligence and ambitiousness that's hidden by her easy laugh. Dining with her is a rare exception to my aversion to meals with people who have a professional relationship with food. Why? Eating shouldn't be competitive. Cooking can be good or bad, but taste is subjective because its original function was instantaneous biofeedback, an instant reaction based on our own personal taste memories of pleasure and aversion.

The last time I'd been here was at the invitation of a rich industrialist who'd made one of my closest friends his mistress. That night, the crowd had a Gaullist smugness that didn't sit well with me, and the metal-bending tycoon not only toyed with my friend, a brilliant and beautiful woman, but made a miscalculated man-to-man assumption that I'd join him in his game. Though the food was delicious, there was no pleasure at our table, and a week later I had only a vague memory of what I'd eaten. Looking at the menu with Dorie, however, my appetite stirred.

Unusually for Paris, you can order half portions of most starters and many main courses, but we went whole hog. It was a good decision, too, since her house-smoked salmon was superb and my thick slab of coarsely ground, beautifully seasoned terrine de campagne was lusciously enveloped in a sticky brown aspic of carmelized meat juices. When you're not very hungry, really good food not only comes as a brilliant surprise but seduces with real power.

Dorie was detailing the latest romantic travails of a mutual friend when a short, rough-looking, unshaved young man came in, sat at the bar, ordered Champagne, and got busy on his cell phone. A few minutes later his friends arrived, and I found myself thinking about how much younger and hipper the clientele at Chez Joséphine had become. The trio sat next to us and included a light-skinned black man in layers of oversized but carefully laundered stone gray sweat clothing. He wore a cap embroidered with an NYC emblem, the international don't-mess-with-me symbol, cocked sideways, and a massive, expensive wristwatch that looked as if it could run a NASA launch. I'm not much of a fan of rap music, but I recognized him anyway—Joey Starr, the most famous French rapper and the former lead singer of a group called Nique Ta Mère, or F——Your Mother.

Our main courses were served, and they were superb. Dorie had a millefeuille de pigeon, a brilliant creation of the young chef-owner, Jean-Christian Dumonet, golden layers of pommes de terre Anna interleaved with boned rare pigeon in a silky dark brown sauce. My boeuf bourguignon came in an enameled poppy-colored Le Creuset casserole and was lush; beef, pearl onions, and button mushrooms were suspended in a rich sauce redolent of wine and meat. Meanwhile, Joey Starr was tucking into a thick slab of foie gras and clearly enjoying it. Just as our cheese course arrived, a lovely assortment from Quatrehommes just down the street in the rue de Sèvres, a massive grilled andouillette (pig's intestine sausage) was served to Starr. I filled Dorie in on our neighbor, his music, and all of his drug convictions, and, as a big-city girl, she was fascinated.

We dawdled over our cheese and had just finished our Bordeaux when an aproned waiter brought Starr a perfect Grand Marnier soufflé, which he accompanied with a snifter of Darroze Armagnac. By now I wasn't surprised when I overheard him say something about the Michelin guide. After all, he'd just scarfed down the same sort of rich, well-constructed meal you'd expect to see served to a priest or a notary.

We paid our bills at the same time, but the rap trio stood up first. Starr glanced at us and flashed the shy smile appropriate to the occasion of our being the last clients left in the restaurant. "Bonsoir, Madame, M'sieur," he said, and stepped into the night. Sometimes even the French forget that few things are more civilizing than good food and good wine, and walking home I couldn't imagine a more hopeful vignette of the country's future than the gourmet meal consumed by the dapper and surprisingly polite rap star.

．　＊　．

IN A WORD: A venerable and much-loved Left Bank bistro has evolved with the times by attracting a younger clientele and adding new dishes to the menu. Perfect for a first or last night in Paris, since the atmosphere is almost as smooth and thick as the foie gras. Also good for business meals, tête-à-têtes, and solo dining. A great address for game lovers, too.

DON'T MISS: Foie gras; salade de mâche; pommes de terre et truffe (lamb's lettuce, potatoes, and truffle shavings, in season only); boeuf bourguignon; millefeuille de pigeon (boned, rare pigeon in flaky pastry with a sauce of its pan juices); cheese tray from Quatrehommes, one of Paris's best cheese shops; soufflé au Grand Marnier.

. . .

[37] 117 rue du Cherche-Midi, 6th, 01.45.48.52.40. MÉTRO: Duroc. OPEN Monday to Friday for lunch and dinner. CLOSED Saturday and Sunday. ▪ $$$

Bistroy Les Papilles

THE LATIN QUARTER HAS A SPECIAL STATE OF MIND. IT'S perenially young, inquisitive, iconoclastic, creative, and cosmopolitan, but as rising real estate prices have pushed students and academics out of the neighborhood and seen many of the cafés where they once gathered converted into clothing shops or fast-food places, this bohemian groove has become increasingly elusive. Happily, there are still a few places where you can channel this delicious sensibility, and one of the best is Bistroy Les Papilles, a wine shop and épicerie (grocery) cum restaurant that quickly became a local favorite after its opening in 2004.

The genial owner, Bertrand Bluy, worked as a pastry chef at Troisgros, Marc Veyrat, Taillevent, and the Hôtel Bristol before deciding to get out of the kitchen, and he's the perfect host, cheerfully explaining the set menu, a single four-course meal that changes daily, and the wines he stocks on shelves that line the attractive brick red dining room. The atmosphere's homey, friendly, and fun, and I often choose this place when we'll be four or more.

We were five the last time I was here, among us Corinne, a professor of architecture who spends a lot of time in Japan and who gave Bluy a hand by translating the menu for a table of Japanese students next to us. This slightly drowsy quartet—it was their first night in town, and they'd read about this place in a Tokyo paper—were astonished to find a Frenchwoman who spoke their language, but on any given evening, this is the kind of place where you might meet an expert in Renaissance brickwork or listen in on friends plotting a trip up the Amazon.

Our meal was superb, too. We began with a tureen of artichoke soup to ladle over oval scoops of foie gras mousse in the bowl each of us was served, a beautifully subtle taste pairing, since the faint sweetness of the artichoke was the perfect foil for the earthiness of the liver. Next, two copper-plated casseroles arrived with the main course—poitrine de porc, or pork belly,

with a crunchy crust and meltingly tender meat, and baby potatoes, mushrooms, black olives, and oven-dried tomatoes. A side
dish of emerald green pistou sauce was the perfect vibrant herbal
finish for this rich meat, too, and our cheese course, a runny
Saint-Maure chèvre with a small salad and a tapenade-spread
tartine was also excellent. Bluy's previous métier was apparent
in a delicious panna cotta (Italian-style baked cream custard)
with a tart, willow-green coulis of Reine Claude plums. Suffice
to say that my papilles (taste buds) always look forward to any
meal at this delightful restaurant.

· · ·

IN A WORD: In the heart of the Latin Quarter, this friendly,
good-value épicerie-wine-shop-and-restaurant captures the
special atmosphere of the neighborhood that's the brain of Paris
and serves a single four-course chalkboard menu daily to a
happy crowd of epicurean locals.

DON'T MISS: Favorites from the changing menu here include
beetroot gazpacho; artichoke soup with foie gras mousse; velouté de carotte (creamy carrot soup) with coriander, cumin,
and grilled bacon; poitrine de porc (grilled pork belly) with
baby potatoes, mushrooms, black olives, dried tomatoes, and
pistou sauce; hanger steak with carrots and spring onions; roast
cod with olive oil and mashed potatoes; chocolate and coffee
pudding; panna cotta with Reine Claude coulis; citrus salad
with Campari gelée.

· · ·

[38] 30 rue Gay-Lussac, 5th, 01.43.25.20.79. MÉTRO: Cluny–La Sorbonne
or RER Luxembourg. OPEN Tuesday to Saturday for lunch and dinner.
CLOSED Sunday and Monday. www.lespapillesparis.fr • $$

Le Petit Pontoise

WHEN YOU LIVE IN PARIS AND DISCOVER A WONDERFUL new restaurant, you're faced with an instant dilemma: to share or not. The reason, of course, is that a review can completely overwhelm a promising table before it's even had a chance to find its groove. When Le Petit Pontoise opened six years ago, we decided this was one to keep under our hats. Why? Not only is it open daily, but the food's delicious and the wine list carefully composed and well priced. Alas, our coterie broke ranks, but despite its popularity with a transient and often gastronomically conservative international clientele, this snug butter yellow dining room remains one of the best bets in the Latin Quarter, an otherwise challenging place to find a good French feed.

On a Sunday night, our quartet was coming from two different Easter lunches and one Passover celebration in different corners of France, so we were surprised to find ourselves eating with real relish. Starters included a superb salad of poached fresh haricots verts (string beans) with meaty crayfish tails; a gratin of tiny dauphinois ravioli, from the mountainous south-central Dauphiné region of France, no bigger than a postage stamp and stuffed with cheese; a first-rate terrine de gibier (game terrine); and a spectacular tarte Tatin d'artichauts. Though I don't like it when the names of specific dishes are used generically—there's a sorry tendency in Paris right now to describe everything stuffed and tubular as "cannelloni," for example—the "Tatin" more or less warranted the name as a brilliant spring dish of young artichoke quarters on a bed of rustic ratatouille on a nice crispy pastry base. (What made it a Tatin, in case you're wondering, is that the vegetables had been braised under the same pastry crust, which became the base of the tart when flipped over.)

At a neighboring table, an adolescent boy from Winnetka, Illinois, refused all attempts by his parents to get him to taste what they were eating and so clearly enjoying, shutting down further entreaties with a warning: "All I wanted was a pizza."

"Okay, but you don't know what you're missing," his mother replied. I love pizza, too, but Mom was right. The parmentier de canard avec foie gras was spectacular—savory shredded duck under a generous cap of panfried foie gras came on a bed of mashed potatoes lashed with a lush mahogany-colored sauce. Scallops in a light saffron sauce, a veal chop sautéed with a branch of fresh rosemary and garnished with marrow bones, and roast chicken with mashed potatoes were similarly carefully cooked and satisfying. Desserts like baba au rhum (pastry sponge soaked in rum with whipped cream) and île flottante, big white tufted pods of meringue on a shallow sea of custard, tasted rather standard issue, and prices have climbed a lot recently, but the service remains outstandingly friendly—it had been a long time, too, since anyone had been so welcoming as to offer me a complimentary glass of white wine while I waited to be seated, and overall this place remains very reliable.

· · ·

IN A WORD: A quality bistro with good traditional French cooking and a nice wine list in the Latin Quarter. Don't be surprised to run into someone you know.

DON'T MISS: Poêlée de grosses crevettes et asperges vertes (sauted shrimp and green asparagus); parmentier de canard avec foie gras (shredded duck and foie gras with pureed potatoes); bar rôti à la vanille (sea bass roasted with vanille); soufflé chaud à la vanille (hot vanilla souffle).

. . .

[**39**] 9, rue de Pontoise, 5th, 01.43.29.25.20. MÉTRO: Maubert-Mutualité. OPEN daily for lunch and dinner. ▪ **$$**

Au Pied de Fouet

WITH VISIONS OF THE SNOWY PEAKS SURROUNDING GENEVA AND the vineyards of the Beaujolais in the snow looking like a tidy patchwork of white corduroy still in my head, I arrived back in Paris from a trip to Switzerland on a smoking cold night last winter and went to meet my friend Judy for dinner at Au Pied de Fouet, a hole-in-the-wall in the Faubourg Saint-Germain, just down the street from my old apartments on the rue du Bac and the rue Monsieur. When I lived in the neighborhood twelve years ago, I never frequented this place, famously known as one of Jean Cocteau's favorite restaurants, because I found the welcome gruff, the food too plain, and the service rushed. But I'd heard it had recently changed owners, and a friend who lives nearby had been raving about the pot au feu, which is exactly what I was hoping to find on the chalkboard menu that changes daily as I walk down the rue du Babylone listening to the crunch of frost beneath my heels. Stepping inside the tiny place, I had a booming "Bonsoir" from the owner behind the bar, and Judy was waiting at a table covered in a red-and-white-checked cloth. Sitting next to her at the same table—you share here—was an elegant older man in a gray flannel jacket with a paisley ascot. He glanced up from his carefully folded *Le Monde* when I sat down and said "Bonsoir," too. There was no pot au feu that night, but we ate a delicious salad of lentils in shallot vinaigrette, crispy confit de canard with crunchy sautéed potatoes, and apple cobbler washed down with a pleasant Côtes du Rhône served in a carafe. The meal was briskly served but delicious, and in a break with the past, you can now have coffee at the table (previously it was only served at the bar to make way for waiting customers). Later, I realized I had finally mastered both the French language and the more arcane rites of Paris well enough to appreciate this place for what it is, a charming little hole-in-the-wall serving very good home-style comfort food in one of the city's most aristocratic and so most pecunious neighborhoods.

I've since been back many times, including this gorgeous April day, when I popped in alone and polished off oeufs mayonnaise (hard-boiled eggs dressed with mayonnaise), asparagus vinaigrette, and chicken in a lemony chive sauce on tagliatelle. Solitary diners are welcomed, and I ate this excellent lunch sitting across from a perfect stranger who broke my musing on why oeufs mayonnaise, one of the homeliest of all French comfort foods, is always served as three halves of egg when he charmingly told me that I could finish the rest of his wine if I liked.

If an anthropologist was looking for the ideal setting in which to study the way that the French relate to each other and food in public settings, he or she could do no better than this place, where everyone is skilled at the art of creating both privacy and conviviality in a small, shared space. Otherwise, it's just about as close as you can get to tasting homey old-fashioned French home cooking without being invited to dinner by a Parisian. And if I'm still some years out of port from being invited to take advantage of the rond de serviettes, or wooden napkin rack where the regulars once stored their napkins between meals, I've graduated to being greeted by the harmlessly ornery waitress as "Notre ami américain" ("our American friend"). P.S., they've recently opened a branch restaurant in the 6th Arrondissement, and it has a similarly winning atmosphere and solid, tasty French home cooking as the maison mère.

IN A WORD: A meal at this tiny cubbyhole in the Faubourg Saint-Germain is like having a comforting pantry supper prepared by an old family retainer—think the real vieille France cooking favored by the local aristocrats.

DON'T MISS: lentil salad; duck gizzard salad; oeufs mayonnaise; confit de canard; sautéed chicken livers; crème caramel.

[40] 45 rue de Babylone, 7th, 01.47.05.12.27. MÉTRO: Saint-François-Xavier. OPEN Monday to Saturday for lunch and dinner. CLOSED Sunday. ▪ $

3 rue Saint Benoit, 6th, 01.42.96.59.10. MÉTRO: Saint-Germain-des-Prés. OPEN Monday to Saturday for lunch and dinner. CLOSED Sunday. ▪ $

Restaurant David Toutain

AFTER HONING HIS SKILLS THROUGH A SERIES OF WORLD-roving apprenticeships that included stints in the kitchens of Bernard Loiseau, Bernard Pacaud (L'Ambroisie), Marc Veyrat, Andoni Luis Aduriz (Mugaritz, near San Sebastian in Spain), and Paul Liebrandt (Corton, New York City), young chef David Toutain first burst onto the Paris scene at L'Agapé Substance, a tiny restaurant in the heart of Saint Germain des Prés, in 2011. Though this restaurant is the size of a railroad car and guests dine perched on stools at a single long table—not exactly the most comfortable of circumstances under which to embark on a long tasting menu—the brilliance of Toutain's cooking delivered in a sequence of small tasting plates with the intricacy, art, and elegance of Fabergé eggs quickly rendered most grumbling mute, however, and this quickly became one of the hardest reservations to land in Paris.

Then, after sixteen months of hard work—Toutain cooked in a miniscule open kitchen at the back of the room—Toutain stunned Paris gastronomes when he resigned and set off to travel the world with his Vietnamese-American wife, Thai. Defying rumors that he might stay on in Asia, he returned to Paris and opened his own restaurant just before Christmas in 2013 on a quiet side street in the plush 7th Arrondissement on the Left Bank.

Walking on my way to dinner on a blustery night across the vast lawns that sweep from Les Invalides down to the Seine, I was curious to see what sort of home Toutain would create for himself now that he's hung out his own shingle. The studied minimalism of his restaurant didn't come as a surprise either when I stepped in off the wet sidewalk, because it was such a perfect reflection of this very talented young chef's planed-down sensibility. Frosted lightbulbs dangled from the high ceiling overhead, and Bruno was waiting for me at a beautiful oak table with a round terra-cotta insert in its center that I correctly guessed could serve as a hot plate. The visual simplicity of sand-colored walls decorated with several varnished slices of a tree, cocoa and ecru leather chairs, and bare floorboards created a soothing atmosphere, and these aesthetics, simultaneously Zen, Shaker, and Scandinavian, tipped the aesthetics of Toutain's cooking.

Since the first course of any tasting menu succinctly announces the chef's intentions, I was intrigued when the rather austere young waitress in a well-cut black pantsuit arrived with curved gray plates that contained roasted ivory-colored salsify roots, which still had an etching of soil around the crown where their leaves had been, and instructed us to dredge them in the artful smear of herb-garnished white chocolate cream that was next to them on the plate. To be honest, I'm not a great fan of white chocolate, which is basically just sweetened cocoa butter, but this garnish surprised by gently amplifying the sweet, mineral rich taste of the earthy vegetables to create a dish that was stunningly original and very satisfying.

"I spent summers on my grandparents' farm in Normandy," Toutain told me the next day when I met him for a coffee. "Every meal began with crudités (raw vegetables) from their garden, and it wasn't until many years later that I appreciated how good these vegetables tasted for having been picked a few minutes earlier. The purity of their taste is a memory I really treasure—they were perfect," said the chef, and the same dewy freshness and innocence of summer deep in the Norman countryside is something that profoundly informs his cooking. Uncommonly for a French chef, Toutain really loves vegetables, and they were given equal billing with the fish and meat that comprised the spectacular menu he'd served me the night before.

If dishes like a slow-cooked egg nestled into a bright yellow cream of sweet corn or an angelic all-white composition of a light soup made with yuba (bean-curd sheet) garnished with finely sliced cuttlefish and translucent Parmesan gnocci made with juices sweated from the cheese during hours of slow-cooking had a winsome originality, Toutain's reflexive earthiness and extraordinary technical skills were showcased by a seared cube of foie gras that acquired a head-spinning potency from black truffle shavings and the shallow pool of baked-potato-skin broth in which it was served. The arpeggio quality of this meal reached an intensely memorable but purring conclusion with a dessert of candied Jerusalem artichokes with an ice cream made from the same vegetable and a praline cream.

Toutain's restaurant is a weather vane for where French cooking is heading in the twenty-first century. Aside from his superb and deeply meditated cooking, it also predicts the demise of aspirationally aristocratic haute-bourgeois comforts and tastes that have been the anointed idiom for serious food in France since the days of Napoleon III. Instead of heavy silver plate and Limoges porcelain, Toutain's knives come from a Belgian metalsmith who cuts down old carving knives to table size—and much of his tableware is likewise Belgian, including homemade pieces from a small potter outside of Brussels and beautiful ceramics from the avant-garde porcelain producer Pieter Stockmann in the old mining town of Genk on the Dutch border. As Toutain sees it, the new French luxury should spin on an axis of sincerity and simplicity, and the concept of *terroir*, that slightly mystical Gallic term that refers to the specificity of seasonal produce from well-defined geographical regions, will always be the rudder of his kitchen.

· ·

IN A WORD: David Toutain is one of the most gifted of a new generation of French chefs, and his deliberately self-effacing tasting menus—"I want my food to be easy to understand, but I don't want anyone to know how it was made," says the chef—are deeply meditated, quietly exciting, and profoundly satisfying.

DON'T MISS: Toutain's menus evolve constantly according to the chef's inspiration and the seasons, but he has a particular gift for making vegetables eloquent.

. . .

[41] 29 rue Surcouf, 7th, 01.45.50.11.10. MÉTRO: Invalides. OPEN Monday to Friday for lunch and dinner. CLOSED: Saturday and Sunday. www.david toutain.com ▪ $$$

Restaurant Jean-François Piège

ONE OF THE MOST INTERESTING AND ORIGINAL RESTAURANTS in Paris is reached via a flight of stairs behind a locked door on the rue Saint-Dominique, the lively main street in the part of the 7th Arrondissement favored by young single executives from good families in the provinces, divorcées, and foreigners looking for a prestigious pied-à-terre in Paris. This street looks the part, too, with lots of glossy boutiques, takeaway food places, and bars and cafés that get busy after office hours. Compared to the bourgeois quietude that prevails elsewhere in this conservative, wealthy part of the city, this lively street politely breaks the prevailing mold, which is exactly what chef Jean-François Piège did when he opened his restaurant here in 2010. A shrewd iconoclast and tremendously gifted young chef, he dropped the traditional template of French haute cuisine dining on the floor, carefully examined every shard, discarded what no longer made sense to him, and incorporated what did into his own new and very personal experience of fine French cooking in the twenty-first century.

Greeted at the top of the stairs by a beautiful young woman in a short, exquisitely cut black dress, you're ushered into a low-lit salon that feels like a politely louche supper club in late-forties or early-fifties Miami or Palm Springs. There's a studied Gal-

lic chic to this midcentury decor, with brass wall sconces, plush chairs and sofas upholstered in velvet in muted jewel tones, and walls covered with white-painted filigreed wooden trellises. At the back of the room is the kitchen, which has a picture window onto the dining room, a thickly carpeted space that accommodates fewer than thirty diners at a time. It certainly doesn't feel like a restaurant, and that of course is the point.

Coming from the opulent splendor of Les Ambassadeurs at the Hôtel de Crillon, where he won two Michelin stars after working for a slate of the best chefs in France, including Bruno Cirino, Christian Constant, and Alain Ducasse, Piège has eschewed the pomp and formality of his former quarters in favor of an experience that's intimate and relaxed but no less tantalizing. Instead he identified and decided to emphasize the element that had gone missing in the French haute-cuisine dining experience: an understated and so rather thrilling sensuality.

Once you're seated, tall, handsome, whippet-thin waiters—
Piège casts his staff for maximum effect—in white shirts and
black suits greet you in low, confidential tones, as if you've
come to attend a private screening. The prix fixe menu begins
with a stylized white-porcelain daisy-shaped lazy Susan with a
tiny cold hors d'oeuvres posed on each petal—perhaps a chunk
of good ham topped with a tiny slice of cornichon and walled
into a fragile pen of nearly transparent, Melba-toast-like wafers
with some butter, which is Piège's riff on France's favorite ham
sandwich (*jambon beurre*), a bonbon of foie gras topped with
grilled eggplant gelée (made from the juices the vegetable has
sweated during cooking), a crunchy codfish ball, and a miniature blini with smoked salmon and horseradish cream. Intended
to arouse your curiosity, they do, so you're fully alert when the
warm hors d'oeuvres start coming.

It was at this point during a recent dinner that my friend
David, a fellow Nutmeg State native with an impressively exi-
gent palate (thanks to years spent working in the kitchen of a
famous San Francisco restaurant), became engaged by Piège's
cuisine. Both of us were astonished by a rectangle of soft brioche
in a shallow pool of tomato water with oregano, slivered Kalamata olives, and burrata, which lit up when the waiter shaved
some frozen anchoïade, a classic Provençal sauce of anchovies
and garlic that melted instantly but left behind the potent punctuation of fish and garlic that made this dish a puckishly edible
cameo of Mediterranean cooking.

It got even better with the next dish, which is perhaps the
one Piège is proudest of—a royale (flan) of chicken livers
with crayfish made according to an 1892 recipe by French chef
Lucien Tendret and garnished with chicken-liver foam. The
sublimated barnyard funkiness of the chicken livers made it

impossible to miss the nobleness of the tiny sweet curls of crayfish tail, and these two dishes together showed off all of the reasons why Piège is the young Paris chef who will most likely step
into the shoes vacated by Alain Ducasse and Joël Robuchon. He
has astonishing technical skills and a lyrically seditious gastronomic imagination.

I've loved the cooking of this deeply trained classicist ever
since I first discovered it at the Crillon. He doesn't need liquid
nitrogen or any other of the clichés of molecular cooking, nor the
caveman antics of the new Scandinavian cooking with its bark,
moss, or raw foods, to create excitement at the table. With a serene
modesty, Piège slyly invites you to meditate on and find pleasure
in the remarkable produce he cooks by parsing out traditional recipes with the miniaturist skills of a watchmaker who knows exactly
how everything fits together or by gently jolting them with unexpected but delightful contrasts of texture or flavor.

To be sure, his puppy-like enthusiasm occasionally wrong-
foots him—a first course of lobster cooked in fig leaves with
an extraction of figs, fresh almonds, cubes of foie gras, and
wild pepper made no sense to me. But my next course, a veal
chop with girolles and fresh almonds on a bed of finely sliced
peaches, was brilliant, amplifying and accenting the taste of the
tender mineral-rich meat so accurately. Even subtler, David's
second main course, duck breast cooked rare with crispy shards
of its own skin, in a sauce of pan juices with black olives and
baby celery, was still masterfully authoritative.

The cheese course is supplied by Xavier, an affineur (cheese
merchant) in Toulouse, and it's a brawny dairy prelude to the
sweet coda of a meal here, a generous assortment of desserts,
including a showstopping "fleur" of nectarines—fine slices of the
fruit rolled into upright petals filled with currant-raspberry gelée

and garnished with a scoop of lemon-verbena ice cream. And the final dish of this dinner, a bergamot flan, was almost maternal, or a gentle reminder of just how contented and well fed I was.

· · ·

IN A WORD: Chef Jean-François Piège is one of the most talented chefs in a new generation of French talent, and his offbeat supper-club-like table coins a new idiom for Parisian chic that will delight anyone willing to dispense with the old-school drills of Gallic haute cuisine.

DON'T MISS: There's no real way of predicting what might be on the menu when you visit this restaurant, but I earnestly hope that you'll have a chance to try Piège's chicken-liver royale with crayfish, which is one of the most elegant but solacing dishes I've ever had in Paris.

. . .

[42] 79 rue Saint-Dominique, 7th, 01.47.05.79.79. MÉTRO: La Tour–Maubourg, Pont de l'Alma (RER), or Ecole Militaire. OPEN Monday to Friday for lunch and dinner. CLOSED Saturday and Sunday. www.jfpiege.com
▪ $$$$

Le Ribouldingue

THE NAME OF THIS AMIABLE LITTLE BISTRO IN ONE OF THE prettiest streets in the Latin Quarter means "The Binge," but this binge is decidedly French, since the menu offers an offal feast that tends to gall those who aren't Gauls. Think extreme eating, as in groin de cochon (the tip of the pig's muzzle, or the fleshy bit with nostrils), tétines de vache (thin, panfried slices of cow's udder), brains, kidneys, liver, and other organs likely to cause even some adventurous eaters to shudder.

To be sure, Nadège Varigny, who worked for many years at La Régalade when it belonged to chef Yves Camdeborde, wouldn't stay in business long if everything on her menu promised an Outward Bound experience on a plate. When my friend Peter, a Scottish antiques dealer whose father was a butcher in Glasgow, came to town with his wife, Violet, she reacted with almost delirious relief and then with real pleasure to her main course of beef cheeks braised in red wine and served with macaroni—from her point of view this was the least horrifying dish on the menu. "This is delicious, although I can barely stand to sit at the same table with the two of you. I mean, really, you can't pretend you actually like eating all of that rubbish, can you?" Well, yes. Peter has no fear of any part of any animal, and though I was hardly to the gizzard born, over twenty years of living in France I've developed a taste for such proverbial nose wrinklers as brains, kidneys, and liver.

If you're more in Violet's camp than mine but vaguely curious, this is the best place in town to lose your offal virginity, since the quality of the produce is impeccable, and it's perfectly cooked and brilliantly seasoned. Interested? Even a little? Let me suggest two delicious dishes that are unlikely to cause a bloodcurdling scream: a starter of carpaccio of calf's head with a nicely made sauce gribiche (a tangy vinaigrette with chopped hard-boiled egg, cornichons, and capers) and perfectly roasted veal kidneys with a side of gratin dauphinois (potatoes baked with onions and cream). You can revert to chicken breasts when you get home, so why not take a walk on the wild side while you're in Paris? And if more encouragement's needed, the tarte Tatin is sublime—"I'd

even willingly fight my way through some of the nasty business
on the menu for another slice of this" was Violet's judgment—as
is the homemade pot-de-crème, a light, creamy chocolate custard.

·   ·

IN A WORD: The best place in Paris to eat something offal, as
in kidneys, tripe, liver, brains, and other bits and pieces inhos-
pitably described as offcuts.

DON'T MISS: Carpaccio of calf's head; roasted veal kidneys;
beef cheeks braised in red wine; sautéed lamb's brains; tarte
Tatin; pot-de-crème.

. . .

[43] 10 rue Saint-Julien-le-Pauvre, 5th, 01.46.33.98.80. MÉTRO: Saint-
Michel. OPEN Tuesday to Saturday for lunch and dinner. Saturday dinner
only. CLOSED Sunday and Monday. www.ribouldingue-restaurant.fr ▪ $$

Le Timbre

EVEN IF THE MANCHESTER-BORN CHEF CHRIS WRIGHT'S COOKING
weren't so good, who'd ever forget having a meal in the same
tiny dining room as Marianne Faithfull? On a beautiful spring
night, the rock-and-roll goddess occupied a corner table in this
minuscule place—*le timbre* is French for "postage stamp," and
after all of us had been listening to a sozzled American steward-
ess recounting a torrid layover in Barcelona, the legend's table-
mate had a word with her.

"It all sounds delicious, dear, but unless you're making a
public confession, you might want to lower your voice."

Midway between Montparnasse and Saint-Germain right in the heart of the Left Bank, Wright's place is ideal for a relaxed, homey meal of first-rate market cooking. His blackboard menu of four starters, four main courses, and four desserts changes weekly, and he prides himself on the quality of his produce—his fish comes from the famous Poissonerie du Dôme in Montparnasse and sparingly used foie gras and truffles from Le Comptoir Corrézien, a speciality shop in the 15th Arrondissement that furnishes many of the city's top tables with these two signature luxuries. Wright also hunts down unusual wines, including the deliciously flinty white Argentinean bottle we chose to accompany first courses of smoked duck breast salad with a citrus vinaigrette and green asparagus in an anise-spiked cream sauce with a few drops of balsamic vinegar and Parmesan shavings. Main courses of daube de boeuf au vin rouge (beef braised in red wine) and trout topped with shavings of country ham and garnished with fava beans were equally satisfying and had a similar homemade sincerity. In a nod to his native Albion, Wright serves excellent cheeses from Neal's Yard in London, including Stilton and Cheddar, and desserts run to fruit crumbles and soups or purees of fresh fruit. All told, a charming place for a relaxed, affordably priced feast.

. . .

IN A WORD: This is an intimate bistro de chef that pulls a stylish, young, international crowd with a friendly atmosphere and homey but imaginative cooking.

DON'T MISS: Brandade de haddock (haddock shepherd's pie); tartines de légumes (country-bread toasts topped with fresh vegetables); guinea hen with tomato and pineapple chutney; millefeuille with vanilla cream; strawberry soup.

. . .

[44] 3 rue Sainte-Beuve, 6th, 01.45.49.10.40. MÉTRO: Vavin and Notre-Dame-des-Champs. OPEN Tuesday to Saturday for lunch and dinner. CLOSED Sunday and Monday. www.restaurantletimbre.com ▪ $$

Le Voltaire

SOMEONE DESERVES A GOOD-SISTER AWARD. "DAD, HE loves you, it's just that he doesn't love your life, and I hope you don't mind if I say this, but instead of just cutting off his allowance, I think the best thing might be to invest in his furniture-making business like a disinterested partner," said the beautiful young blonde, a modern Gibson girl, dining with her parents at the corner table next to us. "That's a constructive idea, darling," said Mom, which left Dad cornered. "Well, maybe. Let me think about it. I just can't get my mind around the idea of anyone dropping out of college to make furniture in the middle of nowhere in Maine," said Dad, serving himself another glass of Bordeaux, a libation that made me optimistic for the wayward New England woodworker.

Few places in Paris offer a more intriguing sociological tapestry than this silk-stocking bistro on the Left Bank of the Seine in Saint-Germain. It's a clubby old place with wood-paneled walls and faded raspberry velvet banquettes, but the global gratin who love it are the same cast who made Truman Capote their lapdog and who tolerate miscellaneous deviance as the necessary fodder for that most essential of social lubricants: gossip. And thanks to these cultivated, tolerant types, most of whom are American, this place has an indestructible buzz, which comes from the fact that everyone feels comfortable here.

When I was a writer working in the Paris office of Fairchild Publications, I was a semiregular, and I never come here without thinking of the dinner or two I had here with Mr. Fairchild, one of the shrewdest old-fashioned newspapermen I've ever met and a daring judge of character with a curiously bashful Machiavellian streak. A bad boy with good manners and famous social antennae, he could never resist pulling the tail of any passing sacred cow and was never afraid to call a spade a spade. In his wake, we staffers frequented this place in search of the casual social crumbs that might make good copy, but during these meals as stalker, I rarely noticed the food. In fact, it wasn't until I'd left the fold and came back here on my own that I realized how good the kitchen actually is and how much fun it is to dine here.

To be sure, you don't come to Le Voltaire for cutting-edge dining but rather first-rate old-fashioned French comfort food, a great crowd, and superb old-school service. If the Italian equivalent of this place is Harry's Bar in Venice, the only American restaurants I've ever been to that approximate it are what Locke-Ober in Boston was when I was a child or, in New York, the now-defunct Gloucester House, the New York Athletic Club, and the Four Seasons restaurant in the Seagram's Building, but if the Gloucester House served better-than-average seafood and the Four Seasons has its moments, none of this quartet has a patch on the Voltaire as a purring, flattering machine that creates evanescent luxury.

The oeuf mayonnaise on the menu at 90 centimes may be its tongue-in-cheek equivalent of a John D. Rockefeller shiny ten-cent tip, but during my last meal here, I pounced

on the poached eggs in sorrel sauce, a vieille France dish I
first experienced when I was invited to Sunday supper by my
landlady, a turban-wearing French countess, and landlord,
a retired British diplomat, when I lived in the rue Monsieur,
a short, chic street in the 7th Arrondissement where Rock-
efeller would have felt right at home. It's basically baby food,
but I loved the sour metallic taste of sorrel, and the perfectly
coddled eggs were glazed with a pellucid layer of Gruyère.
My antique-dealer friend Olivier had beet and apple salad,
which arrived in a pretty, round fan, and then we went for
the meat. My sublime filet of beef with real béarnaise sauce
came with pureed potatoes and carrots, nursing home fodder
that I ignored while plundering the perfect shoestring fries,
some of the best in Paris, that came with Olivier's pert pyramid of steak tartare. The waiter brought us more frites without our asking, and when I finally took a stab at the tartare,
it was impeccable, with high notes of Worcestershire sauce
and Tabasco and discernible chunks of caper or cornichons
(puckery French gherkins). Fat black cherries poached in red
wine with vanilla beans, orange slices, cardamom, stick cinnamon, and mint were succulent and delicious, and the waiter
graciously gave both of us plates and silverware even though
only Olivier had ordered them. The wine list here is a bore,
and the bread should be better, but this reflexively chic hospitality means that I always look forward to a meal here.

Walking home on a balmy night, I mused on the odd but
eternal connection between bohemia and the bourgeoisie signaled at Le Voltaire by the amiably ugly and now priceless
fifties-vintage Vallauris ceramics hanging on the back wall and
was delighted to have found that this place is what it's always
been, which is a bistro wearing Mary Janes.

IN A WORD: Not only does this Left Bank bistro in business for more than sixty years have a stainless-steel chic created by soigné service and a stylish international clientele, the food is surprisingly good. Whether you're casting a romantic tête-à-tête, casual dinner with friends, late lunch on a rainy afternoon, or important business dinner, this place is a perfect one-size-fits-all Paris restaurant. Just come prepared for your plastic to take a beating, and don't expect gastronomic revelations but rather a solidly good Gallic feed.

DON'T MISS: Salad of haricots verts, artichoke hearts, and foie gras; salad of button mushrooms in lemon and olive oil vinaigrette with Parmesan shavings; poached eggs with sorrel; beef bouillon; crab salad; sole meunière; filet mignon with béarnaise sauce; tête de veau (calf's head); poached cherries with fresh mint; peaches poached in wine; chocolate mousse.

. . .

[45] 27 quai Voltaire, 7th, 01.42.61.17.49. MÉTRO: Rue du Bac. OPEN Tuesday to Saturday for lunch and dinner. CLOSED Sunday and Monday. ▪ $$$

Ze Kitchen Galerie

CHEF WILLIAM LEDEUIL IS NOT ONLY MOVIE-STAR HANDsome, he knows how to cook, which is why his offbeat Left Bank restaurant with an unfortunate franglais name is an ongoing hit with the gratin—antiques dealers, artists, book editors, journalists, and celebs—of Saint-Germain-des-Prés. In fact, on any given night, the crowd looks as though it could have just moved en masse from a local gallery opening just a few minutes earlier—think women with severe haircuts and lots of large ethnic jewelry and men with close-cropped beards and the classic outfit of the good-boy, bad-boy Gallic playboy, a well-cut blazer with a white shirt, jeans, and expensive shoes. Ledeuil adds further visual interest to the scene in the loftlike dining room with an open window on the kitchen by employing many Frenchmen of color—in a silk-stocking Paris neighborhood like this one, it is still surprising to see a nonwhite face, which is revealing of the way the French capital remains sociologically cloistered.

Settled at your rust-colored steel table with a sound-blunting block of foam affixed beneath, you'll relax into an affluent contemporary take on bohemian Paris with parquet floors, exposed pillars, and contemporary art on the walls. Ledeuil's menu is as

refreshingly unconventional as his dining room, since it's organized with original and slightly puzzling subheads—instead of
the traditional slugs of starters, main courses, and desserts, the
menu here is organized according to Les Bouillons (soups), Les
Pâtes (pastas), Les Poissons (fish), and so on.

What these menu categories don't tell is that Ledeuil is fascinated by the flavors of Southeast Asia and is one of the most
accomplished practitioners of bona fide fusion cooking in Paris
today. After winning a hot reputation as the launch chef at Les
Bouquinistes, one of chef Guy Savoy's original and very influential "baby bistros" (offshoot tables of haute cuisine chefs that
animated Parisian dining in the eighties) next door, he struck out
on his own a few years back, to emerge as one of the nerviest
chefs in Paris. Consider a starter of maloreddus (rolled durum-
wheat flour Sardinian gnocchi) in a foam of coconut milk scented
with lime leaves and sprinkled with shredded Spanish chorizo
sausage and Mimolette cheese from the north of France. This is
an original and successful dish, since the sweetness of the coconut milk meets the lactic freshness of the cheese, with the al dente
pasta offering a lot of mouth feel, unexpected at stylish Parisian
restaurants, where pasta textures often run to mashed and molle
(soft). Similarly, another starter of chewy bulots (sea snails) in
a lemongrass-and-basil-spiked broth also offers a meaty mouth
feel at pleasant odds with the gentle flavors most often associated in Thai cooking with noodles or braised seafood and fowl.
Ledeuil's ravioli filled with pork, coriander, and galangal root
(a rhizome that's a relative of ginger) and garnished with a condiment of artichokes and wasabi are a brilliant mixing of Asian
metaphors, as is octopus with a marinade of green apple juice
and fennel and superb veal cheeks with udon noodles and a Thai
jus made with lime leaves, ginger, and lemongrass.

Not all of Ledeuil's ideas work—if scallops on a skewer of lemongrass are delicious, "tamarind-lacquered" veal sweetbreads lack the astringent punch that the gum from these seedpods usually offers. There's also no cheese course, for me a serious shortcoming in a country as gifted in the art of milk as France, and desserts are less interesting than the starters and main courses. Still, the wine list is excellent, and Ledeuil continues to push out the boundaries of contemporary French cooking with a fascinating hybrid kitchen that's all his own.

. . .

IN A WORD: When a classically trained French chef develops a passion for Asia, the result is contemporary French fusion at its very best. Stylish, relaxed, and a lot of fun, this is a perfect address for anyone who wants a meal off from traditional French cooking.

DON'T MISS: Gazpacho of red beets with ginger; shrimp and cucumber with Thai herbs; moloreddus (pasta) in coconut milk with chorizo sausage and Mimolette cheese; green asparagus with Buratta (a creamy cheese from Puglia in Italy) croquettes; grilled lamb with lemongrass jus and kumquats; cappuccino of strawberries, pistachios, and lemongrass.

. . .

[46] 4 rue des Grands-Augustins, 6th, 01.44.32.00.32. MÉTRO: Saint-Michel. OPEN Monday to Friday for lunch and dinner. Saturday dinner only. CLOSED Sunday. www.zekitchengalerie.fr ▪ $$$

TABLE FOR ONE

· ·

LEARNING TO EAT ALONE IN PUBLIC WAS ONE OF THE
hardest but most valuable things I've ever done. Why? Because
it freed me from the pitying or censorious judgments I once pro-
jected into the eyes of total strangers ("Gosh, what a loser that
guy must be to be having dinner alone," etc.), and now there's
not a restaurant in the world that's off limits to me. Growing
out of the self-consciousness of being alone in public isn't easy,
but if I can do it, so can you. All it takes is a sense of humor and
lots of practice.

The first time I ate alone in a restaurant wasn't by choice. I'd
been traveling in Europe with a friend when he was called back
to New York a few days early to audition for a play.

At first I panicked—maybe I'd go home early, too. Then the
embarrassment of having everyone know I'd chickened out of
traveling solo shamed me into staying behind. As someone who
cares passionately about food, what really worried me, though,
was how I'd eat. Aside from many forgettable meals in fast-food
places and a New York City coffee shop or two, I'd reached my
early twenties without ever having had a meal alone in a real
restaurant. In fact, the idea was about as foreign as anything I
could imagine. If there was any way to avoid it, who in his right
mind would go to a restaurant alone?

Since I had friends in Paris, I was reprieved until I got to
Brussels, from where I was flying home. Maybe for the sake of
his own fun—many good hoteliers are voyeurs with a repressed

streak of sadism—the portly desk clerk with the wiry mutton-chop sideburns at the Hôtel Metropole, a looming old pile near a railroad station, put me in a honeymoon suite. It was a strange netherworld of rooms with an expectant erotic promise that I never lived up to, conveyed by a flesh-tone decor, lots of mirrors, and an Art Deco boudoir with pink lights. After the porter heaved my hated houndstooth-check tweed-sided American Tourister suitcase onto a luggage rack and left, the first thing I did was check the hotel information to see if they had room service. They did. But not on weekends. So I wandered around the city in a light drizzle eating all the street food I could find—crêpes, paper cones of frites (fries) with curried mayonnaise, and a nasty withered hot dog. After the Musée des Beaux-Arts, it started to pour, so I went to a movie, noticing as I went in at 6 P.M. that it was a three-hour film. My wobbly French meant I'd miss a lot, but I was buying time and vaguely hoped a jumbo bucket of popcorn would be the excuse for skipping dinner.

Two hours later, bored and hungry, I bolted out of the theater with salt-stung lips and became a stalker. Under an umbrella with two shot struts, I cruised by restaurant after restaurant, sizing them up and trying to summon the nerve to go in and ask for a table. Instinctively, I knew better than to try crowded, busy places, which meant, on a Saturday night near the Grand Place, that the pickings were slim. Cold, wet, and ravenous, I almost took the easy way out with a Chinese restaurant, a neutral option since I'd be a foreigner waited on by other foreigners, but I craved one of the Belgian specialties, maybe carbonnade de boeuf (beef braised with brown sugar in beer) or waterzooi (chicken and vegetables cooked in a cream sauce), that I'd salivated over in my guidebook. So I kept circling, and circling, until one of the barkers in a narrow pedestrian lane packed with ratty-looking Greek restaurants laughed at me, probably because he'd already seen me six times within an hour and recognized my predicament. I legged it down a side street and, peering through the tendrils of straggly philodendron in a diamond-paned window, I saw a man sitting alone at a table. I went in immediately.

"Une table pour une personne," I said to the bosomy hostess in a buttoned-up brown cardigan. She smiled vaguely and seated me along the exposed brick wall, lighting the candle in the middle of the table before handing me a menu. I almost snuffed the taper, which seemed to advertise my solitude, but then realized that it gave me something to focus on. I didn't dare look around until after I'd ordered my waterzooi, but when I did I was reassured by the sight of the other solo diner, an older man reading a magazine as he ate. Then I noticed that the table in front of him was also occupied by a solitary diner, as was one by the coat rack. As far as I could see, there was only one couple in the entire place. Everyone else was alone. I laughed out loud.

When he poured my wine, the waiter read my thoughts. "Eh oui, Monsieur, les gens seuls sont très bien chez nous." Since "seul" can mean either solo or lonely, I wasn't sure which he meant, but since I was well and truly both it didn't matter. What did was the way the sturdy rituals of the meal framed and tamed my anxiety. And then, as I settled in, it occurred to me that as far as everyone else in the room was concerned, I was doing something perfectly sensible, if maybe a little dull, which was to go into a restaurant and have a meal when I was hungry.

The food was unremarkable—I think the vegetables in the waterzooi may have even been canned—but everything else about that meal delighted me, including a fleeting linguistic puzzle. After the waiter had served my waterzooi, he shifted from French to the English he was likely studying and asked, "Have you any feather washers?"

"Feather washers?"

"Yes, feather washers."

"I'm sorry, I'm afraid I don't understand."

"I would like to satisfy your feather washers." Oh dear, things seemed to be taking a turn for the kinky. I smiled, shook my head, shrugged my shoulders.

"I really am so sorry. I don't understand."

Fortunately, he wasn't fazed. He wrote down the phrase on his pad and showed it to me: Further wishes.

"No, thank you very much, no feather washers." We shared a chuckle, but the dunce cap was clearly on my head, which was fine. I'd have been miserable if he'd been insulted or felt diminished.

In fact, I loved the seriousness conveyed by his black waistcoat and white apron, folded into sort of a cummerbund at the waist, and the way he promptly refilled my perforated metal bread basket and the reflexive "Bon appétit" that followed the arrival of each course. He greeted my decision to have cheese as proof of my admirable sagacity, and when I ordered a Cognac with my coffee, he summoned the hostess, who followed him to my table with a bottle and waited while he carefully centered a snifter the size of a goldfish bowl on a dopey little lace doily. Madame poured, and, after cocking her head to see that she'd been fair, she added another pour and trilled "À votre service" when I thanked her. What all of these cues taught me was that we were complicit in attempting to accomplish something we'd decided was of mutual importance—my pleasure at the table. Dining alone, I discovered on that rainy night in Brussels, was civilized and civilizing, and though I usually prefer company, there are times when I'm glad for the silence that allows the self-absorption that is one way of amplifying the pleasure of good food and wine.

As is true of most public pleasures in France, eating alone is an art to be learned and perfected. I wish I could claim that my Belgian triumph had left me prepared for a fresh round of solo supping when I arrived in Paris twenty years ago, but since the solution to solitary eating in most American cities remains sitting at a counter, I had to pick up where I'd left off. This time I knew no one and was living in a hotel without a restaurant, so aside from the takeaway lunches from a wonderful but now long-gone traiteur (a French take on the delicatessen) in the rue Cambon, across the street from where I worked—I still crave its delicious céleri rémoulade and succulent slices of the braised ham the owner roasted in the chimney of her girlhood home in the country on the weekends—I was up against it.

I had the major consolation of an expense account, however, and, after a few furtive suppers in cafés, I bought a guidebook and a new jacket, my college-vintage blazer being on its last legs, and doggedly set out to eat my way across Paris. I learned a lot of things about how to eat alone.

For starters, always make a reservation, dress well, go armed with a sense of humor, and never refuse the suggestion of an apéritif before dinner. If you don't want a glass of white wine or a flute of Champagne, order a Perrier (the French never drink hard liquor before a meal)—in Paris, by the way, this famous *eau* is drunk as an apéritif, not with food, *bien sûr*, because its large bubbles are reckoned to disturb the digestion. By having a drink you signal your server that you're not a skinflint and invite better service. Don't mumble or fidget, either—you're the rightful occupant of your table, and don't let anyone rush you.

Bring a book or a magazine if you like, but stop reading once you're settled in and enjoy the show any decent restaurant also provides. Admittedly, single women can attract unwanted attention, but if someone tries to chat you up and you're not interested, send him packing by saying "Dégagez!" ("Get lost!"). Refuse to be bullied, short-shrifted, or patronized, but be generous with smiles and compliments.

Ultimately, mastering the art of dining alone depends most upon cultivating the pleasure of your own company—good mental hygiene under any circumstances—and remembering that the Latin world generally casts a kindly eye on anyone in public pursuit of benign pleasures.

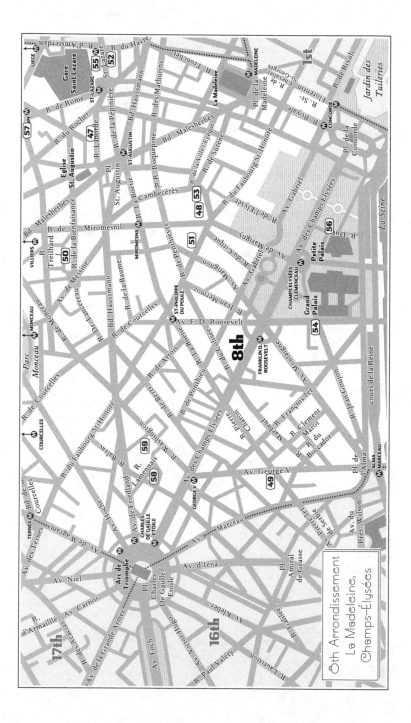

8th Arrondissement
La Madeleine,
Champs-Élysées

L'Abordage

ONE OF THE REASONS I LOVE LIVING IN A GREAT CITY IS THAT they're so propitious for unexpected encounters. This morning, I was sitting at my keyboard in an old T-shirt when my friend Charlotte, an Englishwoman who's been living in Bangkok and elsewhere in Asia for twenty years, called. She was en route to a funeral in the north of England, had the middle of the day free between planes, and wanted to know if we could have lunch. "Since I don't have much time, I'd like a fierce dose of Paris," she said, so I immediately booked us at L'Abordage and told her I'd be waiting on the terrace.

Across the street, the chestnut trees in the Parc Bergson had shed their white flowers, leaving only a long green wick at the center of the flat corsages formed by their serrated green leaves, and I found myself thinking that it was a view of this same lovely European greenery that the great French food critic Maurice Curnonsky enjoyed as he rested his gizzards and penned his jaunty, insightful reviews. As a bronze plaque indicates, the "prince des gastronomes" lived in a house across the way for many years, and I also couldn't help thinking that were he alive today, Curnonsky would surely have been a regular at this wonderful bistro just out his front door.

Arriving, it's not much to look at—just a long bar inside a dimly lit room with a cracked tile floor, some antique winemaking paraphernalia perched on the room divider, and then a second dining room that's equally plain if a bit brighter, but as I waited for Charlotte, it rapidly filled up with one of the sexiest crowds of power brokers to be found anywhere in Paris; bankers, brokers, politicians, newspaper people, PR and advertising people, almost all of them, both men and women, wearing beautifully cut suits. At noon, in fact, this place functions almost as a club of sorts, which is why I prefer to come on Wednesday, the only night it serves dinner and when it becomes the calmer province of discreet bourgeois couples; but I knew that Charlotte would find it fascinating, and there are very few places in town that do a better version of the basic primer of traditional French dishes.

As I rather expected, Charlotte, swathed in filmy Sri Lankan silks and wearing long, dangling Malaysian earrings, caused a stir when she arrived, and the waitress was plainly flabbergasted by her impeccable French. Desperate to get at some good French grub, she ordered marinated herring and grilled calf's liver, while I went with the chicken terrine and an entrecôte. "I say, isn't this a spot," she said, registering the human scenery. "All of these handsome men, a chalkboard menu, the smell of fried potatoes and good bread. This is exactly the Paris I miss when I'm sitting by the pool eating mangoes in Bangkok." She loved her marinated herring, and my chicken terrine, fresh and clearly homemade, was superb, with thick chunks of chicken and sliced carrot suspended in an aspic perfumed by fresh tarragon. Charlotte's liver came pink as ordered and was deglazed with Xérès vinegar, and my steak was tender and beautifully grilled. I almost never order entrecôtes in Paris, because they're often tough and fatty, but this was superb beef, full of flavor and very tender. We finished up with a brilliant baba au rhum, again homemade, for me and a Paris-Brest for Madame. "That was heaven," Charlotte said afterward while we walked to the café where she was meeting another friend, a Laotian princess, for coffee. "Exactly what I wanted, true French food with its proud quality and genius for simplicity," Charlotte concluded, and I'm certain that Curnonsky would have wholeheartedly agreed with her assessment of L'Abordage.

·   ·   ·

IN A WORD: With no decor to speak of, this clubby workaday bistro excels at a menu of French classics, which is why it's packed with one of the most intriguing Parisian power crowds in the city noon and night. Very few places take the basics as seriously as it does, with impeccable quality and cooking.

DON'T MISS: Oeufs mayonnaise; terrine de campagne; terrine de poulet; marinated herring; saumon tartare; côte de boeuf (rib steak) for two; côte de veau (veal chop) for two; calf's liver; entrecôte; Paris-Brest; crème brûlée; baba au rhum.

·   ·   ·

[47] 2 place Henri-Bergson, 8th, 01.45.22.15.49. MÉTRO: Saint-Augustin. Lunch served Monday to Friday. Dinner only on Wednesday. CLOSED Saturday and Sunday. • $$

La Cave Beauvau

ON A NIGHT WHEN AN AUTUMN RAIN HAS APPLIQUÉD THE shiny black trottoirs (sidewalks) of Paris with slippery but beautiful golden and bronze leaves, I arrive at La Cave Beauvau before my friends, order a glass of pleasantly flinty white Touraine wine and a small plate of Serrano ham at the bar, and savor a private moment of leisure in public, indulging in the pleasure of people watching and paddling around in my own random, idyllic thoughts. On this Friday, the front bar is lined with short dark men in dark suits with that pinched and uncomfortable-looking French cut that comes from small, high armholes; a couple of bawdy types in tweed jackets and corduroy trousers, whom I correctly guess to be winemakers; and a single pair of women, both with blond bobs, hair bands, and Hermès scarves (gallery owners).

What surprises me most about this mise-en-scène, however, is that I'm part of it. When I first moved to Paris, I'd walk by similar happy, busy, slightly bawdy bistros and as much as I yearned to, I didn't dare to insinuate myself into such profoundly French places. Twenty years later, my timidity's burned off, my French is pretty good, and nothing could keep me away from such rustic places, which worryingly have become as rare as pearls.

La Cave Beauvau also casts a nostalgic spell, because absent the stink of cigarette smoke, it still looks and smells like the city I moved to so long ago. Best of all, no one designed it this way, it just happened. With its stone-paneled copper-clad bar up front and the swirling Bordeaux-bordered cut-out ceiling that could be part of a set for Cocteau's film *Orpheus*, the ancient cash registers, and the straw-lined tray of temptingly runny cheeses on a counter, this place speaks of an eternal France that respects thrift and treasures conviviality over more strident versions of modernity.

Eventually I fall into conversation with owner Stéphane Delleré, who's one of the best bistro-keepers in France. Cheerful with a pair of winemaker pals, he sighs deeply after they leave, and after making sure everyone else who's sipping and nibbling on either side of me has been well looked after, he stops for a chat.

Tonight, he's rattled by family problems on his home turf in La Sarthe and wearied by the Herculean effort necessary to keep a small, honest, independent, and really good bistro going. (He would throw himself in front of a train before he used any industrial shortcut food products.) Delleré always remembers me in a blur, which is fine with me, because a certain anonymity is crucial to the way I work. Still, I'm flattered that something in him comes to life when we start talking, urgently and passionately, about food and wine.

The next thing I know, he is serving me a saucer of bulots (sea snails), anxious for me to try them. So I pick a first spiraled crustacean out of its shell with a sharp pin and pop it in my mouth. Chewy but crunchy and a little creamy, this tiny iodine-rich sea beast is redolent of real old-fashioned court bouillon, or broth made with white wine, carrots, celery, parsley, and other seasonings, and deliciously dredged in the rouille (spicy mayonnaise) Delleré served with them. Though just bar nibbles, the bulots speak volumes about his attention to detail.

When my friends arrive, we move to a booth with brown leatherette banquettes in the cozy if wanly lit back dining room, and begin a long, happy bacchanalian feast. We pore over the menu, which is an anthology of bona fide bistro cooking, and decide to start with jambon persillé, the Burgundian classic of shredded ham in savory parsleyed aspic, oeufs à la mayonnaise, and two homemade terrines, chicken liver and pork, both of them outstanding and served with good bread and a fine bottle of Crozes-Hermitage.

"He makes his own mayonnaise!" a friend says with delight, and we order another round of the eggs while waiting for our main courses, steak tartare, steak au poivre, and andouillette (chitterling sausage), all of which are excellent. "I have a friend who works at the Elysée Palace (just across the street) who eats lunch here every day, and now I know why," adds my pal Anne. "C'est vraiment fabuleux!"

Before stepping out into the night, I tell Stéphane Delleré I've decided he reminds me of Asterix, the iconic French comic-strip character (a little blond Gaul with a winged helmet) who resists the Roman occupation, and he blushes. "C'est très gentil," he says, before slipping away to top up another customer's glass of Morgon. I'm glad, though, that he instantly knows what I mean, which is that he's very much a keeper of a certain precious French flame.

· ⚜ ·

IN A WORD: This is a bona fide, old-fashioned bistro, so don't come expecting anything fancy. If you love simple, traditional, meat-oriented bistro cooking, good wine, and a lot of atmosphere, however, you'll probably be very happy here.

DON'T MISS: Terrine de campagne, terrine de foie de volaille (chicken liver), jambon persillé, andouillette, steak tartare, steak au poivre, onglet aux echalottes (hanger steak with shallots cooked in red wine), Saint-Marcellin cheese, baba au rhum.

. . .

[48] 4 rue des Saussaies, 8th, 01.42.65.24.90. MÉTRO: Miromesnil or
Champs-Elysées—Clemenceau. OPEN Monday to Wednesday and Saturday, until 8 p.m. Thursday and Friday until 11 p.m. CLOSED Sunday. ▪ $$

Le Cinq

EVEN THOUGH SOME OF THEM ARE STUNNINGLY BEAUTIFUL, hotel dining rooms in Paris used to be dispiriting places for anyone who loves good food. Heavily patronized by an Anglo-American clientele wary of garlic and other menaces, they became the refuge of timid types who were content with white fish in white sauce in the company of potted palms and somnolent waiters. To be sure, the Hôtel de Crillon has long had a line of superlative chefs and one always ate well at the Ritz, but it wasn't until the Bristol shook up the scene by hiring chef Michel del Burgo away from Taillevent that the conventional wisdom about hotel food started to change, slowly at first and then at such a gallop that every luxury hotel in Paris today that's worthy of the adjective now has a serious talent in the kitchen.

When the Four Seasons George V reopened after a multimillion-dollar renovation in 1999, it instantly aimed for a place at the top of the local food chain by shrewdly hiring chef Philippe Legendre away from Taillevent, and studiously recasting the experience of grand hotel dining for a new century so successfully that Le Cinq, its restaurant, has now become one of the best tables in the French capital.

Some twenty years later, a meal at Le Cinq is among the most unfailingly exultant experiences Paris has to offer. Chef Eric Briffard is one of the most talented classically trained chefs in France, and perhaps only Jean-Jacques Rousseau could have imagined a better hybrid of New and Old World, here expressed by the ballet-like service in this elegant Wedgewood-inspired dining room.

The visual drama of the dining room comes from its spectacular flower arrangements, an idiom of single blooms placed at rakish angles in dramatic vases, which are the widely copied work of Jeff Leatham, a former male model from Utah who discovered his floral genius while working at the Four Seasons in Beverly Hills. When I arrived for lunch on an autumn day, the entrance to the dining room contained tall vases of long-stemmed roses of such an elusive and hauntingly beautiful color, they stopped me in my tracks. A dark dusty pink like an old woman's memories of being a young girl, they were some of the most magnificent flowers I'd ever seen.

My friend Enrica Rocca, who runs a popular cooking school in Venice, was waiting for me on the banquette. A low-key countess who lived in Cape Town for many years after graduating from the Lausanne Hotel School, Enrica has one of the most discerning palates of anyone I know, and she'd said she wanted food she couldn't get in London. As we studied our menus, Enrica's eyes were darting everywhere. "I'm starting to panic," she said. "There are so many things I'd like to try."

At last we threw the dice, and we were thick in conversation when a complimentary starter began the meal—an exquisite miniature terrine of wild mushrooms garnished with several slices of grilled cèpe and a dribble of parsley-and-shallot vinaigrette. "This little display of Gallic prowess gladdens my heart, but the acidity of the rivulet of dressing is a distraction from the earthy tones of the terrine," Enrica correctly observed.

This tut-tut-ing didn't worry me, though. If Briffard's cooking can be so disciplined and polite it occasionally seems academic, his talent shines when he unleashes his imagination and lets it guide his encyclopedic knowledge of culinary technique, as was made perfectly clear when our first courses arrived. Enrica's duck foie gras roasted with citrus fruits and garnished with sliced pear and a gingerbread crumble was sublime. "The citrus punctuates the richness of the foie gras, and the sweet garnishes elaborate the liver's buttery taste." My veal carpaccio with shavings of white Alba truffle, fresh chestnut, and aged Parmesan came with warm potato purée, a ravioli filled with sautéed onions, a shot of ginger broth, and an egg yolk—a magnificent composition of subtly, sensually interacting flavors and textures. Knowing that eggs, potatoes, and truffles comprise a umami trinity, Briffard quietly lit up this trellis of tastes with Parmesan and then shrewdly rode the gustatory brake a bit with the ginger broth, which I'd guess was there to disrupt the perfect flow of pleasure so that it could be so thrillingly renewed a few seconds later.

Then, almost as an answer to our curiosity about how to design dishes that will not only satisfy but titillate a worldly international clientele, our main course arrived, a stunningly beautiful Pithiviers, or golden pastry case, named for the town in the Loiret region an hour south of Paris and filled with succulent pieces of gray pheasant, wild duck, and grouse that had been cooked in chestnut honey with autumn fruit, including quince and grapes. The waiters displayed it to us before they served it tableside with great art, a performance that had Enrica swooning. "C'est magnifique, c'est vraiment magnifique," she raved as they went about their work, deftly slicing the tender pastry and serving it in tidy slices with a jus pressé à l'Armagnac.

After we began eating, it was some time before we spoke, since my mind took off on a flight of solitary pleasure, mulling over the idea that this Pithiviers could easily have found a place in one of those meticulous medieval Flemish still-lifes of the feasts of prosperous burghers in Bruges. The faint fumes of

Armagnac in the sauce had the effect of scaring a whole flock of wild birds to life every time I ate another mouthful of this dish, and I was also dumbstruck by the quality of Briffard's pastry, which was just plain sumptuous. "I think he must have cooked all of the birds separately before boning them and then quickly sautéing them before enclosing them in the pastry case," said Enrica, more engrossed in her plate than I've ever seen her. We both ate quite a bit of the Pithiviers, but a good third of the dish remained when we were sated. "Caro," Enrica said, and motioned for me to lean forward. "I think the couple next to us are on their honeymoon. Let's offer them the rest of the Pithiviers." Indeed I had noticed the fresh-faced young couple who were obviously fascinated and perhaps a tiny bit appalled by our recent moaning and mewling. They politely refused our offer, we adamantly insisted, and our waiter promptly served them.

Now Enrica came clean. "To tell you the truth, tresoro, I wasn't expecting much from this meal," she confessed. "I thought it would be very corporate, but instead it was fabulous." Knowing that it usually contains a sublime Beaufort millésime I couldn't pass up the cheese trolley, and then we were delivered to quiet bliss by our desserts, a Sambirano black chocolate soufflé with chunky pineapple preserves and a coconut-milk emulsion for Enrica, and baked Reinette apple with saffron pistil ice cream, green-apple sorbet, and a rosemary honey meringue for me.

"Excuse me, Sir, Madame." It was the young man to whom we'd given the rest of our Pithiviers. "I just wanted to thank you for the best thing that's happened on our honeymoon." Like a wolf eyeing a lamb, Enrica lifted her eyebrows and cocked her head. "*The* best thing?" "Well, one of the best things," he replied, his cheeks blazing.

IN A WORD: Le V is the hole in one of Paris haute cuisine restaurants, a place that's as perfect for a marriage proposal as it is to ink a major contract, and chef Eric Briffard is one of the most consistently original but stunningly refined chefs in Paris.

DON'T MISS: Cèpe risotto with eggplant; duck foie gras roasted with citrus fruit and served with pears and a gingerbread crumble; veal carpaccio with Alba truffle, fresh chestnuts, Parmesan, and potato purée; frog's legs with watercress in vin jaune sauce; sea bass with shellfish, wasabi, and Granny Smith apple juice; Pithiviers de gibier; veal chop cooked en cocotte with capers; roast shoulder of lamb with cocoa beans and sun-dried tomatoes; Sambirano black chocolate soufflé with pineapple preserves and a coconut-milk emulsion.

. . .

[49] Hôtel Four Seasons George V, 31 avenue George V, 8th, 01.49.52.70.00. MÉTRO: George V OPEN daily for lunch and dinner. www.fourseasons.com ▪ $$$$

Dominique Bouchet

I LOVE TO COOK, WHICH IS WHY ONE OF THE MOST INTERESTING days I've ever spent in Paris was with chef Dominique Bouchet when he was head chef at the Hôtel Crillon. I arrived in the immaculate kitchens after a very early breakfast and proceeded to shadow Bouchet all day as he inspected the daily delivery of produce, met with his sous-chefs, worked on some shellfish stock, and ate a quick slice of cheese before the lunch service started. He personally inspected every plate, tweaking a whisker of chive here, blotting up an errant dot of sauce there, before it was sent upstairs by dumbwaiter to the opulent dining room. Perched on a stool in a corner to stay out of the way, I was fascinated by the coordination and concentration required to produce haute cuisine. By the end of the day, I'd found my culinary mantra, too, as I listened to Bouchet good-naturedly telling his staff again and again, "Great food tastes of what it is." This may sound obvious, but in fact it took a long time for top Paris chefs to dare to do simplicity, and few do it better than Bouchet.

Even though he has an impressive résumé—he worked at Jamin before Robuchon arrived, then at La Tour d'Argent and in his own restaurant in the Charentes region on France's Atlantic coast before becoming head chef at the Crillon, and he trained Eric Ripert, one of New York's star chefs, at Le Bernardin—Bouchet is the quiet man of the Paris restaurant scene, much happier in his kitchen than he is in front of television cameras. He's an old-school cook's cook, and this explains why his eponymous restaurant, which opened in 2005 after he left the Crillon, quickly became a hit with both Paris power brokers and epicureans.

Not only is this a handsome adult restaurant with exposed stone walls, a relaxed decor of beige and brown, and an open kitchen, but Bouchet's brilliant restraint when working with first-rate French produce leads to some quietly spectacular cooking. Consider his delicious warm terrine of Beaufort cheese, artichoke hearts, and country ham, for example. Instead of trying to transform these ingredients, he has created a harmonious composition of taste and textures that makes each one distinct and delicious, and this subtlety, which comes from a desire to respect the natural tastes of food, is Bouchet's signature. Likewise, his charlotte of crabmeat, tomatoes, and basil, a starter, makes all three of these ingredients sing, and his roasted cod on a bed of tomatoes and red peppers in a luscious jus de poulet (reduced chicken stock) is a magnificent marriage of the sea and the barnyard. I also love his spit-roasted pigeon with raisin-studded polenta and a honied jus, and pasta stuffed with lobster and mushroom puree and sauced with a jus made from its own carapace is superb, too.

The last time I was here, I overheard a woman from Atlanta complaining that the food was "too simple." I suspect that she's one of the many people who still expect French food to be elaborate, when what's guiding it at the beginning of this new century is the elegance of simplicity. One way or another, her husband, who'd ordered the pigeon (she had steak), wholeheartedly disagreed, and Madame seemed wildly happy when her orange and raspberry soufflé arrived, although I also recommend the poached peach with Champagne granite and raspberry gelée.

.　.　.

IN A WORD: This stylish, well-mannered adult restaurant has two distinct clienteles: bankers, brokers, and politicians at noon and chic bourgeois couples in the evening. What makes everyone happy is chef Dominique Bouchet's brilliantly simple and understated contemporary French cooking.

DON'T MISS: Sautéed cherry tomatoes with foie gras ice cream; terrine of Beaufort, artichokes, and country ham; charlotte of crabmeat, tomatoes, and basil; roast cod with tomatoes and red peppers in a jus de poulet; pasta with lobsters and mushroom puree in lobster jus; spit-roasted pigeon with raisin polenta; aile

de raie (skate wing) with capers and lemon on a bed of baby pota-toes; roasted duck with turnip confit; raspberry and orange souf-flé; poached peach with Champagne granite; raspberry gelée.

. . .

[50] 11 rue Treilhard, 8th, 01.45.61.09.46. MÉTRO: Villiers or Miromesnil. OPEN Monday to Friday for lunch and dinner. CLOSED Saturday and Sun-day. www.dominique-bouchet.com • $$$

Epicure

"IT'S THE HARDEST LEVEL TO COOK AT, BECAUSE AT ITS BEST, all of its complexity should be invisible," says Eric Frechon, rolling an empty espresso cup between his large, meaty hands. He's referring to traditional French haute cuisine, and he's right. Within the last ten years, the Spanish have reconfigured global expectations of high-wire European cooking, which is now meant to startle and delight like a magic show, leaving the endless cycle of hard work necessary to achieve and sustain a classical French haute cuisine kitchen profoundly unknown and underappreciated. Consider that the Bristol makes all of its stocks—fish, shellfish, chicken, veal, and beef—from scratch every single day. As Frechon explains, "Fresh, perfectly made stock is at the core of my cooking." Does the flavor really change all that much from day to day? "Yes." Wouldn't it be easier to make large batches every couple of days—I mean, who'd really know? "I'd know, and actually, I think you would, too."

I've known Frechon for a long time, ever since he first thrilled Paris with some really ballsy but elegant cooking—until he came along no one knew that food could be refined and high testosterone at the same time—at the eponymous bistro he opened in the remote 19th Arrondissement in 1995. The Bristol recruited him in 1999, and he shut down the bistro to take a chance on haute cuisine. On this particular Monday night, Frechon joins us at one of the last tables in the dining room of Paris's most discreet luxury hotel, Le Bristol, and we have a gab. I compliment the stunningly good food I've just eaten, especially his tête de veau, calf's head, which he serves in two different preparations—a crispy croquette of skull meat spiked with anchovies and capers and then a hunk of head, or a square of gelatinous tête (calf's head removed from its skull), with a traditional ravigote sauce (a vinegar-based sauce with onions, capers, and herbs).

Delicious though Frechon's is, I'm honestly not a big fan of tête de veau. What gave me a frisson was finding it on the menu of one of the world's most elegant and exclusive dining rooms. As an ancient, hairy-chested stable hand's sort of a treat, offering it here is smart, gutsy, and provocative, since it surprises the

French ruling class clientele (the Bristol is one of their favorite tables), at the same time that it appeals to their culinary chauvinism and not so subliminal nostalgia for a lost, idyllic Gaul of happy villages, crowing cocks, and ruddy good eating just a step from the barnyard. This knowing earthiness has always been Frechon's signature, and, like the honest, hardworking craftsman he is, he hones it lovingly, constantly, and carefully while knowing exactly when to break to über seriousness with a sling-shotted conker of gastronomic irreverence.

A perfect example is his "cochon fermier," or farm- as opposed to battery-raised pork, parsed out in four declensions—pig's feet, pig's trotter, fatback, and sausage, a potent piggy quartet on one plate. The dish that stunned me that night, however, was sea bass in a thin, glossy gray coat of minced oysters with fork-mashed baby potatoes sauced with flat-parsley jus. What made it so spectacular was the tone-on-tone maritime theme, with the iodine-rich shellfish teasing every bit of flavor out of the more subtly flavored fish by framing it so potently.

After Frechon's earthy acrobatics, desserts are wily, ambitious, and bold—in season, try the fresh Victoria pineapple with a miniature tarte Tatin and lemongrass sorbet or, in the fall, the flambéed Mirabelle plums with almond ice cream. While a meal at Epicure is a heart-pounding extravagance, it's worth every centime.

· ⬩ ·

IN A WORD: The Bristol not only is discreet and chic but has one of the hardest-working and quietly sensual chefs of any top-flight restaurant in Paris. Come here to dwell on the riddle of a sexy dichotomy: one of the best places in Paris for a top-flight business

meal is also one of the city's best addresses for romantic dining. This is also a lovely place to treat yourself to a spectacular meal if you're traveling alone, since the service is absolutely impeccable and tables are well spaced and have very comfortable sight lines. Don't be surprised to spot a famous face or two in the crowd, too, since the surrounding neighborhood is dense with French ministries and this dining room is a favorite retreat for power brokers, along with celebrities who honestly don't like the limelight. Note, too, the spectacular wine list and the fact that it serves one of the best breakfasts in Paris, a sort of early-bird splurge with a groaning buffet of delicious treats with which to start the day.

DON'T MISS: Macaronis farcis d'artichaut; truffe noir et de foie gras (pasta tubes packed with black truffle, artichoke heart, and duck foie gras and then glazed with Parmesan); poitrine de canard challandais au sang (duck breast in blood sauce); filet d'agneau de Lozère rôti aux branches de thym (lamb roasted with thyme); pigeon farci aux foie gras (pigeon stuffed with foie gras and garnished with black pudding made with apples and hazelnuts, carmelized onions, and a sauce of its own blood); homard breton et gâteau au foie blond avec taglierini (Breton lobster with a cake of chicken livers and baby clams); ananas et banana en compote et flambés aux vieux rhum (fresh pineapple and bananas baked and flambéed in aged rum); soufflé chaud au Grand Marnier (hot Grand Marnier soufflé).

. . .

[51] Epicure, Hotel Bristol, 112 rue du Faubourg Saint-Honoré, 8th, 01.53.43.43.00. MÉTRO: Miromesnil. OPEN daily for lunch and dinner. www.lebristolparis.com ▪ $$$$

Garnier

RIGHT IN THE HEART OF PARIS, I CAUGHT A SURPRISING WHIFF of leaf meal, the winey rotten-apple smell that means summer's over. It was a perfect Indian summer day, with the chestnut tree leaves just starting to curl bronze at the edges, but the surest sign that the seasons had shifted was that the stainless-steel banc à huîtres (oyster stand) on the stone-paved sidewalk outside Garnier was filled with mounds of crushed ice, tassels of bumpy brown seaweed, and big plump oysters from all over France. After a summer of salads, I wanted a real lunch.

The success of any meal depends on good casting and clear intentions. In this case, I was meeting Melissa, a clever writer from Dayton, Ohio, now living in India, and the plan was to treat ourselves to a really fine feed. This is why I chose Garnier—it's one of the most reliably satisfying restaurants in Paris.

We were seated on the glassed-in sidewalk terrace at a large round table covered with a crisply starched white tablecloth, and menus were presented by the stout, silver-haired waiter in a black vest with a long white apron. We ordered flutes of Champagne rosé to start and provoked a first sign of interest from the waiter. Sitting opposite us, a pretty older woman with her meringue hair swept up in a chignon gave us a pursed smile when the bubbly arrived; in no other city in the world do people take more pleasure in observing others in search of same than in Paris.

We studied our menus and picked tiny sea snails, a complimentary hors d'oeuvre that rewarded our Champagne, out of their shells with long steel pins. The salty marine taste of the crustaceans met the remote floral edge of the Champagne with a thrilling elegance we both noticed; I knew Melissa would love Garnier, and few things are more fun than sharing a favorite restaurant. We ordered a half-dozen spéciales Gillardeaux and a half-dozen fines de claire No. 2 from the Charente-Maritime, both among the finest French oysters, plus a bouquet of crevettes roses (boiled red shrimp). Afterward, I took the cod steak with girolles mushrooms and Melissa chose a charlotte d'avocat et de tourteau, avocado cream with crabmeat, a starter, as her main course. We drank a fairly priced Quincy, a nice Loire Valley white wine, and some Chateldon, the mineral water favored by Louis XVI. From the muscle tension that grew in his lower lip as he scribbled down our order, it was obvious that the waiter thought we had constructed an admirable meal, the results of which were little attentions like finger bowls, which weren't offered to a table of Germans across the way.

"What's with the decor, though?" Melissa asked, as I knew she would. I explained that in Paris, restaurants are invariably remodeled just at the precise moment when their decor-to-be-destroyed is teetering on the brink of becoming charming, camp, vintage, or, in the case of Garnier, all of the above. Until a few years ago, this curiously overlooked fish house—it's just across the street from the Gare Saint-Lazare, the busiest train station in France, but almost no one knows about it—had a winsomely weirdo appearance that came from a unique hybrid between its original Art Deco interior and a ham-handed seventies makeover. What did the seventies look like in France? Visit any RER station (the RER is the suburban train network that compliments the Métro) in the Paris area to feast on oddball ceramics, extruded aluminum ceilings, and dumpy color schemes like orange and brown or yellow and cobalt blue. At Garnier, the minuscule oyster bar just inside the front door, one of my favorite places in Paris for the world's best fast food—a dozen oysters and a glass of Muscadet—previously had massive grooved half-glazed brown tiles on the wall, and the last time I saw them I remember commenting on how winningly ugly they were. Tragically, they vanished during the summer of 2001, but at least the little oyster bar survived, and in the main dining rooms, French colonial furniture and a silly parquet floor just became the last visual layer of a restaurant that always seems to be trying too hard, which is completely unnecessary, since it serves the best oysters in Paris. The young chef, Ludovic Schwartz, who learned on star chef Joël Robuchon's knee, is a brilliant fish cook, ably riffing on classics like sole meunière by adding a garnish of preserved North African–style lemon or spiking a tempura of langoustines with Espelette pepper from the Basque country.

It's tough to be a good fish cook, since the best are utterly self-effacing, correctly obsessed with proper timing, and parsimonious but creative with the garnish that brings the natural tastes and textures of a first-rate catch of the day into perfect focus. The baba au rhum, a sponge cake dosed with excellent Saint James rum from Martinique and slathered with vanilla-speckled whipped cream, is the only possible way to end a meal here.

· · ·

IN A WORD: Open daily, this is a first-rate fish house with a motley clientele and decor right across the street from the Gare

Saint-Lazare. As suitable for a business meal as it is for a tête-à-tête, it's also perfect for solitary dining, either at the oyster bar just inside the front door or in the main dining room.

DON'T MISS: Oysters, crab, shrimp, mussels, and clams from the stand out front; langoustine tempura; cod with girolles mushrooms; sole meunière with preserved lemons; turbot cooked with seaweed; baba au rhum (sponge cake soaked with rum and topped with whipped cream).

. . .

[52] 111 rue Saint-Lazare, 8th, 01.43.87.50.40, MÉTRO: Saint-Lazare. OPEN daily for lunch and dinner. www.restaurantsparisiens.com • $$$

Le Griffonier

PARIS IS SEXY BECAUSE IT'S SUBTLE. IN THE FRENCH CAPI-tal, the loom of eros is driven more by what's hidden than by what's displayed, with the possible exception of the first two weeks of September. Then the city's streets are filled with people proudly exhibiting their tans, sun-streaked locks, artfully grown-out but trimmed summer beards, and fresh relaxed faces bearing the frank mien of hard-earned and well-spent leisure. In French, this happy, energetic period on the calendar is called *la rentrée* (the return), which refers to getting back to work after holidays spent in the country, at the beach, or in the mountains. It marks the start of the city's collective urban calendar much more than does New Year's Eve, since the French have never really taken to the latter holiday, mostly preferring quiet dinners with friends that night to the staged public hilarity with which the New Year is met in other Western countries.

During the rentrée, which fades by mid-October, there's a wholesome erotic charge to the city, as everyone rediscovers their appetites, and this is why it was a pleasure to renounce a summer of barbecues and salads and head for a serious bistro feed with a fellow food chronicler who loves traditional Gallic grub as much as I do. When we decided to have lunch, he'd proposed a couple of newly opened places, but I had my heart set on Le Griffonier, because this bistrot à vins just across the street from the French ministry of the interior with a rock-of-ages menu and an impressive wine list has never let me down. Then, too, I love the masculine fug of this place at midday, when it's packed with a huddle of powerful, well-groomed men in well-cut dark suits taking a break from their nation-ruling and banking duties over glasses of good Bordeaux and Beaujolais. To be sure, there are some women in the crowd, too, but they're as lean and mean as the men, since this place is an establishment watering hole par excellence.

If my distance from the wheelhouses of French political and corporate power makes me a perennially bemused voyeur at this place, the reason I come is the food, which is an authentic roster of high-quality bistro standards including oeufs à la mayonnaise, foie gras, escargots, charcuterie, steaks, calf's liver, blanquette de veau, and choucroute garnie. The most unfailing way of eating well here, however, is to have the plats du jour, proposed on a little chalkboard that's brought to the table if you sit upstairs—which I prefer, as it's a bit too crowded downstairs around the bar, where owner Cédric Duthilleul keeps the regulars well poured—by a bemused waitress of a certain age in a white blouse and black skirt who's such a perfect example of this nearly extinct genus, the professional Parisian waitress, that it's always a pleasure to see her.

I find the seriousness with which she does her work impressive and sort of moving, because it cues the food that follows—honest, generous, and straightforward, with an understated desire to please. Inspecting the specials, the professor of psychiatry from Baltimore with whom I was dining—a fine example of another threatened genus, the wise, good-humored East Coast liberal—immediately pounced on the girolles as a first course. Since they were expensive, I wanted to know their provenance, and when I asked the waitress if they were from somewhere in central Europe, as most wild mushrooms are in Paris these days, she looked aghast. "Mais non, Monsieur! They're from La Sologne," she said with a reverential intake of breath appropriate to this wooded region of central France, famous for game and mushrooms. Sautéed with finely chopped shallots and parsley, they were firm and pleasantly feral, a first taste of autumn.

Then we parted ways with our second courses. Though the confit de canard from the main menu was perfect—the crunchy golden skin redolent with rich duck fat, the bird's meat gently gamy and tender—this is a great place to eat beef, which comes from the nearby Boucherie Nivernaises, one of the best butchers in Paris. So I had the plat du jour, a just-warm slice of steak with sides of homemade mayonnaise and a salade piémontaise that propelled me back twenty years to the days when I worked in an office on the rue Cambon and ate lunch from the expensive traiteur across the street almost every day. The reason I went is that the woman who ran this pretty tiled shop (sad to say, now a boutique) made absolutely everything from scratch, including the salade piémontaise, a sort of retro throwback to the days of the overdressed picnics depicted by Manet and made up of a sublime mixture of potatoes, olives, chopped cornichons, and tomato in a soft pink-tinted (from tomato paste) mayonnaise, also homemade.

Accompanied by lots of good bread and a bottle of Chiroubles, one of the less expensive wines on a pricey list, this was a luscious and deeply satisfying calories-be-damned feast, but that didn't keep me from ordering cheese—a generous slice of tangy golden yellow Salers from the Auvergne, which came with a nicely dressed salad and a pat of silver-wrapped Au Bonne Beurre butter, from the butter-loving north of France. My friend's apricot tart was excellent too, and coffee came with a canelé—small caramelized tarts with custardy centers that come from Bordeaux—because the pride of this place is that it babies you from the moment you step in the door. Quietly elated after such a good meal, I realized on the way home that Le Griffonier offers a textbook-perfect example of why the world loves Paris bistros: superb produce, lovingly prepared, and abundantly served, along with a wick of conviviality that informs the entire meal.

·   ·

IN A WORD: Just across the street from the French Ministry of the Interior and in the heart of a high-powered banking district, this convivial old-fashioned bistro is an establishment bolt-hole with excellent old-fashioned bistro cooking, great wines, and charming service. Hardly cheap, but definitely worth it.

DON'T MISS: Céleri rémoulade (grated celeriac in mayonnaise dressing), escargots, foie gras, confit de canard, steak tartare, steak, blanquette de veau, choucroute garnie, cheese plate, fruit tart.

. . .

[53] 8 Rue des Saussaies, 8th, 01.42.65.17.17. MÉTRO: Miromesnil or
Champs-Elysées–Clemenceau. OPEN Monday to Friday for lunch. Thursday
for dinner. CLOSED Saturday and Sunday. ▪ $$–$$$

Lasserre

WELL BEYOND ITS INDISPUTABLE CREDENTIALS AS THE IN-
ternational capital of fashion, Paris is loved the world over for
being the ultimate incarnation of urban elegance. The polite
rituals, aesthetic rigor, and nonchalant glamour of daily life in
the French capital not only fascinate visitors but also leave them
aesthetically refreshed.

The very word "Paris" induces an expectant spell of beauty
that makes many people want to dress up a bit and take leave
of their daily lives just for the time of a single transporting
meal. Given the vertiginous prices attached to luxury meals in
the French capital, nothing could be more disappointing than
one that falls short of the mark. This is why I love Lasserre, an
elegant old luxury liner of a restaurant that still practices the
courtly good manners of the beau monde set who began to frequent it when it opened in 1942 and made it one of the choic-
est tables in Paris during the palmy fifties, when the famous
roll-open roof was installed over the main dining room, a peren-
nial showstopper that still delights today for offering a sud-
den view of the sky overhead—and even some stars on a clear
night—at the end of every dinner service. Graciously well run,
humbly customer centered, and with a solidly experienced and

talented chef—Christophe Moret, who was formerly head chef at Restaurant Alain Ducasse at the Hôtel Plaza Athénée—in the kitchen, this is a restaurant that never lets me or anyone else down. And with the recent launch of an excellent vegetarian tasting menu, its charms are now available to almost anyone who can manage the stiff prices that are the inevitable result of lavish staffing in a country with expensive labor laws and also a menu that offers only the finest produce Gaul has to offer.

For obvious financial reasons it's a challenge for me to cover the top of the Paris food chain, so I was thrilled when a very old friend—we grew up together in Connecticut—called to say that she and her white miniature poodle were coming to Paris from the well-known Mediterranean seaside enclave where she currently lives, a place popular with the tax-averse wealthy, and could she invite me to lunch at Lasserre? The life of this brilliant, elegant woman, a Scottish-Danish American who married her elderly godfather when she was still a relatively young woman, would make good fodder for a novel. Now that her husband is gone, I miss him, but I always enjoy seeing my friend and sharing a fine meal with her.

Not having been to Lasserre for a while, I wondered how chef Christophe Moret had evolved since my last visit, and also wondered if the restaurant would have changed under the command of a new owner. Well, it hadn't. The liveried porter was so prompt I didn't have time to touch the well-shined brass handle on the front doors, and the same kindly lady as last time took my coat and gave me a chit before I was ushered upstairs in the carpet-lined lift. The dining room, which is arranged around a sunken central atrium, had been freshened up with elegant bronze fabric on the walls, but there were pots of white orchids around the room as always, and the very serious brigade of professional middle-aged waiters in fitted black jackets stood in attendance like guards in a palace.

Our meal began auspiciously with a starter of langoustines in a ginger-and-lime-spiked seafood bouillon, four perfectly poached little curls of fluffy marine flesh in a rich broth of deeply reduced but very refined shellfish stock brightened by the Asian seasonings, including coriander and lemongrass. Next came tender but firm slices of alabaster sea bass with a thrillingly extravagant garnish of black truffles shaved at the table by a waiter wearing white gloves, and then venison filets cooked perfectly rare with pepper and juniper berries, and finally a sublime croustillant aux pommes façon Tatin, glace vanille (tarte Tatin–style caramelized apple in flaky pastry with home-made vanilla ice cream) by brilliant pastry chef Claire Heitzler. "Exquisite, this," said my friend, and then, "Isn't it nice we still enjoy all of the same things after so many years?" Well, yes, we'll always have Lasserre, even if it's an only occasional—but deeply treasured—experience for me.

.   .   .

IN A WORD: Lasserre is a restaurant that will live up to your idea of what a special night out in Paris should be. The service is stunning, and chef Christophe Moret's exquisite cooking satisfies those yearning for the classical magnificence of French haute cuisine as ably as it does those in search of something more adventurous.

DON'T MISS: Langoustines in ginger-lime-flavored bouillon; sea bass with black truffles; turbot with cèpes in parsley jus; roasted Challans duck with turnips; crêpes Suzette; caramelized apple in flaky pastry.

. . .

[54] 17 avenue Franklin Roosevelt, 8th, 01.43.59.02.13. MÉTRO: Champs-Elysées–Clemenceau. OPEN Monday to Friday for lunch. Saturday dinner only. CLOSED Sunday. www.restaurant-lasserre.com ▪ $$$$

Lazare

I'VE ALWAYS LOVED TRAIN STATIONS, PROBABLY BECAUSE Grand Central Station in New York City was a permanent fixture of my early life. This Beaux Arts terminus in midtown Manhattan is one of the most magnificent buildings in North America, and it was the portal of discovery through which I passed on eager journeys to the great metropolis down the tracks from the quiet suburban town in Connecticut where I grew up.

When I moved to Paris, I quickly developed a similar affection for the city's seven major train stations, each of which serves a different region of France, along with long-distance European routes. They capture the emotional expectancy of travel, and they also preview the turf they serve. In my mind's eye, the pavements in front of the Gare du Nord are often rain-slick like those in Lille, Brussels, and Amsterdam; the Gare de l'Est seems to echo the tidiness of Alsace and German cities; and there's something soft, even palmy, about the Gare de Lyon, from which trains leave for the Côte d'Azur and Provence.

The human vitality and engineering of the Gare Saint-Lazare, a short walk from my front door, fascinated Impressionist painters including Édouard Manet, Claude Monet, and Gustave Caillebotte, for whom it was the subject of many canvases. It has recently been renovated, and to my relief, the handsome etched and painted glass windows in the main concourse depicting destinations once (and sometimes still) reached from the station have been cleaned up and preserved. Recently, however, the reason I've been going to the station most often is to eat, which isn't as odd as it might first sound.

Paris has a long-standing tradition of good dining in and around its train stations, and because I've had dozens of meals at the Oyster Bar in New York's Grand Central, the idea of good food in a train station was never foreign to me. Rather, it made great sense for being so convenient and also for offering a comfortable setting in which to observe the spectacle of life in a great city while enjoying a good meal.

The Gare Saint-Lazare never had a great restaurant like other Paris stations, but following the opening in September 2013 of Lazare by Eric Frechon, who holds three stars as the chef of Epicure, the elegant restaurant at the Hôtel Le Bristol, it does now. Frechon, a native of Le Tréport in Normandy, shares my love of train-station dining, and it was his intention to revive the tattered tradition of great Parisian brasseries with a fresh take on the genre for a new century.

"I love the unexpected mixture of people you find in a train station restaurant," says Frechon, who purposely designed a menu that would be accessible to almost all wallets. "Like all good brasseries, Lazare is for both travelers and Parisians," the chef adds, and along with a clever decor that makes a few feints at what Paris brasseries have always looked like—a big copper-clad circular bar, marble-framed service stations, and a black-and-white fan-pattern mosaic floor in the entryway—it's this heterogeneity that gives it atmosphere.

Neither interior designer Karine Lewkowicz (who created the look of the restaurant by renovating old storage rooms on the main floor) nor Frechon trades in nostalgia, however. Lewkowicz left the pipes overhead exposed and painted them white, then lined the walls with wooden built-ins filled with stacked plates and copper cookware, while Frechon came up with an alluring menu of artfully modernized French comfort food dishes that he says are what he'd want to eat if he were a traveler passing through a train station.

Though Bruno and I had traveled only a few blocks on foot the first time we ate here, we loved our starters of céleri rémoulade (grated celery root dressed with mayonnaise, *bien sûr*,

brightened with Granny Smith apple) and a succulent terrine of mackerel marinated in white wine, served with horseradish cream. That rainy night, we followed with a textbook-perfect sole Dieppoise—sole in a sauce of fish fumet, mussels, and button mushrooms—for me, and a huge veal rib steak with girolles and baby potatoes for Bruno.

On other occasions—I go often—I've sampled the daily specials, including calf's liver, which is a nice big slab of juicy pink organ meat in a sauce of deglazed cooking juices and aged vinegar, and the saucisse de Toulouse with potato puree, a dish I could happily eat once a week. Among the many excellent desserts I've tried, including sautéed mirabelles (tiny yellow plums from Lorraine) with lemon verbena and dark chocolate tart, the one I can never resist is the Paris-Deauville, which Frechon created especially for Lazare. It is his homey Norman riff on the famous Paris-Brest, the choux pastry filled with hazelnut cream that was created on the occasion of a bicycle race in Brittany. Based on a Frechon family recipe, it resembles a creamy soufflé cooked in a round mold, then reversed and drizzled with a light caramel sauce. Just like this unconditionally generous and endearing restaurant, it's as comforting as a grandmother's hug.

. . .

IN A WORD: Three-star chef Eric Frechon reinvents the Paris brasserie with a cozy, friendly restaurant tucked away in the Gare Saint-Lazare. The beautifully prepared menu of shrewdly updated French comfort food favorites and the reasonable prices have made it popular with Parisians, who consider it a destination in and of itself.

DON'T MISS: Shrimp beignets with homemade ketchup, mackerel terrine, potato salad with andouille, céleri rémoulade with Granny Smith apples, calf's liver deglazed with aged vinegar, saucisse de Toulouse with potato puree, veal steak with girolles and new potatoes, sole Dieppoise, mussels in cream sauce, roasted quail with buttered cabbage, Paris-Deauville (baked soufflé with caramel sauce).

· · ·

[55] Parvis de la Gare Saint-Lazare, rue Intérieure, 8th, 01.44.90.80.80.
MÉTRO: Saint-Lazare. OPEN daily. www.lazare-paris.fr • $$

Ledoyen

AT NOON ON A WARM APRIL DAY, I'M SITTING IN THE WORLD'S most elegant tree house, the olive green dining room of Ledoyen. Heavy Bordeaux velvet curtains frame picture-window views of the crowns of the flowering chestnut trees in the gardens of the Champs-Élysées, and every breeze sends a few brief sprays of tiny white blossoms into the air from these fleeting floral torches, a natural confetti that couldn't possibly be a more accurate portent of the lunch to follow.

I'm on time for a change, which means that I have the luxury of some woolgathering while waiting for Alain and Margaret. For several minutes I muse on how lunch is unfailingly the better meal at any haute cuisine restaurant. Not only does it favor leisurely, gentle digestion, but by boarding the long, luxurious cruise of an extraordinary meal in the middle of the day you make a serious commitment to its specialness since it's an experience that can't and shouldn't be hurried. I also think most kitchens are in peak form at noon, when the brigade is as fresh and bright as the produce they're about to prepare. It's also obvious that midday dining rooms have a very different intrigue from what they become in the evening, when many Parisian power brokers are at home eating scrambled eggs or order-in sushi in front of the television.

To my right, the ambassador to France from some Spanish-speaking country and the sommelier are having the sort of elegant verbal duel that makes restaurants such unfailingly intriguing places to eavesdrop. They parry ideas about the perfect wine for the meal that's just been ordered, and I savor this civilized and satisfying exchange that advances according to keenly observed signals, where the suspense comes from the reciprocity of their mutually menaced egos. Their voices grow lower and lower before a happy truce is reached and the diplomat hands the heavy tome back to the sommelier. Later, I'm not at all surprised to see a superb bottle of Vosne Romanée, an excellent choice for a festive but important lunch on a spring day, on the table. To my left, two elegant young Japanese women with obviously new Louis Vuitton handbags (the zippers are still shiny yellow brass) methodically photograph each

dish as it arrives at the table, and the only word I understand from their conversation is "Chanel." Otherwise, aside from a jolly quartet I'm not surprised to later learn are from Mougins on the Côte d'Azur—one woman was wearing silver leather shoes, the other gold—the dining room hums with the diligence of corporate dining punctuated by the laughter of special occasions.

I've just been thinking about how well decorator Jacques Grange's Napoleonic decor, a tented ceiling and lovely motifs of Pompeian inspiration painted onto the wood-paneled walls, has stood the test of time since I first saw them more than a decade ago, when Margaret, one of my favorite tablemates, arrives. A native Londoner and natural wit who's lived in France for many years, she not only knows and loves her food but takes a childlike delight in the luxury of haute cuisine. When natty Alain is seated, we're served hors d'oeuvres with our flutes of Champagne rosé, and instantly I see how much chef Christian Le Squer has grown since my last meal here. These are brilliant little Fabergé bites—two mauve globes of beet meringue stuck together with horseradish cream, an exquisite bonbon of foie gras encased in buckwheat wafers and topped with tangy passion fruit gelée, and green-drizzled white globes on wooden spoons that turn out to be mozzarella skins filled with mozzarella water and a few drops of pesto, a mouthful as stunning in its technique as it is deliciously simple in its suave lactic burst of taste.

We order, and the meal begins with the slow, thrumming, luxurious anticipation of an ocean liner leaving port. It has taken us a while to negotiate our meals among ourselves—the three of us love to eat, often do so together, and have evolved our own unstated code for creating a successful meal, beginning with the minuet of who's-having-what. We never order the same thing, because forks usually fly among us, and so we take turns letting the other go first, which means you should always have a backup choice if your first one is taken.

So it was a surprise when the charming maître d'hôtel, Patrick Simiand, arrived with a complimentary first course that none of us had been tempted by—smoked eel topped with chopped beets, a dish of curiously central European inspiration from a Breton chef. The sweetness of the beets with the subtle smoke of the eel worked brilliantly, though, and the play of textures was curious but exquisite. Next, Alain's plump, snowy langoustines, two grilled in their split shells and three wrapped in a crunchy brown crust of kadif, the same fine golden pastry threads used to make Middle Eastern sweets, came with a superb citrus foam. We agreed that Margaret's medley of spring vegetables in red radish jus looked like an illustration from a Beatrix Potter book and was lovely, but though my lobster tail was beautifully cooked, I was underwhelmed by the pistachio ice cream that melted in a pale green puddle around it; the meeting between the taste of lobster and pistachios was intriguing, but I didn't much care for the contrasting temperatures.

So often in haute cuisine restaurants, the flirtatious starters are followed by main courses as solid and solemn as great-uncles, but the middle ring of Le Squer's circus is the most interesting. I first ate Le Squer's food when he was chef at the gorgeous and now sadly extinct Restaurant Opéra, a Napoléon III dining room in the Grand Hôtel with stunning views of the Opéra Garnier, and have been a fan ever since because he's one of the most gifted seafood cooks in Paris. My darne de bar poché was a perfectly poached rolled sea bass filet delicately stuffed with spring vegetables and served with grilled carmelized pink grapefruit slices and crunchy green asparagus, and Margaret's perfectly roasted pigeon stuffed with dates in a pan sauce brightened by Moroccan spices and preserved lemon was succulent and elegant. Happily, Alain had chosen the most curious dish on the menu: jambon blanc, morilles, parmesan aux spaghettis. What arrived was a small coffer made of spaghetti filled with morel mushrooms in cream and topped with a thatch of melted Parmesan and several chunks of ham, an elegant and unusual echo of the food children like best. It was delicious, but, startlingly priced at the euro equivalent of $130, it launched a brief discussion of the alarmingly vertiginous prices of haute cuisine dining in Paris. The three of us agreed that the sums required for the finest French dining are reaching an altitude that risks tipping the whole category into irrelevance, since it's become an exercise in casuistry—the science of difficult moral issues—to justify spending so much money on a single meal.

Le Squer, a pleasant man with an elfin face, stops by just in time to discover us in ecstasy over a dessert of grapefruit millefeuille, a refreshing composition of candied grapefruit rind, pink grapefruit, and carmelized pink grapefruit sections. He explains that the spaghetti coffer was created to cater to foreigners timid about the wilder reaches of French gastronomy represented by eel and veal sweetbreads and says his greatest pleasure is cooking fish and shellfish. "My earliest memory is of walking on the beach in Brittany with the strong clean smell of the sea in my nostrils, and this purity is what I try to communicate when I cook fish," he says. Twenty minutes later, as I'm walking past the beds of sentrylike tulips in the gardens leading to the Place de la Concorde, my newest memory, that of a perfect lunch in Paris on a beautiful spring day, starts to emerge from the immediacy of recent experience, and as it takes form, I know it's one I'll treasure.

.   .   .

IN A WORD: With one of the loveliest settings in Paris, a beautifully decorated Napoléon III pavilion in a grove of trees just off the Champs-Élysées, this excellent restaurant is a perfect choice for a well-dressed splurge. The gifted chef, Christian Le Squer, remains a dark horse on the Paris scene, but he's one of the best fish cooks in France.

DON'T MISS: Langoustines in a citrus-flavored olive oil emulsion; smoked eel with chopped beets; hare terrine with meat jelly; truffe en croque au sel, quenelle onctueuse de foie gras (black truffle cooked in salt with Jerusalem artichokes and foie gras mousse); gujonettes de sole (strips of sole in bread crumbs) with vin jaune sauce; turbot with truffled potatoes; sautéed suckling pig with gnocchi and dried tomatoes; roasted pigeon with Moroccan spices; grapefruit millefeuille.

. . .

[**56**] **1 avenue Dutuit, 8th, 01.53.05.10.01.** MÉTRO: **Champs-Élysées–Clemenceau.** OPEN **Monday to Friday for lunch and dinner.** CLOSED **Saturday and Sunday. www.ledoyen.com** ▪ **$$$$**

Neva Cuisine

THERE ARE NOT A LOT OF FORGOTTEN OR OVERLOOKED neighborhoods in central Paris anymore, but the quartier de

l'Europe, that curious hive of streets between the Place de Clichy and the Gare Saint-Lazare that bear the names of various
European cities, is still quiet and relatively unknown. To be
sure, the neighborhood was once home to the headquarters of
many big French insurance companies, which was why it was
known as "le quartier des assurances," but most of them have
decamped to unlovely suburban office buildings overlooking
the *périphérique* these days.

When I lived here ten years ago, it was a veritable restaurant
desert aside from a half-decent Indian place in the rue de Moscou.
With the opening of the puckishly named Neva Cuisine—the
Neva is of course the river on which Saint Petersburg is located
and also the largest street near the restaurant—this stolid island
of nineteenth-century urban planning, including the train cut
leading into the Gare Saint-Lazare that fascinated the Impressionist painters, finally has a really good destination table.

Arriving for a social blind-date lunch with a Californian in
Paris, another journalist, I was a bit crestfallen when I realized
that the restaurant was right next to the postal-sorting station
just north of the Place de l'Europe, but inside, it's a lovely Art
Moderne space with a big zinc bar, beautiful parquet floors,
detailed moldings, and thirties-vintage wrought-iron chandeliers with big globe lights that would cost a fortune if you came
across them in a flea market.

The welcome was warm, and the spacious, sunny dining room
was filled with business diners who were clearly already in the
know. I dawdled over a glass of good sauvignon blanc and read
the menu, which looked terrific, while waiting for my date and
thinking about how a restaurant is a great setting for a first meeting, because so much is revealed by how a stranger eats and drinks.

It turned out that my date—we'd been set up by a mutual

pal, a New York magazine editor who thought we'd enjoy each other's company—was pretty and very smart, and we immediately tumbled into a long, interesting conversation about everything from urban planning in Paris to U.S. politics. Still, when our first courses arrived, we were riveted by the food. My ravioli were filled with crunchy chunks of ginger-spiked shrimp and came in a pretty, tangy sauce decorated with razor-fine slices of baby beet. They were light, bright, and delicious. Since my new friend had had a late rosé-sodden dinner the night before, she was grateful for her delicate, creamy fresh pea soup, which was made with an earthy ham-bone bouillon and garnished with an organic egg yolk and a delicious wand of toasted baguette garnished with finely sliced baby onions and crumbled bacon. "This is just what the doctor ordered," she sighed with a grin.

Main courses were excellent, too. My half-salted fresh cod steak was perfectly cooked and seasoned, and came on a bed of delicious smoky eggplant caviar, while her monkfish was generously served and beautifully presented inside a wreath of delicate gnocchi and girolles with a few sprigs of tarragon and an impeccably made sauce that was gently acidulated with citrus.

By that point we were curious about the chef. I'd come here on the recommendation of my banker, a refreshingly good-natured gastronome who, like myself, would much rather talk about food than money, and I knew nothing about this place beyond his enthusiastic appraisal. Somehow neither of us was surprised, however, when our friendly waiter told us the chef was a woman, Beatriz Gonzales, a delightful Mexican who cooked at Senderens and most recently at La Grande Cascade. Why? Because this food was so sweet, sincere, and thoroughly devoid of ego.

We stalled before the idea of dessert, since both of us were soon to be revealing perilously podgy selves on Mediterranean beaches, but the waiter urged us to try something, because they have a serious pastry chef in the kitchen, Yannick Tranchant, who'd also worked at La Grande Cascade. So we shared a pretty little lemon meringue tart that was so good it produced the only moment of tension during the meal as our forks vied for more.

"That was a terrific lunch, Alec," exulted my new pal, and we parted with the pleasant sensation of having agreed on all things important but especially Beatriz Gonzales's excellent cooking.

· ·

IN A WORD: Mexican-born chef Beatriz Gonzales is a rising talent at this Art Moderne–style bistro for the excellence and imagination of her delicate contemporary French cooking.

DON'T MISS: Shrimp-stuffed ravioli, pea soup with bacon-flavored egg yolk, cod with smoked eggplant caviar, monkfish with gnocchi and girolles, ris de veau with artichokes barigoule, wild duck with a reduction of red wine and beets, lemon me-ringue tart, "sphère du chocolat déstructurée," a sort of pear belle Hélène that's contained in a chocolate sphere.

· · ·

[57] 2 rue de Berne, 8th, 01.45.22.18.91. MÉTRO: Europe or Liège. OPEN Monday to Friday for lunch and dinner. Saturday dinner only. CLOSED Sunday. ▪ $$

Pierre Gagnaire

BEING USHERED TO TABLE AT PIERRE GAGNAIRE SETS OFF A surge of serious high-voltage anticipation, which comes from the imminence of being indoctrinated into a select sect of epicureans, those who dare the outer limits of taste. You're not drubbed into the role of aspiring acolyte, however, but received with velvet charm and the respect due to anyone who has both the means and the curiosity to undertake a voyage of gastronomic initiation. Pierre Gagnaire is probably the most innovative chef working in France today—a bold, brilliant, restless, and endlessly curious cook who ceaselessly pushes back the frontiers of gastronomic experience. Ever since he opened his first restaurant in the south-central industrial city of Saint-Étienne, Gagnaire, who trained with Jean Vignard in Lyon and then Paul Bocuse, has stunned and dazzled—and occasionally flummoxed—the clubby summit of French gastronomy.

Why? Gagnaire's ambition is to recoin the idiom of haute cuisine, the highest form of gastronomic pleasure, for a new century. Every dish he creates is a profoundly reasoned and studied construction rather like a Fabergé egg—beautiful to behold, intricately wrought, and unique.

I've eaten at his restaurant a dozen times since he moved from Saint-Étienne to Paris in search of a more receptive clientele, but my last meal was the one I most enjoyed. I went alone to lunch and so finally had the occasion to muse over every seed, drop, foam, and frond during the course of what was a truly spectacular meal. I'd even go so far as to say that dining

solo, or at most as two, is the best way to experience Gagnaire's cooking, since conversation is a distraction from the wonderment that every course brings on. There's quite simply no other chef in Paris who demands such intent concentration at the table, an experience that's a revelation in itself, since usually we briefly register the taste of what we're eating and then resume our conversation.

Consider my starter, the aptly named "Insolite" ("Unusual"). It was listed on the menu in a four-line description:

Tsarkaya oysters, culatello ham, broccoli, and agria
    (potato) with smoked eel
Galette of canaroli rice and sumac berries, sautee of
    espardeignes (sea cucumbers) with parsley
Violet shrimp and red tuna, interleaved
White turnips with koktxas (hake cheeks) with crispy garlic

Each layer of this stunningly beautiful and delicious dish parsed out a different refrain on one main theme, which is the contrast of flavors from the sea and flavors from the earth. The silky culatello ham, for example, amplified the marine flavors of the meaty Tsarkaya oysters, so named because this variety of oyster was the favorite of the Russian czars, with the sweetness of the potato and the smoke of the eel adding some gustatory punctuation. The next layer of this dish was an intriguing study in textures, contrasting the crispy rice and sumac berries with the soft gelatinous feel of the sea cucumbers, while the pairing of prawn and tuna expressed the incredible delicacy of these products and the crunchy turnips and tender cod cheeks reiterated this dish's sensual terre et mer (earth and sea) theme.

Gagnaire works closely with his friend Hervé This, a molecular biologist whose specialty is the physiology of taste, and this collaboration explains his astonishing ability to tease, incite, and orchestrate such unique sensory experiences. In fact, every time I come here, I feel like an infant who's tasting everything for the very first time.

My main course, le veau de lait, forced me to think about what veal actually tastes like. Of course, I know what veal tastes like, but I'd probably never actually thought about what it tastes like—its sweetness, its milkiness, its herbaceousness. This dish was composed of a veal sweetbread grilled with coffee and cardamom with a puff pastry galette sprinkled with tiny chunks of praline, a miniature blanquette with carrot and ginger, and garnishes of baby cabbage, potato puree, and buffalo-milk mozzarella with bergamot (a small pear-shaped citrus fruit grown mostly in Italy). It was one of the most poignant dishes I've ever had, tender with nostalgia—blanquette de veau (veal in a lemony cream sauce) is a homey classic the French associate with their grandmothers and their childhoods—and the sweet fragility of youth that veal represents.

While waiting for my cheese course, I savored the almost monastic calm of the dining room—a few tables were clearly business lunches, but the majority were occupied by people who were embarked on the same quest I was: a short but intense journey to learn more about how we taste what we taste. This is very much the theme of the way that Gagnaire serves cheese, too. My aged Comté cheese came with thin languettes (little tongues) of white chocolate and a chutney of Moroccan peaches, and these garnishes worked to create an exquisite primal lesson in the taste of a single cheese. The chocolate drew out its sweetness, butteriness, and vaguely waxy quality, while the peaches played off of its graininess and gentle acidity.

Speaking about the métier of chef, Gagnaire, an amiable man who's a major Chet Baker fan, once told me, "We're very much like jazzmen in the way we work." I found myself reflecting on this comment over dessert, a remarkable caramel and angelica soufflé, which was an edible expression of jazz. The caramel soufflé was garnished with Pondicherry pepper and came with an angelica (a bittersweet herb)-flavored vacherin and a compote of preserved fruit and licorice ice cream, and was served with a glass of dry oloroso sherry that magnified the tastes of burnt sugar, winy fruit, and strong, masculine herbs. The combination was absolutely brilliant, a lyrical cameo that made me think of the plaintive melancholy notes of a jazzman's trumpet and also the comforting fugue of an old-fashioned English men's club. Interestingly, it was also an echo of Gagnaire's own favorite dish: warm oysters with fine shavings of ham and Xérès vinegar, which offers a similar riff on various tones of sweetness framed by the taste of maderized wine. More than any other chef in the world today, Gagnaire knows how to unlock the emotional content of taste, which is why a meal in his restaurant is a profoundly moving and completely unforgettable experience.

.   .   .

IN A WORD: Pierre Gagnaire is the most extreme chef in Paris, producing dishes that are remarkably intricate and as cerebral as they are sensual. Everything you eat here insists on your full attention and concentration as part of a stunning lesson in how we taste what we taste. Since Gagnaire is globally renowned, advance reservations, plus a willingness to spend a startling sum on a single meal, are imperative.

DON'T MISS: A reflection of his astonishing imagination, Gagnaire's menus change four times a year, but no one presents cheeses in a more imaginative way, and his "grand dessert," a tasting plate of desserts, is a grand experience indeed.

.   .   .

[58] 6 rue Balzac, 8th, 01.58.36.12.50. MÉTRO: Charles-de-Gaulle-Étoile or George V. OPEN Monday to Friday for lunch and dinner. CLOSED Saturday and Sunday. www.pierre-gagnaire.com • $$$$

Taillevent

THE FRAGILE GOLDEN PASTRY CASE WAS SHAPED LIKE Venus's breast but incised with a fine swirling spiral that issued from a central nipple like a perfect architectural element. I cut it open, and inside was an impeccably cooked veal sweetbread wrapped in a mantle of wilted sorrel leaves, which had impregnated the pastry with a faint but sublimely sour perfume. I forked a slice, waved it through the green comma of sorrel sauce the waiter had spooned onto my plate from a silver sauceboat, and then tasted something so exquisite that it produced an instant primal groan of pleasure. The rich buttery pastry, the quiet muscle tension in the sweetbread, the galvanizing metallic taste of the sorrel sauce fused into a potent if evanescent moment of pleasure that left me elated. What I'd just tasted was a nearly transcendental expression of the way cooking can capture and convey human genius as surely as an oil painting or a symphony. And if I'll never have the pleasure of living with one of Degas's magnificent paintings of ballet dancers, for example, this dish may have cost a thumping $100, but it was all mine and an experience of dumb animal bliss I'll never forget.

Just forty-five minutes earlier, I'd been sitting in the Métro picking at a tiny gravy spot on the sleeve of a blazer I'd been too busy to take to the dry cleaners and my thoughts were the usual filigree of anxieties that come from having too much to do and not enough time to do it in. Then I arrived at Taillevent, where you're admitted to a chic and very discreet club with the deference due a distinguished long-standing member, even if your membership begins only when you step through the front door and ends when the door closes behind you. After a little tinkering—the first table Bruno, a delightful Frenchman with one of the most sensitive and well-versed palates of anyone I know, and I were shown to flanked the busy service door, and since I knew my meal would be ruined by the distraction of waiters sorting silver and hurrying into and out of the kitchen, I summoned the courage to ask if we might be seated better. We were, very graciously, and over a flute of Champagne, the machine of daily life went still and we embarked on a three-hour cruise in another world, a privileged place of exquisite manners, courtly charm, and impeccable elegance.

The Japanese trio sitting next to us were, in fact, the most elegant people I'd seen in a long time, and studying them occasionally while we nibbled gougères, tiny puffy cheese pastries, and discussed the menu, I was reminded that elegance is the art of omission, something almost everyone else in the room appeared to understand, too. A handsome older southern woman in a simple but immaculately tailored black dress with a square neckline wore a simple choker of turquoise beads nearly

the same color as her eyes, and her distinguished, rather leonine husband sat on the other side of Bruno, and a strikingly attractive English family—Mum in a vintage shantung suit that had probably been run up in Hong Kong, Dad in a blazer, and their three pretty, poised daughters in loose silk shifts—occupied the table in front of us. Together, our neighbors formed a quietly glamorous tableau that only heightened the implicit exclusivity of being seated in this cosseted dining room with caramel-colored wood paneling and polite modern art on the walls.

My first course of tiny tender ravioli stuffed with fresh goat cheese and fine ribbons of arugula and mousserons (wild mushrooms) no bigger than thumbtacks in a puddle of rich veal stock was a perfect example of chef Alain Solivérès's style. Solivérès, an intensely talented cook, is a gifted, gutsy miniaturist who composes his dishes with an almost surgical precision that often belies his exceptionally lyrical culinary imagination. It was the finely sliced arugula, for example, that made this dish so good by adding texture and tiny vegetal dashes of punctuation to the earthy tones of the stock and mushrooms and the soothing lactic background of the goat cheese. Bruno's petit farcis, a riff on a traditional Niçois dish of stuffed baby vegetables, came as an edible still life that included a tiny eggplant, onion, tomato, and round zucchini, each of which had been perfectly cooked and contained a different stuffing. I could have sworn that tweezers had been needed to compose the mesclun (mixed baby salad leaves) that accompanied this dish, since some of the greens were so fine and feathery that they were almost invisible.

Similarly, the delicate scattering of freshly cracked peppercorns on the thick, exquisitely cooked slice of duckling that was Bruno's main course was applied with such pharmaceutical artistry that it completely transformed the succulent fowl into something one was tasting for the first time. The garnish of sour cherries skewered on vanilla beans and a gossamer sauce of pan juices further rendered this one of the most remarkable dishes I've ever tasted. Since we wanted only one wine, I had initially planned on a red Meursault, but the delightful sommelier highly recommended a Givry, an excellent but less expensive red Burgundy, and although it would have benefited from being carafed, it was a brilliant choice. The wine list alone is a reason to come to Taillevent, since few restaurants in the world offer a more imaginative, approachable—the price range for a restaurant of this caliber is surprisingly friendly—and original carte.

Though many of the other customers that night seemed to have decided on one of the two tasting menus offered, I think food as ethereal as Solivérès's should be consumed homeopathically. I wouldn't have wanted both a fish and a meat course, and as magnificent as the cheese course may be, I was quite content with three courses.

Desserts are divided between those based on fruit and those based on chocolate, and wanting a conclusion that was more adagio than arpeggio, I ordered the croustillant d'abricots et roses de Damas. The tartness of the apricots met the residual sourness of the sorrel sauce on my sweetbreads perfectly, and perfumed notes of rose petal flattered the buttery richness of its caramelized tuile base. Bruno's baba au rhum, that most masculine of Gallic desserts, was the best one I've ever tasted, too, since the round sphere of fine sponge cake had imbibed just the right amount of syrup and smoky, ambered old rum, and a spoonful of ivory-colored vanilla-bean-flecked whipped cream referred back to the richness of his duckling.

As happens in the enclosed and pampered world of a luxury cruise ship, you become keenly observant of the smallest details, and some of them here were wanting. I can't understand why Taillevent doesn't serve better bread, and I shouldn't have had to ask for more of the luscious sorrel sauce for my sweetbreads. The wait for dessert also teetered on the brink of being uncomfortable. But I suspect that the late Jean-Claude Vrinat, who founded Taillevent in 1946 and who oversaw its ascent to becoming an international benchmark of gastronomic luxury, would have almost been flattered by these complaints, since they issue from subscribing to the context of perfection he so magnificently succeeded in creating at this restaurant, a place where hugely pleasurable and very personalized experiences are the coin of the realm. Oh, and just in case you were wondering about the occasion of this very special meal—knowing that I needed an infallible benchmark of gastronomic brilliance to pilot by, it was the first one I ate specifically to write this book.

. . .

IN A WORD: If you've ever looked at old photographs of the Duchess of Windsor or Maria Callas in fancy Paris restaurants and yearned to have an approximate experience of the taut postwar glamour they represent, you'll love Taillevent, which rather impressively manages to be the diva of dining in Paris without being remotely stuffy. Alain Solivérès is an extraordinarily talented chef, the restaurant has one of the world's top ten wine lists, and the service is superb.

DON'T MISS: Taillevent's menu follows the seasons, but dishes to look for include lobster boudin (lobster sausage); scallop rémoulade; ravioli aux mousserons (cheese-and-arugula-filled button-sized ravioli with mousseron mushrooms in veal stock); petits farcis (stuffed baby vegetables Niçois style); cream of watercress soup with Sevruga caviar; spelt risotto with bone marrow, black truffle, whipped cream, and Parmesan; caillette de porcelet aux épices et raisins de Malaga (a sublime dish of pork sausage wrapped in caul fat and tiny pork chops with carmelized cabbage and Puy lentils in a sauce studded with plump, juicy raisins); John Dory stuffed with olives; duckling roasted with cherries; chausson feuilleté de ris de veau (veal sweetbreads in pastry with sorrel sauce); chocolate ravioli; baba au rhum; croustillant d'abricots et roses de Damas (braised apricots on a caramelized crust with rose essence).

. . .

[59] 15 rue Lamennais, 8th, 01.44.95.15.01. MÉTRO: Charles-de-Gaulle-Étoile, George V, or Ternes. OPEN Monday to Friday for lunch and dinner. CLOSED Saturday and Sunday. www.taillevent.com • $$$$

EATING THE UNSPEAKABLE

·   ·

T MAY SURPRISE YOU, BUT I'LL CONFESS THAT I STU-
diously avoided the lobsters served by my grandmother at
her Rhode Island summerhouse for twenty years, or until I
celebrated my twenty-first birthday by realizing what a fool
I'd been. Instead, as the others cracked and tugged and dug
and splattered, I sat quietly in my picnic-table corner eating
a cheeseburger. Why? I was a shy kid who hated messes and
strong tastes and smells; crimson, scalded lobsters were just too
"other" for me.

The fear of unknown victuals is often experienced as visceral, but during a couple of decades in Paris, I've learned
that such an aversion is almost always cultural. This is why a
substantial appendix would be needed to list all of the famous
French delicacies I wouldn't have touched at gunpoint when
I arrived in Paris. Suffice it to say I wasn't wild about game,
found offal awful, and nothing could pry my shell open when it
came to oysters and mussels, to say nothing of bulots (sea snails,
or whelks). Most fish flopped, too.

So my first weeks in town were perilous. As the new correspondent for a fashion-mongering American press group, I
was invited to some of the grandest tables in town. The locals
wanted to size me up and make a good impression—and almost
to a one, their good intentions induced a gastro trauma or two.
How vividly I remember the first ambush. An elegant attaché de

presse with a particule before her surname—the telltale "de," "de la," or "du" that always indicates aristocratic aspirations if not a family tree that will stand up to rigorous genealogical investigation—organized a dinner with a set menu in a private dining room at Lucas-Carton, then one of the most opulent restaurants in the capital. As she rather heavy-handedly hinted, it would be my opportunity to meet a carefully selected group of very important Parisians. Yikes.

I can't say that I was much looking forward to the dinner, and I took an immediate dislike to the countess on my right with a face as taut as an expertly pitched tent when she confided that she found Americans amusing because we're mongrels. Right. The lady on my left kept correcting my French, making it nearly impossible for me to finish a single flawed sentence, and the very elderly man in front of me required shouting-level conversation due to an apparently faulty hearing aid. After I'd made some innocuous remark about the beauty of Paris at the top of my lungs, he said he preferred to speak in German or Russian. Mais, bien sûr (Yes, of course), I thought with some exasperation—after all, it's perfectly normal to expect an American to speak both of these languages.

When the first course was served, I was relieved to have a reason to withdraw from the conversation. On a large cobalt blue glass plate, a variety of the tiniest vegetables I'd ever seen surrounded a thatch of salad frilled with various herbs. I ate a dollhouse-sized carrot and a skinless cherry tomato and then prodded the pretty mound of leaves. For a few seconds, I couldn't believe my eyes. A tiny stiffened claw attached to the minute leg of something was nestled in the brush. God knows how this hideous little object had found its way onto my plate, but I didn't want to embarrass anyone, so I tucked it under a usefully large spinach leaf. And got busted. "Ah, la-la, Alexandre! You must try, it's so good, it's a grive," said the countess. She twiddled a little grive leg between thumb and index finger and started gnawing at the joint's pitiful quantity of dessicated meat. I twiddled, too, and then, with the lightning speed of an escaping convict, I landed the critter in my jacket pocket.

Then, just after the main course had been served, over the shoulder of the I-prefer-to-speak-German-and-Russian man, I caught a glimpse of someone in the mirror who looked amazingly like the main figure in the Edvard Munch painting *The Scream*. Moi. There was a dead bird—a pelican?—with a long beak on the plate in front of me. "Ah, quelle bonheur, une bécasse!" The countess was speaking to me, but I didn't look up. I was too busy starring in my own little version of *The Birds*. By the time this pterodactyl had invaded my porcelain, I was ravenous, so I picked up a knife and fork and went at it. The taste? Old wet dog and spoiled hamburger with a whiff of earthworms crushed on the road after a summer rain.

On the heels of this ornithological nightmare, I opted out of the beau monde circuit for a while, and, by following my basest instincts, I busted open a brave new world. Let me explain. If good manners (not wishing to offend), the fear of social disapprobation (being thought a rube), or plain old curiosity occasionally impel someone to try something he finds unspeakable, it's the possibility of love—and more specifically sex—that probably sees off more self-inflicted food taboos than any other motivation.

We were walking on a flat beach in Normandy next to an army green sea on a sunny September weekday after having spent a whole fugitive morning in bed. On any walk, one leads, the other follows, and on this day, I let myself be led. We didn't speak because we didn't need to, and I hoped this was the sign of a newborn complicity, so even when the walk started to get longer than I had in mind, I held my peace. Then, on the other side of a headland, there was a weathered wooden cabin just off the sand with striped umbrellas shading the handful of tables on a sandy terrace. "Oh, how charming—shall we have lunch?" Fine by me, or at least it was until we were seated and I realized we'd just dropped anchor at an oyster bar. Sipping Muscadet, I hastily plotted a dozen different ways of escaping the bivalves but couldn't coin anything credible ("I love you so much that all I want is a big ham sandwich, darling"—nope) before a big beaten-up aluminum tray filled with crushed ice was set on a stand and I found myself faced down by two dozen of 'em. Oh boy. "Tu aimes les huîtres?" "Oui, oui, oui, oui," I love oysters. Okay, here goes, and wow, I'm egg-beatered in the surf of love with a mouth full of seawater. And I love it. I really do. Punctuated by yellow butter grainy with sea salt and smeared on small pieces of rye bread, the oysters are almost as good as the sex that preceded them.

The relationship ended, but I licked my wounds in the possession of a real prize—a passion for oysters. And so it went. In the hope of pleasing a lover at the beginning of an affair or battening down the supply of good sex in one that had been well and truly launched, I ended up eating many of the foods I had once found repugnant—elvers, reindeer, Czech Christmas carp (really dreadful), the list is long. I didn't end up liking all of them, of course, but I became enough of a bona fide omnivore to happily travel thousands of miles to sample things spooky and unknown—fruit bat curry in the Seychelles, for example (bony, smoky, and gamey are all you need to know).

But why am I telling you all of this? It's because I used to be afraid to eat lobster, and if you recognize yourself in the timorous twit I once was, I want you to know you can change. To wit, why fly all the way to Paris to eat chicken breasts or steak? Push your limits instead. At worst, you'll have a gruesome gastro tale of your own to recount when you get home. More likely, you'll be amazed to discover that you actually *like* pig's feet, beef muzzle salad vinaigrette, and calf's brains. P.S. I'm still not wild about bécasse.

LA NOUVELLE ATHÈNES, GARE DU NORD, GARE DE L'EST, CANAL SAINT-MARTIN

· ·

Abri

ONE OF THE MOST INTERESTING AND SALUTARY RECENT CHANGES in the Paris restaurant scene is the internationalization of the city's gastronomic talent pool. This mirrors what happened long ago in the Paris fashion business, where the importance of being French-born has been eclipsed by a global trawling for seriously gifted young designers. In much the same way that the French capital has long been the global beacon for fashion, it's now attracting ambitious young chefs from other countries in such numbers that it's no longer a surprise to learn the chef who just cooked your dinner is Mexican or Italian or American or, most likely of all, Japanese.

The Japanese, you see, continue to revere French cooking with a seriousness and passion that's dwindled in other countries. This is why young Japanese chefs come to France in droves

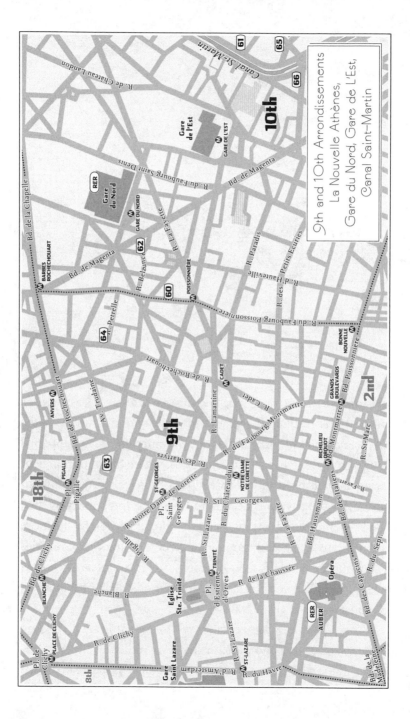

9th and 10th Arrondissements
La Nouvelle Athènes,
Gare du Nord, Gare de L'Est,
Canal Saint-Martin

10th

Gare de l'Est
GARE DE L'EST

Canal St-Martin

61
65
66

R. de Château Landon

Bd. de Magenta

RER
Gare du Nord
GARE DU NORD

R. du Faubourg Saint Denis

R. La Fayette

Bd. de la Chapelle

BARBÈS ROCHECHOUART

Bd. de Magenta

62
R. Belzunce

POISSONNIÈRE
60

R. Paradis

R. des Petits Écuries

R. d'Hauteville

R. du Faubourg Poissonnière

BONNE NOUVELLE

R. Petrelle

64

Av. Trudaine

Bd. de Rochechouart

ANVERS

R. de Rochechouart

CADET
R. de Rochechouart

R. Lamartine

R. Cadet

GRANDS BOULEVARDS
Bd. Montmartre

2nd

Bd. Poissonnière

RICHELIEU DROUOT
Bd. Montmartre

R. St-Marc

R. Favart

9th

R. des Martyrs

NOTRE DAME DE LORETTE

R. du Faubourg Montmartre

63

ST-GEORGES

R. Notre Dame de Lorette

Pl. Saint Georges

R. St-Georges

R. du Châteaudun

R. La Fayette

Bd. des Italiens

PIGALLE
Pl. Pigalle

Pigalle

18th

Bd. de Clichy

BLANCHE

R. Blanche

R. Pigalle

R. St-Lazare

Église Ste. Trinité

TRINITÉ

Pl. d'Estienne d'Orves

R. de la Chaussée

Bd. Haussmann

Opéra

RER
AUBER

Bd. des Capucins

R. du Sept.

Pl. de Clichy

PLACE DE CLICHY

R. de Clichy

8th

Gare Saint Lazare

R. d'Amsterdam

R. St-Lazare

ST-LAZARE

R. du Havre

Bd. de la Madeleine

to apprentice in the country's restaurant kitchens and also why so many of them stay on to open their own restaurants. It makes great sense, too, since the culinary cultures of the two countries are so similar—they both venerate best-quality produce, admire the technical elements of cooking, and are profoundly fascinated by the aesthetics of everything edible.

An impressive example of why France is so lucky to be on the receiving end of all this talent is young chef Katsuaki Okiyama, who worked at Robuchon, Taillevent, and L'Agapé Bis before opening Abri, his bare-bones hole-in-the-wall storefront restaurant in the 10th Arrondissement, not far from the Gare du Nord. Meeting a friend for lunch, I walked right by, since the plastic sign hanging overhead at this address says City Café, and when I first stepped inside, I wasn't sure if I was in the right place either, since it only just barely presents itself as a restaurant. Instead, the decor (which I like a lot, actually) is sort of Berlin proletariat coffee shop, with a few bare wood tables up front, along the wall, and in back. Okiyama works in an open kitchen with a grill and a griddle, which occasionally fills the narrow space with a mist of finely aerated cooking oil; this would be vexing were it not for the fact that the food he cooks is not only intriguing but deeply satisfying.

The only choice we had to make on the lunch menu was between fish and duck as our main course—I went with the fish, she chose the duck, and after ordering we resumed our vaguely tongue-in-cheek conversation about the future of gastronomic journalism and how blogging has so righteously pummeled the former hegemony of professional expertise.

Then our first course arrived and stopped our chatter. Composed of a thin slice of beet, a succulent tomato, and crabmeat in a gently nutty miso vinaigrette, this salad was stunning for being so vivid, light, and fresh. To be sure, the earnest Zen master small-plate aesthetics were similar to those deployed by many of Paris's most ambitious young chefs these days, but that didn't stop them from being pretty and sincere.

When our next course arrived, a potato potage with coffee-cardamom foam, its miniature palette of flavors was as witty and playful as a netsuke. Suddenly it made perfect sense that half of the people at lunch that day were the sort of journalists, artists, and food bloggers who respond immediately to such creativity. Next up, grilled yellow pollack with spinach, Chinese cabbage, and yellow squash in smoked-salt butter sauce with a dusting of cayenne—a subtle composition of delicate and potent flavors and soft and sinewy textures that was exceptionally satisfying. My friend's duckling with duxelles, spinach, artichoke, and carrots in a velvety-looking sauce of pan juices was superb, too, and I immediately decided I'd return for the six-course dinner tasting menu (I have, too, and it's even

suaver than the lunch menu, for it allows Okiyama to create and elaborate intriguing liaisons of unexpected but complementary tastes between courses). And then dessert delivered the knock-out punch, perhaps the best millefeuille I have ever eaten—a magnificent rubble of delicately caramelized buttery brown pastry leaves garnished seconds earlier with vanilla-flecked crème pâtissière and laser-fine slices of dried and fresh nectarine.

To be sure, anyone whose idea of Paris is Saint-Germain-des-Prés might be discombobulated by the scrappy if perfectly safe 10th Arrondissement neighborhood where this restaurant is located, and some people might be put off by the ur-bohemian setting and underpowered ventilation of the open kitchen, but if these aren't obstacles, you'll likely love this place as much as I did. Note that one of the best sandwiches in Paris is served here at lunch, albeit only on Monday and Saturday—grilled bread stuffed with vegetable omelette, pickled cabbage, tonkatsu (Japanese breaded pork chop), and a secret sauce.

.   .

IN A WORD: Die-hard Parisian food-lovers are flocking to Japanese chef Katsuyaki Okiyama's hole-in-the-wall restaurant in a scruffy 10th Arrondissement side street for the excellence of his subtle and precise contemporary French cooking with a lyrical Japanese sensibility.

DON'T MISS: The menu evolves constantly here, but signature dishes include marinated mackerel and beets in a honey-and-cocoa-flavored vinaigrette, veal steak with grilled eggplant and Savoy cabbage, yellow pollack in smoked salted butter sauce, millefeuille with apples or nectarines, and a sublime fondant au chocolate (runny chocolate cake).

. . .

[6O] 92 rue du Faubourg-Poissonnière, 10th, 01.83.97.00.00. MÉTRO: Gare
du Nord, Poissonnière, or Cadet. OPEN Tuesday to Saturday for lunch and
dinner. Monday lunch only. CLOSED Sunday. ▪ $$

Le Galopin

I LOVE THE 10TH ARRONDISSEMENT, BECAUSE IT STILL HAS
a lot of authentic but unselfconscious Parisian atmosphere and
hasn't yet become riddled with Starbucks and Subway sand-
wich shops. Instead, this until recently forgotten corner of
Paris is continuing to emerge as one of the city's most inter-
esting food neighborhoods, mainly because of the fortuitous
chicken-and-egg situation that low rents make it a great location
for young chefs setting up shop on their own, and the creative
types who've been colonizing the quartier steadily for the last
ten years provide them with an eager local audience.

Having lived most of my life in large cities, I'm a keen
student of urban ecology, and walking to dinner at this res-
taurant recently, I concluded that the east bank of the Canal
Saint-Martin has achieved that fragile equilibrium between
renewal and decrepitude that usually presages a tipping point.
The last time I was on the rue Saint-Marthe, where this won-
derful bistro is located, was almost a year earlier, and this nar-
row cobbled street, so Parisian it looks as though it could be a
Hollywood back lot, had changed noticeably. Many of the little
stone houses that line it had a brightly painted front door and
had clearly been recently renovated. There were also several

lively new cafés and interesting recently opened restaurants. To be sure, I still passed two drug dealers, but they're part of the urban ecosystem, too, and they wouldn't be around if demand wasn't creating supply.

Le Galopin occupies a corner space that was once a café, and it has a jaunty teal-blue façade and big picture windows overlooking the street, which made it look both appealing and sort of Edward Hopper–esque when I spotted it from afar. Inside, though, the place was packed with a noticeably good-looking young crowd and a table of three—Dorie, Michael, and Molly, the last a well-known blogger from Seattle—who were patiently awaiting this latecomer.

On a cool night, the little dining room was warm and smelled of good cooking. Since dishes on the prix fixe menu were listed as haiku-like lists of ingredients, the two friendly waiters patiently explained them. We'd be served two amuse-bouches, a starter, a fish, a meat, and then two desserts. The first dish to arrive was a crunchy prawn from Madagascar with mustard leaves in an airy white foam of smoked mozzarella. It made a terrific first impression of yearling chef Romain Tischenko's cooking and immediately heightened our expectations.

We crabbed a bit about American politics, which drew an appreciative grin from the handsome African man sitting at the table next to us, and then our second course arrived—a clear and deeply ruddy guinea hen bouillon with sliced green onions, several slices of pretty crimson carrot (the vegetables here come from well-known organic farmer Annie Bertin in Brittany or the game-changing company Terroirs d'Avenir, which is supplying many of the best new Paris restaurants with high-quality produce from small, environmentally correct producers), tiny cubes of fowl, and groseille de mer, or sea gooseberry.

I had no idea what a sea gooseberry might be, and because the explanations I found on Google were so far beyond my scientific ken, I suggest you do your own research. As far as I could make out, however, these tiny sea creatures were present more for their texture than for their taste, but one way or another the bouillon was excellent. Just two courses into this meal and I was already impressed by the imagination of Romain Tischenko, who was working away like mad in his tiny open kitchen in the corner of the room.

Next up, an unusual but curiously successful composition of white button mushrooms, watercress, nubbins of colored cauliflower, marigold petals (unexpected but adding some potent autumnal punctuation to this dish), and foie gras cream. Crisply grilled brill on a bed of crushed potatoes with grains of lemon, shiitakes, and griddled baby leeks followed, and then two of us had duckling and two of us veal, both of which came with parsnip puree, pea shoots, and slices of raw daikon and parsley root, an elegantly nuanced cameo of flavors and textures.

Though they read enigmatically on the menu—"apple/walnut/chestnuts" and "vodka/grapes/lovage"—Tischenko's desserts were brilliant, too. The first one turned out to be a financier made with ground walnuts, spelt flour, and honey, topped with a slice of pear, three types of chestnuts (crushed, candied, and fresh), and some fresh chestnut cream, and the second was a textural study of crunchy bran and buckwheat with sliced red grapes, vodka-spiked cream, and lovage. The first time I'd ever run into this particular idea of a sandy or ashy texture for food was at Mugaritz in Spain six or seven years ago, and it was interesting to note that it's now crossed the Pyrenees and made its way to Paris.

Both desserts were refreshing, original, and slightly mysterious, which is a very good place for any chef to sign off. Walking along the Canal Saint-Martin after dinner, I couldn't help thinking that Paris is currently being swept by a brilliant wave of talented new chefs and wonderful new restaurants. Before we parted, Dorie said, "Paris is a more exciting place to eat right now than it's been for a very long time." She's right, and Romain Tischenko at Le Galopin is very much part of this gastronomic excitement.

·   ·   ·

IN A WORD: Young chef Romain Tischenko serves a different prix fixe tasting menu every day at his casual, friendly, well-run bistro in a gentrifying corner of the 10th Arrondissement. A wonderful address for anyone who's interested in the new generation of gastronomic talent in Paris.

DON'T MISS: There's no telling what Romain Tischenko might be serving from one day to the next, but he's an especially original fish cook and his minimalist desserts are as intriguing as they are satisfying.

· · ·

[61] 34 rue Sainte-Marthe, 10th, 01.42.06.05.03. MÉTRO: Goncourt, Belleville, or Colonel Fabien. OPEN Tuesday to Saturday for lunch and dinner. CLOSED Sunday and Monday. ▪ $$

Chez Michel

THIERRY BRETON IS A BRILLIANT CHEF. AMONG OTHER talents, he's one of the best fish cooks in Paris and an absolute master of the edible detail that lights up his consistently careful, caring, but ultimately lusty cooking, so it's always a pleasure to return to his funky and rather chaotic restaurant, one of Paris's most deservedly popular contemporary French bistros. Breton is a Breton, and his menu, which has a chalkboard addendum that changes regularly, often features riffs of traditional dishes from Brittany and Breton foods rarely found in Paris, where the inaccurate perception of the cooking of France's westernmost province still runs to oysters and crêpes.

After training with Christian Constant when he was chef at Les Ambassadeurs, Breton struck out on his own by opening a good-value bistro in what was then a rather improbable setting, a 1939-vintage half-timbered building in a slightly scruffy neighborhood near the Gare du Nord. As his renown has grown, however, this tatty part of town has pulled up its socks, and Chez Michel has become a destination table, pulling Parisians of all stripes from all over the city.

I've eaten here many times and unfailingly come away

delighted by the food but also hopeful that he might move to a more comfortable setting and spend a little more time training his staff. The trade-off for great eating here remains a certain discomfort—the tables are too tightly spaced—and a willingness to accept that expediency rather than polish is the priority of the waitresses. Ultimately, however, I'll gladly excuse these shortcomings for such exceptional food.

I especially love Breton's gift for simplicity and the way he jolts homey dishes like the sauté of veal with spring vegetables I had here the other night with haute cuisine levels of quality, refinement, and precision. Served in a copper-clad saucepan, the veal was tender and full of flavor, bathed in a cream sauce based on excellent veal stock, sprinkled with chives, and garnished with a delicious mixture of crunchy broad beans, string beans, baby carrots, and onions, which had obviously been cooked independently of the veal and added at the last minute.

I was dining with Suzy, a self-described "shopping goddess" and the author of the "Born to Shop" guidebooks who was in town for a night en route from her base in San Antonio, Texas, to her house in Provence, and, as is our custom, we freely foraged in each other's plates. Her starter of crabmeat in a creamy gelée made with shellfish stock had deep, ruddy marine notes but was vividly fresh and light, while my Corsican charcuterie, served on a cutting board with a small salad of purslane, a crunchy salad green, was outstanding. Corsica produces the best charcuterie in France, and a hunk of chestnut-wood-smoked mule sausage with a big hunk of some of the best bread in Paris—the restaurant bakes its own—spread with the country's best butter, from Jean-Yves Bordier in Saint-Malo, was an exquisite lesson in the virtues of simplicity. Bordier's bright yellow butter is so good that you eat it like a condiment, savoring its rich, vaguely herbaceous taste. Suzy's cabillaud (cod) also featured Bordier's handiwork, since it had a slight sauce of Bordier's hauntingly good seaweed-flecked butter, an ideal garnish for fish. She sulked briefly when I forked into her Paris-Brest, easily the best in Paris. Choux (puff) pastry filled with hazelnut buttercream and sprinkled with slivered almonds, it was created to commemorate a bicycle race between Paris and Brest in 1891 and is one of my favorite desserts. The shopping goddess was somewhat consoled by a slice of my kouign amann, a flat, layered, buttery Breton pastry served on a small cutting board, but that missing piece of Paris-Brest rankled enough that she booked a table for dinner on the night of her return trip through Paris, a meal I doubt we'll share.

· ༺ ·

IN A WORD: Chef Thierry Breton is one of the best young chefs in Paris, and the quality of his regionally inspired contemporary bistro cooking is consistently outstanding, especially given the relatively modest price of his prix fixe menu. Definitely worth traveling to no matter where you're staying in Paris, this place is also a superb choice for lunch if you're before or after the Eurostar train from London or trains to Brussels and Amsterdam, since the Gare du Nord is just around the corner. Reservations essential.

DON'T MISS: Sautéed ormeaux (abalone); scallops cooked in their own shells with salted butter and herbs; tuna steak with coriander; roasted John Dory with potato puree; kig ha farz (a Breton specialty of boiled buckwheat flour with pork and vegetables); roast veal with baby turnips; rabbit braised with rosemary and Swiss chard; Breton cheese tray with cider jelly; Paris-Brest; kouign amann.

. . .

[62] **10 rue de Belzunce, 10th, 01.44.53.06.20.** MÉTRO: **Gare du Nord.**
OPEN **Monday to Friday for lunch and dinner.** CLOSED **Saturday and Sun-**
day. ▪ $$$

Le Pantruche

FOR ALMOST TEN YEARS I LIVED IN A TINY BUT CHARMING
apartment on the rue du Bac next door to the Couvent de la
Medaille Miraculeuse (a convent built on the spot where a
miracle occurred) and Le Bon Marché department store. This
cozy space on the top floor of an old stable in the courtyard of
a stuffy building with an almost comically nasty concierge was
barely forty square meters, but it included a bedroom that was
just big enough for a bed, a miniature living room with a work-
ing fireplace, a dining room cum office, a hobbit's kitchen, and a
bathroom with a coffin-sized tub blazed with blue (copper) and
burnt-orange (iron) stains on enamel so worn it was velvety.
Best of all, it had a washing machine, which would deliver me, I
desperately hoped, from laundromats forever more.

Despite the operatically unfriendly owner, Madame Rosa—
who, dressed in carpet slippers and floaty on-duty smocks with
alarming religiously themed prints, watered the plants from a
hose in the courtyard and could never stop herself from direct-
ing an errant squirt at any tenant she didn't like when she or
he (me) was walking by—I loved this place and would prob-
ably still be there if I hadn't met Bruno. We lived there together
for six months in the first blush of it all, and then one day we

went for oysters and discussed the obvious, which was that we needed more room. That's how we bit the bullet, decided to buy, left the Left Bank, and ended up in the 9th Arrondissement. Previously terra incognita to me, this pretty, quiet Right Bank neighborhood is also known as "La Nouvelle Athènes," a reference to the vaguely Hellenic architecture of many of its original buildings when it was developed in the early 1800s and also to the affection for ancient Greece of the many artists who once lived here.

This was the spool of thoughts that played in my head the first time I walked to dinner at Le Pantruche, a delightful neighborhood bistro not far from Pigalle. Arriving for dinner with Judy, a New Orleans native, one of my oldest Paris friends, and a scribbler like I am, I liked this place immediately for the fact that the dining room offered a winsome tableau of local residents—a good-looking couple in tweeds with their two adorable sons, an elegant older man who had an orange blossom

pinned to the lapel of his ancient but beautifully tailored jacket and who was accompanied by his wife in a pale blue cardigan and three perfectly draped strings of pearls ("Elles sont fausses, you know," she said to us—her words exactly—on her way out), dating couples of all stripes, and a single man in a trilby hat with a broken feather in its band (a fight with his mother?) at the counter. I also liked the service, which was, for this trendy Parisian neighborhood, studiously polite and reflexively friendly.

We contemplated the chalkboard menu, aware that the busyness of the dining room meant that our options were rapidly dwindling—everything is cooked to order in small quantities—so we threw the dice. To start, Judy had the coddled egg on a bed of creamed leeks with salt cod, and I went with the fowl-studded terrine de foie gras. Since both dishes took a while to arrive, we ate a lot of really good Poujauran bread, some of the best in Paris, and this had dented our hunger a bit by the time our excellent starters finally arrived. The marine scent of salted cod was a subtle spark to the obvious pleasure of Judy's dish—what's more irresistible than a coddled egg on a bed of creamed baby leeks? My foie gras was topped with the lemon-yellow layer of fat that announced it as both fresh and homemade; it was exquisitely well cooked and seasoned, and very generously served.

Next, sea bass with tandoori spices and preserved lemon for Judy, and a free-range pork chop with sautéed baby potatoes for me. Both were excellent, although I'd have liked the spices and lemon in Judy's dish to be a little more assertive. Under a bed of salad, my chop was a terrific piece of meat—juicy and full of flavor in the way that only meat from animals that have been properly fed and humanely raised can be.

Over coffee, we fell into conversation with chef Franck

Baranger, who earned his stripes at Christian Constant's Les Cocottes and is a well-drilled talent whose own style is just beginning to coalesce. I asked him why he chose my neighborhood, and he replied, "The 9th is a great mixture of creative types, young families, and old hippies, and everyone loves to eat. I wanted to do a real neighborhood bistro where people become habitués." All I could say was, count me in as one of the lucky local pantruches ("pantruche" is an old slang word for a Parisian).

·   ·

IN A WORD: Chef Franck Baranger's friendly contemporary French bistro in a former café with a seventies decor is a hit in the rapidly gentrifying 9th Arrondissement for its good-value, market-driven chalkboard menu. Reserve well in advance.

DON'T MISS: The menu here follows the seasons and markets, but pounce if you see the black truffle risotto, oyster tartare, côte de cochon (pork chop), or Grand Marnier soufflé on offer.

. . .

[63] 3 rue Victor Massé, 9th, 01.48.78.55.60. MÉTRO: Pigalle, Saint-Georges, or Anvers. OPEN Monday to Friday for lunch and dinner. CLOSED Saturday and Sunday. www.lepantruche.com • $$

Le Pétrelle

WITH ITS ENCHANTINGLY RAMSHACKLE PROUSTIAN DECOR, including a cat snoozing on a side table and a wonderful mix of nineteenth-century bric-a-brac that the owner, Jean-Luc André, has collected all over France, the oriental-carpeted dining room of this delightful bistro in the 9th has a slightly theatrical, authentically bohemian atmosphere. In fact, it feels more like a writer's study or even a psychiatrist's office than a restaurant. The space was originally the workshop of a picture frame maker who specialized in gilding, the minute application of small, fluttering squares of gold to elaborately carved woodwork. This palpable past adds to the blowsy, baroque charm of the place, and on a warm summer night, it was no surprise to spot the fashion designer Christian Lacroix—he's on record as saying that this is his favorite restaurant—dining with a friend. Le Pétrelle is, in fact, a new celebrity favorite in Paris, since Madonna showed up with her husband, Guy Ritchie, the following week.

What's pulling the famous faces are the delicious market menus that André, a self-taught chef, serves up and the wonderfully louche bohème redux atmosphere of the 9th Arrondissement, dubbed La Nouvelle Athènes, or New Athens, during the nineteenth century because it was home to a dense concentration of artists and eccentrics. Now, with the beau monde bailing out of Saint-Germain-des-Prés because it's become too expensive and touristy, the 9th is blossoming all over again, which explains this restaurant's intriguing clientele—here a rare-book dealer, there a costume historian, with only a sprinkling of young bankers.

Le Pétrelle is as diverting visually as it is gastronomically. A donkey's head made from straw hangs on the wall, there are two stunning wooden chandeliers plus crimson wall coverings that look as though they were originally ecclesiastical, and, at every table, miscellaneous flea market chairs, flowers from a country garden, and a little stack of books. On ours, *Les Années Pop* by Pierre Le Tan, another regular, with charming pen-and-ink drawings of le tout Paris in those days when they were young and went to clubs every night—Valentino, Karl Lagerfeld, Gilles Dufour, Loulou de la Falaise, Yves Saint Laurent, the whole seventies gang whose aesthetic sensibility—a spontaneous mixture of flea market, ethnic, and modern—still informs Parisian life.

Within minutes of being seated, the gracious waiter served us a saucer of radishes with a ramekin of fleur de sel, the finest French sea salt, for dipping, and two thimble-sized goat cheeses sporting sprigs of thyme as an amuse-bouche, exactly the sort of stylish rustic hors d'oeuvre you'd expect at the table of a smart young hostess during a weekend in the country. On a still July night, two superb starters—a salad of poulet du Gers en gelée (cold jellied chicken, a dish it's easy to imagine Balzac eating) topped with summer truffles (more for their texture and perfume than their taste) and another one of rabbit terrine garnished with grilled eggplant slices, zucchini ribbons poached in lemon verbena broth, and a round zucchini roasted and stuffed with ratatouille immediately made indifferent appetites alert.

André's signature is a lavish but intelligent use of fresh herbs—long green whiskers of chive, aromatic sprigs of fresh tarragon and chervil, and other seasonal herbs from the Ile-de-France (the region in which Paris is located) instead of the Mediterranean trio—thyme, rosemary, and bay—that have come to dominate contemporary Parisian cooking. These neglected French herbs punctuate the originality of his disciplined and passionate market menus, too, highlighting the superbly fresh produce and the precision of his cooking and seasoning. They also give it a geographic marker—this is clearly the seasonal produce of the Ile-de-France—as did the garnishes of fork-mashed new potatoes and a mix of baby vegetables, including a crayon-sized carrot, a baby beet, a slender leek, and a roasted tomato that came with a tournedo of beef, and a succulent wild Scottish salmon steak served with pan juices deglazed with Xérès vinegar.

The black cherry clafoutis I had for dessert made me think of Colette. The ripe cherries bled sweet purple juice when I bit into them and were mounted in a perfect eggy custard; I think this dessert would have made her swoon, since she craved simple, sensual country cooking. Similarly, white peaches poached in lemon verbena syrup and accompanied by roasted apricots and a luscious iced vanilla meringue were something Sarah Bernhardt might have served to friends at a summer lunch in the garden at her country house on Belle-Ile, the magical island off the coast of Brittany. Then, just before the coffee, the waiter toured the dining room with a tray of warm, crumbly, buttery sablés (shortbread cookies), each one topped with a single raspberry, a final elegant flourish to a deeply satisfying meal.

. . .

IN A WORD: A dreamy, well-mannered, and very personal candlelit restaurant that offers some outstanding market-driven contemporary French cooking, along with a lot of romance in its eclectic decor. Très Parisien.

DON'T MISS: Sautéed white asparagus and morel mushrooms; artichauts en poivrade (marinated artichokes) with chervil root chips; scallops with truffles (in season); sea bass roasted with fleur de sel and crispy herbs; roast baby lamb with lemon thyme and fava beans; moelleux au chocolat (runny chocolate cake); rhubarb compote with strawberries.

...

[64] 34 rue Pétrelle, 9th, 01.42.82.11.02. MÉTRO: Anvers or Poissonnière. Dinner only. CLOSED Sunday and Monday. www.petrelle.fr ▪ $$

Philou

PARISIANS LOVE THE CANAL SAINT-MARTIN AS A RARE AQUEOUS ribbon of tranquility in an old working-class neighborhood, but the barge waterway that once linked the Seine to an inland system of other canals and is today a pretty industrial relic is little known to visitors. Within the last ten years, however, this formerly forlorn part of the city has become fashionable with young creative types, and in their wake, many restaurants have opened in the neighborhood. Some of them, like Philou, an archetypal Parisian neighborhood bistro even though it's only a few years old, are a good reason to discover this atmospheric part of the city.

The only things that would lure me out of my warm lair on a wet and very wintry night in Paris are the possibility of eating really good food and spending time with a favorite friend, so on an icy January evening I bundled up and headed off to the 10th Arrondissement for dinner with the delightful Dorie and, as it turned out, an excellent meal at Philou, a little bistro on a side street just off the Canal Saint-Martin. Stepping through the heavy red velvet curtains at the front door, I knew right away that I'd like this friendly and cozy place.

This is the most recent address of amiable restaurateur Philippe Damas, who formerly ran the fashion-industry crowd

favorite Le Square Trousseau, so I arrived with solid expectations. Dorie, a well-known cookbook author who divides her
time between New York, Connecticut, and Paris, and I studied the chalkboard menu for a while and finally decided on two
starters. Both of them, an oyster-and-scallop tartare for me and
winter vegetables sautéed in salt butter with sea snails and a
vivid herbal pesto for Dorie, delighted when they arrived.

The iodine brightness of the chopped oysters was a perfect foil for the sweet, creamy scallops, which were mixed
with finely diced baby endives and a few scattered lingonber-
ries that added some color and bright sweet-and-sour notes to
this light and quietly elegant winter preparation. The finely
dressed herb salad atop the tartare was a nice touch, too. Dorie's
vegetables—salsify, daikon, parsnip, potatoes, and snow
peas—were perfectly cooked, and the plump, chewy sea snails
gently poached in a court bouillon brought a touch of oceanic
succulence and texture to this beautifully conceived dish.

Our main courses were outstanding, too. My cod on a bed of
Le Puy lentils with chopped carrots, celery, and lardons was at
once fresh and stick-to-the-ribs consoling on a cold night, while
Dorie's wild duck came with a wonderful half of honey-braised
eggplant, a perfect garnish for the rich wild meat.

Desserts were less successful. My caramelized banana
millefeuille with coconut ice cream was a good idea, but the
pastry tasted commercial and cardboard-like, while Dorie's
lychee gelée garnished with raspberries, a ladyfinger, and some
black-tea ice cream, while conceptually wonderful, was not
perfectly executed, since the tea in the ice cream was astringent and the glazed ladyfinger was dull. Service is efficient and
amiable, and this place attracts an exceptionally good-looking
crowd of arty young Parisians, many of whom repaired to the

canvas-enclosed terrace out front for a smoke. Desserts not-withstanding, if this bistro were in my neighborhood, I'd eat here often. One way or another, it's found a solid place on my to-go list, especially since it's also a very good buy.

· ⁓ ·

IN A WORD: Well-heeled bohemians have made this really good bistro near the Canal Saint-Martin in a still under-the-radar part of Paris their canteen because the modern French cooking is so good.

DON'T MISS: The chalkboard menu here changes almost daily, but the oyster-and-scallop tartare, roasted duckling with honey-brushed eggplant, and cod on a bed of lentils stewed with carrots, celery, and other vegetables offer a great taste of contemporary French comfort food.

. . .

[65] 12 avenue Richerand, 10th, 01.42.39.04.73. MÉTRO: République. OPEN Monday to Friday for lunch and dinner. CLOSED on Sunday and Monday. ▪ $$

Le Verre Volé

FOR BOTH LOCALS AND VISITORS, PARIS'S THRIVING BIS-trot à vins scene offers both great eating and excellent value for the money. Among the new generation of bistrots à vins—bistros with interesting wine lists and menus designed to flatter these bottles—my favorite is the funky and very trendy Le Verre

Volé, on a side street near the atmospheric and unexpected Canal Saint-Martin in the 10th Arrondissement. The problem with this place once was that its popularity made it so tough to snag a table, but a recent expansion of the dining room has now made it incrementally easier to enjoy one of the city's best bistrots à vins without having to call a week or two ahead of time.

This is a perfect choice when you want to eat a good casual meal without making too much of a fuss about it. The young team in the kitchen not only uses the best produce but is constantly coming up with excellent new dishes, like the grilled pork belly with a curried cream sauce, baby beets, and grilled green peppers I had the last time I met a friend here for lunch.

Le Verre is also usefully open on Sundays and many holidays, so my most recent meal here was with Bruno, François, and Tina on Armistice Day. The recent addition to the dining room is a narrow alcove to the right of the kitchen, and it's preferable to the busy, lively, and often noisy front room if you want to have a quiet conversation. At the back of the main dining room, an international staff works in an open kitchen, while twin wooden étagères displaying the wines served and sold here—they specialize in organic and natural wines—line both walls. The price displayed is retail; if you drink it in-house, it's a few more euros for corkage.

Even though I hadn't been here for a while, I was hoping the lamb-and-fig terrine I'd loved the last time I came might be on the menu, but alas, no such luck. So instead I started with a salad of sliced oranges, flaked salt cod, garlicky croutons, and fleshy black olives, while the others went with the Thai-style green papaya and beef salad, finely sliced veal carpaccio with shavings of Mimolette cheese, and grilled octopus with a salad of herbs. With forks and knives flying, we all tried everything, and these dishes were excellent for offering such original but logical constellations of taste and texture.

Next, it was a neat split between couples, with one pair having the grilled duck breast with roasted turnips and an intriguingly piquant side slaw of sliced radishes and onions in light mayonnaise, the other choosing the plump and wonderfully tangy saucisse de Toulouse with potato puree and a lively little salad of mixed baby organic greens and herbs.

Aside from the fact that it was so cleverly conceived and well executed, what I appreciated about this cooking is that it was perfect social food, pleasant comfort dishes that serve as a backdrop to good conversation and good wine—we chose the organic Crozes-Hermitage, one of my favorite bottles.

The others finished up with apple-and-pear crumble and chocolate cream, but I ordered the cheese—Comté, Abbaye de Citeaux, and Brin d'Amour—as my grand finale, all of which were perfectly aged and generously served. "That was a fun night," said Bruno in the car on the way home, "but I'm sorry they didn't have the lamb-and-fig terrine you were so looking forward to." When I told him I was glad it wasn't on the menu, he looked puzzled. "Now we have a good reason to go back again soon," I told him.

· ·

IN A WORD: Le Verre Volé, one of the best bistrots à vins, or wine-oriented bistros, in Paris is a delightful address for a reasonably priced casual meal, and also offers the opportunity to discover one of city's lesser-known but appealingly bohemian neighborhoods.

DON'T MISS: The chalkboard bill of fare changes almost daily, but dishes to look out for include the lamb-and-fig terrine, veal carpaccio with Mimolette cheese shavings, grilled octopus with Thai herbs, grilled pork belly in curry sauce with baby beets and grilled green peppers, saucisse de Toulouse with potato puree, and apple-and-pear crumble. This is also a great address for cheese-lovers.

. . .

[66] 67 rue de Lancry, 10th, 01.48.03.17.34. MÉTRO: Jacques Bonsergent, République, or Temple. OPEN daily. www.leverrevole.fr ▪ $$

THE FRENCH FOREIGN LEGION:
THE PARISIAN PASSION FOR
NORTH AFRICAN COOKING

· ·

THE FRENCH HAVE A COMPLICATED RELATIONSHIP WITH foreign food. When I first moved to Paris more than twenty years ago, foreign restaurants were still regarded as night-off standbys or places you'd go for quick, cheap, exotic eats instead of a serious meal. Today, even though most Parisians still insist on the primacy of French cooking, this attitude has changed enormously, the result of the deeper integration of Europe and also the travel that has broadened the gastronomic horizons of many Parisians.

Though Italian food is very popular in Paris, it's not what I'd generally recommend to anyone who wants something other than French cooking during a visit to the capital. Why? The French still prefer their pasta well cooked and their risotto mushy. Sidelining Italian food, then, the city's signature foreign cooking is North African, a result of France's long, intimate, and complex relationship with the Mahgreb—the North African countries of Algeria, Morocco, and Tunisia, all of which were once French colonies.

The French are in fact so besotted with North African cuisine that surveys of national eating habits regularly reveal that the country's second favorite dish—steak frites remains number one, *bien sûr*—is couscous, that most emblematic of North African recipes: steamed semolina grains variously garnished with roasted lamb, spicy lamb sausage (merguez), chicken, fish, or vegetables and sauced with vegetables (carrots, zucchini, and turnips) cooked in bouillon.

This passion for couscous is very much a reflection of French history. France's colonial adventures on the other side of the Mediterranean began in 1830, when it took control of Algeria. During the century that followed, Algeria became so much of an appendage to France that it was a shock to the Gallic psyche when a bitter war for independence broke out at the end of the 1950s. This ugly struggle culminated with the independence of Algeria in 1962 and the repatriation of hundreds of thousands of French colonists, unkindly dubbed pieds noirs (dirty feet) by the mainland French. Similar exoduses followed the independence of Morocco and Tunisia in 1956, and there was also heavy immigration of North Africans to France to work in the country's factories, mines, and fields. Following the arrival of the ex-colonists and immigrants, restaurants opened to serve them the food they'd left behind, and as the French began vacationing in Morocco and Tunisia en masse, these expat tables slowly moved into the mainstream.

Today, Paris has the best selection of North African restaurants of any city in Europe. While most all of them offer a satisfying feed, the cooking of Morocco is perhaps the most refined and varied. In addition to couscous, other Moroccan specialties include tagines—meat or fish braised with prunes, olives, preserved lemons, figs, and other garnishes in a ceramic dish with a cone-shaped ceramic top—and pastilla, which is boned fowl, usually chicken, squab, or pigeon, cooked in layers of flaky pastry. The condiment that all North African kitchens share is harissa, a hot red pepper paste that also includes garlic, caraway seeds, cumin, tomato puree, salt, and olive oil. Traditionally, it's used to garnish couscous, with a spoonful or two being dissolved in a ladle of bouillon before being poured over the dish. Here's a list of my favorite North African tables in Paris.

L'ALCÔVE. Run by a friendly former butcher, it's the quality of the meat in the Algerian dishes here that's made this simple hole-in-the-wall restaurant so popular. The spit-roasted lamb couscous is one of the best in Paris—the meat is crusted, tender, and full of flavor, and the tagines are excellent, too. A friendly welcome and full-bodied Algerian wines add to the good-times atmosphere. 46 rue Didot, 14th, 01.45.45.92.02. Métro: Alésia, Pernéty or Plaisance. Open daily.

L'ATLAS. This popular and long-running Left Bank Moroccan restaurant has an attractively decorated dining room and a reliably good kitchen. Try the salad of eggplant and artichokes, pigeon pastilla, and tagine of grouper with saffron. 10 boulevard Saint-Germain, 5th, 01.46.33.86.98. Métro: Maubert-Mutualité. Open Wednesday to Saturday for lunch and dinner. Tuesday dinner only. Closed Monday and Tuesday lunch.

LA BOULE ROUGE. Popular with showbiz personalities and fashion industry types, this lively Jewish-Tunisian restaurant serves up a variety of dishes not found elsewhere in Paris, including l'akoud (tripe cooked with tomatoes and cumin), minina (chicken soufflé with eggs), couscous bkaila (with spinach and beans), and couscous with dried apricots and pumpkin. It also serves delicious Tunisian-style grilled fish. 1 rue de la Boule-Rouge, 9th, 01.47.70.43.90. Métro: Grands Boulevards or

Cadet. Open Monday to Saturday for lunch and dinner. Closed Sunday.

CHEZ OMAR. The Algerian restaurateur Omar Guerda got his start in Paris working as a waiter at La Coupole, and then took over this old-fashioned bistro when this now-trendy corner of the Marais was still a sleeping beauty. Through the years, he's turned Chez Omar into one of the liveliest and friendliest places to discover high-quality North African cooking. The star dish here is the couscous royale, grilled merguez sausages (spicy lamb links) and roast lamb served with fluffy semolina and a big bowl of vegetables in bouillon. Don't miss the Arabic pastries for dessert either, since they come from La Bague de Kenza, Paris's best oriental pâtisserie (pastry shop). 47 rue de Bretagne, 3rd, 01.42.72.36.26. Métro: Arts et Métiers or Temple. Open Monday to Saturday for lunch and dinner. Closed Sunday. No credit cards.

WALLY LE SAHARIEN. Tucked away in the 9th, this attractive restaurant is decorated with kilim pillows, carved wooden armchairs, and rich fabrics. Formerly a camel driver in Algeria before he moved to Paris and became a restaurateur, owner Wally Chouaki serves his couscous Algerian style, or dry rather than with bouillon and vegetables, and it is excellent with mechoui (roast lamb). Other dishes not to miss include grilled sardines with a sauce of capers and basil, tchatkhouka (grilled eggplant, peppers, tomatoes, and garlic), and a delicious chicken pastilla. 36 rue Rodier, 9th, 01.42.85.51.90. Métro: Anvers or Notre-Dame-de-Lorette. Closed Sunday and Monday.

ZERDA CAFÉ. As the 10th Arrondissement becomes trendier and trendier, I worry that this delightful Berber table might be edged out of the neighborhood by rising rents. Before that happens, make a beeline for this simple but good-looking spot with a riad-like decor to sample its generous and seriously good cooking, including chorba (Moroccan soup), Berber vegetable couscous, and lamb tagine with quince or pears. 15 rue René Boulanger, 10th, 01.42.00.25.15. Métro: Strasbourg-Saint-Denis. Open for lunch and dinner Tuesday to Friday. Monday and Saturday dinner only. Closed Sunday.

Astier

I CAN'T THINK OF BETTER PROOF OF THE RELIABILITY OF my dictum that Paris restaurants with red-and-white jacquard cotton tablecloths never serve bad food than the fifty-something-year-old Astier, a tremendously popular bistro on a tree-lined pedestrian street in the trendy Oberkampf district of the 11th Arrondissement. Given the expedient popularity of bare-wood tables in newer bistros (no laundry bill), these well-starched and -ironed spreads—here also embellished with the restaurant's name—invariably signal a well-run restaurant with a serious kitchen, which is why unfurling one of Astier's heavy, oversized red-and-white jacquard napkins is always a happy occasion.

I also treasure the debatable taste of the drop lamps made from panels of lemon-lollipop-like tropical seashell, the fifties-vintage corduroy-style wooden paneling, and the plum velvet curtains of this busy dining room, since they send the message

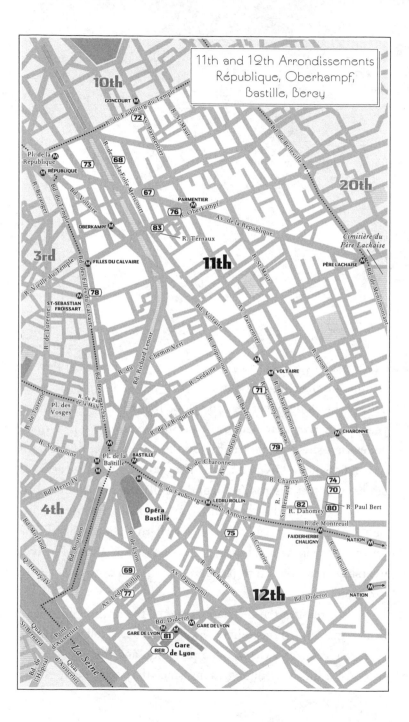

that what really counts is what you find on your plate. Happily, Frédéric Hubig-Schall, the shrewd, hardworking, affable young restaurateur who bought Astier two years ago, innately understood that the regulars would be heartbroken if anything changed. So today chefs Cyril Boulet (ex-Robuchon, Troisgros, and Marc Neveau) and Nicolas Frezal (ex-Ritz Hotel) work to perpetuate the much-loved bistro tradition here while shrewdly giving it a modern tweak here and there.

The last time I dined here, the front door still stuck the way that it did when I first ate here twenty years ago, and inside the dining room was packed, mostly with Parisians but also with foreigners who'd heard of its famous holy cow, the serve-yourself cheese tray that's part of the prix fixe menu. Studying the menu over a nice cool glass of white Sancerre, I was impressed by the way it had been discreetly reset to the twenty-first century without any overt changes that might ruffle the feathers of diehard traditionalists. House classics like the marinated herring with warm potato salad and fricassee of rabbit in mustard sauce were still available, but a variety of other more stealthily modern dishes tempted.

Curious, I ordered the oeufs cuits durs et coeur de sucrine aux deux mayonnaises as a first course, and it turned out to be a delicious and witty take on one of my favorite French starters, the deceptively homely bistro classic of hard-boiled eggs served with mayonnaise. In reality, this simple-as-water dish has a quiet genius, because it offers a brilliant miniature of the art of cooking by contrasting the nude perfection of nature, a boiled egg, with a sauce that stars the same ingredient transformed by human ingenuity. In Astier's new version, the four halves of egg came with two different mayonnaise-based sauces, one green with herbs, the other given a red tint and a roguish edge by the addition of some sauce vigneronne, red wine and shallot sauce. The tweaked sauces were delicious, as was the addition of a centerpiece of hearts of gem lettuce, which weren't just a feint at healthy eating but a nice contrast of texture and taste— when they're this small, sucrine has almost the same bewitching crunch of something deep-fried, with a tauntingly sweet taste. Bruno's starter, a salade de racines (salad of roots), turned out to be a pleasant summer salad of carrots and beets with mixed greens, including some baby beet greens, in a light mayonnaise with a risqué tint created with beet juice.

My onglet de veau (veal hanger steak), a thick, juicy cut of meat packed with flavor, came with potatoes sautéed in duck fat to give them a savory richness, while Bruno's main course of plump grilled shrimp with fine strips of Niçois lemon and tapenade (a southern French condiment of finely chopped black olives and anchovies) was a delicious seasonal nod at Mediterranean cooking on a summer night. It took a while for the famous cheese tray to reach our table—no one's ever in a hurry to see this lovely array spirited away—but, buoyed by the infectiously jovial atmosphere of this place, we were in no rush.

The owner, Hubig-Schall, buys the cheese himself at the nearby Aligre market and also sources directly from the main Paris food market in suburban Rungis, and his assortment is so perfectly composed, beginning with a gentle chèvre or two, running through a variety of cow's milk cheeses, and concluding with a blue or another strong cheese, that it's a superb opportunity to deepen one's knowledge of French cheeses. The cheese tray is also a very generous gesture as part of a menu that's one of the best buys in Paris.

In recognition of the fact that most diners will have sated themselves with cheese, desserts tend to be light, including refreshing watermelon soup (small chunks of melon in its own juice) with vanilla-scented fromage blanc ice cream that Bruno chose, and my own airy fresh apricot yogurt, which was topped with luscious lemon verbena cream.

At a time when many young French chefs have taken a detour down the road of a mannerist creativity inspired by the intriguingly Dalí-esque cooking of the Spanish chef Ferran Adria, this very good meal was deeply reassuring, proving as it did that contemporary French cooking succeeds through subtle and refined evolution rather than revolution.

IN A WORD: This boisterously popular fifty-year-old bistro in a once quiet, now-trendy corner of the 11th Arrondissement has been given a clever new lease on life by the talented restaurateur Frédéric Hubig-Schall. The appealing menu of traditional French classics and a few contemporary dishes changes regularly, but the legendary cheese course survives as part of a prix fixe menu that's one of the best buys in Paris.

DON'T MISS: Marinated herring with warm potato salad; cream of lentil soup with smoked duck breast; foie gras terrine; fricassee of rabbit in mustard sauce; entrecôte with frites; turbot with béarnaise sauce; the cheese tray; crème caramel; prune tart with ice cream; pear and apricot crumble.

. . .

[67] 44 rue Jean-Pierre Timbaud, 11th, 01.43.57.16.35 MÉTRO: Parmentier. OPEN daily for lunch and dinner. www.restaurant-astier.com ▪ $$

Auberge Pyrénées-Cévennes

BOOMING THUNDER ON A NIGHT IN EARLY MAY MADE IT a relief to slip through the front door of this epic bistro in an old working-class neighborhood behind the place de la République just before the downpour. Aside from serving up a truly gargantuan and generally very good feed, this cozy old slipper of a place with a decor of copper pans, antlers, alarmingly long sausages hanging from pegs, and a rare and very fine example of the intriguingly ugly wallpaper once commonly found in

French hotels and restaurants (flowers and gourds in red, spearmint, and pumpkin) offers a revealing sociological snapshot of how Paris is changing.

The husky voice of the pretty blond hostess is muffled by the halting but charming efforts of some English tourists who've dusted off their university-vintage French. More locally, her old-fashioned French diction—unself-conscious, a little loud, and often resorting to snorts of laughter, stands out against the perfectly denatured version of Molière's tongue spoken by the Bobos (bohemian bourgeois types, as they're somewhat derisively known in Paris), young, affluent, educated professionals with a taste for the accoutrements if not the reality of a bohemian lifestyle, who flock here to satisfy a craving for the same authentic Old Paris they're so swiftly and unwittingly destroying.

A good meal is always in the details, and for me the most important one is often the welcome. Greeted with smiles when I arrived, I was set up with a glass of cold white Macon wine and a complimentary saucer of delicious saucisson (sausage) within a minute or two of being seated. While waiting for my friends, I started chatting with Françoise Constantin and learned that she's a Lyonnaise who went to work at that city's famous Café des Fédérations when she was seventeen. She waited tables there for thirteen years, met her husband, Daniel, and they moved to Paris and eventually bought this bawdy old trooper of a bistro. Daniel later explained that business is good because the "young kids moving into the neighborhood have a yearning for the food their grandmothers made. A lot of their mothers might have been liberated working women who spent as little time in the kitchen as possible, but these kids know and love good food."

The British tourists flinched with every thump of thunder, and Françoise attempted to reassure them that disaster wasn't imminent. "Au moins il n'y a pas de neige ce soir" ("At least it's not snowing tonight"), she said, which left them mystified. At last, Judy, Bob, and Lynn arrived, and our practiced quartet à table was hungry. We ordered frisée au lardons, caviar du Puy, and terrine de maison. The frisée (curly endive) salads came with perfectly coddled eggs, hunks of salty, chunky bacon, and a grinding of black pepper, and they were delicious. The "caviar," as the Auvergnats, who founded many of Paris's most venerable bistros when they migrated to the capital en masse from their south-central region at the beginning of the twentieth century, puckishly named the earthy lentils that grow out of the stony soil of their home turf, was nicely seasoned with good olive oil, chunks of carrot, and sprigs of thyme, and the earthy garlicky country terrine brightened when eaten with a few cornichons (gherkins pickled in vinegar) fished out of a salt gray crock with a pair of wooden tweezers.

If there was anything flawed about the meal, it was the daunting abundance of the main courses. Judy's quenelles (pike perch dumplings) came as a pair and overwhelmed her, while Lynn barely touched the copper-clad saucepan of sliced sautéed new potatoes that accompanied her ris de veau (veal sweetbreads) in port sauce. Bob and I weren't able to make a dent in the massive servings of the cassoulet that is the kitchen's pride, and all of us felt a little wilted, because we hate to waste.

Even after this avalanche of white beans, sausage, and preserved duck, however, I couldn't pass up a Saint-Marcellin from La Mère Richard, a spark plug of a woman who's built a whole life on aging these small, puffy raw cow's milk cheeses from the Dauphiné region to perfection and who has a stand in the main market of Lyon. Judy never eats dessert, but Bob ordered a Colonel—lemon sorbet with a shot of vodka—and Lynn was delighted by fresh raspberries with a dainty sprig of mint that held out a promise of refreshment after this fine, ample feed, a meal that came as much from the hearts of this passionate young couple as it did from the shiny copper-clad saucepans in Daniel's kitchen.

· · ·

IN A WORD: This is a bistro that defines the genre—rustic, friendly, generous, and with a menu of well-prepared regional French classics. Come with a big appetite and a desire for a relaxed, friendly meal in a sepia-toned setting.

DON'T MISS: Foie gras; frisée au lardons (curly endive salad with coddled egg and chunks of bacon); harengs pommes à l'huile (marinated herring with boiled potatoes); brandade de morue (shepherd's pie made with salt cod and garlic); cassoulet (casserole of white beans, sausage, and preserved duck); ris de veau au Porto (veal sweetbreads in port sauce); Saint-Marcellin cheese.

. . .

[68] 106 rue de la Folie-Méricourt, 11th, 01.43.57.33.78. MÉTRO: République. OPEN Monday to Friday for lunch and dinner. Saturday dinner only. CLOSED Sunday. ▪ $$

A la Biche au Bois

AFTER A POLITE EXCHANGE OF BUSINESS CARDS AT A NOVEMBER gallery opening in Saint-Germain-des-Prés, I was surprised the following day by a phone call from Mr. X, who suggested lunch at A la Biche au Bois. I accepted instantly because he was handsome and smart and told fascinating stories about his abbreviated childhood in Tunis. Originally from Burgundy, his family owned a department store in the Tunisian capital, and his earliest memories were of jasmine-scented nursemaids, streetcar rides to Mediterranean beaches, and favorite foods, including couscous and un poisson complet (grilled fish with various garnishes) in the style of La Goulette, a popular seaside suburb.

So we met for lunch, and in retrospect, he knew what he was doing. While I was silently panicking before a menu that was mostly gibier (game)—in season, this is one of the best addresses in town for a wild feast—he cornered me right off the bat. "You're not one of those idiot Americans who don't eat game, are you?" So with quiet trepidation on my part, we shared thick pink meaty slices of roebuck paté and then lièvre à la royale, or hare stuffed with foie gras and truffles and served

with an unctuous glossy mahogany-colored sauce of its giz-zards. The latter may just be the ultimate expression of Gallic culinary genius, too, since a dozen different flavors are melded into one that's so rich and nuanced it produces a strong jolt of primal pleasure.

If I never go to A la Biche au Bois without thinking of that long-ago lunch when a stupor of good food and wine found me dumbly nodding in agreement with the declaration that it's only natural to have more than one lover at a time, I've had many decidedly delicious if considerably more innocent meals here through the years, most recently in the fine company of John and Sue, an erudite and good-humored couple from Baltimore.

On an Indian summer day at noon when this snug old-fashioned place was packed with hungry businessmen, John had game terrine and a gorgeously juicy venison steak, I loved my oeufs en cocotte with cream and tarragon and then dove into a casserole of stunningly good coq au vin, and Sue contented herself with a nicely cooked salmon steak. The three of us shared a platter of perfect golden frites and a bowl of potato and celery bulb purée that came as sides. An excellent cheese course was included in the Euro lunch menu, one of the best buys in Paris, and I finished up with a pleasantly eggy crème caramel. A complimentary pour of Armagnac was the final punctuation of this feast, and we went off into the afternoon with renewed affection for this honest, generous, old-fashioned bistro, which is just the kind of place that makes people fall so hard for Paris.

IN A WORD: Though the décor of brown vinyl seats and antlers hung on the walls won't win prizes, this friendly bistro has a seriously good kitchen, and is one of the best buys in Paris, especially when game is in season.

DON'T MISS: Terrine de chevreuil (roebuck); céleri rémoulade; foie gras; coq au vin; wild duck in black currant sauce; partridge with green cabbage; venison with prunes.

[69] 45 avenue Ledru-Rollin, 12th, 01.43.43.34.38. MÉTRO: Gare de Lyon. OPEN Monday to Friday for lunch and dinner. CLOSED Saturday and Sunday. ▪ $$

Le Bistrot Paul Bert

SOME PARIS RESTAURANTS ARE INSCRUTABLY SEXY. THIS mysterious frisson never comes from exposed skin, or too much of it anyway, to say nothing of a waiter or a waitress wearing bunny ears and a cotton ball on their tail. No, in Paris eroticism is usually implied, which is why there are few better vehicles for expressing it than food. There's no surefire way to explain it, but some Paris restaurants find their erotic groove when the holy trinity comes together—a good-looking staff serving great food generates a receptive crowd that gets off on their vibe and, in doing so, puts a hot spin on a place. It's this deceptively low-ball formula that explains why this bistro on a short, quiet street in the 11th Arrondissement has become almost irresistible. Ask any Parisian food writer where to eat in Paris right now, and Le Paul Bert always figures.

The problem with this accelerating celebrity is that by the time it reaches your ears, the hype has generated impossible expectations. So let's set the record straight. Le Paul Bert is a very good restaurant, but if most of the meals I've had here have been excellent, a couple have been clunkers. In the end, beyond the buzz, it's nothing more than a well-intentioned

neighborhood bistro with an able kitchen working with good produce, a happy calculus that's accentuated by pleasant service, a charming dining room, and an excellent wine list, period.

This being said, no one I've ever brought here has been disappointed. For starters, there are the sassy young waiters in low-slung jeans and the great human salad of bohemians and bourgeois types, the latter being explained by the fact that this place is sort of the home away from home for many French winemakers when they come to the capital, hence the fantastic wine list. Then there's the nonchalantly retro and decidedly Parisian decor, including vintage cheese box covers, enameled advertising panels, and winsomely amateur still lifes picked up at the flea market. This scene creates a laid-back Gallic groove, and the punters at the old-fashioned wooden tables with scuffed-up legs get off on eyeballing one another, especially since the good food, great wine, and heterogeneous fauna make for fine flirting fodder.

The chalkboard menu changes regularly but ensures an unfailingly toothsome run of well-prepared seasonal comfort food at reasonable prices. On a cool late spring night, I loved my eggs sunny-side up in a ramekin with first-of-season morels and a morel-flavored cream sauce, a rich and thoroughly satisfying starter for someone who'd been able only to graze through the course of a busy day. Bruno, my partner, went for the salad of ris de veau (veal sweetbreads), nicely browned pieces of veal sweetbread on a bed of haricots verts and spring vegetables napped with a suave Xérès-vinegar-spiked vinaigrette, and then had an entrecôte dotted with pearly buttons of moelle (marrow) and accompanied by a mound of crispy golden homemade frites. My cod steak was thick and flaked apart into nice firm white petals of fish that were a pleasure to eat when seasoned with a drizzle of olive oil, some of the gray (unprocessed) sea salt placed on the table in a little jar, and a little fresh lemon juice; flanking the fish was a fan of roasted white asparagus and baby carrots no thicker than a pencil. Justified by the first-rate produce that makes up its ingredients, the cooking at Le Paul Bert tends to be simple, even plain, which is why it is such a welcome table for anyone craving a good, convivial feed without a lot of bells and whistles. Desserts are superb, including a locally famous île flottante (floating island), a big cloud of fresh meringue floating on a pool of yellow custard sauce (crème anglaise) and garnished with a scattering of crushed pralines, and a massive Paris-Brest, a round choux (puff) pastry filled with hazelnut and mocha cream. And for my money, the Cairanne Domaine de l'Oratoire Saint-Martin, a fruity red with good bones, is easier, and much more fun, to drink than water.

· ·

IN A WORD: A very popular, stylish, and convivial bistro with a great crowd and atmosphere. It has a terrific wine list at very fair prices, and the kitchen sends out wonderful French comfort food and bistro standards.

DON'T MISS: Eggs with morels; salade de ris de veau (salad with sweetbreads); head cheese with pickled girolles mushrooms; cod steak with olive oil; tuna with baby vegetables; entrecôte with bone marrow and frites; ris de veau; terrine de campagne; tarte fine aux pommes et glace rhubarbe (apple tart with rhubarb ice cream); Paris-Brest; île flottante.

· · ·

[70] 18 rue Paul Bert, 11th, 01.43.72.24.01. MÉTRO: Faidherbe-Chaligny. OPEN Tuesday to Thursday for lunch and dinner. Friday and Saturday dinner only. CLOSED Sunday and Monday. ▪ $$

Bones

ARRIVING AT AUSTRALIAN-BORN CHEF JAMES HENRY'S HUGELY popular new restaurant-bar in the 11th Arrondissement on a snowy night not long after it opened in January 2013, I wasn't surprised to see a whole roasted suckling pig displayed on the white marble bar in the front of what previously had been an Irish pub before it was stripped back down to its good Parisian bones. Though the young, hip crowd who'd packed the bar area and steamed up the front windows while drinking craft beers, artfully mixed cocktails, and natural wines and scarfing down freshly shucked oysters might not have known it, the beautifully golden-crusted piglet was making a major statement about modern Australian gastronomy and what Henry has brought to the Parisian dining scene since he first got noticed while working as chef at Au Passage, a trendy bistrot à vins (bistro with a special vocation for wine) in the 11th Arrondissement.

Australia doesn't have the same gastronomic hierarchy as France—to wit, there's no Michelin-star-lit, critically curated pyramid of gastronomic pleasures to ascend in that vast, fertile, food-loving country. In Oz, as in America or Canada for that matter, a great meal can be a simple one, and there's also that recurring undertow of Anglo-Saxon suspicion of food that's too fancy for its own good rather than just plain good and wholesome, although the high Victorian British Empire idea of virtuous wholesomeness has recently given way to the trendier concept of locavorism.

True to his home turf, then, Henry presents himself more by his skills as a cook than as a chef. He bakes his own bread and makes his own butter and charcuterie, all of which reminded me of the earnest hives of culinary industry I came across during a recent visit to Hobart, the capital of Tasmania, the stunningly beautiful island that looks as though a piece of Australia snapped off and floated 150 miles south of the mainland. In that handsome old seaport, the locals have taken to the unselfconscious and sinewy genius of the head-to-tail, farm-to-table ethos, and at Bones, a new generation of Parisian food-lovers weary of the country's gastronomic establishment are lapping up the French-inflected version of same, served by Henry on a chalkboard menu that evolves regularly according to the seasons and his culinary intuition.

Meeting another American in Paris, Meg from Kansas, for dinner, I offered my explanation for the instant success of James Henry's restaurant. She listened with interest and then supplied one of her own. "Interesting, but there's also the fact that Henry is very handsome," she said, identifying a likely contributing factor. There were a lot of familiar food-and-wine faces in the crowd that night as well, but there was nothing that suggested this place would become a scene. Then, too, the lighting is harsh, with two old factory lamps casting everyone in sort of a cold, metallic rail-siding-in-the-suburbs-of-Birmingham glow. One way or another, there's zero attitude here and the staff are quick with a smile, which gives this place a laid-back, democratic vibe that has a lot more in common with Hobart than Paris.

Henry's food is very nice, too. Despite all of the forearm tattoos in the room and the punk-rock soundtrack, he's a very serious eye-on-the-ball chef, which is why his constantly evolving prix fixe menu is a challenge he lives up to.

I really liked the flirty little hors d'oeuvre of shaved celeriac with smoked trout and trout roe and was happy to taste his griddled squid with baby onions and squid's ink again. His yellow pollack with tricolor carrots from potager princess Annie Bertin, whose organic vegetables, produced on a small farm in Brittany, show up often on the menus of many of the most ambitious young chefs in Paris right now, was very good eating, too, as part of the prix fixe menu served in the dining room, which is on a raised platform behind the bar. Live shrimp sautéed in dashi broth and garnished with snippets of smoked eel showed off the more delicate spectrum of Henry's style, but the dish that really bore his signature was a pan-roasted pigeon with kale—a big crinkly leaf of this vegetable, still little known in the Old World, was a sight for sore eyes—served alongside salsify with a punch-you-in-the-nose-mate funky sauce of blood, bird juice, and gizzards, which I loved.

In fact, I think Henry likes giving his clients the bird, as it were. When we chatted, he told me that he plans to serve a lot more offal and other bits and pieces, with the idea that it might rough up a young French crowd that's been slowly succumbing to one of the most heinous of all American vices—chicken breasts. I'm all in favor of his plan, since the only reason I learned to love eating snouts, feet, and innards of all sorts is because I moved to France, and the idea that a younger French generation is becoming disaffected with barnyard eating is a heartache for me.

Dessert, a composition of almonds, coffee, and lemon, was

fine but nothing memorable. My take on Henry is that he's just not as interested in the sweet end of any meal. Instead he's all about the energy and agitation of baking, butchering, smoking, brining, and churning his own food, along with the work of making sure you're well fed. He succeeds beautifully.

. . .

IN A WORD: Australian-born chef James Henry's hip restaurant-bar offers a produce-centric prix fixe menu that includes his own bread, butter, and charcuterie, and he has a deft hand with all things offal.

DON'T MISS: Pan-roasted pigeon with kale, salsify, and a sauce of its own gizzards; grilled squid in a sauce of its own ink with charred baby onions; roasted suckling pig; grilled quail with a side of herbed Greek yogurt for dipping.

. . .

[71] 43 rue Godefroy Cavaignac, 11th, 09.80.75.32.08. MÉTRO: Charonne or Voltaire. OPEN Tuesday to Saturday for dinner. Bar up front open from 7:00 p.m. to 1:00 a.m. CLOSED Sunday and Monday. www.bonesparis.com
▪ $$

Le Chateaubriand

INAKI AIZPITARTE HAS A LONG, GENTLE, AND SLIGHTLY vacant face, sort of like that of a medieval monk, or maybe a shepherd, who has gone for a very long time without seeing or speaking to another person. Originally from the French Basque country, he's a self-taught chef who washed dishes in Tel Aviv and bounced around Latin America before becoming interested in food and moving to Paris. Since he couldn't afford to go to cooking school, he learned by working instead, making his way through a variety of Paris kitchens before he found his way to Montmartre and a job as chef at La Famille. This long, narrow restaurant furnished with fifties- and sixties-vintage flea market finds was where Inaki was discovered, and five years later, the experience still seems to have left him slightly stunned and privately puzzled. He'd be a deer caught in the headlights, but he's not so much afraid of the media as much as he is bewildered by it.

Now settled at Le Chateaubriand, an atmospheric old bistro created from an old-fashioned grocer's, he seems to have found both a quiet perch from which to continue developing what he describes as his "cuisine de vagabond" and a highly appreciative audience. This formerly working-class neighborhood in the 11th Arrondissement has been flooded by stylish young couples in search of that rarest of urban prey—a charming apartment

made affordable by its need for major renovation—and it's the energy of these smart young things that gives this place the feel of a come-one, come-all party night after night (the restaurant is much quieter at noon, when it serves a short, simple menu to people who work locally). Frédéric Peneau, formerly the proprietor of the Café Burq in Montmartre, hosts the crowd from behind the long bar just inside the front door with smiles, guffaws, and backslapping, while Aizpitarte makes only an occasional rare appearance, which is slightly frustrating, since it's only natural to be curious about the man behind the stunning contemporary food served here.

Aizpitarte is a brilliant miniaturist, composing original, origami-like compositions of taste that are often potent and pretty. In fact, if he weren't a chef he could easily be a brilliant jeweler, so striking is his talent for the minutiae of aesthetics and taste. His starter of raw fresh peas, diced daikon (Japanese radish), and a raw egg yolk, all sprinkled with rice vinegar and hidden in a pale green foam flavored with nori, the Japanese seaweed, was hauntingly good as a set of tastes and textures never before encountered or even imagined. Similarly, a recent creation of raw foie gras enclosed in transparent slices of daikon and dotted with magenta buttons of beet was a remarkable dish, almost aesthetically pure but stunningly sensual at the same time.

The bawdy atmosphere of this restaurant, with its suspended globe lamps, bare wooden tables, and bluff waiters, creates an odd foil to what comes to the table, too, since the basic experience of Aizpitarte's food is to taste everything like a newborn baby, or with a suddenly virgin palate.

The menu changes constantly—Aizpitarte serves a single menu nightly, but everything is clean, assertive, and delicate, which makes a meal here a source of real meditation. Weeks after trying his coarsely chopped tartare of beef with ground peanuts, I wondered why no one had ever thought of it before, and his saddle of lamb with smoked eel and pork breast with grated celery root and réglisse (a licorice-flavored root) stopped conversation. Two weeks later, friends visiting from San Francisco were stunned by the lamb "retour de Maroc" (just back from Morocco) with its emulsion of green tea and a scattering of coriander flowers.

One of Aizpitarte's recipes from his stint at La Famille, peach gazpacho, a superbly balanced and refreshing pureed soup that I often make when white peaches and tomatoes coincide in the market, perfectly sums up the winsome naiveté in his cooking. If the peach and the tomato meet in perfect balance, the sweetness of the former surprises by tempering the acidity of the latter. This recipe is as simple but perfect as a grade school math lesson, one plus one equals two, but now the two are one.

.   .   .

IN A WORD: Inaki Aizpitarte is one of the most interesting and original young chefs working in Paris today. Not everyone will like the noise and crowding at this place, but Aizpitarte's food is more than worth a little discomfort.

DON'T MISS: The menu changes constantly here, but some dishes make repeat appearances. If you spot them, don't pass up: julienned cucumbers with smoked fish; blanquette de veau à l'orange; mackerel ceviche with Tabasco; veal mignon sautéed with potatoes; tuna with asparagus and chorizo; black chocolate cream with emulsified red pepper.

. . .

[72] 129 avenue Parmentier, 11th, 01.43.57.45.95. MÉTRO: Goncourt. OPEN Tuesday to Saturday for lunch and dinner. CLOSED Sunday and Monday. www.lechateaubriand.net ▪ $$$

Cartet

AT CARTET, A SUPERB OLD-FASHIONED BISTRO NEAR THE PLACE de la République, I was reminded yet again just how much the company you have, or don't have, at a meal affects the way you perceive your food. To wit: this ornery little restaurant, which wonderfully recalls a dentist's waiting room in Clermont-Ferrand in 1959. It's not the shelf of bottles of peculiar aperitifs no one drinks anymore but which are still advertised on fading signs on the sides of barns in the French countryside that invites this comparison. Rather, it's the dark wood-paneled walls, pale tile floor, and atmosphere of professional solemnity that makes this an obstinately different sort of table with a clientele of insiders who'd like to keep it a secret.

Due to the excellence of the cooking here and also its random exclusivity, it's a favorite of many French food writers, even though, or perhaps because, it's pointedly ignored by the major Gallic gastronomic guides, probably for the reason that they're uncertain about sending a guileless and miscellaneous general public to a place that doesn't play by the rules of the ,conventional restaurant. Here, you don't just call up and make a reservation, though of course that's necessary. Instead, you call to request a table and the owner agrees to receive you. Or not. It's his restaurant, you see, and he does all of the cooking, so

he sees it as his prerogative to decide whom he feeds and entertains in his very intimate dining room. Perplexing though this may sound, most people get reservations without a problem, and Cartet isn't one of those power spots like L'Ami Louis that deliberately stokes its desirability by making it tough to land a table. Instead, the obstacle is that the owner may decide for one reason or another that he doesn't like you and wave you away.

If this caveat exasperates you, Cartet may not be for you. On the other hand, if you love traditional French cooking enough to cast yourself in the role of good-humored gastronomic supplicant—something I wouldn't hesitate to do in this case—you may very likely love this place as much as I do.

Indeed, I'm still thinking about the remarkable lunch I had here the last time I went. That day, when I arrived a little late, I saw my friend before she saw me. Dressed in a plain gray dress with a white collar like a subject in a Grant Wood painting, the New York magazine editor was seated alone in the small, empty dining room; we were the only table for lunch. Her head was tilted sideways and dipped as she read a magazine, so the rich September light softly polished her blond hair, which was tightly pulled back, allowing me to study her profile. The shyness of my attraction to her, chaste but muddled with respect and affection, made me cerebral. So I resorted to art history to try to frame her. Rembrandt's Saskia? Something of the scrubbed rectitude of a Saxon Madonna in a Dürer drawing? No, that day she was Vermeer's *Woman in Blue Reading a Letter,* except that there was nothing docile or dreamy about her. Viewed from afar, she was coolly beautiful and intimidating, as still and carefully posed as a porcelain doll, except that her deep concentration conveyed a crackling intelligence.

Then she looked up and smiled, and when the butterflies left my stomach, I remembered I was hungry, very hungry. She was, too—she always is, which is one of the many reasons I like her so much—and so I sat down and we ate. I think we surprised the chef-owner, whom I admire too much to identify beyond his first name, Dominique, and in any event his surname has no place here, since this restaurant is all about his food. After we ordered, he promptly returned with four shoe-box-sized white porcelain terrines—chicken liver, pâté de tête (head cheese), terrine de campagne, and jambon persillé (ham in parsley-flecked aspic). He didn't need to tell us to help ourselves, since we knew this is how every meal here begins.

Since we were the only table for lunch and unobserved, both of us ate a thick slice of all four, a meal in and of itself. It's rare to find chest-beating Gallic grub of this quality in Paris today. It takes hours to produce these dense, rich masterpieces—these dishes were invented when thrift was more pressing than time. I'm sure I detected a wisp of a smile on Dominique's face when he cleared away the terrines—like any true cook, he likes to make people happy. Then he served us lightly creamed morels in meat jus on brioche toast, one of the best things I've ever eaten, at once so feral but fancy, but then that was the unstated theme of our lunch: a rutting harvest feast à deux.

So what did we talk about? I don't remember, since the food dulled the usual playful dueling of our wits. What I won't forget, though, is this lady laying waste to a thick, lightly crusted slab of perfectly cooked calf's liver, deglazed with red wine vinegar and served with a potato puree so silky it must have been at least half butter. Meanwhile, I was trouncing a monument of my own, ris de veau (veal sweetbreads) that were improbably crispy on the outside but custard-like within. After twenty-five years of living in Paris, I'll take ris de veau over a steak any day, but I won't eat them just anywhere, only at a handful of restaurants, like Cartet.

Sometimes we were so happy during this meal that we forgot each other, only to laugh together when we emerged from the private ardors of the plates in front of us. But when the table was spread with a buffet of desserts, all homemade—including chocolate mousse, crème caramel, bugnes (flaky ribbons of confectioner's-sugar-dusted pastry popular in Lyon), oeufs à la neige, lemon tart, what is perhaps the world's best rice pudding, and pâte à choux (puff pastries) filled with rum-spiked cream and drizzled with caramelized sugar—she told me what I'd known without giving it words since I first saw her from the door, which is that she was pregnant (with a beautiful son with medicine-bottle-blue eyes, as it turned out), and that she hoped her child was enjoying the food as much as we were. The wish I made on the spot is that my friend, her son, and I will be able to return to Cartet on his tenth birthday and eat exactly the same remarkable meal.

· · ·

IN A WORD: A confidential address among dyed-in-the-wool bistro-lovers, this politely standoffish restaurant serves some of the best old-fashioned French comfort food in Paris, much of it Lyonnais.

DON'T MISS: Morels on brioche toast, ris de veau (veal sweetbreads), veal chop with morels, boeuf à la ficelle (beef poached in bouillon), chocolate mousse, and rice pudding.

· · ·

[73] 52 rue de Malte, 11th, 01.48.05.17.65. MÉTRO: République, Oberkampf, or Filles du Calvaire. OPEN Monday to Friday for lunch and dinner. CLOSED Saturday and Sunday · $$$

L'Écailler du Bistrot

AS FAR AS I'M CONCERNED, PARIS IS THE BEST SEAFOOD CITY
in the Northern Hemisphere. Why? Supply and demand. Parisians love fish and insist on top quality, which, happily, doesn't
always cost an arm and a leg here either. Then, too, France
has one of the largest fleets of artisanal fishermen in the world.
These small boats land fish by line instead of using the long nets
of industrial trawlers, a practice that avoids damaging the catch,
and they put into port regularly to rush what they've landed to
market.

The fish served at this charming wood-paneled dining room
come from Le Guilvinec in Brittany, one of France's premier
ports, and the oysters from one of the country's best producers, Cadoret in Riec-sur-Belon, also in Brittany. So to discover

just how good the local catch of the day can be, this is an ideal address. The sister restaurant of its next-door neighbor, Le Paul Bert, one of my favorite bistros, this place has a terrific chalkboard menu that changes daily, a guarantee of impeccable quality and great eating. My most recent meal began with the excellent house-smoked salmon and a dozen fines de claire oysters, served room temperature instead of chilled so that you can really taste them, followed by a thick pollack steak sautéed in salt butter and served with baby spinach and an outstandingly meaty turbot with cèpes mushrooms, a lovely terre et mer (land and sea) combination. The caramel apple dessert—a baked apple lashed with salted caramel sauce—is a homey treat, and the white Saumur Champigny, a nice dry Loire Valley pour that's ideal with seafood, not only is delicious but keeps the bill down.

· · ·

IN A WORD: An excellent fish house with moderate prices and friendly service.

DON'T MISS: Tuna tartare; house-smoked salmon; oysters; turbot with cèpes mushrooms; the assorted shellfish platter; fresh crab with avocado; roasted sea bass; lobster.

· · ·

[74] 22 rue Paul Bert, 11th, 01.43.72.76.77. MÉTRO: Faidherbe-Chaligny. OPEN Tuesday to Saturday for lunch and dinner. CLOSED Sunday and Monday. • $$

La Gazzetta

UZÈS IN THE GARD IS ONE OF MY FAVORITE TOWNS IN THE south of France, a handsome, unspoiled place in the sun that you still won't find in Peter Mayle. I have a wonderful friend there, too, Calista, a retired English novelist with a Burne-Jones face who taught me a course in Victorian literature when I was a student in London a long time ago. Among her many good qualities is the fact that she loves to eat, and so a summer or two ago, when she called for a chat, I was intrigued by her enthusiasm for a new local chef, a Swede named Petter Nilsson. "His food is just lovely, he's a real Nordic angel," she said, and as it turned out she was absolutely right. The next time I was in Uzès, we went to dinner at Les Trois Salons, and I was aston-

ished by his sugared and salted cod with pumpkin water and juniper berries in a sauce of sweet Cévennes onions, and Lozère lamb with a walnut-breadcrumb crust and a sauce of pan juice, lamb sweetbreads, and dates.

Next I heard, Nilsson was cooking in Paris at La Gazzetta, an appealingly laid-back place in the 12th Arrondissement behind the Bastille. This part of the city had an urban edge fifteen years ago, but, rather like SoHo in New York, it has calmed down now that the original pioneers have had children and stopped clubbing. They like their food, though, and since New York is their favorite shadow city, or the foreign city they understand best, the loftlike downtown atmosphere at La Gazzetta won them over right away.

Since the arrival of Petter Nilsson, La Gazzetta has been all good news, too. He does a simple menu at lunch, and then in the evening he serves up a short carte that puts his talent on show. His dinner offer changes regularly, but dishes like a starter of caramelized endive with dill, horseradish, lemon, and almond puree, and grilled cod with a mash of Brussels sprouts, tarragon, and capers, show off his gift for creating subtle but fascinating juxtapositions of flavors and his love of contrasting textures. If it's on the menu, don't miss his superb dessert of ricotta ice cream with shavings of Corsican brebis (sheep's cheese) and unusual but exciting garnishes of hazelnuts and olives. Since he's arrived in Paris and found a larger audience for his winsome but audacious and very personal cooking, Nilsson just gets better and better, so go now to catch a rising star.

· ·

IN A WORD: The loftlike dining room with low lighting and friendly service provides a perfect setting for Petter Nilsson, a

very talented young chef who cooks in a pure, clean, contemporary bistro idiom that's unique in Paris. This is an ideal choice when you want really interesting food in the context of a reasonably priced, low-key meal.

DON'T MISS: Nilsson's chalkboard menu changes all the time, but dishes that'll tip you off to his style include caramelized endive with dill, horseradish, lemon, and almond puree; cod with a mash of Brussels sprouts, tarragon, and capers; pizza with daikon and wild watercress; veal with bulgur, cauliflower, and broccoli; ricotta ice cream with Corsican brebis, hazelnuts, and olives.

. . .

[75] 29 rue de Cotte, 12th, 01.43.47.47.05. MÉTRO: Ledru-Rolliuor Faidherbe-Chaligny. OPEN Tuesday to Saturday for lunch and dinner. CLOSED Sunday and Monday. http://lagazzetta.fr • $$

Pierre Sang Boyer

THE FIRST TWO TIMES I TRIED TO GO TO PIERRE SANG BOY-
er's restaurant in the Oberkampf district of the 11th Arrondissement, my luck wasn't with me. Since they don't have a public
phone number or take reservations, we showed up one night
only to find that the restaurant was "exceptionally" closed.
Then another time, the crowd waiting to be seated at this compact counter-service first-come-first-served restaurant was so
huge that it would optimistically have been an hour before we
were seated. So my interest drifted away, because this place
seemed just too hard to get into.

Since he opened in 2012, however, the amiable South
Korean–born chef had received glowing reviews in the French
press from colleagues I respect, so at the end of a busy week
when we were too tired to cook, Bruno and I decided to roll the
dice again and headed once again to the 11th Arrondissement.
Arriving just after they opened at eight o'clock on a Friday
night, we found the place packed, but they promised a half hour
wait, so we ordered glasses of white wine and milled around
on the sidewalk for twenty minutes before we were ushered
inside. Given the throngs waiting to get in, the first thing that
impressed me about this place was the exceptionally courteous
and well-organized service. Though there was no written list,
the nice young waiters respected the proper rotation of waiting customers and the kitchen even sent out complimentary
hors d'oeuvres—thick slices of toasted country bread topped
with pale slices of summer truffle that tasted pleasantly like wet
leaves.

Once inside, we sat at the big oak bar on comfortable stools (there are only a couple of tables for two here, unless you book the one much larger table down in the basement, which is the only reservation they'll take) in front of a big burlap-wrapped sack of delicious-looking butter and a huge wheel of Laguiole cheese. The chef himself greeted us, and one of the friendly and impressively efficient waiters set us up with cutlery and the slabs of slate that serve as place mats. Staring at the cheese, I found myself thinking that I could very happily make a meal for myself by shamelessly plundering this monument to all good things dairy.

Instead our meal kicked off with two delicious little salads—haricots verts topped with micro greens, and then a chunk of sesame-seed-coated tuna with a small salad of fennel garnished with wasabi peas and a pool of mustardy mayonnaise. Both of these nibble-sized dishes were exceptional for their intricate layering of flavor, intriguing contrast of textures, and beauty. What made them even more impressive is that they were cooked at the speed of light in a kitchen the same size as a galley in an airplane. Open kitchens fascinate me, but I know from friends who are chefs that they impose an additional layer of pressure on a cook, since everything happens in the public eye. So adding this constraint to the mix made these first dishes even more remarkable.

Every chef has his or her palate, of course, and I immediately liked the way Sang Boyer backstops the umami richness of his cooking with refreshing but subtle tones of acidulated tastes. And for a small, crowded, and very busy restaurant, the service was outstanding, at once playful and professional. The rhythm of the meal was flawless.

Next up, a rich octopus ragout served on a bed of quinoa

with a light vinaigrette and garnishes of chopped yellow tomato and crunchy ficoïde glaciale, which was a deeply satisfying dish. Both this course and the fascinating sauté of pork and white beans in a rich tomato broth garnished with fresh anchovies and finely sliced radishes that followed it were suavely cosmopolitan, at once Mediterranean and then sort of winsomely Asian, a style that's very much a reflection of the chef's multicultural culinary roots. He grew up in the rugged Auvergne region as the adopted child of a food-loving French family, worked at a French restaurant in South Korea, where he'd gone to explore the food ways of his birth country, and has also worked in Lyon and London.

Throughout this meal, there was a joyous atmosphere in this diminutive dining room, too, and if it was mostly generated by the cheerful staff, another part of this glow of well-being came from an intriguingly diverse crowd who hailed from all over Paris and points beyond and who had clearly come here to discover one of the city's best and most interesting new chefs. From the snatches of conversation overheard, everyone else was as impressed by the cooking and the overall experience of this restaurant as I was.

After a generous serving of the Laguiole cheese I'd been eyeing for an hour and a half—the chef's only overt reference to the region where he grew up—which was plated with a streak of spiced chestnut puree and more of the same good country bread that we'd wolfed down all during our meal, we finished with an unusual but really good dessert. "This is sort of a riff on riz au lait [rice pudding], but it's not my grandmother's recipe," the chef said puckishly as we tucked into this grand finale, which was made with sticky Japanese rice and eschewed the usual sweet, soupy richness of the French version. Instead a rice ball was dressed up with a silky sabayon, slices of nectarine, squash puree, yuzu sorbet, a shard of crispy caramelized biscuit, and a dried orange slice to create a sophisticated, palate-cleansing coda to the medley of gentle acidities that had animated the meal.

"I come here every other night," said the single man sitting next to Bruno. "Please don't think I've been listening to your conversation, but it made me happy to hear people who like Pierre's food as much as I do." I told him that since I so often dine on my own when traveling to report on the food in other cities and countries, I was sorry our conversation had been so doggedly food-centered instead of offering the entertainment of, oh, I don't know, maybe a bit of squabbling or a spicy anecdote or two. "No need to apologize," he said with a grin. "You talk great food porn." This stumped me for a second, but then I decided to take it as a compliment, and in any event, Pierre Sang Boyer is the kind of place that'll bring out the dirty food talk in anyone.

· ·

IN A WORD: Korean-born, French-raised chef Pierre Sang Boyer's witty market-driven tasting menus change daily but reflect a delicious and very personal inflection point between French culinary traditions and the kitchens of Asia.

DON'T MISS: The menu here changes almost daily, but dishes to hope for include octopus ragout on quinoa en vinaigrette; sautéed foie gras with honey, vinegar, and pomegranate seeds; and Sang Boyer's superb Asian riff on rice pudding. And don't leave the premises without a solid serving of the huge wheel of Laguiole cheese in the middle of the table d'hôtes.

...

[76] 55 rue Oberkampf, 11th, no telephone. MÉTRO: Oberkampf or Parmentier. OPEN Tuesday to Friday for lunch and dinner. Saturday dinner only. CLOSED Sunday and Monday. www.pierresangboyer.com • $$

Le Quincy

SUDDENLY IT'S 1972 ALL OVER AGAIN. EVERY TIME I VISIT this small, cozy bistro near the Gare de Lyon, I have the pleasure of confirming the pith of truth at the core of my memories of my first visit to Paris. This is how the city smelled—a whiff of coal, beef bouillon, honest sweat, damp wool, sour tobacco smoke—and this is how those long-ago meals unfolded, and still unfold here, with a waiter in a black vest pouring a glass of white wine as an apéritif and then cutting a thick slab of dried sausage onto your serving plate to nibble as you study the menu. Then *le patron*, a sturdy gray-haired man with thick blue-framed glasses and an indigo cotton serving jacket arrives, offers the menu— "Un peu de lecture?" ("A little reading material?"), sizes you up, and launches into his commentary, teasing you toward certain choices, making sly but harmless jokes about your American accent, asking where in the States you're from, and then plunging back into the menu. "Just because it's almost Easter is no reason not to have the rabbit, the foie gras is made here, the caillette d'Ardèche are meat patties made with Swiss chard and wrapped in caul fat, served with salad and really delicious, the oxtail's been cooking for ten hours, tonight's not a good night for fish. Do you need a little more time? Of course you do, there's no hurry, don't worry, we don't want to upset your digestion."

On the second pass, things become more serious. There's more consultation, punctuated by a joke or two about how young people have become lazy and don't know the meaning of work. His sharp pencil is poised on his pad. We order the house terrine with a cabbage salad dressed with garlic cream, the caillette d'Ardèche, the rabbit in shallot and white wine sauce and the poularde en sauce vin jaune (fattened chicken sautéed with a sauce of vin jaune, the maderized wine from France's eastern Jura region), and a bottle of Saint-Joseph, an amiable Rhône valley red.

Now there's time to savor this vest-pocket restaurant fronted by a small terrace, with red checked curtains in the windows, faux wood varnished walls, and the main dining room with its gray and white Belle Époque tiled floor, tables dressed with pink and red jacquard tablecloths that include the restaurant's name, and a pleasant clutter of the bric-a-brac accumulated over the course of one man's life as a restaurant owner. In this case, the attractive detritus—a mounted stag's head, a series of framed pay stubs showing how the taxes and social security charges imposed on the French workingman and -woman have grown continuously over the course of thirty years, and a faience plate that says "The best clock is your stomach"—all tell the story of owner Michel Bosshard's career, and it's a tale that's as jovial, opinionated, and joyously French as he is.

If the terrine's a little fatty, its accompanying cabbage salad, a nice mix of white cabbage and Savoy finely grated and dressed in a delicious garlic cream, saves it, while the caillette, a patty in neat slices on top of a bowl of perfectly dressed mixed salad leaves, is succulent and perfectly seasoned. So is the rabbit, a whole rack of it, meaty and moist, served on a plate in a shallow bath of rich shallot-scented sauce with a side dish of noodles and croutons. The poularde is a succulent bird that comes in a copper saucepan, and its mushroom-rich sauce has a lovely dry edge of vin jaune. A complimentary tasting portion of another house specialty, brandade de morue, salt cod flaked into garlicky potatoes, arrives, and the meal turns into a feast. After such a meaty meal, dessert seems improbable, but no one who has had the chocolate mousse here will be able to pass it up. Because he's had some fun with us, Bobosse, as Bosshard is known, swings by again at the end of the meal to offer us complimentary glasses of plum eau-de-vie, which he flames inside big snifters to release its ambered perfume of fruit, leather, and tobacco. We take a sip, and Bobosse stands by, grinning. "Vous ne pourriez pas me dire que la vie n'est pas belle, non!" ("You can't tell me life isn't beautiful, right?"). Right indeed.

IN A WORD: The jovial Michel Bosshard is an old-school restaurateur who's made this cozy bistro one of the best and longest-running tables in town. Go for his sly sense of humor, the way-we-were atmosphere, and the menu of beautifully prepared traditional bistro dishes.

DON'T MISS: Terrine de campagne with cabbage salad; foie gras; caillette d'Ardèche (a patty of pork and Swiss chard); stuffed cabbage; rabbit and shallots braised in white wine; chicken in vin jaune sauce; brandade de morue (baked salt cod, garlic, and mashed potatoes); veal chop with morel mushrooms; chocolate mousse.

. . .

[77] 28 avenue Ledru-Rollin, 12th, 01.46.28.46.76. MÉTRO: Gare de Lyon. OPEN Tuesday to Friday for lunch and dinner. CLOSED Saturday, Sunday, and Monday. No credit cards. www.lequincy.fr ▪ $$$

Le Repaire de Cartouche

DINNER TONIGHT WITH JUDY, A CHARMING NEW ORLEANS— born journalist who has lived in Paris for thirty years and is one of my most regular dining companions, at this long-running hit of a bistro between the Place de la République and the Place de la Bastille, left me stumped. Why? In spite of chef Rodolphe Paquin's impressive track record, there was one serious misfire during the meal—Judy's otherwise lovely miniature cast-iron casserole of succulent guinea hen with spring vegetables had been dosed with truffle oil, which is the culinary equivalent of spraying insect repellent on wholesome, fresh food.

In the Métro on the way home I chewed on this one for a while. To wit, I'm lucky, I live in Paris, and I know what a good cook Rodolphe Paquin is, but what about you? What if you decided to have a meal here on my recommendation and it ran aground on one of the saddest cheats in contemporary cooking ("truffle" oil, which is nothing more than olive oil spiked with synthetic flavor)?

This is the quandary that lurks between the lines of all books about food, although I've never seen anyone take it by the horns before. There's nothing more subjective than taste, especially where food's concerned, since it is grounded in the most indisputable biological righteousness: everyone knows what tastes good because they eat only things they like. But what if I say it's delicious and you say it's not, or vice versa? Who's right? Both of us, which is why it is important to admit that any of the cooks I praise can have an off night and any of the restaurants might not cast the same spell for you that they have for me. On the other hand, I've been to all of the places I recommend many times, and so these chefs have won my confidence despite those occasions when I've ordered badly or the kitchen was having a bad day, which is why I decided to include Le Repaire de Cartouche in this book.

When Paquin gets it right, which he usually does, he's a brilliant chef. Consider my starter of pork pâté with foie gras enclosed in a pastry crust. A layer of luscious chestnut-colored gelée, the natural juices of cooking meat, had set inside the baroque curls of the pastry cap on this beautifully made concoction, which was deliciously seasoned and obviously prepared with real passion and skill. My tuna steak with grilled eggplant and a light sauce of tomatoes, black olive slivers, and olive oil was delicious, too, and if Judy's main course misfired, her starter terrine of grilled eggplant layered with red pepper mousse was rich, earthy, and very satisfying. In season, Paquin is also one of the best game cooks in Paris, and he has a winning way with desserts, including a sublime cranberry and chocolate chip clafoutis (baked custard pudding with chocolate chips) cooked to order.

The white stucco decor of the main dining room is a bit drab, but a very good wine list, including one of the best all-purpose reds around, Domaine Gramenon Côtes du Rhône "Poignée de Raisins," and Paquin's generous, hearty cooking make this easy to overlook. Overall, Le Repaire de Cartouche remains one of the better bistros in Paris—just give that truffle-oil-drizzled guinea hen a wide berth.

. . .

IN A WORD: This popular bistro between the Place de la Ré-publique and the Bastille pulls a hearty, happy crowd who come to feast on chef Rodolphe Paquin's generally excellent and very imaginative cooking.

DON'T MISS: Pâté de porc au foie gras en croûte (pork and foie gras pâté in a pastry crust); cold pea soup with ham; ter-rine of eggplant and red pepper; timbale of potatoes and sea snails; pan-fried foie gras; roast suckling lamb with white beans; grouse cooked in cabbage; tuna steak with grilled eggplant; pi-geon roasted with baby vegetables; chocolate mousse with gin-ger; cranberry and chocolate chip clafoutis; chestnut mousse millefeuille.

. . .

[78] 8 boulevard des Filles-du-Calvaire, 11th, 01.47.00.25.86. MÉTRO: Saint-Sébastien Froissart or Filles du Calvaire. OPEN Tuesday to Saturday for lunch and dinner. CLOSED Sunday and Monday. • $$

Septime

IT'S PEONY TIME IN PARIS, AND WE HAVE A BIG VERMILION
bunch in the living room, and some ivory-colored ones in a
smaller vase on the kitchen table. Every time I trot out of my
office to make tea or rustle up some lunch, these flowers swing
a winsome punch of pleasure. This is exactly what I experienced the first time I went to dinner at young chef Bertrand
Grébaut's restaurant Septime in the 11th Arrondissement.
While established chefs sometimes rest on their oars, fledgling
ones are often like puppies in their eagerness to play and please.
To be sure, Grébaut is a considerably experienced cook, having worked at Alain Passard's L'Arpège for two years, also at
Joël Robuchon, and most recently at L'Agapé Bis, a pretentious place in the 17th Arrondissement that I never cottoned
to, but his cooking still exhibits a delicious earnestness and a
sincere desire to delight.

Grébaut reboots his short menu almost daily but is obses-
sively committed to working with the best seasonal produce and
also does smart and slightly seditious riffs on the Escoffier canon
he had to master as an apprentice chef. A perfect example from
a springtime dinner was the wonderfully crunchy white asparagus with an oyster-spiked sauce gribiche I had as a first course.
The iodine in the bivalves at once brightened and softened the
acidity of the sauce gribiche, with trout roe and artfully chosen herbs (tarragon, chervil, chives) adding witty gastronomic
punctuation to this deeply considered and carefully composed
dish.

Bruno loved his grilled couteaux (razor-shell clams) in a

light vinaigrette with a shower of fresh herbs, too, and they were perfectly cooked (probably sous-vide), remaining tender and juicy.

Our main courses—chicken on a bed of lentil puree with grilled baby onions for me, cod with green asparagus for Bruno—were cooked impeccably and beautifully garnished, but possibly in need of more assertive seasoning to temper their choir-boy sweetness.

Charmed by both the food and the atmosphere at this great new restaurant, Bruno and I shared a homey dessert—a financier-like bar of cake with fresh strawberries, elderberry ice cream, and strawberry sorbet. And so the meal ended as it had begun, with another delicious cameo of the talent and irresistible sincerity of a young chef trying hard to make his mark and very much succeeding. Though the location of this restaurant is decidedly outlying for anyone whose ground zero in Paris is Saint-Germain-des-Prés, as someone once said, it's well worth the trip, especially since this atelier-style dining room is a handsome space with an artfully staged post-industrial decor of workbench lamps, an open kitchen, tables made from recycled wood, and beautiful neo-Danish-modern armchairs, and because the service is so prompt and charming.

IN A WORD: A committed locavore, chef Bertrand Grébaut is one of the most talented young chefs in Paris right now. Ever since it opened in 2011, his arty atelier-like restaurant way beyond the Bastille has been packed with an international crowd that loves his fresh, clean contemporary French cooking, which is informed by a deep respect for and knowledge of traditional cuisine bourgeoise.

DON'T MISS: Grébaut's menus change constantly, but he has a real affection for vegetables, fresh herbs, and fruit, so dishes featuring these ingredients are especially good.

. . .

[79] 80 rue de Charonne, 11th, 01.43.67.38.29. MÉTRO: Faidherbe-Chaligny, Ledru-Rollin, or Charonne. OPEN Tuesday to Friday for lunch and dinner. Monday dinner only. CLOSED Saturday and Sunday. www .septime-charonne.fr ▪ $$

Le 6 Paul Bert

EVEN THOUGH I'VE LIVED IN PARIS FOR A VERY LONG TIME and go out at least five nights a week, there are still a few restaurants I always look forward to going to again and again. Bistrot Paul Bert in the 11th Arrondissement is one of them. I've loved this place ever since the first time I stepped in the door six years ago, because it's such a studiously perfect example of a genus very dear to my heart, the Paris bistro, *bien sûr*. This place isn't some sort of forgotten off-the-radar cat-sleeping-on-a-pie restaurant, though, but instead is an exactingly rendered summary of everything the whole world imagines when it thinks of Paris bistros, from the saucy service to the zinc bar and wonderfully assorted (but again mostly artfully styled) flea-market-enriched decor, and a menu that's meant to be a primer of great bistro dishes but which truth be told, somewhat undershoots this mark for lacking many *plats mijotés*, or long-simmered stews and casseroles like boeuf bourguignon or coq au vin. Instead, most of the cooking at

Bistrot Paul Bert consists of prepped starters and à la minute grills, and it's still very good indeed.

To be sure, I've had good and less good meals at Bistrot Paul Bert, but I have such profound respect for and confidence in owner Bertrand Auboyneau, who also owns the very good L'Écailler du Bistrot seafood restaurant a few doors down from Bistrot Paul Bert, that when I heard he'd opened Le 6 Paul Bert, a sibling to the original Bistrot Paul Bert, I picked up the phone and booked immediately. Arriving at this very handsome new restaurant, we were promptly seated by a charming young waitress.

The menu came as a surprise. It consists of an assortment of small plates in the idiom of such recently opened Paris restaurants as Pierre Sang Boyer or Roseval, but these rather cryptically written-up compositions—as is true at Septime and many other new Paris restaurants— are described haiku style as lists of their ingredients. They sounded great, so we quickly decided to go with the dinner menu of three plates and dessert. We negotiated the who was getting what, and then with a bottle of one of my favorite white Crozes-Hermitage wines (Les Bâties from Dard et Ribo) and better bread than I've eaten from baker Jean-Luc Poujauran in a long time to keep us happy, I mused on a more immediate dilemma—should I say hello to fearsome *Le Figaro* food critic François Simon, who was sitting at the table next to me, or desist for fear of calling attention to him if he was hoping to remain as assiduously anonymous as possible? I decided to desist, and this decision made, it was very easy to relax in this exquisitely decorated and well-lit room. With a small selection of groceries up front and a service bar, young Québécois chef Louis-Philippe Riel and crew cook in a small open kitchen at the head of the room, and tables come in a variety of different sizes, including a rectangular one for six up front.

Our first two dishes—my "ravioli" of daikon radish, chopped raw beet, tangerines, and oysters in a delightfully gentle citrus vinaigrette, and Bruno's grilled squid in an herb oil coulis with baby salad leaves—were beautifully conceived, intriguingly referencing the collective culinary imagination of young chefs around the world. While very much his own creations, these gastronomic miniatures indicated that Louis-Philippe Riel is doubtless aware of what colleagues including David Chang (Momofuku, New York City) and René Redzepi (Noma, Copenhagen) are doing, to say nothing of other young Turks in Paris, including Gregory Marchand at Frenchie, James Henry at Bones, or Braden Perkins at Verjus. To wit, these plates were sort of raffishly elegant, exhibiting a suave play of acidities and different textures, and packed some powerful pleasure with the freshness of exquisitely sourced produce.

Bruno's next dish, rollmops (herring) with a cucumber pickle, pickled scallion, beets, and cream, leapt back across the Atlantic to the deli traditions of Eastern seaboard cities at the other end of the steamboat-borne East European diaspora a century ago, especially to New York and Montreal, and was really fascinating for being framed by Paris, a city where Ashkenazi dining traditions have been fading for a long time. I liked my chunky veal tartare, too, although the seasoning was off balance due to too much mustard oil. Both dishes were worldly, well prepared, and, in the context of Paris today, shrewdly daring. Or in other words, anyone who knows what's cooking in New York, Copenhagen, and other cities right now might not find these preparations especially original, but in Paris they're politely changing the gastronomic conversation, and that's a good thing.

With the arrival of our third course, something fun and unexpected happened: I suddenly found myself in the presence of the first "dude food" I've ever eaten in Paris. People in other cities are actually a tad weary of this David Chang cum M. Wells style of eating, but for me, an assimilated Parisian, it was bracing and delicious. Bruno let me taste his succulent pork belly with baby clams and Japanese artichokes (*crosnes*, in French) and it was terrific—an immaculately conceived and cooked little still life that just left you wanting more. My barbecued pork on a carrot crêpe sounded sort of awkwardly effete, but on the other hand I love meat, smoke, everything fried, most fats, and anything that's crunchy and edible. Like many people these days, I'm trying to eat more healthfully, but without sacrificing taste, and this is why I loved getting a pass with the carrot crêpe, which was really nicely seasoned root veg mash with some good crusting. So Louis-Philippe knows how to do North American dude food to suit a European sensibility, and that's an impressive gastronomic hat trick.

· ·

DON'T MISS: The menu here changes constantly, but chef Louis-Philippe Riel has a special talent with seafood and pork.

IN A WORD: This excellent contemporary French bistro is a game-changer for Paris. Chef Louis-Philippe Riel has the really long gastronomic antennae needed to cook in the context of what's happening in other cities right now, along with a nascent but accomplished cooking style of his own and impressively solid kitchen skills.

· · ·

[8O] **6 rue Paul Bert, 11th, 01.43.79.14.32.** MÉTRO : **Faidherbe-Chaligny.**
OPEN **Tuesday to Friday for lunch and dinner. Monday dinner only.** CLOSED
Saturday and Sunday. • **$$**

Le Train Bleu

IT WASN'T UNTIL I ARRIVED IN PARIS THAT I REALIZED I
was starving for grandeur. It's not that there wasn't any in
New York City, the hub of the tentacular metropolis in which
I grew up—Grand Central Station remains one of my favorite
buildings in the world, and the quiet exultation associated with
crossing its vaulted limestone concourse is one of my earliest
memories—but it wasn't until I got to Paris that I learned what
grandeur was really all about.

On a frosty January evening in 1975, I lugged my much
loathed tweed-sided American Tourister suitcase up the stair-
case leading to Le Train Bleu after reading in *Let's Go Europe*
that it overlooked the main hall of the station and was one of
the most beautiful restaurants in the world. I couldn't afford to
eat there, but the guidebook tipped me off that I could at least
afford a coffee.

Coming through the doors, I was stunned by a vision of the
nineteenth-century opulence that had made Paris the envy of
the world. Waiters in black tie and fitted black waistcoats, most
of them with mustaches, raced through the room bearing trays
overhead, a few shiny potted palms offered a hopeful suggestion
of imminent southern luxuriance, and the vaulted ceiling with
balmy pastel scenes alluded to the cities you could exchange
Parisian grit and gray for—Antibes, Marseilles, Nice, and Men-

ton, among others. Rock crystal bud lamps punctuated lavish gilt floral moldings, the herringbone oak parquet stretched for what seemed to be at least a mile, and the various quadrants of the dining room were demarcated by massive oak-framed banquettes.

Taking it all in, I forgot my rain-dampened ski jacket and my fear that the $300 in my wallet might not be enough to travel comfortably from Paris to Athens and back over the course of a month. My coffee came, and when I noticed a tiny chocolate wrapped in gold foil on the edge of the saucer, my heart melted. So this was Paris, a place where a pauper could become a prince for a few francs. The mingling smells of tobacco smoke, roast lamb, perfume, sweat, wine, an odd and ancient whiff of coal smoke, vinegar, and drawn butter made me wildly happy, and when I dug into my pocket for a cigarette, I was startled by sulfur and looked up to find that the bartender with the pencil mustache and finely oiled streaks of hair stretched over his bald dome was waiting to light my smoke. "C'est magnifique, Le Train Bleu, n'est ce pas?" he said with a grin.

Almost twenty-five years later, on a warm April Sunday night, something bit me and I invited Bruno to dinner here. En route, I qualified the excursion: it was unlikely that the food would be very good, and the place was likely to feel wilted on a Sunday night—it might even be almost empty—but a stiff shot of grandeur would do us both good before the onslaught of a busy week.

So we arrived and were met with a jolly welcome and shown several possible tables before deciding to sit at the head of the busy dining room near a window overlooking the station's main concourse. Flanked by a Russian family on one side and two Dutch businessmen on the other, we sipped Champagne and were mutually surprised by the restaurant's gracious and solid service.

Bruno subsequently spotted the husband of his psychiatrist, a well-known French actor dressed in a crumpled black velvet jacket, being fawned over by the waiters, and we wondered where his shrink, "Le docteur de ma tête" (his head doctor), might be, perhaps in their country house in Provence on this long weekend.

We ordered smoked salmon, saucisson de Lyon (pork sausage studded with pistachios) with warm potato salad, steak tartare, and, with some reluctance—the actor's roast lamb served in thrilling rare slices tableside from a silver-domed gueridon was very tempting—guinea hen with buttered Savoy cabbage and a garnish of Morteau sausage, plus a nice bottle of Delas Saint-Joseph, a reliably suave red Côtes du Rhône.

In the meantime, we were both impressed by the handsome cheese tray purveyed to the Dutchmen, who made more than the most of it, and it was fun to watch the waiter pouring hot chocolate sauce from a silver-plated teapot with a side-mounted spout over two plump ice-cream-stuffed profiteroles for the Russian ladies and explaining to their men that the bottle of Saint James rum brought to table with the baba au rhum wasn't for drinking but for sprinkling on their sponge cakes, which were flanked with fat vanilla-bean-flecked rosettes of whipped cream. I said nothing to Bruno but cautiously decided that we might actually eat well.

And I was right. My saucisson—five thick slabs of sausage covering a full dish of parsley-and-oil-dressed baby potatoes— was delicious, as was Bruno's thick slice of smoked salmon with a side of lentils, mixed salad greens, and whipped cream, which, we agreed, would have been improved by a bit of horseradish.

The next surprise was that Bruno's steak tartare was prepared tableside—the waiter splashed olive oil and an egg yolk into a deep glass bowl, added capers, parsley, and chopped onion, plus dainty dashes of Tabasco and Worcestershire sauce—Bruno had ordered it doux, or not too hot—and then folded in the coarsely ground beef, kneading it all together and then transferring it to a plate, where he formed a tidy pattie. Decent fries and a side of salad accompanied the meat. My guinea hen was moist, nicely crusted, and flavorful, and even if someone had been a little heavy-handed with the white peppercorns in the cabbage, it was a very satisfying dish. The profiteroles were surprisingly good, too, and coffee came with a tiny meringue and a miniature chocolate bar that reassured me that even if the computerized female voice announcing TGV departures below was woefully current, this grand monument to everything that ever made France such an irresistible destination had barely changed at all.

Mind you, this is not a gourmet destination but rather a place to wallow in timeless Gallic grandeur and have a decent feed while doing so. And as I observed during this meal, the magnificence of this restaurant, a place unique in the world, continues to leave children, pensioners, and everyone in between absolutely awestruck.

· · ·

IN A WORD: Even if you're not about to board a train, the nineteenth-century splendor of this magnificent restaurant at the Gare de Lyon is worth seeking out for its surprisingly decent cooking and spellbinding decor.

DON'T MISS: Saucisson de Lyon with warm potato salad; smoked salmon; pied de cochon (breaded pig's foot); veal chop with wild mushroom lasagne; steak tartare; roast leg of lamb; baba au rhum; vacherin; profiteroles with hot chocolate sauce.

. . .

[81] Gare de Lyon, place Louis-Armand, 12th, 01.43.43.09.06. OPEN daily for lunch and dinner. www.le-train-bleu.com ▪ $$$

Au Vieux Chêne

"I DON'T SEE ANYTHING WRONG WITH HAVING SLEPT WITH both sisters. In fact, it's rather amazing how different they are in bed," chuffed the man, apparently an architect on the basis of his mane of curly red hair and elaborate titanium-framed eyeglasses. Marie-Odile and I exchanged raised eyebrows. "Mais bien sûr" ("But of course") Marie-Odile said, and the woman sitting on the other side of us, who'd also overheard the architect's declaration to a bunch of colleagues, laughed out loud at Marie-Odile's sardonic verbal dart. "That crew really needs to go back to the drawing board," Marie-Odile whispered to me, nodding her head at the architects. And then, "When did everyone find out about this place? I've never seen Hermès scarves in here before."

Food as good as chef Stéphane Chevassus's never remains a secret for long, so this dark horse of a bistro in a residential corner of the outlying 11th Arrondissement has become a word-of-mouth address among the creative tribes of Paris—filmmakers, producers, photographers, artists, writers, architects, and designers. The menu makes a few alluring promises right up front, since chef Chevassus, ex–Michel Rostang and Guy Savoy, states that he uses only the freshest seasonal produce from the most ecologically correct farmers. There's nothing precious about this manifesto, either, since his goal is food that's as naturally delicious as possible, right down to the last petit lardon (little bacon bit). What these good intentions don't convey, however, is the unself-conscious sincerity of the cooking. Quite simply, Chevassus and his crew know and love food and wine and earnestly want you to have a great meal. But as the sign on the wall that says "A day without wine is a day without sunshine" gives away, this is a happy, easygoing place with a homey decor created by antique enameled advertising signs, soft lighting, a big zinc bar inside the front door, and stenciled nineteenth-century floor tiles.

I loved my simple starter, a terra-cotta ramekin filled with a coddled egg, a few strips of smoky piquillo pepper, and some frizzled slices of country ham, and Marie-Odile's langoustine tails rolled in crispy browned angel's hair pasta and garnished with fresh mango slices were superb, too. Though Chevassus's elegant pigeon sautéed with Chinese cabbage and garnished with galangal-spiked mushrooms is a favorite, I chose a snowy filet of cod with chive-dressed potatoes as my main course, and it was perfectly garnished with olive oil and brined lemons, the latter being one of the best and most popular French borrowings from the North African kitchen, since pickling concentrates and mellows the fruit. Marie-Odile's monkfish with lentils in a creamy shellfish sauce was outstanding, too, but both of us looked on longingly as our neighbors were served two whole, deliciously crusted legs of baby lamb, which came to the table sliced on wooden chopping boards with sides of salad and pommes dauphinoise.

"It was a great experience. I had lots of sex and saved a lot of money, plus the food's wonderful, but after three years in Sydney you miss the rest of the world," said a woman at the

architects' table. "Maybe I should try Sydney, then," quipped Marie-Odile, just as her dessert and my cheese course from Alléosse, one of the city's best cheesemongers, was served. She loved her rhubarb and strawberries with almond milk, and my Loire Valley chèvre, Saint-Félicien, and Roquefort were superb. "Australia does sound like it has its advantages, but I could never give up these cheeses," I replied. "And I'm not going anywhere until I've been back here to try that lamb," said Marie-Odile. You shouldn't either.

IN A WORD: Located in the rapidly gentrifying 11th Arrondissement, this is a stylish bistro serving excellent contemporary French cooking. A welcoming atmosphere and intelligent, friendly service in a pleasant old-fashioned dining room with a certain funky charm make this place well worth going out of the way for.

DON'T MISS: The menu here changes regularly, but outstanding recent dishes include coddled egg with roasted piquillo peppers and grilled country ham; langoustines wrapped in angel hair with fresh mango; quail with green asparagus and oven-dried tomatoes; monkfish with lentils and shellfish sauce; cod garnished with olive oil and preserved lemons; roast agneau de lait (baby lamb) with salad and pommes dauphinoise; lamb shoulder in date juice on a bed of braised spinach; pigeon sautéed with Chinese cabbage with a side of galangal-seasoned mushrooms; strawberries and rhubarb with almond milk.

. . .

[82] 7 rue du Dahomey, 11th, 01.43.71.67.69. MÉTRO: Faidherbe-Chaligny. OPEN Monday to Friday for lunch and dinner. Saturday dinner only. CLOSED Saturday and Sunday. www.vieuxchene.fr • $$

Le Villaret

IN THE CONSTANT CHURN OF THE NEW, SOME EXCELLENT Paris restaurants fall between the cracks. As I was reminded by a superb dinner at a sidewalk table on a balmy May night, Le Villaret is one of them. Though it doesn't generate much buzz, it's quite simply one of the city's best bistros.

Le Villaret's been around for a while and in fact was one of the first tables to take a serious contemporary approach to bistro cooking. To wit, the talented chef, Olivier Gaslain, serves bistro dishes that are cooked with the same care, precision, and imagination as anything you'll find in a haute cuisine restaurant, and the service is friendlier and more engaged to boot.

As the funky old working-class Oberkampf (the name is that of a French industrialist of German descent best known for creating toile de Jouy, one of the most famous French textile prints) neighborhood of the 11th has grown younger and trendier, Le Villaret has become something of an anomaly, a serious table in a part of town where the most popular restaurants serve pennywise spins on ethnic eats—Latino, Brazilian, North African—and sound tracks are de rigueur. Still, even though we were early, this place filled up completely on a Wednesday night, and many of its well-dressed customers, quite obviously from other parts of Paris, arrived by cab, a sure sign of an address with seriously good word of mouth.

Some came from even further afield, including the deeply tanned mother and father from Philadelphia and Miami who were dining with their Paris-based son. His brother from New York was also on hand, which led me to guess that they were in Paris for an important family occasion. "Okay, sweetheart, she's very nice, but would she ever be willing to live in the U.S.? You can't stay over here forever, you know, and the kids, when they come, they should learn English," said Mom, and an impending wedding became clear. The groom-to-be continued to dutifully translate the menu for his parents and brother before he answered her question. "She wants to live in Israel," he said while leafing through the wine list. "Israel? What's wrong with Philadelphia? Or Miami? And what are joues de lotte again?" "Monkfish cheeks." "Who knew fish have cheeks? Do they smile, too? And so tell me, what's wrong with Philadelphia? Or Miami?"

Elsewhere in the half-timbered dining room, a solitary French woman executive read a neatly folded copy of Le Monde between courses, there were several besotted young couples on dates, and everyone else seemed to be wearing neatly pressed linen on the occasion of the year's first really warm night.

Since I've become enough of a Parisian that people watching is one of my favorite pastimes, I love sidewalk dining, and for this, Le Villaret is ideal, since the rue Terneaux has little car traffic but a constant motley stream of Parisians on foot. Just as Hugh and I were served our first courses, the concierge of the building in which the restaurant is located trundled by with the big, recently emptied green plastic garbage bins that are one of the city's less acknowledged emblems. A stout older woman with salt-and-pepper hair in a pine-tree-print rayon housedress, she paused and looked at our plates. "Bon appétit, Messieurs. Il est très bien, ce cuisinier" ("He's good, that cook").

My tangle of seared girolles mushrooms and finely sliced baby squid served in a shallow white bowl and flecked with tiny bits of parsley and garlic was superb, and when Hugh finally stopped ranting about his boss at UNESCO, he tucked into his homemade terrine de tête (pig's head cheese, also known as brawn, and made from meat recovered from the animal's head after boiling) with wild asparagus and girolles and rolled his eyes. "This is just so good, which is why I always bring friends from Brisbane when they come to town. Everyone in Australia's always going on about how great our cooking is. And it is, but you'd be hard put to find anything this wonderfully funky and old-fashioned even in Sydney or Melbourne."

My firm, fleshy monkfish cheeks—these fish do have cheeks, and they're prized meaty morsels—had been pan-seared before being posed in a pool of smoky bacon-flavored bouillon with first-of-season peas, and the contrast between the smoke, the sweetness of the peas, and the light crusting on the fish was delectable. Hugh's boneless jarret de veau (veal shank) came with tender sliced baby carrots and artichokes in a lemon-brightened, stock-dashed sauce of Isigny cream (Isigny in Normandy is reputed for the quality of its cream and is also the ancestral seat of a famous American with French origins, Walt Disney).

My cheese course was a stunner, presented in a wooden case with four shelves filled with chèvres, Coulommiers, Camembert, and a deliciously nutty Comté. Hugh's first-of-season cherries were sautéed in salt butter and brown sugar and served with a huge dumpling of buttery mascarpone cream, a truly sublime dessert, and as we were dawdling over coffee, I heard the woman from Philadelphia and Miami over my shoulder. "You know what, dear, this food's just too good to be ruined by your wedding. Let's talk about it again tomorrow," said Mom, a wise lady with the right priorities.

IN A WORD: Hidden away in the trendy Oberkampf district, this friendly, well-run contemporary French bistro serves outstandingly good food and is a real dark horse on the Paris restaurant scene.

DON'T MISS: Winter vegetables in chicken stock with foie gras; asparagus and artichokes in bouillon with a poached egg; terrine de tête with wild asparagus and girolles mushrooms; lotte (monkfish) cheeks with baby peas in bouillon; roast chicken with cabbage in Arbois wine sauce; roast shoulder of lamb with white beans and potatoes; strawberry and raspberry soup with a salt-butter sablé (shortbread biscuit); sautéed cherries with mascarpone cream; pear clafoutis.

. . .

[83] **13 rue Ternaux, 11th, 01.43.57.89.76.** MÉTRO: **Parmentier.** OPEN **Monday to Friday for lunch and dinner. Saturday dinner only.** CLOSED **Sunday.** • **$$**

THE RISE AND FALL OF
THE PARISIAN BRASSERIE

. .

THE AFFAIR MAY BE WANING, BUT THIS DOESN'T DIMINISH my pleasure in remembering that in 1986 it was love at first bite.

Returning from three exhausting weeks of work in Italy to Paris and an apartment in the Latin Quarter where I'd spent only one night—I'd left for Milan the day after I moved in—I gazed disconsolately at the contents of my refrigerator: a bottle of duty-free aquavit, the Danish spirit distilled from caraway seeds—a houseguest gift I'd yet to open—a flat half bottle of white wine, and a jar of anchovies from the previous tenant.

No possible recipe came to mind using these ingredients, so I looked up a pizza delivery place. When I called to order, I was told, "We're not delivering tonight. Il neige." It's snowing. I'd slept all afternoon that Sunday after getting home and so was surprised when I went to the window and saw that the city was covered with deep snow, with more falling so fast and furiously that I could barely see the Sorbonne across the street.

I had three choices. I could drink a large glass of aquavit and nibble an anchovy or two; I could bundle up and set out in search of an open restaurant in a neighborhood I didn't know; or I could toss in the towel and jump back into bed. I sat by the window and watched the snow coming down on a fast diagonal into the pretty amber penumbra of a streetlight and pondered. Though tempted by the last option, it seemed sort of lame to duck a first chance to learn something about my new neighbor-hood. So I had a fortifying shot of aquavit and went out to see what I could find.

Under its white mantle, the city was still, stately, and stunningly beautiful. I walked to the corner without passing another soul and turned left toward the busy boulevard Saint-Michel. A few more steps and I stopped to peer through the lace curtains and streaky patches of condensation in the windows of a well-lit restaurant. It wasn't very busy, but it was open and the small dining room was attractive. I'd only gone around the corner

from my apartment, which didn't seem very adventurous, but I liked the looks of the place and there'd be other occasions to go further afield.

As I'd lived in Paris for only a few months, my French was wobbly and I wasn't yet comfortable eating alone in restaurants, so I rather dreaded going inside. Happily, my apprehension was misplaced. When I asked the owlish maître d'hôtel in a black spencer jacket by the door if they had a table for one, he smiled and said, "Mais bien sûr!" ("But of course!"). Settled on the saggy red leatherette banquette of a table for two, I sipped a kir (white wine with crème de cassis) and studied the menu, quietly pleased with myself for not having settled for an anchovy supper. "Quel sale temps!" ("What awful weather!") said the older waiter in a snug white apron when he came to take my order—a gratinée (onion soup), filet of beef with béarnaise sauce, frites and sautéed spinach, and a half bottle of the house Bordeaux.

Just a table down from mine, a pretty older woman with a spray of glossy red plaster cherries pinned to her gray dress and some soft white curls peeking out from under her gray angora cloche hat caught my eye and smiled. "Bonsoir, Monsieur!" she said, and I felt completely at home in this small dining room with a cantilevered mirror running the length of one wall just below the ceiling and a tarte Tatin sitting on the bar next to stairs that led to the téléphone et toilettes in the basement. The older man sitting across the table from her appeared to be reading a book, but then I realized that he was reading to her and craned to see if I could read the title of his volume—Baudelaire, the great romantic French poet. With the possible exception of one rainy afternoon in a coffeehouse in Cambridge, Massachusetts, I'd never seen anyone reading poetry to his dinner companion before, and it struck me as desperately romantic.

I'd folded open next to my fork one of the two rolled-up *New Yorker* magazines I'd brought with me, but it was more fun looking around. There was still a crust of snow melting on top of the big fur hat of the beautiful young woman across the aisle. Her boyfriend, who wore a heavy black cabled turtleneck and a peacoat, ate his salad without taking his eyes off her, pausing between bites to draw hard on his cigarette. I watched as she was served what I later learned is choucroute garnie, sauerkraut garnished with sausages and other cuts of pork. She nibbled a shaggy forkful of shredded cabbage, then speared a brick-colored sausage with her fork and held it out to her boyfriend. He bit it in half, she laughed, and I looked away.

My soup came and was piping hot under a cap of molten, blistered cheese, which released a puff of potent steam redolent of beef and onions when I pierced it with my spoon. My Bordeaux was good, too, maybe even a little too good, since I had only a glass left by the time my steak arrived. After the nice old lady and her husband a table down bade me good night, I noticed they'd barely touched their bottle of excellent Médoc and was thinking about how good it would be with my meat. "Est-ce-que vous avez jamais vu une bouteille du vin volante?" asked the waiter who'd just served me. It took a minute to register what he'd said— "Have you ever seen a flying bottle of wine before?" "Non," I said, thinking I must have misunderstood him. He looked left and right like someone pantomiming a burglar, then quickly picked up the bottle of Médoc and planted it on my table. "Et maintenant vous l'avez vu!" ("And now you have!") he said with a wink.

I'm sure I blushed, surprised by his solicitude and also dumbstruck by my luck in finding this place. Dessert—a big slice of tarte Tatin with a spoonful of crème fraîche that was udderly (*sic*) fresh and rich—was superb, too, and after I paid my bill, I thanked the maître d'hôtel effusively for a lovely meal. He shrugged. "Mais c'était mon plaisir de vous recevoir, et bien sûr, Monsieur, il n'y rien au monde qui est mieux que les brasseries de Paris" ("But it was my pleasure to have you here tonight, and of course there's nothing better in the world than the brasseries of Paris"). I asked for a card, and during my brief walk home in the snow, I gloated in anticipation of revealing my find the next day at the offices of the style-driven publishing company where I was the newest editor.

Every Monday we had a meeting to discuss the weekly churn of assignments and suggest new story ideas. I let everyone else go first, waiting to show them that the new boy in town had a card up his sleeve. When my turn came, I announced I'd discovered a remarkable restaurant in the Latin Quarter, a discreetly stylish, convivial place with great food, a fascinating crowd, and wry, complicit service. "Sounds fantastic—what's it called?" asked the bureau chief. I fished the card out of my pocket. "Brasserie Balzar." "Oh, please!" they groaned almost in unison, with someone adding, "Alec, it's one of the best-known restaurants on the Left Bank."

I was crestfallen for a few minutes, but later, in the quiet of my office with the door closed, I retrieved my initial elation, knowing that this solitary meal on a snowy night in Paris was something I'd treasure for many years to come.

So I learned that the Balzar was one of the great brasseries of Paris and eventually what a brasserie is, something I couldn't have told you that day either. All I knew after my dinner at the Balzar was that it channeled everything I love about Paris, its spellbinding chic and animation, a certain metropolitan glamour at once winsome and wistful, and most of all the nonchalant but reflexive sensuality that quietly exhilarates daily life in the French capital. Looking at Monet's paintings of Parisian streetscapes, I'd often wondered where and what the throngs on those damp gray boulevards ate or exactly what sort of room you'd have stepped into if you were hungry after shopping and caught in a rain shower at the end of the nineteenth century. So now I knew, later understanding that the brasserie is a quintessentially Parisian institution, usually a large and lavishly decorated place where waiters in long white aprons worn over fitted black jackets dash around delivering big aluminum trays studded with freshly shucked oysters bedded on mounds of crushed ice, along with steaks, grilled fish, and choucroute garnie.

Invented during the second half of the nineteenth century to feed the hungry crowds generated by the growing affluence of industrializing France, the birth of tourism, and a boom in rail travel, brasseries, along with their cozy, homey cousin, the bistro, are the culinary incarnation of Paris. Swift-paced but friendly, anonymous but communal, they offer up a vivid palette of intriguing vignettes of urban life and its endless possibilities along with a gastronomic refrain of how culinary pleasure can be casually democratic in one of the world's greatest cities—for a long time, brasseries weren't expensive.

The first Parisian brasserie was founded by Frédéric Bofinger in 1864. Bofinger's innovation was to serve draft beer with plates of charcuterie (sausage and cold meats), and after his simple place became popular, he remodeled and dressed it up, feeding a new rage for this format of restaurant.

Many of the most famous Parisian brasseries were founded by Alsatians who sought refuge in the capital following the disastrous Franco-Prussian War (1870–1871), when a big slice of eastern France came under the rule of the German kaiser. In Alsace, brasseries, or breweries in French, served their suds in taverns adjacent to their brew halls with plates of charcuterie and hearty local specialties like choucroute garnie, juniper-berry-scented sauerkraut garnished with sausage and various cuts of pork, including kassler (pork loin), bacon, and occasionally a jarret (pork knuckle). Choucroute garnie became the Parisian brasserie's signature dish, but brasserie menus evolved to suit Parisian tastes. Since Parisians love oysters, many brasseries added bancs à huîtres—sidewalk oyster stands where écaillers, or oyster shuckers, in blue cotton smocks and rubber boots prepare lavish trays of fresh oysters and other fresh shellfish, including langoustines, shrimp, mussels, cockles, and clams.

From 1890 to 1930, dozens of brasseries opened in Paris. Since they served similar menus, their owners competed by commissioning jaw-dropping decors, initially in the same resplendent, sinuously floral Art Nouveau style used by the Paris Métro and, after World War I, in the sleek Art Deco style that epitomized the Roaring Twenties.

Perhaps the apotheosis of the brasserie occurred on December 20, 1927, when a festive crowd of some 2,500 Parisians thronged the boulevard Montparnasse on the Left Bank in the 14th Arrondissement to celebrate the opening of La Coupole, the sprawling brasserie that became one of the epicenters of Parisian life during Les Années Folles, or the Roaring Twenties. The merrymakers got through some 1,200 bottles of Mumm Champagne that night, and the sleek new Art Deco–style brasserie's reputation was instantly made as the Parisian press reported their bibulousness, the mountain of oyster shells produced by the opening-night feast, and the naughty shenanigans of the arty crowd that then made Montparnasse its home.

During my first years in Paris, I was a regular at many of the city's storied brasseries. I loved their liveliness, they served late and on weekends, and they were perfect for dining with a gaggle of friends and blowing off the blues on a Sunday night over a plateau de fruits de mer. Everyone I knew had their favorites. Christa liked La Coupole and Julien, while Christophe was keen on Le Vaudeville, Jutta had a soft spot for Brasserie Flo, and I loyally championed the Brasserie Balzar. I also liked Saturday lunch at Brasserie Lipp and Au Pied de Cochon for onion soup after hours—this brasserie serves round the clock, twenty-four hours a day—and Chez Jenny for its good choucroute on a wintry day.

Though I never went to any brasserie with lofty gastronomic expectations—they were more about good times, people watching, and simple, tasty food—I couldn't help but notice when their quality started slipping at the beginning of the 1990s, by which time most of them had been bought up by two restaurant groups, Groupe Flo and Frères Blanc. After founder Jean-Paul Bucher bought Brasserie Flo in 1968, Groupe Flo became a brand name that gobbled up one grande old dame after another, including La Coupole, Bofinger, Julien, Le Boeuf sur la Toit, Le Vaudeville, Terminus Nord, and Brasserie Balzar, while the rival Frerès Blanc's stable ran to Au Pied de Cochon, Charlot, La Lorraine, Chez Jenny, Le Procope, and l'Alsace, among others.

Eventually, however, the mediocrity of the brasseries' food became so flagrant that I reluctantly concluded that most of them had become unfrequentable. The problem was that behind the scenes, it was accountants, not cooks, who edited the menus and order sheets and who eliminated expensive kitchen staff by enthusiastically embracing almost every industrial shortcut devised by France's booming food service industry, notably mass-produced sauces, soups, salads, frites, and desserts. Every year, it seemed, there was less real cooking going on behind the swinging doors, maybe just a bit of grilling, frying, and reheating.

Today, there are only a handful of brasseries left that warrant a meal by a traveler to Paris, and the luster of the city has been slightly dimmed by their decline. Still, a new generation of inspired restaurateurs seem to have recognized that this profoundly Parisian institution is as valid today as it was a century ago, and the opening of Lazare, an excellent new brasserie at the Gare Saint Lazare, has raised my hopes that the genre will be reborn. I certainly hope so.

PLACE D'ITALIE, GOBELINS, MONTPARNASSE, GRENELLE, CONVENTION

L'Avant Goût

THOUGH IT ENJOYED A BRIEF BLAZE OF COUNTERCULTURE glory in the sixties as a popular address for soixante-huitard types (what the French called the student protesters who tore up the Latin Quarter in May 1968), the pretty La Butte aux Cailles

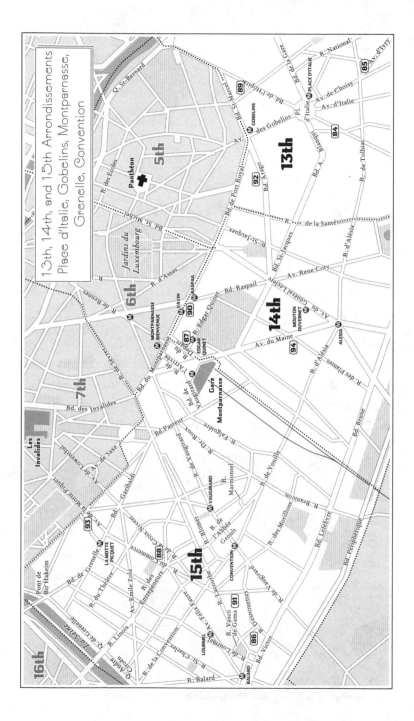

13th, 14th, and 15th Arrondissements
Place d'Italie, Gobelins, Montparnasse,
Grenelle, Convention

5th

6th

7th

13th

14th

15th

16th

Panthéon

Jardins du Luxembourg

Les Invalides

Gare Montparnasse

Pont de Bir-Hakeim

La Seine

Q. St-Bernard

R. des Écoles

Bd. St. Michel

R. d'Assas

R. de Rennes

R. de Sèvres

Bd. des Invalides

Av. de Saxe

Av. de Lowendal

Av. de la Motte Picquet

Bd. de Grenelle

Q. de Grenelle

Q. Branly

Q. André Citroën

R. Linois

R. du Théâtre

Av. Émile Zola

Bd. de Grenelle

R. du Commerce

R. de la Croix Nivert

R. des Entrepreneurs

R. St-Charles

R. de la Convention

R. Balard

Bd. Victor

Av. de Lourmel

R. Vasco de Gama

R. de Vaugirard

R. de l'Abbé Groult

R. Blomet

Bd. Pasteur

Bd. du Montparnasse

R. du Départ

R. de l'Arrivée

Bd. de Vaugirard

R. Falguière

R. Dr. Roux

R. Marmontel

R. de Vouillé

R. des Morillons

R. Brancion

Bd. Lefèbvre

Bd. Brune

Bd. Périphérique

R. des Plantes

R. d'Alésia

R. d'Alésia

Av. du Général Leclerc

Av. René Coty

Av. du Maine

Bd. St-Jacques

R. St-Jacques

R. de la Santé

Bd. Arago

Bd. de Port Royal

Av. des Gobelins

Bd. St-Marcel

Bd. de l'Hôpital

R. de Tolbiac

Bd. A.

Av. d'Italie

Av. de Choisy

R. de la Gare

R. National

Av. d'Ivry

Pl. d'Italie

Edgar Quinet R. Edgar Quinet Bd. Raspail

LOURMEL

GARIBALDI

PLACE D'ITALIE

GOBELINS

MONTPARNASSE BIENVENUE

VAVIN

RASPAIL

EDGAR QUINET

MOUTON DUVERNET

ALÉSIA

VAUGIRARD

CONVENTION

LA MOTTE PICQUET

BALARD

85

89

92

84

90

87

94

93

88

91

86

(Hill of the Quails) neighborhood in the 13th Arrondissement has been quiet ever since these rebels settled down as academics, researchers, artists, and writers and decided they'd rather own stones than throw them. In fact, one of the newsiest things to have happened in this quartier lately was the opening of L'Avant Goût a few years ago. Suddenly, rave word of mouth about chef Christophe Beaufront's cooking meant this off-the-beaten-track part of town had a restaurant that was pulling Parisians from other parts of the city. Beaufront, who trained with Guy Savoy and Michel Guérard, converted an old café into a great-value modern bistro where his husky-voiced wife ran the dining room and the menu ran to edgy dishes like his signature pork pot-au-feu with fried ginger chips. The place quickly became a roaring success—in fact, it was often so noisy you had to shout at your tablemates, a problem since rectified with an acoustically tiled ceiling, and it became tough to snag a table.

I hadn't been for a while but joined South African friends, winemakers from Paarl, who'd come to town with the nearly impossible task of peddling their wares to the French, most of whom still refuse to take any wine but their own seriously, for dinner on a Saturday night. Wedged in between a large table of Franco-Cambodians celebrating a birthday and an elegant older Parisian couple dining with the son of an English colleague and his wife, we ate very well indeed, but not every dish was a success. Ravioli filled with fresh cod in a foamy sauce of shiitake mushrooms were delicious, with an intriguing contrast of textures, but a ball of herbed goat cheese surrounded by radishes, Nyons olives, and broccoli florets in a shallow jar came off like one of those "I hate to cook" recipes you see in women's magazines, and shrimp wrapped in kadif, crunchy Lebanese pastry threads, were bland enough to make eavesdropping on the next table more tempting. It turned out that the natty older gent was a nuclear scientist recruited to teach at Columbia in 1940, just before the Nazis invaded France, and he went to great lengths to point out that the Americans liked Philippe Pétain before the Germans invaded and he became the leader of Vichy France, the Nazi puppet state.

Happily, the main courses showed why Beaufront remains a talent to be reckoned with. A snowy filet of cod had been marinated in herbed crème fraîche before cooking, which made it wonderfully moist, and it was served on a bed of perfectly cooked lentils. Duck breast with date chutney was succulent and perfectly seasoned, and the South Africans loved their pot-au-feu—various cuts of pork, sweet potato, fennel bulb, ginger chips, and a glass of the spicy bouillon in which it had been cooked. Desserts were excellent, too, including melon sprinkled with anisette and garnished with a ball of tarragon ice and a candied sweet potato with pineapple compote. L'Avant Goût may no longer be avant-garde, but it's a very good restaurant that's well worth the trouble of booking the requisite week or two in advance.

IN A WORD: Chef Christophe Beaufront's popular bistro isn't as cutting edge as it once was but it still offers an excellent feed for a very reasonable price. With his creativity anchored by classical training, Beaufront's contemporary French cooking remains extremely appealing.

DON'T MISS: The menu changes regularly here but usually includes Beaufront's signature dish of pot-au-feu de cochon aux épices, braised cuts of pork in a spicy bouillon with sweet potatoes, fennel, and a garnish of fried ginger. Other good dishes include ravioli with fresh cod in shiitake mushroom sauce;

piquillo peppers stuffed with smoked haddock rillettes; cod marinated with crème fraîche and herbs with lentils.

. . .

[84] 26 rue Bobillot, 13th, 01.53.80.24.00. MÉTRO: Place d'Italie. OPEN Tuesday to Saturday for lunch and dinner. CLOSED Sunday and Monday. www.lavantgout.com ▪ $$

Le Bambou

FOR DAYS AFTER MY FIRST MEAL AT LE BAMBOU, I WAS desperate to return to this crowded, chaotic restaurant in an inconvenient corner of the 13th Arrondissement, Paris's most Asian neighborhood. I'd been invited by my friend Nancy, a Vietnamese-American woman living in Washington, D.C., with the caveat that you go there only to eat, since they don't let you linger at the table or take reservations and the decor and lighting are awful. She was correct on both points. Still, the chance to see her and meet her Paris relatives was too good to pass up, and so I found myself in this superb Saigon hash house in excellent and truly charming company.

What Nancy didn't prepare me for was some of the best Vietnamese home cooking I've ever had outside Vietnam, a country I've visited a half-dozen times. As the only non-Vietnamese at the table, I was shy about ordering but plunged in with a gluttonous request for Vietnamese ravioli, green papaya salad with shrimp, and a big bowl of pho topped with sliced nems (deep-fried spring rolls). Everything I ordered was exceptional, sending me back to the tiny Saigon restaurants where I'd squatted on knee-high fluorescent plastic stools and stuffed myself with some of the best food I've ever eaten. The dishes her family ordered were spectacular, too, including Saigon-style omelettes brimming with bean sprouts, squid and shrimp, and duck in a caramelized sauce with fresh pepper. Our meal occurred in a blur, as almost every meal here does, but as someone who passionately loves Vietnamese food, I'm more than willing to put up with the noise and often slapdash service. So come early or very late, and in as large a number as possible to sample some of the best Vietnamese home cooking in the French capital.

· · ·

IN A WORD: Though it's as crowded, noisy, and uncomfortable as a rush-hour subway car, this clamorous Vietnamese in Paris's modern "Chinatown" serves some of the best Vietnamese food in town. Just remember that you're going on a tasting mission rather than in search of a cosseted dining experience.

DON'T MISS: Vietnamese ravioli; green papaya salad with shrimp; bo bun (nems and pho, or beef noodle soup); Saigonese omelette.

. . .

[85] 70 rue Baudricourt, 13th, 01.45.70.91.75. MÉTRO: Tolbiac. OPEN Tuesday to Sunday for lunch and dinner. CLOSED Monday. ▪ $

Le Beurre Noisette

DURING THE LAST TWENTY YEARS, THE QUIET, LEAFY, residential 15th, Paris's largest arrondissement, has become terra nova for young chefs looking to hang out their own shin-

gles. Why? Rents are lower than in the single-digit arrondissements, this prosperous part of town provides an instant clientele, and Parisians from other neighborhoods have gotten used
to traveling to offbeat corners of the city in search of great eating at good prices, all of which means that Le Beurre Noisette,
the talented chef Thierry Blanqui's amiable modern bistro, is
booked solid at lunch and dinner.

It's an address that's very much worth the trek, too, since
Blanqui, who trained at La Tour d'Argent and with Christian Le
Squer at Ledoyen, easily awed the palates of my friends Bert and
Noël from Los Angeles. They have two of the world's most experienced and discerning palates, but on a hot summer night, none
of us thought we were very hungry until our first courses arrived.
"This is terrific," said Noël after tasting her fresh pea soup with
mint and crumbled bacon. My sautéed supions, or baby squid,
were spectacular, too—lightly crusted by perfect grilling and seasoned with fresh herbs, shallots, lemon, tomato cubes, and sesame

seeds. Burt loved them, too, and Bruno's pressé de jarret de porc et foie gras, terrine of boned pork shank with duck foie gras, was brightened by a small salad of mixed baby lettuce leaves and fresh herbs, and the contrast between the unctuous foie gras and chewy meat was sexy and elegant.

Our waiter clearly enjoyed Bert's impeccable French and punning sense of humor, and the small, pretty dining room buzzed with the pleasure of people having a good meal. Main courses were excellent, too. Two of us had the John Dory, which was served whole, a welcome change from the lamentable Parisian trend to fish filets, with a medley of vegetables à la Greque, or poached in vinaigrette, and drizzled with a vividly herbal pesto sauce, and roasted cumin-dusted lamb shoulder was garnished with Moroccan-style preserved lemons, a lovely foil for the rich meat. Noël, one of the lustiest eaters I know, reveled in her assorted pork plate, which included a juicy chop, a length of grilled Auvergnat sausage, a slice of grilled smoked filet and crispy bacon topping a mound of mashed potatoes. While we were eating our chocolate quenelles with crispy carmelized tuiles, or cookies, and soup of summer fruit, we heard a woman at the next table tell the waiter, "Vous êtes au bout du monde ici, mais la cuisine vaut vraiment la peine de venir" ("You're at the end of the earth, but the cooking's really worth the effort of getting here"), and we agreed wholeheartedly.

IN A WORD: Though it's a chore to get here, chef Thierry Blanqui's bright, fresh contemporary French bistro cooking is worth it. Moderate prices, friendly service, a nice selection of wines, and a few sidewalk tables during the summer add to the pleasure of a meal here.

DON'T MISS: The menu changes regularly, but dishes to look for include sautéed rolled tête de veau (calf's head) with salad; sautéed supions (baby squid) with tomatoes; shallots, herbs, and sesame; cold pea soup with bacon; calf's liver with Parmesan polenta; pressé de jarret de porc et foie gras terrine (pork and foie gras terrine); John Dory with légumes à la Grecque (marinated vegetables) and pesto; grilled pork plate; roasted lamb shoulder with cumin and preserved lemons; quenelle de chocolat (scoops of chocolate-and-cream mousse); summer fruit soup.

. . .

[86] 68 rue Vasco de Gama, 15th, 01.48.56.82.49. MÉTRO: Lourmel. OPEN Tuesday to Saturday for lunch and dinner. CLOSED Sunday and Monday. ▪ $$

La Cerisaie

AMONG THE REGIONAL KITCHENS THAT ARE THE GLORIOUS bedrock of French cooking, the food of southwestern France is the brawny macho towel snapper. This is why French presidents feel compelled to demonstrate their love of such emblematic dishes as cassoulet (preserved duck, sausage, pork, and white beans) and the region's more arcane dishes, including roasted ortolans, or tiny birds, that the late François Mitterrand gobbled down under legally dubious circumstances on his last New Year's Eve.

The gastronomic posturing of politicians to one side, Parisians love this rich, hearty cooking, too, which may seem surprising in view of recent trends to healthier, lighter eating. When it comes to good food, though, they have a contrarian weakness for such atavistic pleasures, which is what explains the popularity of La Cerisaie.

To be blunt, this broom closet of a restaurant in Montparnasse isn't for everyone. There's no decor to speak of (a forgivable sin in my book when the food's this good) and the tiny room gets as crowded as a rush-hour Métro car at both lunch and dinner. But if overpacked dining rooms don't put you off, you're in for a treat, since the young chef Cyril Lalanne's take on the southwest is tender, sincere, and absolutely delicious, and his wife, Maryse, who runs the dining room, is a charming, good-humored hostess.

I'm still savoring the foie gras raviolo in pot-au-feu bouillon I had the last time I had dinner here. The single tender pasta pillow contained a stunningly good piece of foie gras, and the bouillon was rich, deeply flavored, and ancestral, just the sort of simple, consoling pleasure you might be served at a farmhouse supper in the heart of la France profonde. My friend Nanette's white asparagus from Les Landes was brilliantly bathed in a parsley-infused oil that amplified its natural bittersweet taste, and her spiced goose breast with roasted peaches was sublime, too. I loved my tuna with piperade (the Basque garnish of sautéed peppers, onions, and tomatoes), and my baba à l'Armagnac was a clever regional riff on the classic sponge cake in rum syrup and came under an alluring cloud of whipped cream. Nanette claimed that her chocolate tart with coffee ice cream was worth the price of her airplane ticket from New York and booked for dinner again two nights later after we paid our bill. "If I ate like this every day, I'd be shopping at Lane Bryant [the plus-size clothing shop] before I knew it. But hey, summer's still a few months away and I've always said I want a man who loves me for my mind," she said over after-dinner coffee at Le Select, a café just a few streets away in the heart of Montparnasse.

.   .

IN A WORD: Though this minuscule restaurant in Montparnasse isn't a good place to share secrets, it's worth putting up with the elbow-to-elbow seating for chef Cyril Lalanne's excellent southwestern French cooking.

DON'T MISS: The menu changes constantly here, but dishes I've enjoyed include squash soup; velouté de châtaigne et foie gras (chestnut and foie gras soup); terrine de confit de canard (preserved duck terrine); sautéed foie gras with polenta; tuna steak with piperade (Basque garnish of tomatoes, onions, and peppers); sautéed goose breast with roasted pears; roasted pigeon dove with foie-gras stuffed ravioli; baba à l'Armagnac; chocolate tart with coffee ice cream.

. . .

[87] 70 boulevard Edgar-Quinet, 14th, 01.43.20.98.98. MÉTRO: Montparnasse. OPEN Monday to Friday for lunch and dinner. CLOSED Saturday and Sunday. www.restaurantlacerisaie.pagesperso-orange.fr ▪ $$

Le Cristal de Sel

ONE OF THE CONUNDRUMS OF WRITING ABOUT FOOD IN PARIS is that I rarely have the opportunity to return to a restaurant I've already reviewed as often as I'd like. Why? The insistent churn of the new and the fact that I won't do more than five dinners out during any given week (weekends I not only love to stay home and cook but also want to give my girth a respite) mean that it's hard to get back to places I'm already familiar with. So I was delighted when a friend who lives in the 15th Arrondissement recently suggested dinner at Le Cristal de Sel.

I liked this contemporary French bistro a lot when it opened three years ago, but hadn't been for a while, so this was the occasion to see how talented chef Karil Lopez's cooking had evolved. Lopez trained with Eric Frechon at Hôtel Le Bristol before he went out on his own, and I was charmed by his cooking, which is notably sincere, delicate, and almost maternal, all quite unusual for a male chef.

On a warm spring night, it was a pleasure to come up from the Métro on the rue du Commerce, since it's one of the sweetest streets in Paris and has a real village feel, convivial but peaceful. The restaurant, just remodeled after a fire, looked terrific, with bamboo floors, generously spaced zinc-topped tables with comfortable wooden chairs, good lighting, and votive candles burning inside niches gouged into pink blocks of salt.

Meeting Corinne, another expat scribbler who loves great food as much as I do, we studied the chalkboard menu while it was helpfully explained by Damien, the charming maître d'hôtel here. Lots of things looked good, but I started with shrimp wrapped in crisp phyllo pastry and served with a delicious tandoori-spiced mayonnaise and a lively salad of fresh herbs, and Corinne went for the crab lasagna, which was terrific—perfectly dressed crabmeat with fava beans and fine matchsticks of Granny Smith apple that shot the dish through with a pleasant tanginess. Next, langoustine-filled ravioli in a foamy nage on a bed of buttered cabbage for me—a dish that was at once comforting and quietly luxurious—and for her, a perfectly cooked gray mullet in a brilliant sauce of rosemary honey that played perfectly with the delicate flavor of the fish, accompanied by green asparagus tips and squid rings. "You know, it really gets on my nerves when people naysay this city's gastronomic reputation as faded. The fact that you can easily find food of this caliber in a quiet residential neighborhood for reasonable prices is why Paris still runs circles around any other major Western city," my friend stated emphatically, and I heartily agreed.

She finished up with fromage blanc from Jean-Yves Bordier, who produces France's best butter and a range of other excellent dairy goods, in Saint-Malo. It came with a choice of homemade jams—Lopez loves making jam. I had a nice aumônière (the fancy name for a crêpe folded up like a purse) filled with apples that had been cooked in salted caramel, a wonderful dessert. Le Cristal de Sel is a charming restaurant and a place I look forward to returning to again soon.

· ︵ ·

IN A WORD: Talented Karil Lopez's stylish but relaxed contemporary bistro is a perfect example of how Paris's legendary gastronomic laurels are being renewed, with elegant Gallic discretion, by a new generation of chefs.

DON'T MISS: Pastry-wrapped shrimp with tandoori mayonnaise, grilled pork with sweet potato and wild garlic puree, langoustine-filled ravioli on a bed of buttered cabbage in a langoustine nage, cheese course by Jean-Yves Bordier, riz au lait (rice pudding) with lemon cake, aumônière filled with stewed apples in salted-butter caramel sauce.

. . .

[88] 13 rue Mademoiselle, 15th, 01.42.50.35.29. MÉTRO: Commerce. OPEN Tuesday to Saturday for lunch and dinner. CLOSED Sunday and Monday. www.lecristaldesel.fr ▪ $$

Les Délices de Shandong

BEFORE I SING THE PRAISES OF THIS VERY GOOD RESTAURANT, it seems appropriate that I present my credentials as a critic of Chinese cooking. The regional kitchen of Shandong, an eastern coastal province of China, is one of what the Chinese call their country's "eight cuisines." Alas, as much as I feel qualified to write authoritatively on the American, French, Italian, and other Western kitchens, it's best to admit that my knowledge of Chinese cooking is based very much on a personal primal reaction to what tastes good. Oh, to be sure, I grew up eating and loving "Chinese" food of a sort: Sunday night takeout meals from the excellent West Lake, a Cantonese place in downtown Westport, Connecticut, next to the public library, or the also good Golden Door restaurant, in a shopping center on U.S. 1, were a treat I craved as a suburban child with an insatiable hunger for new tastes and flavors, textures, and ingredients.

Mom would save the printed takeout menu from one order to the next in a drawer next to the wall-mounted phone in the kitchen, and around 7:00 p.m. on a Sunday, I'd poke my head around the corner every five minutes to see if she was sitting at the kitchen table filling out the menu before calling in the order. Mom understandably felt she deserved a night off from shopping and cooking for a family of six, so Sunday was often takeout night, and the promise of favorite foreign foods blunted the habitual melancholy I always felt on the seventh day of the week.

We almost always had the same things, too: egg drop soup, egg rolls, shrimp toast, barbecued pork spare ribs, fried rice, moo goo gai pan, egg foo yung, shrimp with cashew nuts and broccoli, I think, which no one ever ate, with a grand finale of fortune cookies that no one actually ever ate, either. These were great kitchen-table meals with plastic packets of the hot Chinese mustard my father liked, sweet duck sauce, and soy sauce, the food packed in waterproof white paper boxes with thin wire handles. Little did I know that most of what we were eating was heavily Americanized Cantonese cooking.

So my real education in the Chinese kitchen began with a first few revealing forays to restaurants in Boston and New York's Chinatowns as a college student. It galloped forward when I was living on the Upper West Side at the time when a blaze of hot peppers was being unleashed on Manhattan by the sudden popularity of Szechuan cooking, making everyone rather embarrassedly aware that China had regional kitchens like, well, Italy, and that what we'd thought was Chinese food was tasty but timid stuff edited down to politely tempt our American palates.

I don't think I advanced much, however, until Joe Fox, the brilliant and courtly editor for whom I was editorial assistant at a New York publisher, invited me out for lunch on a long-ago birthday. It was a beautiful fall day, but in the space of a sudden ill-defined social occasion I labored to create conversation that I thought would interest him as we walked up Third Avenue and then cut over to Shun Lee Palace. There I tasted my first Peking duck, a dish so good I stopped caring if my conversation with a man my father's age seemed smart or interesting and just ate, greedily wrapping duck, crispy duck skin, finely slivered scallion, and cucumber in hot rice-flour pancakes smeared with plum sauce. This was one of the best things I'd ever eaten, and I just couldn't stop. "The best companions at the table have real appetites," Joe said elliptically as we were walking back to the office, and if I was momentarily worried he'd found me dull, I also had the rest of our lunch in a brown paper bag to look forward to for dinner, and I instinctively knew I'd have plenty of time to puzzle over his bon mots in the years to come. Suffice it to say that I finally figured out that he loved good food and, as the father of four sons, had enjoyed the relaxed quietude of sharing a really good meal with someone else who was also immersed in the pleasure of the plate.

So am I a reliable judge of Chinese cooking? I'd like to think so, and this is why I'd say that if you were only going to go to a single Chinese restaurant in Paris, it should be Les Délices de Shandong, where I've eaten many times with Bruno, who lives in terror of red pepper (or, if money is no object, perhaps the Shang Palace at the Shangri-La Hotel).

I love the low prices and animation of the brightly lit dining room at Les Délices de Shandong, though, and, accustomed to the usual turn-those-tables brusqueness of Asian restaurants in the 13th Arrondissement, I'm always surprised by the polite service. Every time we go, however, we have to negotiate a meal for two very different appetites. I always want the tangy smoked-pork-and-cabbage-stuffed dumplings, while Bruno avoids fire by ordering noodles in sesame sauce.

Main courses require similar calculation. Even though it's good, I have little interest in the shrimp with cashews he likes, craving instead the sauté of smoked pork and tofu with lots of red peppers, celery, Savoy cabbage, and a few fermented black beans. I also like everything offal, a house specialty. So with all due respect to the long-suffering Bruno, I'd recommend coming here with someone who loves hot food and who also doesn't mind noise. One way or the other, this is a terrific restaurant. And to think it all started out over egg rolls with duck sauce in Westport, Connecticut.

IN A WORD: If you want a Chinese fix while in Paris, or are curious to discover the fiery lesser-known cuisine of the Shandong region, join a mostly Chinese crowd around the Formica tables in this simple, noisy, popular place.

DON'T MISS: Smoked-pork-and-cabbage-stuffed dumplings; eggplant with garlic; tripe with peppers; smoked pork and tofu sautéed with peppers; sautéed eel; Chinese-style steamed turbot.

. . .

[89] 88 boulevard de l'Hôpital, 13th, 01.45.67.23.37. MÉTRO: Campo-Formio. OPEN Thursday to Tuesday for lunch and dinner. CLOSED Wednesday. www.delicesshandong.com • $$

Le Dôme

AH, LA VIE EN ROSE: IT'S THE METROPOLITAN LURE OF THE French capital, a spontaneous mixture of chic, frivolity, and sensuality that fills Paris-bound jets from cities around the world daily, and amazingly enough it's still around if you know where to find it. Long after the flame has guttered out in Montparnasse, where the cafés and restaurants of legend are now the province of tourists and clock-watching out-of-towners (the last train or Métro is the virtual hourglass on many of their tables) who still cast themselves as hopeful voyeurs at a now much diminished bohemian scene, this grand and stunningly extravagant seafood restaurant keeps the magic alive.

It's shocking, really, to pay such prices for fish, but then it would be foolish not to. Here, the price of admission is not only a really good meal but a brief passage on a grand old barge that remains one of the best addresses in town for anyone who wants to eat from Neptune's spear.

Assiduous students of Paris history will quickly tell you

that the Dôme wasn't always this way, a place where most of the blazers tossed over chair backs are cashmere and the janitor finds a Christian Dior scarf or two under the tables as he brooms the room before heading for the night bus. No, the Dôme was once a smoky workaday café where people like Trotsky jotted down their oddball and sometimes dangerous ambitions on paper napkins while nursing a coffee for hours as a way of escaping the cold reality of cheap lodgings.

This high-minded seditiousness is long gone, but a whiff of bohème still hovers over the cultivated Parisians—politicians, artists, and editors—who come here to change the world for at least the time it takes to devour a big tray of some of the best oysters in the city or tuck into a perfect sole meunière line-caught off the Ile d'Yeu on France's Atlantic coast. This is why I knew it would be perfect for dinner with my friend Catherine, a book editor from New York. She also loves fish, and I think Paris is the best city in Europe for anyone who loves seafood, which is explained by the fact that France makes a fetish of freshness and has two coastlines, Atlantic and Mediterranean, both of which yield up different delicacies, as well as a proud, hardworking fleet of traditional fishermen who catch fish by line rather than in nets, which damage them.

Catherine instantly took to the glittery crowd and festive atmosphere created by the busy dance of serious waiters in aprons and the wonderful burble, my favorite metropolitan noise, of people eating well. We ate delicious tiny, sweet pink shrimp from Brittany with flutes of Champagne, and then, knowing I could filch one or two, I left the meaty Gillardeau oysters to Catherine and ordered ormeaux (abalone) as my first course. Fished off the Channel Islands, they rarely appear on Paris menus because they're quite rare and not easy to cook, since too much heat makes their succulent flesh rubbery. Here they were exquisite, cut into fine strips and gently sautéed in salted butter with a bit of garlic and parsley. Catherine's sole was "sublime," and my freshly salted cod with aïoli (garlic mayonnaise) was gorgeous. To oblige our waistlines, we split a slice of the very good fresh raspberry tart for dessert and enjoyed the wake of a truly excellent meal over coffee.

IN A WORD: Few restaurants in Paris offer a better take on classical French seafood cooking than this soignée grande dame in Montparnasse. Its catch of the day is just that, and it's impeccably cooked and served in a simple but festive setting that thrums with a worldly crowd having a good time. You'll also net a big bill here, but it's worth it.

DON'T MISS: Breton shrimp; oysters; smoked salmon; ormeaux (abalone); sole meunière; grilled sea bass; roast turbot with hollandaise sauce; raspberry tart.

· · ·

[90] 108 boulevard du Montparnasse, 14th, 01.43.35.25.81. MÉTRO: Vavin. OPEN daily for lunch and dinner, except during July and August, when it's closed on Sunday and Monday. ▪ $$$

Jadis

TO MY SATISFACTION, THE SAME SCRIPT PLAYS OUT THE SAME way every time I meet friends for a meal at Jadis, a storefront place with a simple décor of dove-gray and white walls with Bordeaux-red trim in a quiet residential neighborhood on the outskirts of the 15th Arrondissement. Invariably, they arrive late and exasperated, muttering about the godforsaken location and grumbling that the food had better be good, and then a couple of hours later, I see them off into the night cooing with pleasure over chef Guillaume Delage's superb cooking and the pleasure they feel at having "discovered" such an offbeat destination.

Delage is one of the hardest-working and most intensely focused young chefs in Paris today. His dual-speed menu lets you choose between bistro classics or a smaller range of dishes that are the fruit of his experience and imagination. If I've eaten superbly well when opting for Delage's own creations, I have a weakness for his traditional dishes for the simple reason that they're so brilliantly executed.

Jadis is a place I often take visiting food professionals, and my most recent meal was with a delightful couple of chefs who live in Providence, Rhode Island, and who have a Paris pied-à-terre and very demanding palates. There were four of us at the table: two had the delicately acidulated oyster velouté (creamy soup) with shavings of Cantal cheese that accentuated the milkiness of the bivalve and the other pair a very original salad of Puy lentils with bulots (sea snails) and chunks of smoked bacon. I loved the unexpected but brilliant detail of pairing cheese with oysters to fully express the milky nuances of their taste, and also the way Delage had created a bridge of vegetal richness between the earthy lentils and iodine-bright snails by cooking them in the same rich court bouillon. Next, a spectacularly good roast shoulder of lamb served in a copper casserole on a bed of fat white Mogette beans with black olives and sun-dried tomatoes and ocean perch in a rather timid but pleasant wasabi sauce with a delicious side of fluffy sweet-potato purée, and then the grand finale, Delage's sublime warm bittersweet chocolate soufflé for dessert.

· · ·

IN A WORD: In an out-of-the-way location in the 15th Arrondissement, a talented young chef has created an outstanding bistro that offers a changing roster of contemporary French and traditional bistro dishes.

DON'T MISS: The menu changes regularly, but dishes not to miss include pâté en croute, lamb's feet and button mushrooms in lemon sauce, terrine of artichokes and foie gras, oyster velouté, shrimp with black rice, roast shoulder of lamb, île flottante à la pistache, and dark chocolate soufflé.

. . .

[91] 208 rue de la Croix-Nivert, 15th, 01.45.57.73.20. MÉTRO: **Porte de Versailles.** OPEN **for lunch and dinner Monday to Friday.** CLOSED **Saturday and Sunday.** www.bistrot-jadis.com ▪ $$

L'Ourcine

EVEN BEFORE YOUR FIRST COURSE ARRIVES, L'OURCINE, IN a funky corner of the 13th Arrondissement that reminds me of New York's West Village, is a very easy place to like. The

staff is smart and friendly, and the rustic dining room with generously spaced wooden tables, a small bar inside the front door, and a tomettes (clay tile) floor cue you that chef Sylvain Danière has an auberge state of mind. What you wouldn't know unless you'd been here before, of course, is just how wonderful the food is going to be. Danière trained with the bistro wizard Yves Camdeborde, the chef whose La Régalade, now under new management, daringly renewed the idiom of Paris's most beloved restaurant category, but if he remains one of Camdeborde's most loyal lieutenants, chef Danière is starting to spin his own style, with very exciting results.

The chalkboard menu changes regularly, but Danière's precise, passionate cooking doesn't miss a beat, whatever you choose. On a balmy May night, my meal led off with a complimentary shot glass of scallop mousse topped with tiny fried croutons (these tasty little bread cubes are a signature of the Camdeborde school if ever there was one), and the way the mousse concentrated the flavor of the mollusk was more exciting than anything I'd eaten in a haute cuisine restaurant for a long time. The cute young couple from Houston next to us ordered exactly the same first courses as we did—the terrine of fennel bulb and foie gras for me and the young Texan woman and a pressé of pig's head (meat from the pig's head pressed into a loaf) for my friend Arnaud and the young woman's husband—and all of us loved these fully flavored but delicately composed dishes. The fennel bulb and foie gras terrine was real art, with fresh chervil separating each layer of perfectly cooked liver and vegetable, and an accompanying crouton-topped salad of slivered beet root, mizuna, and other herbs brightening the dish. Arnaud, a professor of physics who, given my knowledge of his field, is, happily, very interested in food, insisted that I try his pig's head terrine, which was crunchy, earthy, and exact.

Our main courses were exquisite, too—brandade de cabillaud, Danière's riff on the famous garlicky potato dish of whipped potato and salt cod from the southern city of Nîmes, and a juicy breast of duckling on a très vieille France (old-fashioned France) bed of baby peas and wilted lettuce. I found it interesting that a young Turk like Danière was doing a dish as classically French as the duckling breast, and when I mentioned it to the waiter, he said, "Mais c'est ça que les gens veulent manger aujourd'hui" ("But this is what people want to eat these days"). While chatting with the young Texans, edgy types with a lot of curiosity about the world, the birthday cake of a Bolivian politician visiting France and his table of seven was served, and after the whole room had applauded, everyone was offered a glass of Champagne. L'Ourcine is that kind of place, profoundly Parisian, charmingly low key, generous, and dedicated to good times and great food.

· ·

IN A WORD: An outstanding contemporary bistro with relaxed, friendly service, an appealingly rustic atmosphere, and chef Sylvain Danière's remarkable market-inspired cooking.

DON'T MISS: Danière's menu evolves constantly, but dishes to pounce on if they're available include fennel bulb and foie gras terrine; spider crab ravioli with endives; rabbit rillette with pickled girolles; yellow pollack roasted in olive oil; stuffed chicken breast with Chinese cabbage; brandade de cabillaud; duck breast with baby peas and lettuce; filet mignon of pork with whole garlic cloves and baby potatoes; chocolate quenelles with saffroned crème anglaise.

. . .

[92] 92 rue Broca, 13th, 01.47.07.13.65. MÉTRO: Les Gobelins or Glacière. OPEN Tuesday to Saturday for lunch and dinner. CLOSED Sunday and Monday. www.restaurant-lourcine.fr • $

Le Père Claude

THOUGH THE DECOR'S MORE REMINISCENT OF AN AIRLINE office than a Paris bistro—think a bland modernity with no real character—it's hard not to love Claude Perraudin's place, which explains why it's one of the most popular restaurants on the Left Bank. Perraudin, a contemporary of the better-known Guy Savoy, the late Bernard Loiseau, and Jean Ramet, learned his trade with some of France's greatest chefs, including Jean and Pierre Troisgros, Michel Guérard, and Paul Bocuse, but instead of reaching for the stars, he contented himself with firing up a gas rotisserie in this tranquil corner of the Left Bank and serving generous portions of the sort of rustic country comfort food city dwellers crave.

Thirty years later, this place is still packed with a mix of silk-stocking locals and politicos. Both the conservative former president Jacques Chirac and the socialist former prime minister Lionel Jospin are fans, evidence that carnivores' credentials are still essential to the credibility of French politicians and that perfect roast chicken crosses party lines. Sport stars like Zinédine Zidane, smart tourists, and UNESCO staff fill out the crowd, which has become noticeably younger since Perraudin put his son-in-law in charge.

Interestingly, the plancha (flat metal grill) is now as busy as the rotisserie, a sign of the popularity of fish in Paris.

The menu is tweaked seasonally, which meant a terrific sauté of first-of-season cèpes (porcini mushrooms) as a starter on an early September night. Girolles mushrooms with Iberian ham were another excellent starter, but go with a first course only if you're really hungry, since portions are huge. The meat—beef, rack of lamb, and one of the best veal chops in town—comes to the table with perfect mashed potatoes, while tuna steak rides in on a mound of nicely seasoned salad greens.

The pot-de-crème au chocolat, velvety chocolate custard, is the favorite dessert, and service is brisk. The wine list is uninteresting, but the house Bordeaux is easy drinking with this food. Reservations are essential. It's hard to think of a better choice for a Sunday night or a relaxed meal during the week when you're suffering from a surfeit of gastronomy and crave just meat and potatoes.

IN A WORD: Great Gallic comfort food is the draw at this rotisserie-oriented bistro with a stylish clientele that often includes a famous face or two.

DON'T MISS: Escargots; terrine maison; frogs' legs sautéed with garlic and fresh herbs; entrecôte with mashed potatoes; veal chop, assiette du Père Claude (rotisseried beef, lamb, veal, chicken, and blood sausage); clafoutis aux pommes (baked custard with apples); crème brûlée.

. . .

[93] 51 avenue de la Motte-Picquet, 15th, 01.47.34.03.05. MÉTRO: La Motte-Picquet. OPEN daily for lunch and dinner. www.lepereclaude.com • $$

Le Severo

THOUGH THERE ARE STILL A COUPLE OF GOOD STEAK houses at La Villette, once the site of Paris's abattoirs, there's no need to trek to that remote part of town for some really good meat when you can head for this charmer with a jaunty red-painted facade in Montparnasse.

Owner William Bernet once worked at the famous Nivernaises butcher shop in the 8th Arrondissement, and he really knows his viande, which is why this place is packed to the rafters daily with a very stylish Left Bank crowd. As I discovered the last time I went, it's also the perfect place to ponder the delicious contradictions that compose a perfect Parisienne.

Two tables down from us I spotted Loulou de la Falaise, who was once Yves Saint Laurent's muse. With her caramel-colored hair, lapis lazuli blue eyes, and Roman nose, the delicate de la Falaise is a character out of a Colette novel, which is why it didn't really surprise me to see her tucking into a thick, juicy steak with a big side of mashed potatoes. At a time when many women seem to subsist on bowls of wispy greens, it was almost erotic to watch her happily wielding her knife on a gorgeous piece of beef and seemingly oblivious to all of the tediously clinical tenets of "healthy" eating.

"I'm hoping there's a message here," said my TV producer friend Alison from Los Angeles. "If she can eat like that and look so good, maybe I can, too?" My favorite meals are those with no limits of any kind, so I was delighted when Alison threw caution to the winds and we shared a big platter of mixed charcuterie to start—andouillette (sausage made from the pig's colon and intestines), rosette (dried pork sausage), and sublime homemade pork rillettes (pork preserved in its own fat). "This place has a great buzz," said Alison as she smeared a slice of baguette with rillette. "And it's pretty, too." Next, I indulged my inner caveman with a superb mound of impeccably sea-soned steak tartare topped with chopped shallots and capers and accompanied by a massive heap of hot, crisp, freshly made frites. Getting into the scheme of things, Alison plumped for the boudin noir, a blood pudding sausage. "This is incredible. I haven't eaten like this since I used to visit my grandmother in Pennsylvania," she confessed. "You know, in L.A., it's all about the fear of gaining weight, and then there's the bizarre relation-ship to food that so many entertainment industry people have. Every other person in my office brings their lunch—sprouts, tofu, and fruit—which is just fine, but all of this fabulous lusti-ness goes missing. Do you know what I mean?" I do indeed, which is why I unpacked my suitcase twenty-two years ago and never went home. I doubt you'll be surprised to hear that we both ordered chocolate mousse for dessert and that it was superb. "Oh, well, I've been thinking about breaking up with my boyfriend anyway," said Alison as she tucked into the airy wave of cream and dark chocolate.

· ⸛ ·

IN A WORD: This very popular bistro in Montparnasse is car-nivore central—it serves some of the very best meat in Paris. It's also a terrific address for wine lovers, since more than two hundred bottles are listed on the chalkboard wine lists that line the walls of the pretty tiled-floor dining room with its glossy wooden tables set with crisp linen napkins.

DON'T MISS: Salade de chèvre (goat cheese on a salad of mixed baby greens); terrine de pot-au-feu; charcuterie plate; côte de boeuf; steak tartare; foie de veau (calf's liver); boned pig's foot; boudin noir (blood sausage); crème caramel; chocolate mousse.

. . . /

[94] 8 rue des Plantes, 14th, 01.45.40.40.91. MÉTRO: Alésia or Mouton-Duvernet. OPEN Monday to Friday for lunch and dinner. CLOSED Saturday and Sunday. • $$

FASHION PLATES:
A BRIEF HISTORY OF
STYLISH DINING IN PARIS

· ·

PARIS WAS THE CITY THAT MADE EATING FASHIONABLE
and perfected not only the art of public preening but two of the
most popular metropolitan settings for participating in this
urban rite, the café and the restaurant. Le Procope, the city's
first café, opened in 1685, and the popularity of its convivial
atmosphere quickly inspired dozens of similar establishments.
Within a century, idling over a coffee or other refreshment and
watching the world go by had become a quintessential part of
stylish Parisian life.

Paris was also the birthplace of the modern restaurant. In
1765, a soup maker named Boulanger opened a shop near the
Louvre where he sold bouillons restaurants, meat-based con-
sommés intended to restaurer, or restore, a person's health.
Given the heartening motto over the door of his restaurant,
"Come unto me, all ye that labor in the stomach, and I will
restore you," it's not surprising that Boulanger's place was a hit.

The first restaurant, in the modern sense of a place where
people sit at tables during fixed serving hours and order from
a multichoice menu, was La Grande Taverne de Londres,
opened by Antoine Beauvilliers in 1782. According to the great
French gastronome Jean-Anthelme Brillat-Savarin, the reason
it became a roaring success was that it was "the first (restau-

rant) to combine the four essentials of an elegant room, smart waiters, a choice cellar, and superior cooking." Fed by growing affluence and leisure time, the Paris restaurant scene blossomed during the nineteenth century, with certain tables becoming de rigueur places for fashionable types to see and be seen.

The Café de Paris on the boulevard des Italiens and Restaurant Durand at the corner of the Place de la Madeleine and the Rue Royale pulled a glittering crowd of artists, politicians, and writers, including the novelists Anatole France and Émile Zola, but the most celebrated restaurant of nineteenth-century Paris was the Café Anglais on the boulevard des Italiens. Its crowning moment was the Three Emperors Dinner, served on June 7, 1867, to the Russian tsar Alexander II, his son the tsarevich (later Tsar Alexander III), and King William of Prussia, the first emperor of Germany, when they were in Paris to attend the Universal Exposition of 1867. The Paris press breathlessly reported every aspect of their meal, including the menu the trio

dined on—soufflés with creamed chicken, filet of sole, scalloped turbot, chicken à la Portugaise (with tomatoes, onions, and garlic), lobster à la Parisienne (medallions of decorated, gelatin-glazed lobster), duckling á la Rouennaise (boned slices of its breast, its grilled legs, and liver in a red-wine and liver sauce), and ortolans (tiny songbirds known as buntings that are roasted and eaten whole), all washed down with eight different wines. Needless to say, on the heels of this feast the renown of this restaurant spread to every corner of the globe, and it became an essential reservation for not only modish Parisians but elegant foreigners visiting the capital.

When the Ritz Hotel opened in 1898, it set a new standard for both luxurious accommodations and refined dining. Chef Georges-Auguste Escoffier's superb cooking delighted everyone from the crowned heads of Europe to the writer Marcel Proust, who dined here almost nightly after his beloved mother died in 1905. The beau monde's other favorite address during La Belle Époque (1890–1914) was Maxim's, which almost more than any other single Paris address codified the modern idea of the fashion restaurant, or a place that people went to see and be seen as much as they did to eat and drink.

After World War I, the burgeoning popularity of movies and the rise of celebrity journalism turned a handful of Parisian restaurants, including Fouquet's, Lapérouse, and La Coupole, all of which are still in business today, into household names as the haunts of the rich and famous. Television further fueled the public interest in restaurants patronized by celebrities, as did the heady nightlife and fashion scene in Paris during the 1970s, when fashion designers started to become as famous as the clients they dressed. By the 1980s when I moved to Paris, the complicit code-pendency between the international fashion tribe—models, journalists, designers, hairdressers, photographers, and stylists—and the aristocrats, socialites, and movie stars whose patronage could make or break them meant that restaurants you went to because they were fashionable were thriving as never before. Everyone wanted to be in the same big room, and restaurant owners understood the game, too, since a well-circulated photograph of, say, the designer Yves Saint Laurent and his muse Loulou de la Falaise dining at a place brought a cachet that was almost as precious as a Michelin star. At that time, there were two main types of see-and-be-seen tables—old-school places like Le Voltaire, an excellent Left Bank bistro, and funky, individual, off-the-beaten-track places such as Anahi, an Argentinean steakhouse with excellent meat in the appropriate setting of an old butcher shop in the Marais. Aside from the buzz in the room, what all of these places had in common was that they served good food—this was Paris, after all.

Little did I know at the time that this fundamental truth— that even the most fashion-conscious Parisians wouldn't go anywhere where the food wasn't good—was about to be upended by Gilbert and Jean-Louis Costes, a shrewd pair of brothers from the south-central region of the Auvergne, who'd recently opened a very trendy café in Les Halles, the neighborhood surrounding the old main food market of Paris.

The first time I went to the Café Costes, I loved it. In the late eighties, it was boldly, bracingly different from the usual drab, smoky French café, and though I'd never heard of Philippe Starck, now one of the world's best-known interior designers, I loved his decor for this place. Apparently inspired by a Budapest train station, it had creamy walls with dark-varnished wooden tub chairs at round caramel-colored tables, a dramatic mezzanine, and polished aluminum furniture on the terrace out front. Oh, and the food? Forgettable sandwiches, salads, and omelettes, but somehow it didn't matter. The Café Costes was cool, and it was always packed.

By the time it closed in 1994, this café had made the reputations of both Starck and the Costes brothers. On its heels, the Costes launched an eponymous hotel in 1996 that completely recoined the idiom of stylish lodgings. Instead of liveried doormen, there were men in black, and the usual tall oak front desk was replaced by a leather-topped desk softly lit by a lamp with a pleated raspberry-colored silk shade. When I checked in to write it up for a travel magazine, I fell instantly for interior designer Jacques Garcia's lush, Napoléon-III-cum-New-Orleans-bordello decor, but I had a rude shock when I went downstairs for dinner. A beautiful but snake-eyed hostess told me the restaurant was *complet*, full. I protested that I was staying in the hotel, but she just shrugged and walked away. I was dumbfounded. The restaurant wasn't a famous Michelin-starred

table, and no one had told me a reservation would be necessary when I checked in, so I assumed I could just show up and be seated. Wrong.

Eventually I managed to get a table by sidestepping the officious hostess and appealing to her male colleague, and this only confirmed my worst suspicions. The social currency of this place was in-your-face New York–style attitude, period, the end. My high dudgeon aside, the dining room offered some first-rate people watching, but my meal—maybe an arugula salad with Parmesan shavings and perhaps some Thai-style grilled chicken?—was forgettable. Observing the scene that night, it dawned on me, however, that something socially seismic was shifting in Paris. Despite the snooty service and dull food, the room was packed, and from my perch, I watched the hostess raise the blood pressure of hopeful diner after hopeful diner. All she seemed to know how to say was "Non, complet," but then this was the point. With nightlife out of fashion in Paris since the beginning of the 1980s, the Costes brothers had co-opted the New York, and to a lesser degree Parisian, formula of velvet-rope discotheque disdain and applied it to the restaurant.

As someone who passionately loves the conviviality of good food and the weird and wonderful randomness of any roomful of strangers eating together, I found this newly minted and zealously enforced formula depressing. What it said was that appearances matter and food doesn't—what is most important is making the scene, or just being there.

Unfortunately, my consternation seems to have made me part of an unfashionable minority, since today the Costes run several dozen thriving Parisian hotels and restaurants—Georges, atop the Centre Pompidou; Café Marly at the Louvre; L'Avenue on the swanky Avenue Montaigne; and L'Esplanade across the street from Les Invalides among them, and they've all succeeded by baiting the same social hook with an arbitrary and ersatz exclusivity and hiding it in sleek and sexy settings with great lighting by name-brand interior designers. Their success has inspired a whole subgenre of Costes knockoffs, too. These places have become so common that even though I still love arugula, there are days when I suspect you could roof every building in Paris with the amount of the stuff that the Costes's tables run through in a week. I also wonder if the ubiquity of out-of-focus Asian cooking and upmarket fast food like saumon tartare will be the death knell of real French cooking. Why? The first generation of French who haven't had stay-at-home mothers and grandmothers to tutor them in their country's culinary heritage have come of age in a state of gastronomic oblivion and indifference, and the Costes and other restaurateurs who peddle style over substance have appropriated them as happy and perplexingly loyal customers to the detriment of real restaurants, places where the food still comes first and there are real old-fashioned cooks in the kitchen.

The huge success of the Costes empire, along with the proliferation of other superdecorated restaurant-bars where food plays a minor supporting role to decor and atmosphere, has made the fashion restaurant the most visible and successful category of restaurant in many central Paris neighborhoods, too, most notably in and around the Champs-Élysées in the 8th Arrondissement. But the phenomenon has spread to the city's outlying neighborhoods, too. Now, almost every other corner café that closes for a revamp reemerges with a lounge-bar look featuring velvet-upholstered banquettes and low lighting, a disc jockey compilation soundtrack, and a deracinated international menu running to sliced tomatoes with mozzarella—a pretty sad choice in the middle of winter, when the tomatoes come from Belgian or Dutch greenhouses; hamburgers; a few vaguely Asian dishes; and inevitably something with, you guessed it, arugula.

There's some hope on the horizon, however. Fashion thrives on impermanence and the ruthless repudiation of what was only recently coveted. By embracing this process of creative destruction, and even mocking it, the Hôtel Amour, a laid-back but very hip hotel-restaurant in the 9th, has become tremendously popular. It helps, too, that the Amour is a relaxed and reasonably friendly place, and if the menu served in the lobby cum restaurant is simple, it is also pretty good.

A new generation of restaurant-going Parisians seems to have lost interest in the Costes' formula, too. They prefer small-plates dining at trendy bars like the excellent Le Mary Celeste in the 3rd Arrondissement or serious but simple bistros like chef James Henry's Bones.

So it looks like the twenty-year disconnect between food and fashion in Paris is being repaired, since it's becoming fashionable to insist on eating really good food again.

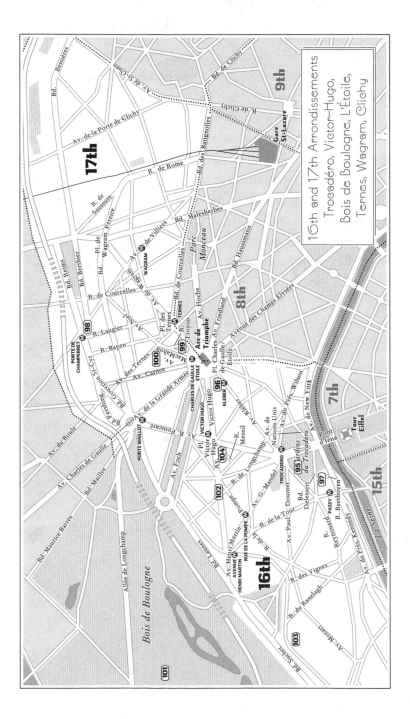

16th and 17th Arrondissements
Trocadéro, Victor-Hugo,
Bois de Boulogne, L'Étoile,
Ternes, Wagram, Clichy

L'Abeille

ON A WARM SUMMER NIGHT, THE FRENCH DOORS OF THE DINING
room at L'Abeille, the gastronomic restaurant at the Shangri-La
Hotel, were open onto the emerald lawn of the hotel's newly
created courtyard garden, and the night sky was indigo as
Bruno and I were finishing our brilliant desserts—fleshy black
Burlat cherries stuffed with a creamy chutney and served with
beer sorbet, a sugar-dusted waffle, and a warm cherry compote for me, an intriguing composition of apricots poached in
their own juices and filled with apricot cream, grilled popcorn
ice cream, and apricot gelée for him. This was the finale of a
three-hour-long meal that was a perfectly scored crescendo of
pleasure, from the stunningly good contemporary French haute
cuisine to the beauty of the dining room itself and the exquisite
service—the staff here have been coached to avoid the tiresome
shirt-cardboard pomp of many haute cuisine dining rooms in

Paris in favor of a warm and spontaneous serving style that is neatly trellised to a respectful grid of formality.

I was musing on the sophisticated palette of flavors in my dessert—the gentle bitterness of the beer sorbet was a superb way of creating a foil to the sweetness of the cherries—when a gentle, shy-looking man, chef Philippe Labbé, who had just cooked our meal, did a dragonfly-like feint at our table as part of the chef's rounds that are often customary in such exalted restaurants. I think he received my fulsome praise with a mixture of mortification and pleasure, but he didn't remain long enough for me to decide. He was swiftly off to the next table, a party of six, where he displayed a touching mixture of anxiety, bashfulness, and delight at hearing their almost operatic expression of how much they'd loved their meal.

The reason, of course, is that Labbé is a serious old-school chef who has no intention of building a gastronomic empire in Paris or anywhere else. No, as we'd experienced during our meal, he passionately loves his work and practices the art of cooking with a ferocious self-exigence that comes across in every dish that leaves his kitchen. His culinary imagination may often be passionate, but he clips its wings with a sincerity, craft, and delicacy that have made him one of the best haute cuisine chefs in Paris since he arrived three years ago from the Château de la Chèvre d'Or in Eze, in the south of France, to man the kitchens of this elegant luxury hotel in the opulent limestone mansion built in 1896 by Napoleon's nephew on a hillside over-looking the Seine. The Bonaparte connection explains the restaurant's name, too, since *abeille* is the French word for "bee," Napoleon's symbol.

You don't just pull a serious, full-fledged haute cuisine restaurant out of a hat, of course, and it's been fascinating to observe L'Abeille evolve into one of the city's best. Beyond setting the stage with well-spaced white-linen-dressed tables, perfect low lighting from wall sconces, and artfully arranged vases of flowers, creating a restaurant is about good casting and developing an *esprit d'équipe* around a shared and deeply under-stood mission. Though it may sound obvious, the goal here is for you to have not only a spectacular meal but a very good time as well, and the success of this ambition was the pleasant back-ground noise of laughter and the Christmas morning sound of surprised pleasure from all over the room that greeted every course. And since haute cuisine dining so often ends up being a laborious chore that pricks your conscience with its astronomi-cal prices while leaving you sort of desperately eager for all of the hidebound ritual to end so that you can go home and relax, this restaurant is a real standout.

Wisely, Labbé keeps his menu short, not only because

everything is cooked to order but also because this allows him to assiduously cook the best seasonal produce France has to offer. Chef Labbé is a gifted classicist—he previously cooked with Bernard Loiseau, Gérard Boyer, and Eric Briffard—but he also has a wily gastronomic imagination that exalts the remarkable produce he works with. That night I began with plump langoustines served just warm on a bed of seaweed-flecked aspic with a tomato sorbet whose gentle acidity amplified the natural sweetness of these luxurious crustaceans, while Bruno tucked into a luminous composition of Breton crabmeat dressed with ponzu and served on a royale, or fine custard, of crab juices with a shellfish gelée and marinated seaweed and cucumber. These dishes may sound elaborate, but they tasted so instinctively logical that they seemed simple, and this is the ruse that makes Labbé's cooking as sensual as it is satisfying.

Next, the best salmon I've ever eaten—line-caught wild fish from the Ardour River in southwestern France, one of the country's rarest delicacies—was impeccably cooked and served on a bed of pureed fresh almonds that emphasized its natural flavors. Bruno loved the tender mauve meat of his roasted Bresse pigeon, which was accented by a fine crust of anise-brightened spices and served with baby turnips and onions that punctuated the richness of the tender bird with alternating notes of astringency and sweetness. L'Abeille has one of the best cheese trolleys in Paris—it's a tantalizing display of several dozen cheeses from Alsatian maître fromagers Bernard and Jean-François Antony that come to the table under glass cloches and are served tableside by waiters with an enthusiastic and encyclopedic knowledge of each fromage.

Walking down the avenue de President Wilson under the chestnut trees after dinner, Bruno could barely contain his enthusiasm. "That was such a good dinner. The food was so light and so interesting without being fussy or pretentious, and best of it all, it was a really good time." Since an haute cuisine meal in Paris is an extremely rare pleasure for being so vertiginously expensive, I think one is entitled to a relaxed and celebratory atmosphere, and by delivering the same in a subtle and shrewdly calculated rejection of the usual withering ceremony connected to great food, L'Abeille has become one of the city's best and most modern restaurants.

·   ·   ·

IN A WORD: Located in the Shangri-La Hotel, chef Philippe Labbé's restaurant L'Abeille is an outstanding choice for a grand-slam experience of the very best French gastronomy.

DON'T MISS: Langoustines with seawater gelée and tomato sorbet; foie gras served as two courses: mi-cuit with a light crust of praline and cocoa and a salad of beets, and cooked in a crust of salt and served with a duck jus; Ardour salmon with almond puree; Aveyron lamb in two services: a roasted saddle with garlic and black shallots with a spiced jus, and lamb sweetbreads with baby fava beans, gnocchi, fresh cheese, and a milk foam; chutney-cream-stuffed black cherries with beer sorbet, a waffle, and cherry compote; poached rhubarb with goat-cheese ice cream, rhubarb gelée with lemon verbena, and a meringue.

· · ·

[95] 10 avenue d'Iéna, 16th, 01.53.67.19.90. OPEN Tuesday to Saturday for dinner. CLOSED Sunday and Monday. www.shangri-la.com • $$$$

Akrame

PERHAPS BECAUSE MANY OF ITS AFFLUENT RESIDENTS OFTEN prefer traditional French cooking to anything more inventive, the elegant tree-lined streets of the 16th Arrondissement are a relatively uncommon setting for gastronomically unorthodox restaurants. This makes Akrame the appetizing exception to the rule. Run by the talented chef Akrame Benallal, French-born but raised in his parents' native Algeria until he was thirteen, this intimate dining room with a cool, mostly black-white-and-gray low-lit contemporary decor has succeeded in seducing a regular following of suit-wearing business diners at noon and then re- laxes a bit at dinner, when it's popular with well-heeled profes-

sional couples from the surrounding neighborhood behind the Arc de Triomphe.

"I think of my restaurant as my atelier, since it only seats twenty-five and every dish is cooked to order," says Benallal, an earnest, hardworking cook who is one of the very rare French chefs of North African origin to make a name for himself. "Since I work in a small open kitchen, I'm in contact with the dining room throughout every service, and this intimacy is important to me, because I receive my guests here as I would in my home. I don't like pretentious restaurants, and I don't think they're modern." Benallal began his Parisian career making pastry at Pierre Gagnaire. His next stop was an apprenticeship with chef Alain Solivérès at Taillevent, and then he went off to Spain to do a stint working for Ferran Adrià at the legendary and now-closed El Bulli.

Returning to France from Spain, he opened his first restaurant in Tours, but the locals there were indifferent to the gastronomic wizardry he'd learned at El Bulli, and the restaurant was not a success. "After Tours, I rediscovered that simplicity is the genius of all great cooking," says Benallal, reflecting on the experience of trying to be too bold in the wrong place at the wrong time, and then adding, "In the end, all of the best food is an affair of the heart. You only cook well if you really want to make people happy."

Today, the Benallal signature is spontaneity and a sort of puckish culinary wit. This was beautifully expressed by the debut dish I had as part of one of his recent tasting menus: "oeuf mimosa," or riced egg yolk and riced egg white on a puddle of fresh mayonnaise and black-bread croutons, a delicious riff on one of the great French bistro classics, oeufs mayonnaise—which also shows how the canon of traditional bistro cooking remains a reference for nervy young chefs like Benallal. In a similar vein, he turns a salad of haricots verts, another bistro classic, into a dramatically different dish by sprinkling them with crunchy black South African marula fruit seeds and garlicky toast crumbs.

"A great dish is often made by a single detail or two," says Benallal, sounding decidedly Escoffier-like and perhaps referring to his own shrewdly angelic dish of steamed line-caught whiting on a sheet of rice-flour gelatin spread with buttermilk and garnished with oxalis, a sour clover-like herb, and nanami togarashi, the Japanese seasoning of pepper, orange rind, and sesame seeds. Nothing about the innocent-as-a-convent looks of this dish prepared me for the complexity of its intriguingly subtle flavors and contrasting textures. Desserts like fresh strawberries with sorrel ice cream and margarita ice offer an amusing coda to this imaginative young chef's sophisticated cooking.

· ·

IN A WORD: Akrame Benallal, a Frenchman of Algerian origins, is winning an ever larger reputation for the clever and very personal contemporary French cooking he does at his intimate storefront bistro in the silk-stocking 16th Arrondissement.

DON'T MISS: Chef Benallal's daily menus evolve constantly, but the best way of discovering his cuisine is through the six-course tasting menus, which showcase his love of seafood and vegetables.

. . .

[96] 19 rue Lauriston, 16th, 01.40.67.11.16. MÉTRO: Charles-de-Gaulle–Étoile, Victor Hugo, or Kléber. OPEN Monday to Friday for lunch and dinner. CLOSED Saturday and Sunday. www.akrame.com ▪ $$$

L'Astrance

CHEF PASCALE BARBOT AND MAÎTRE D'HÔTEL CHRISTOPHE
Rohat of L'Astrance, the most exciting modern French restaurant in Paris, will forever associate me with bread crumbs. Let me explain.

Some ten years ago, I went to dinner one night with no expectations. A London newspaper had asked me to write about Lapérouse, an old warhorse of a restaurant overlooking the Seine on the Left Bank—it was doing historic Paris restaurants, and this one's been around forever. I politely suggested that there might be better candidates, because as far as I knew, this place was still a slumbering tourist table flogging its past: it has several charming tiny private dining rooms with badly scratched mirrors—as the legend goes, these cuts were made by ladies testing the veracity of newly offered diamonds (real diamonds cut glass). The editor was unyielding, so off I went. The stale-smelling dining room was mostly empty on a winter night, and though the young maître d'hôtel was unexpectedly charming and gracious, I was more interested by my friend Anne's gossipy account of a recent visit to Los Angeles than I was by the menu.

Then we were served an amuse-bouche, or complimentary starter, which the maître d'hôtel described rather unpromisingly as "milk soup." The small shot glass was warm to the touch, and there was something black and brown, fine and grainy floating on the frothy surface of the soup. I tasted it and instantly knew what it was—toast crumbs. The chef had scraped toast crumbs into his soup, and I was galvanized by this garnish for being so ingenuous, homely, and oddly delicious. When the maître

d'hôtel came to clear away our shots, he asked if we'd enjoyed the soup. I said I liked it very much, especially the toast crumbs, and he did a double-take. "Yes," he stumbled—the only time I've ever known him to—"yes, they are toast crumbs," and at the end of the meal, which was superb, the chef, a slight, elfin man with a wry but gentle smile stopped by our table. We chatted, and he told me that he and his colleague had previously worked at Arpège, chef Alain Passard's thumpingly expensive place in the rue de Varenne, and had just moved over here. A few weeks later, however, eager to repeat the experience and discover more about them, I booked at Lapérouse again, and my hopes were dashed by exactly the type of polite, ordinary, expensive meal I'd originally been expecting. They were gone.

A few months later, though, I had a postcard from them (I'd left my card). Chef Pascal Barbot and maître d'hôtel Christophe Rohat were opening a little restaurant in the rue de Beethoven in the 16th Arrondissement. I was there the first week their new place, L'Astrance—named for a wildflower in Barbot's native Auvergne—was open and had one of the best meals I've ever eaten. I also had a much longer conversation with Barbot, who once cooked for the admiral of the French Pacific Fleet and lived in Sydney for a while, experiences that had changed him. "While I was in Australia and the Pacific, I became much more interested in fruit and vegetables. The classic ingredients of French cooking, especially cream and butter, didn't taste good in these settings, so I started experimenting. Working at Arpège, I was also exposed to Alain Passard's love of vegetables, and all of these things had a big impact on me," said Barbot.

Since every meal I've ever eaten here has been better than the last, I always look forward to L'Astrance, although the difficulty of snaring one of this small dining room's twenty-six places and the rising prices have made it an infrequent pleasure. Still, at the cusp of late spring, which is one of the loveliest times of the year in Paris, and to celebrate the arrival of some of my oldest friends in town from San Francisco, I tackled the reservation process the necessary month ahead of time and secured a table for dinner on a night in late May, peony time, when Paris is floral and flirtatious.

We arrived at this discreet duplex dining room with silvered walls and apricot banquettes and embarked on a wonderful voyage. Christophe Rohat, who has a voice like dark gray velvet, an instrument that perfectly matches his dignified and elegant serving style, suggested a tasting menu with individual wines for each course, and its first note was an amuse-bouche that was spring in a shot glass—warm goat's milk, lemon, fresh peas, and scissored herbs, a vivid, refreshing concoction that foreshadowed the pleasures to come.

Barbot's contemporary haute cuisine is a whimsically cus-

tomized experience. He changes his menu daily, and it varies
from table to table according to what Rohat and the kitchen
decide you should try. Next up for us was a miniature brioche painted with rosemary butter and accompanied by a tiny
ramekin of Parmesan cream, a stunning but potent miniature
that brilliantly demonstrates the difference between France's
culinary avant-garde and that of Spain. France, thank goodness, is not Spain, where dry ice and exploding bonbons have
become the norm. No, even at the most creative outer limits
of a new, widely traveled generation of chefs, French cook-

ing remains guided by a rigor and refinement that profoundly respects the palate, and instead of chemistry-set antics, Pascal Barbot astonishes with his winsome love of flowers, berries, herbs, and seeds.

A plump oyster sitting on a slice of roasted beet on a bed of shredded oxtail in a pool of Camembert foam offered a tiny universe of taste so harmonious and sensual I thought of *The Ripening Seed,* Colette's novel of quickening adolescent sexuality set on the beaches of Brittany. All of these flavors were naive but together they formed a composition that was racing with desire. Another dish, tuna belly cooked sous-vide (individually vacuum-packed in plastic at a very low temperature) and served with fresh peas, nasturtium flowers, and blazes of a sauce made with ground dark orange Espelette pepper and Chorizo sausage drippings—Barbot sweats the sausage to recover its rich, paprika-flavored fat—was vivid and smoldering like a flamenco dance, while turbot cooked with an oxalis (red clover) condiment and garnished with crunchy green cabbage and a lemon-ginger sauce had an almost geisha-like allure.

As these cameos of color, taste, and texture succeeded one another, my San Franciscan friends were astonished. "What I find most amazing about this food is that even when it's knowingly sensuous, it remains innocent and sincere," one of them said, and as if to prove the point, we were served quenelles of fromage blanc drizzled with pomegranate syrup, a product Barbot discovered in Beirut, in small pools of perfect crème anglaise, a dessert that was the equivalent of watching a belly dancer from the window of a room in a convent.

Luxuriating in the glow of a brilliant meal, we were eating fresh fruit—Barbot doesn't like the traditional onslaught of mignardaises, or sweets and pastries, that follow most of the highest-altitude French meals because he finds them superfluous and unhealthy—when he stopped by. He said he'd recently been inspired by travels to India and was experimenting with techniques, foods, and spices he'd found there, and when I questioned him about his move toward a small-plate format, or meals composed of many small tasting portions, he became momentarily pensive. "I can't express myself on a big plate," he said. "I look for the extreme in terms of flavors. My favorite elements to compose with are l'iodée [the brininess of the sea and all of its minerals], le lacté [the sour edge of dairy products], la terre [the earth, or produce that conveys the primal taste of the soil], and la chair [flesh, in the meatiest sense of the word]. This is my little universe." I can't imagine better contemporary culinary compass points either, which is why every meal here leaves me longing for the next one.

. . .

IN A WORD: Chef Pascal Barbot is the most consistently creative young chef in Paris, with an extraordinary culinary imagination and a mastery of technique that has made him one of the great chefs of his generation. Using almost no added fat in his cooking and starring vegetables and fruit on his menus, he proves that healthy eating can be pleasurable and, by doing so, is one of the most influential French chefs in terms of creating a cuisine for the twenty-first century. Stunningly good service by maître d'hôtel Christophe Rohat succeeds by freeing some of France's best cooking from a pompous nineteenth-century straitjacket. Reservations at least a month in advance are imperative.

DON'T MISS: Barbot changes his menu so regularly that you're unlikely to come upon any of the dishes that I've enjoyed here, but dishes that explain his style include his signature avocado ravioli stuffed with crabmeat and glossed with almond oil; mushroom and foie gras galette; turbot with oxalis (a clover-like herb) condiment; green cabbage and lemon ginger sauce; tuna belly with chorizo drippings; sautéed pigeon with baby potatoes; fromage blanc quenelles with pomegranate syrup and crème anglaise; chocolate biscuit with milk sorbet.

. . .

[97] 4 rue Beethoven, 16th, 01.40.50.84.40. MÉTRO: Passy. OPEN Tuesday to Friday for lunch and dinner. CLOSED Saturday, Sunday, and Monday. www.astrancerestaurant.com ▪ $$$$

L'Entredgeu

TUCKED AWAY IN AN OUTLYING CORNER OF THE 17TH ARrondissement, this charming little bistro would be a perfect set for a scene from a 1950s Simenon detective novel because it is, as the French would say, still very much *dans son jus,* or in its juice, which means an old object or place that hasn't been restored. During my last lunch here I kept expecting the late French actress Simone Signoret to come through the door, since this is exactly the kind of place I always pictured her in—a happy, busy bistro with lace curtains, a checkerboard floor, wooden sconces, a jaunty decor of yellow walls and plum-painted woodwork, an old sign indicating the Lavabo and a bar just inside the front door where a waiter joked with the regulars while drying glasses.

If the mise en scène is deliciously vieux Paris, chef Philippe Tredgeu's edgy cooking offers a delicious, fresh, modern riff on traditional French regional dishes and bistro favorites. Tredgeu previously cooked at chef Thierry Breton's Chez Michel and Chez Casimir, and this background shows up in his outstanding fish cooking. The chalkboard menu changes regularly, but consistently offers a variety of wonderfully earthy choices, like my starter of charred piquillo peppers stuffed with a tender, flavorful beef ragout. Lovely blond Maryse, whom I've known for many years, ordered the daily special of langoustine tails in a bright herbal bouillon and then gorgeously grilled slices of rolled lamb roast served on a bed of mixed spring vegetables

including tiny peas, swiss chard, and broad beans. My John Dory filets were superb. Known as Saint-Pierre in French, this firm white fish is one of my favorites, and it had been perfectly cooked and was served with a delicious compote of chopped tomato, sliced fennel bulb, and fava beans.

Neither of us had been here for a while for the same reason. This place has become so popular, it's always crowded, especially in the evening, when it does two services (book the second one for a more relaxed meal). On this balmy afternoon we had plenty of room for a change, and the service was swift and disarmingly sincere, the atmosphere warm and relaxed.

Just as our desserts were served—an excellent baba au rhum (sponge cake soaked in rum-spiked syrup) intriguingly served with prunes and fantastic stout ice cream for me, and compote de fraise et rhubarb for Maryse—the two nice insurance execs (they were both wearing little AXA lapel pins) at the table next to us asked if we wanted to help them finish a celebratory bottle of Monbazillac, a lovely dessert wine from the Dordogne. I'd never refuse such a friendly offer, and during the conversation that followed, we quickly discovered a thick cross-hatching of common interests and tastes—both Maryse and Jean-Marc were originally from Normandy, while Armand had just discovered one of my favorite places for lunch in New York during a business trip there—Mary's Fish Camp—but the main thing we agreed on was that L'Entredgeu is, in Armand's words, "vachement bon!" or damned good.

·   ·

IN A WORD: Despite its remote location in the 17th Arrondissement, chef Philippe Tredgeu's charming bistro with a decor worthy of a Doisneau photograph is one of the hottest word-of-mouth addresses in Paris. You'll understand why after you've tasted his superb contemporary bistro cooking. Note, too, that this place is one of the city's best buys.

DON'T MISS: The chalkboard menu is revised daily, but dishes I've loved here include piquillo peppers stuffed with beef ragout; langoustine tails in herb bouillon; oyster tempura with a sauce gribiche; fish soup; stuffed squid in a vinaigrette made with their own ink; roast cod; roast lamb with spring vegetables; carmelized pork belly; lièvre à la royale (wild hare in a sauce of its blood and gizzards) with macaroni gratin; colvert (wild duck) with roasted fruit; baba au rhum with prunes and stout ice cream; brioche perdue with carmelized apples; strawberry and rhubarb compote.

. . .

[98] 83 rue Laugier, 17th, 01.40.54.97.24. MÉTRO: Porte de Champerret. OPEN Tuesday to Saturday for lunch and dinner. CLOSED Sunday and Monday. • $$

Guy Savoy

CHEF GUY SAVOY'S PARIS RESTAURANT OFFERS AN EXPERIence of gastronomic luxury that's as solidly engineered as a Mercedes and as consensually tasteful as a string of good pearls. This is why it's filled noon and night with a well-dressed and necessarily well-heeled—this place is bloodcurdlingly expensive—international crowd who keep their perplexed reactions to the designer Jean-Michel Wilmotte's somber, masculine dining rooms to themselves and instead concentrate rather self-consciously on enjoying some of the best-drilled service in the world. Of course the food's very nice, too, but this isn't a place you come if you're craving culinary adventure. Instead, you choose this restaurant when you want a safe, stylish, and unfailingly gracious experience of modern French cuisine, a formula that slyly appeals to people for whom a meal here is usually just one special occasion in lives that are filled with them.

So does it cut the mustard for anyone like me whose nerves are rattled by spending almost $1,000 on dinner for two (mine consisted of two flutes of Champagne, a medium-priced bottle of Condrieu, and two glasses of sublime Jurançon dessert wine in addition to two starters, two main courses, and a shared dessert)? I'm not ducking, but it depends on what you're looking for. The last time I dined at Savoy, the two of us had a delightful time and a very good meal, but as impeccable as the food may have been, what really impressed me was the service. Our dining room was populated by a handsome older American couple celebrating the gent's birthday over a dinner punctuated by several robin's egg blue Tiffany boxes, a very chic young Japanese couple, two Rus-

sian businessmen, and three assiduously elegant Argentinean women whose meringue-colored hair was elaborately coiffed in styles that reminded me of Goya's eighteenth-century portraits of the Spanish nobility, and I was awed by the way the wait staff made subtle calibrations to enhance the pleasure of each of these very different planets. The Japanese, both of whom had heroically embarked on the tasting menu, were served with deference and distance, the Russians with a homeopathic dose of complicit jocularity, the Americans with perfect English and a little flattery, and the Argentines with Gallic gallantry. Oh, and my trophy was being treated as the equal of the very knowledgeable Frenchman with whom I was dining, which I'll humbly admit is a prize indeed for any long-term American resident of Paris, since the limbo bar of Gallic knowingness has a clearance of about a half inch.

The wilder shores of gastronomic creativity to one side, this place falls all over itself to make sure you have a good time, with a steady rain of constant attentions and surprises that make an evening special. Some of them are superfluous—I don't need anyone to pose a napkin in my lap—but most are welcome, including the arrival of a miniature kebab of foie gras and toast to nibble over Champagne and a bread trolley that supplies you with a different bread for every course (curiously, the bread isn't baked on the premises but is bought in from Eric Kayser, one of Paris's best bakers, with headquarters in the 5th Arrondissement).

As is so often the case in haute cuisine restaurants, the starters were much more appealing than the main courses, so just as we were dithering over our choices, the maître d'hôtel arrived and suggested they'd happily serve tasting portions of several appetizers if we couldn't make up our minds. So I had the tuna and asparagus crus-cuits (raw and cooked) and a half portion of Savoy's signature artichoke and truffle soup. I found both the seared slices of raw tuna with shavings of raw asparagus and a node of tuna tartare and the soup underseasoned, but their presentation was lovely. Bruno's oysters with seawater gelée (aspic made from sea water), another Savoy specialty and a more interesting choice than either of mine, and his ladies-who-lunch classic of fresh baby peas with pea mousse and an egg coddled at a very low temperature so that the yolk was glossy alabaster, were similarly polite and pleasant.

Main courses reprised the themes of careful cooking and quality, tripped up by an overzealous culinary politeness. It's almost as though Savoy's modus operandi is to avoid offending any possible gastronomic sensibility, which means he lowballs his recipes, with often timid results. There was nothing I could reproach about my chop of turbot, which flaked easily but was still firm and had a vague nuance of white truffle, which rose from an artful but unfortunate dribble of white-truffle-flavored olive oil in the bouillon beneath a perforated plate posed on a shallow soup dish. Most of the egg yolk of another cooked-at-low-temperature egg dribbled into the bouillon as well, which meant that I was eating a correctly cooked but rather monastic piece of plain fish. Bruno's slices of meaty sole were cooked à la meunière (rolled in flour and sautéed in butter flavored with seaweed), and pleasant as this dish may have been, it would never have driven anyone into the ecstasy one hopes to experience at the summit of the French food chain.

We passed on the rather modest cheese trolley and instead split a "passion de légumes," carrot juice with finely chopped citrus peel, with a long-nosed carrot chip sticking out of a ball of root vegetable ice cream, a very adult dessert making a feint at the modern preoccupation with healthy eating. It was nice enough, especially when followed by the buckshot of luxury mignardises, or various sweet nibbles—marshmallow chunks (when and why did the French ever decide that marshallow was a desirable sweet for anyone over fifteen?), chocolates, caramels, and a delicious miniature strawberry-filled crêpe, but more of a child's sweet good-night peck on the cheek than the suggested lover's kiss. Overall, this meal was a charming but studiously polite performance without a single taste that would startle, tease, or puzzle, which is why I'd heartily recommend Guy Savoy to anyone who wants a perfect business meal or who is at the very beginning of their haute cuisine learning curve. N.B. This restaurant is scheduled to move to new quarters in the Hôtel de la Monnaie in Saint-Germain-des-Prés within a year or so.

.　.　.

IN A WORD: Guy Savoy offers a well-mannered experience of luxurious contemporary French haute cuisine in a sleek modern dining room by the architect Jean-Michel Wilmotte. Soigné service delights the monied international crowd who've made this restaurant so enduringly popular.

DON'T MISS: Artichoke and black truffle soup; huîtres en nage glacée (oysters on a bed of cream in a gelée of their own juices); roasted duck foie gras with red cabbage nage; sea bass with spices; poached guinea hen and vegetables in a vinaigrette made with its liver; vanilla millefeuille.

.　.　.

[99] 18 rue Troyon, 17th, 01.43.80.40.61. MÉTRO: Charles-de-Gaulle-Étoile. OPEN Tuesday to Friday for lunch and dinner. Saturday dinner only. CLOSED Sunday and Monday. www.guysavoy.com ▪ $$$$

Le Hide

EVERYONE WHO LIVES IN PARIS INHABITS BOTH THE CITY of brick and stone and the city of their predilections and imagination, which explains why I so rarely find myself in the leafy, quiet, affluent precincts of the western arrondissements—the 16th and that part of the 17th west of the train cut leading into the Gare Saint-Lazare. For me, the axis of seriously good eating in Paris has shifted eastward during the last ten years toward the younger and artier 10th, 11th, and 12th arrondissements, but this doesn't mean I won't make a beeline for any seriously good new address in those gilded, long-established western precincts.

Curiously, I first heard about Le Hide, which is just behind the Arc de Triomphe, from my barber, a charming *pied noir* (Frenchman born in North Africa when much of it was part of France's colonial empire) who not only takes care of my graying locks but also tends to the thatches of many of the most powerful men in France, a veritable limousine fleet full of cabinet ministers, company presidents, and politicians. Philippe is wry but also discreet about their confidences, so the main subject we share is a love of really good food at really good prices. Not long ago when I fended off yet another of his suggestions that he dye my hair to hide the gray, a cover-up popular with French politicians, by quietly offering a couple of restaurant recommendations, he reciprocated by telling me that many of his clients love Le Hide, a little bistro in the 17th Arrondissement with a Japanese chef. I went and immediately understood the loyalty of these well-coiffed titans.

Japanese chef Hide Kobayashi, who trained with Joël Robu-

chon, Dominique Bouchet, Jacques Cagna, and others before going out on his own to launch this friendly little bistro, has triumphed by learning his French lessons so well that they've become something almost better than what his mentors taught him. As an outsider, he has respectfully sublimated the French kitchen by enhancing it with his Japanese sensibility. So while the register of the good-value menu here may read as grandly Gallic, Kobayashi's cooking is much lighter, fresher, and more precise than traditional French bistro cooking, as I discovered during an excellent springtime meal with Bruno and some friends.

Kobayashi's menu follows the seasons, and our table of four loved our starters of white asparagus with a mimosa (riced hard-boiled egg) vinaigrette, a superb terrine of duck foie gras, and marinated salmon with a warm buckwheat-flour crêpe and a dollop of unctuous crème d'Isigny, an ivory-colored crème fraîche with so much butterfat a spoon stands up in it. Main courses were excellent and generously served as well, including a fork-tender braised shoulder of lamb with white beans and stewed tomatoes, a succulent Limousin faux filet (steak) from star butcher Hugo Desnoyer, and a velvet carpaccio of scallops with white truffle oil and a salad of lamb's ear lettuce.

The saucy waitresses here stoked the bonhomie born of Kobayashi's excellent cooking with their mildly tart and gently pleasing quips—clearing the plates, one of them looked at my steak-eating friend Laurent and asked, "Did you enjoy that?" When he nodded, she said, "I'm sure you did, and now you have the strength to keep that pretty woman [his wife] happy!" Slices of tarte Tatin, one of my favorite French desserts for the way in which the sliced apples tucked under a flaky crust absorb the caramel at the bottom of the pan in this upside-down creation, offered another excuse to consume more of that crème d'Isigny, while île flottante (floating island) with salted-caramel ice cream was bliss. The wine list offers a variety of nicely chosen and

fairly priced bottles, and the service couldn't be friendlier. I left looking forward to my next meal here, and since I'm not alone, make sure to reserve, since word is getting around on this one.

. . .

IN A WORD: Japanese chef Hide Kobayashi has expertly mastered the canon of traditional French bistro cooking and artfully updates it with carefully prepared dishes that can be ordered à la carte or as part of the good-value prix fixe menus. The dining room is a bit snug, but the atmosphere is relaxed and the service friendly.

DON'T MISS: Marinated salmon with céleri rémoulade, sautéed shrimp and bean sprouts on a bed of baby spinach leaves, faux filet (steak), roast lamb with sweet potato puree, sea bass filet in beurre blanc, tarte Tatin, poire belle Hélène (poached pear with vanilla ice cream and hot chocolate sauce), crêpes Suzette with Grand Marnier.

. . .

[100] 10 rue Général Lanrezac, 17th, 01.45.74.15.51. MÉTRO: Étoile. OPEN Monday to Friday for lunch and dinner. Saturday dinner only. CLOSED on Sunday. www.lehide.fr ▪ $$

Le Pré Catelan

TUCKED AWAY DEEP IN THE BOIS DE BOULOGNE, THE VAST park on the western edge of Paris that's one of the city's two green lungs (the other is the Bois de Vincennes on the southeastern edge), Le Pré Catalan is one of the most romantic restaurants

in the world. Since the arrival of chef Frédéric Anton more than ten years ago, it has also become one of the city's best restaurants, since Anton is a boldly inventive cook who delights in creating dishes that are miniature studies in culinary theater—his cooking is carefully staged and decorated and has a lot of drama.

Though there's never a time of the year when I don't look forward to a meal in this sumptuous Belle Époque pavilion, it is especially wonderful during the summer, when it's a pleasure to escape the heat-stunned city. I've been here on many different occasions through the years, but for rather surprising reasons, my last meal was particularly memorable. Let me explain.

The approach of August, the de rigueur vacation month that's always been the anchor of family life, is a potentially perilous season in Paris. As soon as I heard Anna's voice on the phone, I knew what had happened. She and Gérard had been involved for two years but had been seeing less and less of each other since Gérard got a new job that meant he went to New York regularly, and now, just before he'd left for Bali with his family for three weeks, plans he hadn't mentioned before, he'd told her that she deserved much more and he thought it would be better if they stopped seeing each other.

It was a hot, pretty summer day, and aching for Anna, a charming banker from Auckland who'd made the classic mistake of getting involved with a married man, I had an idea. "What are you doing for lunch today?" "I don't much feel like eating right now." "I understand, but a change of scene might do you some good."

I called a friend who's a concierge at one of the best hotels in Paris, asked if he could do me a favor, and two hours later we were sitting in this elegant dining room deep in a forest twenty minutes from central Paris. You might think this romantic bower was a curious place to bring someone with a broken heart, but wait.

Anna had never been here before, and as is true of anyone who comes for the first time, she was impressed and excited. "Isn't this lovely! I feel like we're a thousand miles from Paris," she said as we studied the menu while sipping flutes of chilled Champagne. Around us, besotted couples outnumbered business diners on this gorgeous afternoon when much of corporate Paris had already decamped to idle on Breton beaches or doze in the shade of Provence's olive trees to a scrim of cicadas after lunch. Across the way, however, a man with salt-and-pepper hair was dining with a pretty young woman in a fluttery polka-dot navy blue chiffon dress. Anna instantly seized on this tableau, which included a single wedding ring. "I feel like going over there and telling her to come to her senses before it's too late," she said, while I was mum. In a country with an institutionalized tolerance of adultery, it is easy for a culturally disoriented young foreigner to get caught up in these webs.

Our first courses came, and my grilled scallops in a lime-zest-spiked foam were light, succulent, and sexy. Anna loved her stuffed crab in an elegant gelée of its own coral. And she didn't mention Gérard again during our meal, although her eyes darted often to the table across the way. I had the sole in caramelized mango sauce with giant capers, and Anna, ready to buck herself up, devoured a brilliant composition of lamb that included grilled cutlets, a lamb sausage, a kidney, and a slice of filet in an intriguing licorice-flavored sauce with a side garnish of a large goat-cheese-filled raviolo. "This sauce is really interesting—I'd never have made the association between lamb and licorice, but it really flatters the meat," said Anna.

I couldn't wait for our desserts to come either, since Le Pré Catalan has one of the best pastry chefs in Paris. Young Christelle Brua didn't disappoint. Both of our desserts looked as though they'd been made in Fabergé's workshops. Decorated with quivering bits of gold leaf, my transparent green sugar sphere was filled with baked apple, crumbled shortbread, and whipped cream, while Anna's wild strawberries came under a meringue veil decorated with silver-colored candied almonds. "These are so pretty I could weep," said Anna. "But I've done enough of that for the time being." Over coffee, I gingerly raised the subject of summer vacations. "A friend of mine from London has invited me to a beach house he's rented in Puglia, but I'd been putting off making a decision until I knew what Gérard was doing," she sighed. "But maybe a long weekend down there would be nice. I don't know that part of Italy, but they say it's lovely." She sipped her coffee and glanced at the couple across the way. "I wonder if it looked that obvious when we were together. I hope not." I watched as a welcome breeze slightly ruffled the geraniums. "What a wonderful meal this has been," Anna said. "And I'm so glad I didn't come to such a special place as anyone's mistress."

. . .

IN A WORD: Chef Frédéric Anton has made this famous sylvan getaway one of the best restaurants in Paris. Service in the elegant Belle Époque pavilion is courtly and soigné, and it also has one of the most impressive wine lists in Paris. During the summer, they have one of the prettiest terraces in town, and this lavishly decorated dining room with refreshing views over the surrounding greenery is one of the most romantic addresses in the city. This is just the place for some enchanted evening, although tables are usually easier to snag for lunch. Advance reservations are imperative.

DON'T MISS: Stuffed crab with a gelée of its own coral; grilled scallops in lime foam; l'os à moelle (beef bone marrow) in two preparations, grilled in the bone with black pepper and stuffed with baby peas and morel mushrooms; spit-roasted pigeon with a poivrade sauce and macaroni gratin with petits pois; lamb in réglisse (licorice) sauce with a goat-cheese-stuffed raviolo; sole with caramelized mango sauce; ris de veau (sweetbreads) with morel mushrooms and a Parmesan-glazed soubise (sauce of onions and cream); turbot in an almond crust with capers and baby onions in bitter almond jus; millefeuille; macaroon with bergamot ice cream and carmelized hazelnuts.

. . .

[101] **Bois de Boulogne, 16th, 01.44.14.41.14.** MÉTRO: **Porte Maillot and then a taxi, since the restaurant is located deep inside the Bois de Boulogne, Paris's largest park.** OPEN **Tuesday to Saturday for lunch and dinner.** CLOSED **Sunday and Monday. www.restaurant-precatalan.com • $$$$**

Le Stella

DEEP IN THE SILK-STOCKING PRECINCTS OF THE 16TH ARrondissement, Le Stella is a textbook example of a good brasserie. This is not a part of town where people cook much, so Le Stella babies its bourgeois clientele by shrewdly offering its kitchen-averse regulars a different special dish every night of the week, including delicious hachis parmentier (the French version of shepherd's pie, but better) on Monday and a fine choucroute garnie (sauerkraut with pork and sausages) on Wednesday. Should you arrive by car, a parking jockey spirits away your car, and inside, in the wood-paneled dining rooms, the atmosphere is what the French call bon enfant, or polite and pleasant. The small glassed-in terrace contains the most sought-after tables, which are implicitly reserved for recognizable faces—regulars or politicians, businesspeople or the occasional showbiz personality—but the main dining room also offers some fascinating people watching.

Think *The Discreet Charm of the Bourgeoisie.* Or wealthy middle-aged couples composed of Madame with a helmet of

expensively coiffed and colored hair and Monsieur in a blazer, fiddling with his BlackBerry as a way of forestalling some incipient bickering. With the exception of a few befuddled Japanese tourists, tables of bespectacled businessmen having conversations about "implementing" things, and dutiful adult grandchildren accompanying Grand-mère to a feed that will at the very least allow her to air out her fur coat, the fact is that a faint air of infidelity hangs over this dining room. While we gorged on meaty Gillardeau oysters and the better-than-average house-smoked salmon as first courses, the surgically impeccable brunette in a fringed tweed jacket next to us informed her husband that she was certain he hadn't been alone at their country house the weekend before (she'd been visiting her mother in Marseille). Gulp. Talk about a study in guilt, with a vague reference to "a friend" who'd stopped by and the furrowed brow that wondered, how did she find out? Fortunately, a big plateau of shellfish—oysters, clams, langoustines, sea snails, and shrimp—

arrived in time to keep things on an even keel, momentarily at least, while we supped on a perfectly grilled sole and an excellent steak, accompanied by homemade frites and some rather pallid sauce béarnaise, the only off note in a very satisfying meal.

No one has dessert here, because everyone's counting calories, but it was fun to watch a beautiful young woman in a shaggy shearling coat tucking into a pyramid of ice-cream-stuffed profiteroles slathered with hot chocolate sauce, which are far and away the best choice here, while her companion, an older man, twirled his sour-smelling cigar and looked on with a hunger of his own. Since the restaurant doesn't take reservations, you may have to wait, but this democratic seating system leads to brisk service and means you can almost always get a table here. A perfect Parisian tableau, and a good meal to boot.

"I found a red sock," the aggrieved madame finally blurted out as we were putting on our coats. "And I don't wear socks." Maybe, but she sure knew how to put away the oysters.

·   ·   ·

IN A WORD: A well-mannered traditional French brasserie with better-than-average food and a diverting crowd.

DON'T MISS: Haricots verts with Parmesan shavings; smoked salmon; grilled sole; tarte fine aux tomates fraîches; tuna steak with pistou sauce; grilled cod with olive oil; beef brochette sauce diable; tête de veau; vacherin glacé sauce caramel.

·   ·   ·

[102] 133 avenue Victor-Hugo, 16th, 01.56.90.56.00. MÉTRO: Victor-Hugo. OPEN daily for lunch and dinner. www.brasserie-le-stella.advertory.fr • $$

La Table de Hugo Desnoyer

OFTEN THERE'S NO BETTER TICKET TO HIGH SPIRITS THAN
spontaneity and a little extravagance (deeply considered penu-
riousness somehow just never seems to work). So on a rainy
Saturday morning, Bruno and I set out on a gastronomic ex-
pedition that I was certain would raise our weather-dampened
spirits. We were heading to the new butcher shop that Hugo
Desnoyer had opened in such a remote and very quiet corner
of the remote and very quiet 16th Arrondissement that it barely
seemed like Paris when we got there. Or at least the Paris I
know, but then everyone inhabits the city differently.

Almost from the moment I arrived in 1986, I developed an
indifference to the 8th and 16th Arrondissements, which have
always struck me, with the exception of certain pleasant pockets,
as epitomizing a certain bourgeois self-satisfaction. Still, there's
some handsome architecture deep in the 16th, and it's also very
green. And at this time of year, mid-May, small rain-drenched
purple torches of lilac were tumbling over wrought-iron fences,
and you could catch a glimpse of the occasional bank of peonies
here or there in a private garden.

Monsieur Desnoyer's new butcher shop turned out to be
neat as a pin, with the staff just as polite and helpful as they
are at Tiffany's. And if you find another similarity between
these two businesses, you're not wrong, either: vertiginous
price tags. But our destination was the solid butcher block table
d'hôtes (common shared table) on a raised platform in a corner
of the immaculate white space where meals are served. What
we'd decided, you see, was to take ourselves out for a carni-

vore's feast, something Desnoyer only previously offered in a do-it-yourself version.

So we settled in at the table and decided to share the faux filet for two—the prix fixe tasting menu being more than we wanted to eat at noon—with a very good bottle of Haute Côtes de Beaune. No sooner had we ordered than the handsome and courtly Monsieur Desnoyer arrived with a complimentary plate of charcuterie, not because he knows me from a hole in the ground but rather because, with the opening of the restaurant at the butcher shop where he began his career as a sixteen-year-old apprentice and where he has now become the boss, he's celebrating his good fortune and hard work by sharing. Not only was it a generous and charming gesture, but it reminded me of why he's my favorite Paris butcher. In the suddenly testosterone-fueled big-bad-ego world of star butchers in Paris, Desnoyer is the quiet man who gets on with his craft and whose pride and pleasure is in selling the very best meat he can possibly find. He also supplies many of the best restaurants in Paris, including Le Bristol, L'Astrance, Pierre Gagnaire, and Le Chateaubriand, among others, along with the kitchens of the presidents of the Assemblée Nationale and Sénat.

When our meat arrived—a sublime and perfectly cooked piece of Limousin beef so big we took half of it home and ate it for the next three days (here I advise moderation as the basis for real delectation)—I was delighted by the only element of our meal that wasn't animal-derived: a copy-this-idea medley of tiny new potatoes and radishes sautéed in salt butter. But by the time we'd eaten half of our steak, it didn't even occur to me to wonder if there was a dessert option on the brief table d'hôtes menu. There is, of course, and it's often a nicely made fruit tart, which comes as part of the regularly changing menu découverte prix fixe—the day we were here it was a Brobdingnagian feast that included tomato tart, duck breast with snow peas, beef, and cheese, but dessert can also be ordered à la carte. One way or another, young chef Angie Fouquoire, ex-Crillon, does admirable justice to Desnoyer's meat and has a talent for inventive side dishes and garnishes.

After lunch, we joined the polite but wide-eyed line of customers waiting to be served at the meat counter. Staring into the cases at Desnoyer, one's pulse really does quicken—his meats are magnificent, which is why our usual self-exhortations toward a reasonable thrift promptly derailed the moment a polite young butcher in a pressed white jacket began serving us. So we'd have a veal chop, and some of that gorgeous jambon à l'os (ham on the bone), and a slice of the pistachio-studded veal terrine, which I just can't resist, and some of the head cheese Bruno likes. Oh, and also that nice little rack of lamb, and the pork loins looked good, too, and finally another faux filet to put in the freezer.

Watching the butcher trim the meat that needed it (before he weighed it, thank you), and then wrap it—first in waxed white butcher's paper, then in brown paper, before he tied it up with red string and wrote the name of the contents on the edge of the package in loopy black script—I was very happy, since the precision of these details communicated a solid but humble pride. And he also took the time to offer a warm, low-rolling set of suggestions as to how the morsels we were buying might best be cooked. So not only had I just eaten a wonderful lunch, and not only did I know I'd be eating very well again for a few weeks to come, but I admired the art and grace with which these butchers practiced their craft. Of course, we left after paying a thumping big bill, but that's okay, because the only logo sweatshirt I'd ever be comfortable wearing would probably say "Carpe diem."

· ⁓ ·

IN A WORD: Star butcher Hugo Desnoyer's convivial table d'hôtes in his shop in the 16th Arrondissement is the new go-to address for meat-lovers in search of a generous and seriously good example of France's finest meat. This is a terrific address for lunch with a group of friends.

DON'T MISS: The regularly revised menu découverte is a superb five-course feast that showcases Desnoyer's meat and fowl. You can also order à la carte, in which case start off with a plate of charcuterie and then go with the côte de boeuf or the faux filet.

. . .

[103] 28 rue du Docteur-Blanche, 16th, 01.46.47.83.00. Reservations essential for the table d'hôtes. MÉTRO: Jasmin or Ranelagh. OPEN Monday to Friday from 9:00 a.m. to 6:00 p.m. CLOSED Sunday and Monday. www .hugodesnoyer.fr ▪ $$−$$$

Les Tablettes de Jean-Louis Nomicos

WHEN IT CAME TO CHOOSING A RESTAURANT FOR LUNCH with a discerning editor from a major German food magazine, I knew Les Tablettes, which takes its name from the iPads that contain its wine list and also offers anyone waiting for a late date or dining alone the distraction of watching an interesting little video or two about chef Jean-Louis Nomicos's suppliers, would be a sure bet. Nomicos, a native of Marseille, went to

work for Alain Ducasse when he was eighteen and then cooked at Lasserre for many years before opening his own strikingly designed dining room with bittersweet orange velvet upholstered chairs and an intriguing basketweave wall by French interior designer Anne-Cécile Comar. Best of all, his sophisticated Mediterranean-inspired cooking pleases all comers, since he employs the technical discipline of his Escoffier-style training as the basis of a personal culinary style that is unfailingly light, lively, and cosmopolitan, and the service here is excellent.

I also love the way that he manages to produce dishes like a solacing starter of baby artichokes and squid with a jus barigoule à la bergamote (the cooking liquid used to braise the artichokes—white wine with lardons, onions, and garlic is reduced and then brightened by the addition of the finely chopped citrus fruit), or luscious ravioli stuffed with silky potato puree and black truffles, which delight by being homey but impressively creative at the same time. The harmony of a kitchen that achieves such a delicious equilibrium just might be attributed to Nomicos's hometown. "The melting pot of Marseille, which has restaurants representing most of the countries around the Mediterranean, has had a big impact on the way I cook," says the chef. "I had a classical French culinary education, but as a Marseillais, I'm also familiar with many flavor palettes beyond France."

If a single dish on Nomicos's menu offers a perfect cameo of his refined but politely lusty cooking, it's his fennel-and-sea-urchin royale, a seasonal delicacy (November–April) comprising a flan of fennel, a signature flavor of Provence, enlivened by the iodine-rich punch of fresh sea urchins, a favorite Marseillais crustacean. Not surprisingly for someone who's a son of one of the world's great port cities, Nomicos is also a superb fish cook, as seen in main courses like succulent rouget filets garnished with zucchini, girolles, and a delicate sauce of deglazed cooking juices cleverly brightened by pickled lemon, or roasted John Dory with anise and saffron, sauce vierge, and a garnish of fennel bulb. He has a deft touch with meat, too, including a perfectly roasted saddle of lamb with wild thyme and a puree of baby zucchini drizzled with Moroccan argan oil.

I loved the all-goat-cheese sampler, as did the delightful lady from Hamburg with whom I was dining, and we happily concluded an excellent meal with wild strawberries in rosewater with a Chartreuse granité, and a luscious hot runny chocolate cake with a mascarpone emulsion and cocoa sorbet. Perhaps the surest measure of Nomicos's success is the fact that even though the clientele here is frequently suit-wearing, there's often laughter to be heard in his dining room.

.　.　.

IN A WORD: Marseille-born chef Jean-Louis Nomicos brings a welcome taste of the south of France to the well-heeled 16th Arrondissement with his contemporary Mediterranean-inspired cooking. Though popular for business meals, the warm, relaxed atmosphere prevents it from feeling too corporate.

DON'T MISS: Macaroni stuffed with foie gras and black truffles and gratinéed with Parmesan and jus de veau; fennel mousse with sea urchins; ravioli stuffed with mashed potatoes and black truffles; rougets with girolles, zucchini, and a preserved-lemon jus; roasted John Dory with sauce vierge and baby fennel; goat-cheese sampler plate; wild strawberries in rosewater with Chartreuse granité; warm chocolate cake with mascarpone emulsion and cocoa sorbet.

. . .

[104] 16 avenue Bugeaud, 16th, 01.56.28.16.16. MÉTRO: Victor Hugo. OPEN daily for lunch and dinner. www.lestablettesjeanlouisnomicos.com
▪ $$$$

MONTMARTRE, BUTTES-CHAUMONT, NATION

·〜·

Le Baratin

A CENTURY AGO, L'AMI LOUIS, THE EGREGIOUSLY OVERPRICED Marais bistro that pulls an international crowd of high rollers more interested in a brand-name luxury experience than good

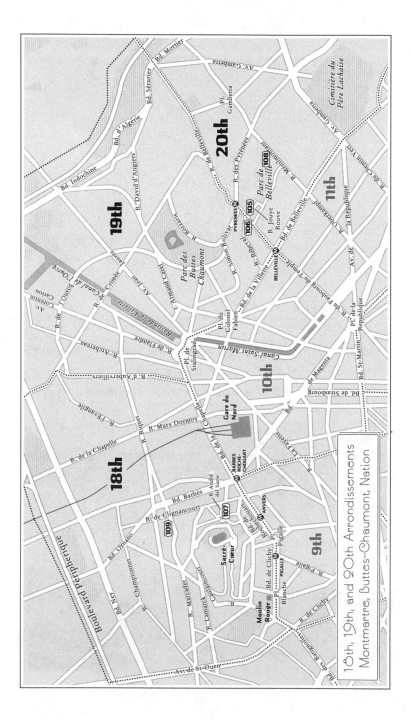

18th, 19th, and 20th Arrondissements
Montmartre, Buttes-Chaumont, Nation

food, might have been something like this hole-in-the-wall in Belleville, the old working-class neighborhood in northeastern Paris where the singer Édith Piaf was born—a buzzy, unpretentious place with a smart, sexy, arty crowd, a fabulous chalkboard menu, and a slightly bluff style.

On a warm night in July, we settled at our bare wood table and started with glasses of a sublime and very unusual pétillant naturel Chasselas de Tavel, a naturally sparkling (no sugar added to promote fermentation) wine made from sweet Chasselas grapes. Le Baratin is a bistrot à vin par excellence, and justly proud of its nervy and very original wine list.

The restaurant, in a steep cobbled side street of crooked old houses and Arab groceries, is a simple pair of dining rooms with cracked tile floors, a service bar under three globe lights, and wonderful faces with stories you want to hear. One of them was that of the Uruguayan dancer and her French lover to our left. Even though she was in the corps of a top-tier company in a small French city, she still didn't have proper work or residency papers after ten years in France and so was on the verge of tears all night about whether or not to risk a trip home to visit her gravely ill mother (by the time coffee was served, she'd decided to go). To our right, a pair of scrubbed but funky Dutch architects discussed green buildings in Rotterdam with a New York–based French arts administrator who said he dreamed of working for the Brooklyn Academy of Music. No one in the room was talking about real estate, private schools, or hedge funds. As much as there's any real vie bohème left in Paris these days, you'll find it here. That being said, Parisian bohemians not only know and love their food and wine but have the scratch to pay for it. In rapidly gentrifying Paris, Belleville is the last and latest frontier, which is why dinner for two at this bistro in this remote and atmospherically run-down part of the city isn't the bargain you might be expecting in such an off-the-beaten-track neighborhood.

Still, the food is so good and generously served I'd go often if it were in my neighborhood. Raquel Carena, the chef, is Argentinean, which explains her brilliantly irreverent approach to bistro cooking. She has a style all her own that defies categories—if it's rooted in Argentinean home cooking, it's also surprisingly creative and international, lit up by her sincerity and desire to please. She often brings dishes to the table herself and beams every time she comes across an empty plate.

We were elated by first courses of hand-chopped red tuna tartare with pitted black cherries and grated cucumber with a scattering of fleur de sel and a little miso, a truly brilliant dish, and a chunky terrine of meaty monkfish livers, which the waiter accurately described as "foie gras of the sea." A soulful bottle of Saint-Joseph from the Rhône valley proved the perfect foil for delicious lemon-braised veal topped with chewy ribbons of grilled eggplant skin and garnished with baby vegetables and olive-oil-dressed rice pilaf. Another main course, a tender and perfectly seasoned souris d'agneau, was bright with Moroccan spices, and afterward, we had slices of the best Saint-Nectaire cheese I'd ever had—it smelled and tasted like the inside of a musty stone church in the country—and for dessert, a gratin of buttered apricots in almond meal.

We lingered over coffee—this a place where you want to spend an evening—and felt that all was solidly right with the world when we stepped out into the animated streets of Belleville a few hours later. This is a wonderful restaurant.

IN A WORD: A first-rate bistrot à vin in a far-from-the-madding-crowd location in Belleville. This is the type of place that Parisians guardedly share with friends, and it's a favorite of chefs on their night off.

DON'T MISS: The menu changes constantly here, but if the following are available, don't pass them by: bouillon de lotte au galanga (monkfish broth with galangal root, a gingerlike

rhizome); barbue poêlé aux asperges vertes (brill sautéed with green asparagus); pudding aux noisettes (hazelnut pudding).

. . .

[105] 3 rue Jouye-Rouve, 20th, 01.43.49.39.70. MÉTRO: Belleville or Pyrénées. OPEN Tuesday to Friday for lunch and dinner. Saturday dinner only. CLOSED Sunday and Monday. ▪ $$

Chapeau Melon

THE CHAPEAU MELON, ONE OF PARIS'S BEST WINE BARS, offers a perfect opportunity to discover Belleville, one of my favorite Paris neighborhoods. For people who really love Paris, and especially those who think they know it well, Belleville comes as a surprise, even a shock. While major cities like New York, Los Angeles, London, and Berlin are immediately and quite visibly international, the center of Paris remains primly French. On any given sunny afternoon in the Tuileries Gardens, for example, the only foreigners you'll see are students, domestics, and other tourists. Head up to Belleville, an old working-class neighborhood in the 19th Arrondissement, however, and you'll be surprised by what an almost antically international city Paris really is. Every fifth shopfront advertises the services that are the umbilical cord of any modern immigrant's life—prepaid calling cards, Internet access, fax transmissions, and money transfers—in Hindi, Chinese, Arabic, and a dozen other languages, and the streets are filled with people from every country in the world.

Recently, however, younger French-born professionals in search of affordable housing and a more richly textured urban experience than that offered in most of the city's single-digit arrondissements have discovered the neighborhood, and their presence is creating a demand for something other than the local Chinese restaurants, gyro stands, and kosher couscous parlors. The Chapeau Melon's chef-owner, Olivier Camus, understands exactly what this crowd likes to eat, too, and crafts a single dinner menu daily that showcases French comfort food and dishes that have a finely tuned international inspiration.

As we settled in for dinner on a Saturday night in this cozy dining room with bare wood tables, celadon-painted walls, exposed beams, and wine displayed in open stock shelves, it was easy to like this place even before the kitchen began performing. Jazz played on the soundtrack, and Camus's wife poured us a welcome glass of Bourgogne Aligoté before she recited the set menu and asked if it suited. The whole atmosphere was decidedly chilled out and reminded me of my first exciting experiences of modern American-style bistros in Northampton and Cambridge, Massachusetts, when I was a pennywise college student. What these New England tables had in common was a guiding belief in the natural democracy of food, the idea that good eating should be stripped of the trappings of power and status that were built into the original French boilerplate for restaurants. This idea of making good food available to as many people as possible also thrived in other places, most importantly San Francisco and to a lesser degree London and Berlin, before finally taking root in Paris, initially in counterculture vegetarian restaurants but more recently at higher levels of the local food chain. Where it's most successful in Paris today is in the new generation of bistrots à vin, wine-oriented bistros, which have cropped up in some of the city's edgier and lesser-known neighborhoods, like Belleville.

Since I wholeheartedly agree that good, healthy, delicious food should be available to everyone, I had no trouble getting in the groove here, and what followed was an excellent meal. We began with artichauts barigoule, tender baby artichokes poached provençale style in a light vinaigrette and sprinkled with delicious piggy-tasting lardons. Next up was red tuna tartare, which had me scratching my head a bit, since I thought this dish was the creation of Raquel Carena at the nearby Le Baratin. Whatever its original authorship may have been, it was excellent, with fat cubes of fresh red Mediterranean tuna marinated in soy sauce, sesame oil, and ginger and garnished with black cherry halves. A delicate saffron-brightened fish bouillon garnished with steamed coques (baby clams) and crab-stuffed ravioli followed and was talented home-style cooking at its best—fresh, sincere, generous, and uncomplicated. My favorite dish on the menu was the paleron (shoulder) of beef, fork-tender but grilled so that it had a light crust of its own juices, and served with a jaunty green sauce of herbs and good olive oil, plus a side of vividly fresh steamed vegetables.

Since the human landscape was so appealing—a large table of diamond dealers and their wives from Antwerp visiting relatives who lived in the neighborhood, two male webmasters on what I'd guess was a third date, an older quartet of university types, and a motley crew at the table d'hôtes (a communal table where strangers sit together)—we decided to linger. I ordered the Pelardon, goat cheese from the Ardèche, with a drizzle of olive oil and a pinch of Espelette pepper, and Bruno had a slice of the rich brownie-like chocolate cake. While we were dawdling over coffee, the friendly, hardworking waitress paused by the table and asked, "Ça va?" ("Everything okay?"), and when I told her we'd had a wonderful meal, she grinned and said, "C'est la moindre des choses" ("That's the least we can do").

.   .   .

IN A WORD: A pleasantly bohemian bistrot à vin with simple, delicious, homey cooking, this place is a good choice for dining as a group and also offers the opportunity to discover Belleville, one of Paris's shaggier and more colorful neighborhoods. This place is also one of the city's best buys.

DON'T MISS: The set menu—everyone eats the same meal—changes constantly here, but do order the Pelardon, a creamy goat cheese, if it's available.

.   .   .

[106] 92 rue Rébeval, 19th, 01.42.02.68.60. MÉTRO: Jourdain or Pyrénées. OPEN Wednesday to Saturday for lunch and dinner. Sunday dinner only. CLOSED Monday and Tuesday. www.chapeaumelon-paris.com • $$

Chéri Bibi

TUCKED AWAY IN A PRETTY COBBLED STREET ON THE EASTERN slope of the Butte de Montmartre, the hill on which Montmartre is built, Chéri Bibi is a sure sign that the appealingly ramshackle and sociologically diverse Barbès-Rochechouart neighborhood is next up for gentrification. The mushroom-colored dining room with a façade of folding glass doors that open fully on warm nights and a hip decor of antique factory lamps, bare wood tables with kraft paper place mats, and found-at-the-flea-market Danish modern chairs has been packed with happy Bobos (bohemian bourgeois types) ever since it opened. Its immediate success is a reflection of the way it channels one of the most urgent culinary yearnings of hip Parisians, which is terroir, or a nostalgic desire to eat the way they did in the days when everyone in Paris still smoked Gauloises, drank wine at lunch, and blew off warnings about cholesterol in the unlikely event they even knew what it was.

Cheri Bibi is pure terroir, which means hearty, earthy, rustic French country cooking. The chalkboard menu leads off with starters like a superb homemade bacon-wrapped pork-and-prune terrine spiked with green peppercorns and served à volonté (help yourself) with a crock of puckery cornichons (miniature cucumber pickles), and there's also a soup of the day (maybe carrot and coriander), marinated herring, lentil salad and head cheese in anise-perfumed vinaigrette, oeufs mayonnaise, and bulots (sea snails) with aïoli (garlic mayonnaise). Mains include boudin noir (blood sausage), andouillette (a sausage made from the pig's colon and intestines), beef braised with red peppers and cocoa beans, sausage, and bavette (skirt steak) with sautéed shallots, and all of them come with a choice of sides—homemade frites, mashed potatoes, sautéed vegetables, or salad. Follow with a serving of Laguiole cheese from the huge wheel in the middle of the dining room, or go for strawberries sprinkled with fresh basil, fresh fruit salad, or the heavenly chocolate mousse. The service by two blowsy waitresses is friendly and fun but professional, and the whole place has a sweet, funky vibe that's très Parisien.

· ⸙ ·

IN A WORD: Fun and frisky, this lively bistro in an authentically bohemian part of Paris is a great choice for anyone who wants a great feed for moderate prices and a buzzy scene that's a living snapshot of the city today. It's also an excellent address for fans of real old-fashioned terroir-style cooking, which runs to hearty, traditional country-style French food.

DON'T MISS: The chalkboard menu changes often, but dishes to look for include terrine de campagne aux pruneaux; marinated herring; lentil salad; head cheese in anise-perfumed vinaigrette; oeufs mayonnaise; bulots (sea snails) with aïoli (garlic mayonnaise); andouillette; skirt steak with sautéed shallots; boudin noir; blanquette de veau (veal in a lemony cream sauce); roasted shoulder of lamb for two; grilled sausage with potato puree; rice pudding; chocolate mousse.

. . .

[107] 15 rue André-del-Sarte, 18th, 01.42.54.88.96. MÉTRO: Anvers or Château Rouge. OPEN Monday to Saturday for dinner. CLOSED Sunday.

▪ $$

Roseval

I LOVE MÉNILMONTANT, WHICH IS WHERE PARIS INTERSECTS with Brooklyn's Greenpoint, or maybe Bedford-Stuyvesant. What I mean is that this neighborhood is a completely unselfconscious showcase of the profoundly tonic human diversity that always had me craving life in a big city in preference to the sociological homogeneity of the Connecticut suburb where I grew up. Though the real estate clouds are gathering over this still relatively ungentrified part of Paris, the motley quality of the neighborhood's housing stock is likely, I hope, to keep it safe from the woeful process of urban threshing that replaces artists and moderate-income people with newcomers in search of bohemian atmosphere. Since this quartier has been chopped up a bit with new low-income housing, it retains a feisty proletarian feel that's profoundly Parisian and a palpable relief from the city's increasingly globalized center. And for the time being, rents are still lower than they are in central Paris, which means creative people can still work and settle here.

The latest delicious addition to the neighborhood's appeal is Roseval, a bistro that opened in an old neighborhood tavern worthy of a Toulouse-Lautrec painting. Right across the street from the curiously moving nineteenth-century church of Notre-Dame-de-la-Croix, the restaurant became an immediate hit. Arriving on a warm summer night, Bruno and I found Richard waiting for us, and as soon as we walked in I liked this place. Why? It's simple, and there was an immediate warm and spontaneous welcome from the staff, with not a single note of pretension or attitude to be found fluttering anywhere in the room, these being afflictions that can manifest themselves with occasional regularity at ambitious newly established modern bistros in Paris.

So once we'd sorted out our wines—a great Viognier and a superb Sangiovese from Emilia-Romagna (how rare to see a foreign wine or two on the list at a place like this) served by Erika Biswell, the Colombian-born sommelier who previously worked at Le Chateaubriand and is one of the best sommeliers in Paris, our meal kicked off with a pretty valentine of a dish—a single flash-grilled langoustine with a bright green velouté of baby peas garnished with a single raspberry delicately cut in half. I didn't find that the tastes of this dish fused together memorably, but the velouté was nicely made and our enthusiastic young waiter set the tone for the evening with his puppy-like eagerness that we enjoy our meal.

There was a great crowd in the dining room that night, too, including a well-known Belgian fashion designer out on a date with a T-shirt-wearing body-builder; a famous furniture designer who'd nicely taken his elderly mother, clearly and very sweetly bemused by the crowd around her, out for a nice meal; and a lot of arty types chattering about gallery shows and their summer holidays.

Then gastronomic thunder struck with a dish made from the restaurant's namesake spud—a sublime puree of smoked potatoes with sautéed onions, baby clams, and a garnish of buttered bread crumbs. This one was so good that conversation died completely until the three of us had mopped up every drop of the puree from our plates. While eating, I found myself thinking that even though the duo of chefs in the kitchen—American-born, British-raised Michael Greenwold and Italian Simone Tondo—have worked at an impressive constellation of some of the best and hippest restaurants in Paris, including Le Chateaubriand, the gentle suaveness of this dish brought to mind Bertrand Grébaut at Septime more than any other chef working in Paris today.

Our main course—sliced sirloin with anchovy cream, riced and pureed cauliflower, and a few tarragon leaves—continued in the same vein of primal innocence, with a real reverence for the natural tastes of the excellent produce the kitchen works with, an earnestly naive aesthetic in terms of dressing the plates, and a quiet confidence expressed by the pair's impeccable technical skills.

An excellent cheese course followed—chèvre, Mimolette,

and an almost winey-tasting Bleu d'Auvergne, with more excellent bread from baker Christophe Vasseur—and then a strawberry-chocolate-praline dessert, which I found too complicated. This muddled finale didn't even remotely diminish the pleasure of the meal that had preceded it, however, and I've been back to Roseval many times since to taste the intriguing dishes that issue from the restless tandem of the chefs' culinary imaginations and to savor their evolving talent.

· · ·

IN A WORD: Two talented young chefs, Michael Greenwold and Simone Tondo, have made this casual modern bistro in one of the last authentically bohemian corners of Paris a go-to address with their stunningly inventive and beautifully executed contemporary cooking.

DON'T MISS: Roseval serves only a regularly revised prix fixe dinner menu, but dishes I've loved here include langoustines in smoky bouillon with bok choy, hazelnuts, and kumquats; smoked potato puree with buttered bread crumbs and baby clams; sliced steak with anchovy cream and riced cauliflower; and pork with smoked eggplant, pomelo, fingerling potatoes, and dill.

. . .

[108] 1 rue d'Eupatoria, 20th, 09.53.56.24.14. MÉTRO: Gambetta, Ménilmontant, or Couronnes. OPEN Monday to Friday for dinner. CLOSED Saturday and Sunday. www.roseval.fr • $$–$$$

La Table d'Eugène

PERCHED ON A HILLSIDE OVERLOOKING PARIS, MONTMARTRE, once a country village and later a bohemian neighborhood known for its lively cabarets and popular with artists like Toulouse-Lautrec and Utrillo, is one of the most-visited districts of the city. The Basilique du Sacré Coeur and the Place du Tertre, where artists once congregated, are its main attractions, but to enjoy the handsome church and the fine views over the city from its steps, I send out-of-town friends to visit early in the morning and also advise them to skip the tourist-heavy Place du Tertre in favor of a long walk with no itinerary through the streets of the neighborhood to savor its particular atmosphere and architecture.

If they think they'll want lunch during their perambulations, I book a table for them at this excellent little restaurant on a side street near the *mairie* (town hall) of the 18th Arrondissement, a lively area with lots of cafés and interesting boutiques. Chef Gregory Maillard worked with Eric Frechon at Epicure, the three-star table at Hôtel Le Bristol, before going out on his own with this intimate and casually chic storefront dining room. The precision and flawless quality of his sophisticated market-driven contemporary French comfort food shows off why Paris still deserves its vaunted gastronomic reputation, since one still eats remarkably well in small neighborhood restaurants like this one all over the city. The haute cuisine background he brings to the modern bistro register is his signature.

Plotting a post-summer-vacation reunion dinner recently with pretty Franco-American Claire and handsome Breton

Denis, a delightful couple we met while staying in the same bed-and-breakfast in Stonington, Connecticut, almost ten years ago, I knew this place would be ideal, since they're as avidly gourmand as Bruno and I are but dislike food that's fussy or too cerebral. So two of us began with the terrine of duck foie gras topped with a fine quince gelée, and two settled on the langoustine tails wrapped in crisply fried pastry parcels and garnished, in a successful feint at the Asian palate, with squid's ink wafers, cucumber slices, sesame seeds, and fresh coriander.

The main courses we chose on a cool night on the edge of two seasons were thick pork chops in a lush sauce of pan drippings with a garnish of elbow macaroni lashed with more of the same deeply rich sauce and chopped cèpes and truffles for the gents, and a juicy rack of lamb with vegetables, including yellow squash and arugula, for Claire.

An exceptionally good cheese plate gave the boys an excuse to order another glass of wine, while Claire tucked into an elegant lemon tart with a fine pane of caramel and a crumbly buttery crust.

The only drawbacks to this fine restaurant are the expensive wine list, service that's a little more formal than it need be, and the fact that reservations need to be made well ahead of time. But these constraints don't stop it from being my favorite restaurant in Montmartre, and Claire and Denis loved it, too.

· ·

IN A WORD: Chef Gregory Maillard trained with Eric Frechon at Epicure, the three-star restaurant at Hôtel Le Bristol, before setting up shop with this small excellent contemporary French restaurant in a stylishly redecorated shopfront on a side street in Montmartre.

DON'T MISS: Maillard's menus evolve constantly, but look for dishes such as his warm white bean salad with piment d'Espelette and pork jowl, crisply fried langoustines with squid's ink wafers and Asian garnishes, pork chop with cèpes-and-truffle-garnished elbow macaroni, sea bream with carrots in a mango and radish jus, and lemon tart.

. . .

[109] 18 rue Eugène Sue, 18th, 01.42.55.61.64. MÉTRO: Jules Joffrin or Marcadet-Poissonniers. OPEN Tuesday to Saturday for lunch and dinner. CLOSED Sunday and Monday. ▪ $$–$$$

BUT WHAT ABOUT? OR WHY CERTAIN FAMOUS RESTAURANTS AREN'T INCLUDED IN THIS BOOK

· ·

Y OU MAY BE WONDERING WHY SOME VERY WELL KNOWN
Paris restaurants are not profiled in this book, so let me briefly
address some of the more obvious omissions.

L'AMBROISIE. Chef Bernard Pacaud is a brilliant cook, and
this intimate dining room on the lovely place des Vosges is quite
beautiful, but the joyless atmosphere and sanctimonious service
have unfailingly dampened my spirits during every meal I've
ever had here. When you're spending this much money, I insist
it should bring on rhapsody.

L'AMI LOUIS. The prewar atmosphere of this power broker's
bistro is indisputably delicious, but even though the food is decent enough, the real thrill comes more from getting a reservation—tables are highly sought after—than anything you'll
eat there. The lofty prices make it a pretty egregious example
of conspicuous consumption, too, especially when you can find
better roast chicken and foie gras elsewhere.

APICIUS. Since chef Jean-Pierre Vigato's handsomely decorated town house restaurant serves as a sort of de facto club-

house for Parisian power brokers, unknown diners often get lost in the shuffle.

BALZAR. I loved this Latin quarter brasserie for many years, but the cooking has become so insipid that it's now best avoided.

BENOÎT. The food's still pretty good at this luxury bistro, which is not far from the Hôtel de Ville, Paris's city hall, and is now part of chef Alain Ducasse's restaurant empire, but the atmosphere was badly wounded when it added a new dining room. I also regret that its uniqueness has been spoiled by branches in Tokyo and New York.

BOFINGER. The beautiful decor at this historic brasserie on the edge of the Marais can't compensate for the kitchen's mediocrity and the offhanded service.

CARRÉ DES FEUILLANTS. Chef Alain Dutournier is a really nice guy, and some of his dishes are excellent (I loved the Jerusalem artichoke and foie gras cake with truffles and veal sweetbreads with oyster sauce). Unfortunately, I can't imagine why anyone would come here unless they were invited, since it's just not a good time.

LA COUPOLE. I love the history of this famous Montparnasse brasserie, but I've never warmed to the heavy-handed renovation of the dining room ten years back, and it has been ages since I've had more than a half-decent meal here. Service is often glacially slow, and it is overpriced relative to the quality of the cooking. If you are a Hemingway fan or just fascinated by Paris during the twenties, stop by for a drink at the bar or maybe just a plate of oysters.

LA GRAND VEFOUR. Yes, the eighteenth-century decor is exquisite, including painted glass ceilings and brass plaques with the names of famous patrons like Colette and Cocteau, and there are few lovelier places in Paris than the Palais Royal. The food is good, too, but nowhere near as memorable as the setting, because chef Guy Martin's cooking suffers from a politesse that negates the primal pleasure that is always at the heart of great haute cuisine.

HÉLÈNE DARROZE. Because Hélène Darroze is a charming woman, I really wish I could like this one-star on the Left Bank. Unfortunately, I've never had a more than better-than-average meal here. The cooking's uneven and imprecise, the dining room's dull, and the bill lands on the table with a disheartening thud.

LE DIVELLEC. Popular with politicians, but it's a total mystery why this stuffy, mediocre, and exorbitantly expensive fish house on the Esplanade des Invalides retains its reputation.

MAXIM'S. Just say no. The Belle Époque decor is the only appetizing thing left about this world-famous tourist trap.

MICHEL ROSTANG. This two-star in the 17th Arrondissement has drifted off into an irrelevant senescence.

PRUNIER. It's been low tide at this handsome Art Deco restaurant, once one of the city's most prestigious seafood tables, for a long time.

RELAIS LOUIS XIII. One can only assume that the Michelin inspectors have forgotten that this dusty old dowager still lurks in their guide. Why it still has two stars is a total mystery.

AU TROU GASCON. Once Paris's temple of southwestern French gastronomy, this well-known place is but a shadow of its former self, with distracted service and a seriously disappointing cassoulet.

ACKNOWLEDGMENTS

I would like to thank the many people who taught me how to eat and also the friends with whom I've shared many happy meals in Paris: Bamma, Emma, my mother and father, Laurie Eastman, Tom Crane, Marc Parisot, David Bruel, Judy Fayard, Michele Loyer, Anne Bogart, Nadine Frey, Bob and Lynn Peterson, Barbara Nagelsmith, Suzy Gershman, Dorie Greenspan, Jean-Marie and Marie-Therese Midavaine, William Sertl, Ruth Reichl, Jocelyn Zuckerman, Nanette Maxim, Charlotte Shagolsky, John Van Ness Philip III, Kato Wittich, and Charles Carroll, among many others. I'd also like to thank Susanna Porter, my editor, and Deborah Ritchken, my remarkable agent, without whom this book would never exist.

RESTAURANTS
BY TYPE

RESTAURANTS
BY PRICE RANGE

EXPENSIVE ($$$)

OPEN ALL OR PART OF WEEKEND

. . .

NOTE: Weekend hours vary. Restaurants marked with an asterisk (*) are closed on Sunday.

INDEX

Restaurant names in **boldface** are the
109 restaurants profiled in the book.

ABOUT THE AUTHOR

· ·

ALEXANDER LOBRANO grew up in Connecticut
and lived in Boston, New York, and London before
moving to Paris, his home today, in 1986. He was
the European correspondent for *Gourmet* magazine
from 2000 until it closed in 2009, and now writes
regularly on food and travel for *The New York Times*
and many other publications in the United States
and the United Kingdom.